PLATO'S CRITIQUE
of IMPURE REASON

PLATO'S CRITIQUE
of IMPURE REASON

On Goodness and Truth in the *Republic*

D. C. SCHINDLER

THE CATHOLIC UNIVERSITY OF AMERICA PRESS

Washington, D.C.

LIBRARY OF CONGRESS CATALOGING-IN-PUBLICATION DATA
Schindler, D. C.
Plato's critique of impure reason : on goodness and truth in the Republic /
D. C. Schindler.
p. cm.
Includes bibliographical references and index.
ISBN 978-0-8132-1534-1 (cloth : alk. paper)   1. Plato. Republic.
2. Reason.   3. Truth.   I. Title.
JC71.P6S35 2008
321´.07—dc22
2008005003

FOR NICK HEALY AND ANDY MATT,

who were there when the "third Plato" first came to light

Thought is all in all for universities. Today there is precious little thought about universities, and what there is does not unequivocally support the university's traditional role. In order to find out why we have fallen on such hard times, we must recognize that the foundations of the university have become extremely doubtful to the highest intelligences. Our petty tribulations have great causes. . . . The essence of it all is not social, political, psychological or economic, but philosophic. And, for those who wish to see, contemplation of Socrates is our most urgent task. This is properly an academic task.
—Allan Bloom, *The Closing of the American Mind*

"Fatigue" is the antithesis of Reason. The operations of Fatigue constitute the defeat of Reason in its primitive character of reaching after the upward trend. Fatigue means the operation of excluding the impulse toward novelty. . . . The power of going for the penetrating idea, even if it has not yet been worked into any methodology, is what constitutes the progressive force of Reason. The great Greeks had this knack to an uncanny degree.
—Alfred North Whitehead, *The Function of Reason*

CONTENTS

ACKNOWLEDGMENTS

There are many people to whom I owe a debt of gratitude for this book. Eric Perl was the one who first opened up the riches of Plato to me, which have since seemed inexhaustible. Though he does not have responsibility for the fruits it bore in this particular case, what he taught me has continued to be an inspiration in all my subsequent reflection. This book, in fact, grew out of the last graduate paper I wrote for him as a student.

The Humanities Department at Villanova has been a stimulating home for thought about important questions. I am grateful to my colleagues there and at Villanova University more generally for their spirited engagement with me on how best to understand the *Republic*. In particular, I would like to thank Mark Shiffman for his illuminating comments on the introductory chapter and Peter Busch and those from the Villanova Center for Liberal Education who participated in Peter's Plato Reading Group in 2005 for discussing chapter 3 and offering helpful suggestions. The staff at the Falvey Library were generous with their time in helping me obtain some of the more obscure secondary materials. I would like also to express my gratitude to two student assistants, Michael Metcalfe and P. J. Gorre, for their many trips to the library on behalf of this project. P. J. also prepared the bibliography. It has been a pleasure working with Jim Kruggel, Theresa Walker, and Elizabeth Benevides at the Catholic University of America Press, and I am grateful for Susan Lantz's invaluable help in copyediting the text. Some of the arguments I make in this book appeared in "Going Down: Founding Reason in the *Republic,*" *Journal of Neoplatonic Studies* 9:1 (2001–2003): 81–132.

Though they may not have been directly involved in the work on this book, others have enriched my understanding of Plato, and of philosophy simply. The students I have taught at Villanova have kept me alive to the original questions. In this context, I would like to give thanks in particular to the 2005–06 "Monks'" crew: Garth Brown, Chris Continanza, Chuck Girard, Dan Larkin, and Chris Varano. I am especially grateful to my friends Michael Hanby, for consistently reminding me, through word and example, of what is most important in the academic world, and Paul Wright, for his unstinting generosity; to my father, for showing me what genuine intellectual piety is; to my family, for their constant support; and above all to my wife, Jeanne, for her sometimes disarming questions about Plato, and for embodying the integration of goodness and truth.

NOTE ON TEXT AND LIST
OF ABBREVIATIONS

The Greek text of the *Republic* used is from Plato, *Respublica,* edited by S. R. Slings (Oxford: Oxford University Press, 2003). All other Greek texts are cited from the volumes in the Loeb Classical Library. Unless otherwise indicated, citations of Plato in English are from translations contained in the *Complete Works,* edited by John Cooper (Indianapolis, Ind.: Hackett Publishing Company, 1997), except for passages from Plato's *Republic,* which are taken from *The Republic of Plato,* 2d ed., translated by Allan Bloom (New York: Basic Books, 1991). English translations have occasionally been altered.

Abbreviations of the Platonic Dialogues Cited

Alc. I	*Alcibiades I*
Ap.	*Apology*
Chrm.	*Charmides*
Cl.	*Cleitophon*
Cra.	*Cratylus*
Cri.	*Crito*
Epin.	*Epinomis*
Euthd.	*Euthydemus*
Euthphr.	*Euthyphro*
Grg.	*Gorgias*
Hp. mai.	*Hippias Major (Greater Hippias)*
La.	*Laws*
Phd.	*Phaedo*
Phdr.	*Phaedrus*
Phlb.	*Philebus*
Plt.	*Politicus (Statesman)*
Prm.	*Parmenides*
Prt.	*Protagoras*

Rep.	*Republic*
Soph.	*Sophist*
Symp.	*Symposium*
Tht.	*Theaetetus*
Ti.	*Timaeus*

Abbreviations of Other Works

De comp. verb.	Dionysius of Halicarnassus, *De compositione verborum*
D. K.	Diels and Kranz, *Die Fragmente der Vorsokratiker*
D. L.	Diogenes Laertius, *Lives of Eminent Philosophers*
Meta.	Aristotle, *Metaphysics*
Nich. Eth.	Aristotle, *Nichomachean Ethics*

PLATO'S CRITIQUE
of IMPURE REASON

MISOLOGY AND THE MODERN ACADEMY

La raison oblige?

When we debate an issue with someone, we spontaneously offer *reasons* for one position or another, and we expect that these have some claim on the other person's assent. If our reasons are strong, we generally assume that some assent is required, unless the person can produce stronger reasons for an alternative, which would then in turn obligate us. Such everyday situations raise fundamental philosophical questions: Why should reason have a claim on us, and if it does, what exactly is it that reason lays claim to in us? To what extent, and by what principle, does it bind? What is the "force" intended in the phrase "by force of reason"? Does truth move us by virtue of its being true, or by virtue of something else? What exactly is a "compelling" argument? How do words compel?

These are basic questions, so basic we could say they are implicitly raised in the raising of any other question, so basic we can never avoid answering them in some manner or other even while we can never claim to have finished answering them. The questions concern the foundation and goodness of reason. While philosophy has always distinguished itself from other sciences by including itself as a central object of its study, and thus occupying itself fundamentally with its own ground, only a handful of major philosophical works have addressed the question of the foundation and goodness of reason in a direct way, in a way that has determined what we might call the collective mind of Western civilization. Plato's *Republic* is certainly the first of these, and no doubt one of the boldest and most comprehensive. To be sure, Plato addresses an abundance of themes in this dialogue, but they all take their bearings in some decisive respect from the idea of the good, which Plato claims to be the ultimate cause of the being, the truth, and the

knowability of all things, and also the end of desire and the universal reason for action. The aim of the present book is to explore the meaning of this
enormous claim specifically in relation to the connection of goodness and
intelligibility and its implications for the nature of reason. Through an interpretation of the *Republic,* we will consider what it means to affirm goodness
as the ground of reason, what this implies regarding reason's responsibility
to goodness in order to *be* reason, and what it entails more generally for the
life of philosophy.

Plato presents this claim about reason in the course of what he offers as
the most adequate response possible, within the parameters of the encounter
in the Piraeus, to the problems generated by both the ultimate a-rationality
of poetic traditionalism and the rootless rationalism of sophistry. What drove
Plato was the desire to address a concrete historical need, but to do so in a
deep and enduring way required him, at the same time, to say something essential about reality and about the human soul. Accordingly, our aim in the
present book is to understand what Plato says in the *Republic* so far as we are
able, certainly, but we pursue this aim out of a conviction that this philosophical dialogue reveals a fundamental truth about reason, goodness, and reality,
and therefore holds significance in relation to our own cultural situation. To
appreciate this significance, it is helpful to explore why our present cultural
situation lends our opening questions a particular urgency.

Is it prudent to raise the question of the source of reason's claim in the
first place? In his *Twilight of the Idols,* written when his attack on reason had
acquired the ferocity of a final assault, Nietzsche asserted that the very act
of asking after the value of something undermines its value. To ask "What
good is life?" is to confess, however unwittingly, that its goodness is not self-
evident, and that one has already fallen outside the reach of life's compelling
power.[1] In this case, insofar as the power of attraction is not compelling unless it is spontaneously compelling, the most enthusiastic response one gives
to persuade oneself of life's goodness will never bring one back inside the
reach of its pull. If Nietzsche's view is correct, attempting to justify a value
would be analogous to attempting to recover innocence; and just as it is impossible to "know" that one is innocent until it is too late, so too is it impossible to "know" ultimately why something is good or compelling.

---

1. Friedrich Nietzsche, *Götzen-Dämmerung,* in *Kritische Studienausgabe,* 2nd ed., vol. 6, edited by Giorgio Colli and Mazzino Montinari (Berlin: Verlag de Gruyter, 1999), 68.

What Nietzsche says here in relation to life would seem to hold even more radically in relation to truth or reason. What reason could one possibly give for reason? If reason itself is not compelling a priori, it has no resource upon which to draw in order to prove itself compelling. Apriority would seem to be essential to something's being compelling: "compellingness" can never simply be lent to something, since that implies it can just as easily be demanded back. And reason without any intrinsic necessity is not reason.

Of all philosophical questions, there may be none to rival this in inducing a sort of intellectual vertigo. On one hand, it seems to exclude the possibility of answering it in any adequate fashion. But, on the other hand, the very incapacity to answer it would seem to lead inescapably (by the force of reason!) to the conclusion that reason lacks any rational justification. Thus the very raising of the question seems at once to deny the possibility of answering and to force a particular answer. In this case, to call attention to the problem is in fact in some respect to cause it. Reason, Nietzsche will say, is at root irrational; truth is a subspecies of falsehood that has been elevated above the other falsehoods for "reasons" that cannot be measured against the standard of reason itself. We cannot get outside of reason to judge it, and even if we could we would by the very same stroke lose the criterion by which to judge.

But if it is imprudent to raise the question of the goodness of reason, it may become far more imprudent to avoid it. One of Nietzsche's proposed remedies for nihilism, namely, to keep all roots buried deep, quickly reveals its inadequacy if there are cultural forces already at work eroding the soil. One may, in fact, argue that refusing to raise the question amounts in this case to the same problem that raising it does: rejecting the possibility that reason can be justified is an admission of its "irrational" origin. It may be the case that "what must first be proven has little worth,"[2] but it may also be the case that certain historical circumstances, in which truth or reason as such seem increasingly impotent, make the evasion of a confrontation with the question irresponsible, not to say irrational.

We thus cannot avoid asking whether we live at present in circumstances that require this confrontation. Doubts about reason have, of course, existed as long as thinking itself, and in this respect, reason has always had some call to justify itself. Nevertheless, there is some plausibility to the suggestion that

2. Ibid., 70.

a certain mistrust in or even contempt for reason has grown beyond isolated thinkers and attained to the roots of more general cultural forms. In the admittedly complex web of intellectual history, two figures stand out in particular as representing a fundamental shift in the disposition toward reason that has been determinative for the modern and postmodern ages. Martin Luther is perhaps the first to turn against reason in a radical and historically significant way. According to him, reason *(ratio)* is "the Devil's greatest whore," and in order to repel the force of her profound seduction, he urges us "to fling dung in her face so as to disfigure her."[3] These are fierce expressions, but it is crucial to recognize that, for Luther, reason was not so much a problem in its own right—indeed, he often affirmed its necessity for the proper ordering of human affairs. Rather, it presented, in his view, an obstacle to what is incomparably greater than it, namely, faith. Implicit in this assessment is the notion that reason stands for human mastery and independence, and for that very reason resists the obedience integral to theological faith. Acknowledging the new set of issues the claim of revelation makes with respect to the claim of reason, which cannot be addressed here, we ought to ponder the implications of taking reason to be something we must essentially *overcome* in our relation to what is ultimate rather than an essential dimension of whatever access we might have to the ultimate, as the Greeks generally took it to be.

Once the cultural horizon recedes from a basically theological order, the exclusion of reason from what is most essential becomes the exclusion of reason from what is most essentially *human*. Jean-Jacques Rousseau is apparently the first figure to turn against reason in a historically determinative way specifically in relation to human nature. Against Hobbes's view that the lust for power and glory is a defining characteristic of human nature, Rousseau championed the natural goodness of human beings, and—breaking radically with the optimistic rationalism of the Enlightenment—fingered reason as the primary corrupting force. Rousseauian nature consists of a pre-reflective sentiment, in which man is in harmony with himself, with others, and with God and the world. Reason disturbs this harmony, and does so more or less irreparably, because it is impossible (as Kierkegaard will eventually say) to reflect oneself out of reflection. Thus, far from being the fulcrum of human

3. Martin Luther, "Die letzte Predigt zu Wittenberg, 17. Januar 1546," in *Predigten*, vol. 7 of *Luthers Werke in Auswahl* (Berlin: Walter de Gruyter, 1962), 411–17, here 412 and 414: Ratio is "die hochste hur, die der Teuffel hat.... [W]irft ir ein dred ins angesicht, ut deformis fiat."

nature, as it was through the Middle Ages and until the rise of fideism, reason now becomes essentially alienating to man.[4] It introduces fragmentation into what was originally whole by nourishing the passions with the food of the imagination until they grow in utter disproportion to the heart's original and *real* desires. For Rousseau, "It is reason that gives rise to egoistic self-love, and it is reflection that strengthens it; it is reason that turns man in upon himself, she that separates him from everything that disturbs or afflicts him."[5] To break the self-imposed bonds of *amour propre*, Rousseau urged the cultivation of feeling *in opposition to* the cultivation of intellect and its "civilization."

The contrast between the notion of reason implied in the charges Rousseau brings against it and the notion taken for granted in classical philosophy is striking. The Greek word for a person "turned in upon himself" is ἰδιώτης, "idiot," and it was used to describe one who in fact *neglects* reason, the *logos* that binds all things and people together.[6] The understanding of the nature of reason has clearly undergone a dramatic shift. Luther and Rousseau do not represent merely a new attitude toward reason, but adopt an attitude that follows spontaneously from a new conception. It is not accidental that Luther's philosophical formation comes from late scholastic nominalism, which introduced a gap between the soul and the real by denying that reason's proper objects, the universals, had any *fundamentum in re*, and that, in Rousseau's intellectual milieu, reason had acquired an increasingly "egological" (i.e., self-centered), form, both in moral or political philosophy (Hobbes) and in theoretical philosophy (Descartes).

It is especially interesting, for our purposes, that the tendency toward an individualistic conception of reason appears to coincide with the marginal-

---

4. To be sure, Rousseau's disposition toward reason is complex. Just as it does in Luther, reason plays an indispensable role within certain delimited spheres in Rousseau's thought, as Robert Derathé is right to argue (*Le rationalisme de J.-J. Rousseau* [Paris: Presses Universitaires de France, 1948]), but Rousseau is nevertheless the first to be able to depict reason as bad and in some respects inhuman. Though Montaigne, for example, had made Pyhrronian skepticism current once again, he still takes for granted that reason is wholly natural: "There is no desire more natural than the desire for knowledge," he says at the beginning of his essay "Of Experience." This is a statement Rousseau would never grant.

5. Jean-Jacques Rousseau, "De l'inégalité parmi les hommes," in *Du contrat social* (Paris: Editions Garnier Frères, 1962), 60.

6. On the original philosophical sense of *logos* in this respect, see D. C. Schindler, "The Community of the One and the Many: Heraclitus on Reason," *Inquiry* 46 (2003): 413–48.

izing of the causal presence of the goodness in the universe. This shift is especially clear, for example, in the Renaissance figures of Machiavelli, who discredited the rational significance of goodness in the human world,[7] and Galileo, who eliminated teleological explanation from the investigation of the material world.[8] If reason possesses a self-centered form in Rousseau, rationality appears as wholly indifferent to goodness in Rousseau's erstwhile friend, David Hume: "It is not against reason," Hume says in his *Treatise on Human Nature,* "to prefer the destruction of the whole world to the scratching of my finger."[9] Whereas reason had earlier been the deepest place of the human soul's encounter with reality, it becomes more and more the mind's encounter with itself alone, and thus becomes more and more of a problem. *If* reason does indeed present an obstacle to what is highest, and *if* reason is the cause of both private and public alienation, then it ought to be rejected; Luther and Rousseau no doubt had such a cultural impact because they offered a response to what had undeniably become a problem. But if the response is simply to reject what has become problematic, then the heart of the problem remains there to be grappled with. By addressing what is merely a conditioned effect, one concedes the root cause and thereby reinforces it.

Apart from certain strands of phenomenology and the revival of Thomism, which largely but not exclusively seek to reinstate the primacy of reason rather than inquire into its foundation and nature, the main intellectual currents in twentieth century continental philosophy have been virtually unanimous in their effort to relativize or even abandon reason.[10] The identification of the project of reason with the tyranny of technology, industry, and bureaucracy, the intrusion of scientific thinking into every realm of human existence, and the rise of fascistic movements in politics are no doubt major causes of this effort. Against what he took to be the technological *telos* of Western rationalism, a judgment that clearly has a resonance with Rousseau's claims,[11] Heidegger called for the recovery of a more originary attune-

7. See Pierre Manent, *An Intellectual History of Liberalism,* translated by Rebecca Balinski (Princeton, N.J.: Princeton University Press, 1995), 10–19.

8. See E. A. Burtt, *The Metaphysical Foundations of Modern Science,* rev. ed. (Garden City, N.J.: Anchor Books, 1954), 72–104.

9. David Hume, *A Treatise of Human Nature,* edited by L. A. Selby-Bigge, 2nd ed. revised by P. H. Nidditch (Oxford: Clarendon Press, 1975), II.3.iii (416).

10. See Stuart Sim, *Contemporary Continental Philosophy: The New Scepticism* (Burlington, Vt.: Ashgate, 2000).

11. For a treatment of the influence of this aspect of Rousseau's thought on Kant, Heidegger,

ment to being, and, to this end, for example, he rereads Leibniz's *"Satz vom Grund"* (Principle of Reason) as a "leap from reason," and thus as the opening of a radically different mode of thinking. The search for an alternative to rationality is evident not only in, say, Sartre's existentialism, but in nearly all of the major figures generally labeled "postmodern." If these figures have any shared "identity," it would no doubt be found in the common embrace of some version of a radical relativization of reason's claims. (It is interesting to observe how often Plato, or the "Platonic conception of Truth," is taken to be the primary opponent).[12] We have, for example, Lyotard's privileging of the figural over the discursive; Foucault's unmasking of the essential connection between knowledge and power, which reveals the modern construction of the concept of reason to be a function of a general will to surveillance and control ("La torture, c'est la raison"); Vattimo's advocating of a more ironic, supple, and accommodating *pensiero debole*; Rorty's neopragmatism; Feyerabend's "farewell to reason" and his urging of "anything goes!" as the proper scientific methodology; Levinas's affirmation of ethics, rather than metaphysics, as first philosophy; and Derrida's free play of reason that cheerfully acknowledges reason's inability to ground itself, but sees this impotence as allowing a more "reasonable"—more modest, more moderate—

---

and others in recent continental philosophy, see Richard Velkley, *Being after Rousseau: Philosophy and Culture in Question* (Chicago: University of Chicago Press, 2002), esp. chaps. 3 and 9.

12. See Kenneth Baynes's observation, in the preface to a collection of essays from prominent postmodern thinkers significantly titled *After Philosophy,* edited by Baynes (Cambridge, Mass.: MIT Press, 1987), 7: "All are agreed in their opposition to the 'Platonic conception of Truth.'" It should be noted that Levinas is more ambivalent in his assessment of Plato than most postmodern thinkers. In his essay, "La philosophie et l'idée de l'Infini," *Revue de métaphysique et de morale* 62 (1957): 241–53, Levinas criticizes Plato's notion of *anamnesis* as a basic example of the "narcissism" of Western thought, but also affirms Plato's notion of the *transcendence* of the desire for the "Good beyond being," and thus of a metaphysics beyond ontology. (Cf. *Totality and Infinity,* translated by Alphonsis Lingis [Pittsburgh, Pa.: Duquesne University Press, 1969], 42–48.) It is in line with this interpretation that he reads *eros* in the *Symposium* as essentially "non-nostalgic," based not on a prior need (Aristophanes) and therefore relative to the soul, but as the wholly unanticipated encounter with the Other. (See *Totality,* 63.) Levinas does a great service in bringing to light the essential nonrelativity of goodness that is often overlooked in Plato. Our interpretation differs significantly from his in showing that the transcendence of goodness nevertheless necessarily *includes* (without reducing to) immanence: thus, metaphysics includes without reducing to ontology, and "exteriority" includes but does not reduce to interiority. Therefore, while goodness (i.e., justice) for Levinas ultimately does violence to reason, we will argue that its transcendence is the necessary *ground* of reason, and thus that the reversal its transcendence entails fulfills rather than destroys reason.

sense of reason. What distinguishes the contemporary situation from earlier times is perhaps that, while attacks on reason had previously come for the most part from figures outside the mainstream university, they now seem to have won a certain level of respect *within* the university. In the *Geisteswissenschaften* at least, it has become common among those on the "cutting edge" to deny any fundamental distinction between *logos* and *mythos,* or philosophy and poetry.

But it is also common to suggest, somewhat wryly, that the more virulent forms of contempt for reason are more or less restricted to certain "inbred" academic circles, and that even members of these circles show symptoms of their contamination only when explicitly addressing the question as such in discussion with colleagues. In other words, some will say that the rejection of reason as described here is merely a professional stance. When professors close up their offices, they spontaneously reacquire a capacity to distinguish between reason and its false imitators, they both appeal and submit to reason in their everyday dealings with others, and they entrust themselves without a pang of conscience to common sense. They return to the world that most people never leave. If students learn to suspend the claims of reason and open themselves to other points of view for the sake of classroom discussions and writing assignments, they do so for the most part with the sense that they are only playing a role; they are saying what one is supposed to say in the classroom. In this respect, if there is a problem with the foundation and goodness of reason, it is the sort of problem that those outside of the academic world would call "academic." In other words, it is not *really* a problem. Justifying the goodness of reason does not seem to be a cultural concern.

What prompts the writing of this book, by contrast, is the belief that the explicit dismantling of reason and its claims that occurs in certain circles within the academy is merely the reflection of a more profound, more subtle, and more pervasive problem: the general acceptance of a radically impoverished conception of reason, both by those who deny *and* many of those who affirm reason's claims. To give some plausibility to this suggestion, let us look more closely at some aspects of our current cultural situation.

Dogmatism and Skepticism

At a recent conference on education, a professor commented on the pervasive relativism and skepticism among both students and faculty in our universities. There was a hum of general assent in the room. Another professor then rose to contradict the statement, saying that, in fact, he had never once encountered a genuine skeptic in all his years of teaching. Even if people claim there is no such thing as absolute knowledge, they nevertheless constantly make assertions they take to be true, and even hold stubbornly to them; they regularly give explanations they take to be more adequate than alternative explanations, and when they do so they invite and normally expect assent. In this respect, the professor suggested, there are in fact no skeptics among students and faculty, despite appearances. Again, there was a hum of agreement. The apparently opposed judgments here are not uncommon: one will often hear at faculty discussions alternating complaints that the students are content with "merely" subjective opinion and that they are too easily satisfied with absolute assertions. Which judgment is correct?

To see why they both are, it is instructive to consider a peculiar feature of the phenomenon of skepticism in the Hellenistic age. The fundamental difficulty with skepticism is that it rests on the assumption—however it may be formulated in different contexts—that reason has no access to anything beyond mere appearance, and so cannot make any legitimate dogmatic statements about what "is" the case. The difficulty is that in order to understand something *as* an appearance, rather than as the reality itself, one must be able to contrast it with what is other than appearance. In other words, in order to "see through" all appearances, conventions, prejudices, and presuppositions—which is the skeptics' pride—one must in fact see *beyond* them. A fish could never "know" it was in water without at some point breaking the surface. What, given this difficulty, does a true skeptic look like? The patron saint of skepticism, Pyrrho of Elis, was especially remarkable because of his heroic attempts at consistency.[13] Some say he was followed by acquaintances to save him from the consequences of his radical renunciation of all judgment—for example, walking off a precipice. On the other hand, such legends are disputed by those who claim his suspension of judgment was consistent only in theory, but not in practice. He is reported to have said, after running from an attacking dog, that suspension of judgment was something one had to struggle continuously to achieve. If one could not carry it through in one's actions, one should try at least to carry it through in one's words.

13. See Diogenes Laertius, *Lives of Eminent Philosophers*, reprint ed., vol. 2, translated by R. D. Hicks (Cambridge, Mass.: Harvard University Press, 2000), IX.62.

But, in saying this, is Pyrrho in fact carrying the suspension of judgment through in his words? Do these very words belie his skepticism? It is worth posing the question whether Pyrrho is more consistently a skeptic when he struggles against convention as mere convention and thus as having no claim on him, or when he ceases to struggle and simply follows appearance, abandoning any need to identify it *as* appearance and thus distinguish it from what *really* is the case. It is illuminating to note that some of his associates and later followers typically insisted that the desirable consequence of skepticism is that it led a person to follow appearances and customs, but to do so free from anxieties and in a gentleness of spirit.[14] In other words, the point of skepticism is not so much to make a point but to achieve a certain state of mind; it represents not so much a doctrine as a way of living. Let us consider the implications of this aim more closely.

Skepticism is rationally impossible; as an intellectual position, it is no less dogmatic than the dogmatism it so easily refutes.[15] Those who would wish to defend reason against skepticism—let us call them, with a nod to Plato, "friends of reason," *philologues*—have the airtight "retorsion" argument ready at hand: it is self-refuting to insist on the truth of skepticism against any and all rival claims. But if this argument is so strong, why does it

14. Ibid., 102–8: "The end to be realized they [skeptics] hold to be suspension of judgement, which brings with it tranquility like its shadow: so Timon and Aenesidemus declare. For in matters which are for us to decide we shall neither choose this nor shrink from that; and things which are not for us to decide but happen of necessity, such as hunger, thirst and pain, we cannot escape, for they are not to be removed by force of reason. And when the dogmatists argue that he may thus live in such a frame of mind that he would not shrink from killing and eating his own father if ordered to do so, the Sceptic replies that he will be able so to live as to suspend his judgement in cases where it is a question of arriving at truth, but not in matters of life and the taking of precautions. *Accordingly we may choose a thing or shrink from a thing by habit and may observe rules and customs.* According to some authorities the end proposed by the Sceptics is insensibility (ἀπάθεια); according to others, gentleness (πρᾳότητα)." (Italics mine.) See also Sextus Empiricus, *Selections from the Major Writings on Scepticism, Man, and God,* rev. ed., translated by Sanford G. Etheridge, (Indianapolis, Ind.: Hackett, 1985), 37: "For we follow a certain line of reasoning which indicates to us, in a manner consistent with appearances, how to live in accordance with the customs, laws, and the institutions of our country, and with our own natural feelings."

15. Even Montaigne's uncertainty with regard to whether he knows or does not fails to evade dogmatism to the extent that it presents itself as a genuine *position:* he *is* uncertain. Montaigne recognizes just this criticism of Pyrrhonism, and for this very reason, consistent with our argument, he points out that skepticism is not, in fact, an intellectual position, but a *therapy,* analogous to the medicine that washes both the disease and itself out of the body. See "Apology for Raymond Sebond," in *Essays and Selected Writings,* translated by Donald Frame (New York: St. Martin's Press, 1963), 229.

invariably fail to convince anyone but those who don't need convincing? Invulnerability is a virtue only if one comes under attack. It is pointless to erect impenetrable walls around a barren corner of space in an uninhabited wasteland; they would have significance only for the poor souls who happened already to be caught inside. To think that one has sufficiently dealt with the issue of skepticism by revealing it to be self-refuting is to fail to grasp the nature of the problem in a serious way, and in fact—as we will eventually argue—to fail to grasp the nature of reason itself.

A skeptic who would be disturbed by the charge that he is contradicting himself is not yet a skeptic, insofar as he shows a residual deference to the demands of reason and the claims of reality as distinct from mere appearance. To keep constant vigil against the claims of reason is clear evidence of a deep respect; it is only when the respect, and thus the vigil, disappears that we can genuinely say reason has been ruined: in this case, it is trivialized to insignificance, even if it remains everywhere present. A full-blown skeptic will simply not bother to dodge the claims of reason, because he does not feel their importance. Before a skeptic of this sort, a philologue cannot avoid becoming fundamentally helpless; he has no resort, and typically falls to the rage and frustration that accompanies impotence. The philologue will no doubt assert that if the skeptic is willing to contradict himself, he must abandon all claims to being a "rational animal" (i.e., a human being); as Aristotle says, the person who denies the principle of contradiction shows himself to be nothing better than a vegetable.[16] But, again, if we take this to be the last word on the matter, we have still not understood what skepticism is. Why would a skeptic agree to renounce his claim to rationality? Only in order to remain intellectually consistent. However, one who is willing to be self-contradictory will have no "reason" not to claim to be just as reasonable as anyone else—and in this case, he would seem in his undisturbed gentleness of spirit to have even more claim than the philologue who is turning blue with frustration.

Using the term in a way slightly different from Plato's usage, let us give the name *misology* to this utterly radicalized skepticism, followed all the way to its practical conclusions. For Plato, misology is what befalls one who has been "burned" by reason and now harbors a deep mistrust and resentment. He refers to misology as the greatest evil a person can suffer (*Phd.,* 89d). We use the term in the present context to indicate a more advanced stage of the

---

16. *Meta.,* IV.4.1006a15–16, 1008b11–13.

experience, wherein the resentment has cooled to the point of fading alto-gether from felt significance, so that one is no longer troubled by reason one way or the other. Misology, as we characterize it, appears most perfectly not in the person who rejects reason altogether, but in the person who accepts it . . . most of the time. He will be happy to make assertions, perhaps even with great conviction, but will be just as happy to abandon them when, for example, in a moment of crisis they commit him to some further claim be-yond what he is ready to admit. Someone who harbored a *radical* contempt for love wouldn't keep himself from professing it in some situations, since reserve in this regard is a sign of respect. Instead, he may be wont to profess it—at the drop of a hat. Contempt for reason is similar. A skeptic in the usu-al sense feels some obligation to the "truth" of skepticism, an obligation that requires the kind of passion and even ascetical devotion that we associate with profound faith. A *radical* skeptic, or misologist in our sense of the term, by contrast, is ready to deny even the truth of skepticism whenever he has "good reason" to do so. As people often say, the real opposite of love is not hatred, but indifference; the real opposite of the philologue is the misologist who has simply grown numb to the claims of reason. If a refusal to make any claim about the way things are is indeed more a concession to reason than a rejection of it, then the misologist is best characterized as one who does not allow reason to make any lasting claim on him, even if he, for his part, makes whatever claims on reason he needs to make given the circumstances.

Misology thus represents the most complete ruination of reason precise-ly because it allows a momentary claim, but always only within a willingness to relativize this claim in the next moment, "whenever necessary." In this re-spect, it does not chase reason off, but allows it to be present everywhere—though only in the form of a weightless ghost: forgotten but not gone. If skepticism preserves the difference between knowledge and ignorance and affirms the latter, the ruined form of reason represented by misology surren-ders even this: it gives up not only any basis for distinguishing what is ra-tional from what is not, but also any felt need to make the distinction. This point cannot be overstated if we wish to understand our present situation.

What, in this case, would be an adequate proof-test for misology? Clear-ly, it would be insufficient to scrutinize any particular claim in its discrete-ness, made at one moment or another. As paradoxical as it may seem, even one's insistence that there *is* an objective truth or that there *is not* reveals lit-tle, insofar as the very next moment may bring circumstances that prompt one to insist differently. At issue here is not the content of a particular assertion, but the meaning it has within the context of one's fundamental relation to the whole of reality. Such a relation cannot be disclosed in an immediate way, but can show itself only over *time*. It is impossible to see whether reason has a claim on us or whether we are simply submitting to reason at a particular instant by the force of some other, nonrational criterion, except over the course of a series of linked episodes in which the consequences of a decision are borne out. Therefore, as we will eventually see, the "truth of truth" cannot come to adequate manifestation through a single claim or argument, a proposition or even an intuition, insight, or inspiration, but only through some form of a dramatic narrative: this is, we will suggest, a principal philosophical significance of the dialogue form of the *Republic*. The criteria that include both truth and time, and thus offer an adequate test for misology, are *fidelity* and *comprehensiveness*. Fidelity represents a being bound by some "more-than-momentary" claim, and comprehensiveness represents an aspiration to, and responsibility for, the whole beyond the fragmentariness of parts. It follows, conversely, that the most decisive mark of misology is precisely a lack of fidelity, an inconsistency, or the absence of any felt need to integrate particular claims into a coherent whole.

What does it mean to relativize the claims of reason moment by moment, "whenever necessary"? It means that we measure reason by some criterion external to it, a criterion that is therefore by definition nonrational. There are a variety of such criteria. We could think of the fideism of late scholasticism and the Reformation we mentioned earlier, which refused to allow reason to take part in what was most essential, or the early modern transformation of reason into the "scout and spy of the passions" (Hobbes) or reduction of it simply to a kind of "custom or habit" (Hume). A more directly familiar and contemporary example is the "emotivism" that MacIntyre has shown to prevail in contemporary moral discourse.[17] Another is the overturning of the rule of reason by the self-imposing authority of history and the subsequent sovereignty of the "present moment," which Manent points to in the thought of Montesquieu.[18]

17. Alasdair MacIntyre, *After Virtue: A Study in Moral Theory,* 2nd ed. (Notre Dame, Ind.: University of Notre Dame Press, 1984), 6–22.

18. Pierre Manent, *The City of Man,* translated by Marc LePain (Princeton, N.J.: Princeton University Press, 1998), 15–17.

The proposal we make here—and it will be amplified in the first chapter—is that once reason loses its ordering to, and responsibility for, the *whole*, it will inevitably become a servant of "whatever works." In other words, its own claims will be trumped by whatever most effectively brings about a desired result. Misology means that "knowledge" becomes a function of power. Reason in this case remains a member of the household, but it does so as the older brother who has been persuaded to sell his birthright and is no longer entitled to make his own demands.

Once we see that a thoroughgoing skepticism is not only compatible with, but in fact necessarily implies, a willingness to submit to "reason" under certain conditions, we can understand how both judgments on the students and faculty in our universities can be justified—they are relativists, yet they are also dogmatists. In one of his letters to Mendelssohn, Lessing laments the widespread tendency to identify the goal of thinking with the point at which thinking falls off.[19] Leo Strauss, interestingly, takes the phrase to be a characterization of dogmatism,[20] but it is not difficult to see that it characterizes relativism just as well. Relativism and dogmatism, however much they are opposed to each other on one level, nevertheless share at a deeper level a common conception of reason: both deny that the natural *telos* of reason *is the comprehensive whole.* Both relativism and dogmatism agree in accepting (either implicitly or explicitly) a partial or fragmented view of reason, one that does not feel any intrinsic obligation to *understand* something as a whole and in the totality of its parts or to get to the heart of a matter.

The problem with dogmatism is that it is essentially relativistic: by making a particular claim definitive in isolation from the integral whole within which that claim would have its reasonable and sense-giving ground, dogmatism ends up absolutizing the relative and therefore making the relative a *ne plus ultra*.[21] The problem with relativism is that it is essentially dogmatic: by equalizing all perspectives in a wholly undifferentiated manner, relativism makes each perspective in itself a kind of self-contained totality, which is

19. G. F. Lessing, "An Moses Mendelssohn, 9 Januar 1771," *Lessings Briefe in einem Band* (Berlin: Afbau-Verlag, 1967), 230.

20. Leo Strauss, *Natural Right and History* (Chicago: University of Chicago Press, 1965), 22.

21. It ought to be noted in this context that the insistence on dogma is not necessarily dogmatism. In fact, some form of "suprapersonal" absolute, within which an individual inserts himself, is arguably necessary ultimately to avoid dogmatism. As used here, the term "dogmatism" means the absolutizing of an individual perspective.

therefore on its own terms incontrovertible and thus definitive. Instead of respecting reason as responsible to the whole, a person, whether he leans in a relativist or a dogmatist direction or both directions at once, takes for granted that reason is merely an "instrument" (a function of something else), which remains the same regardless of the use or nonuse to which it is put; it is no less reason when it satisfies itself with the grasp of some partial aspect. In this case, strong claims made in the tradition on behalf of reason—such as that of Husserl, who accords the life of consciousness an "all-pervasive teleological structure" that drives it beyond merely formal logic to the actuality of evidence[22]—typically fix reason's *telos* too low to overcome either dogmatism or relativism. Again, if reason finds completion in the mere adequation of a particular judgment, it does not so much matter whether one insists (as a "dogmatist") that this partial grasp is "true," or takes (as a "relativist") this partial grasp to be "just my opinion, which is no better than any one else's"; the decisive thing is that one does not see reason's need to be comprehensive in order to be reason at all. If we do not feel a need to follow thinking all the way through to the end—and thus remain faithful to it—because it is the nature of reason to do so, then reason has lost its claim on us.

Misological Habits

One of the troubling paradoxes of misology is that it makes the diagnosis of the failure of reason seem out of place or alarmist. If reason is in fact in crisis, it will for that very reason not notice. When it is corrupted in its foundations, reason will characterize whatever cultural problems it recognizes as anything else but as a problem of reason. If the very nature of the problem is to hide its problematic nature, the charge of misology may appear as foolish as the conspiracy theories that take a lack of evidence as decisive confirmation. Perhaps the best one can do in this case is point to certain cultural habits that evince a trivialization of reason and its claims. I enumerate four such habits in contemporary Western culture below. The list is meant to be suggestive rather than exhaustive. The point is not to provide an analysis of these tendencies—which others have done at great length in different contexts—but to see that these tendencies share a unity; they reflect the same

22. See Edmund Husserl, *Formal and Transcendental Logic*, translated by Dorion Cairns (The Hague: Martinus Nijhoff, 1978), §§16, 46, 59–60.

problem from a different angle. In each case, we find what we could call a form of "intellectual impatience" (a disinclination to follow reason to its end and on its terms).

First, perhaps the most obvious cultural habit is the general tendency toward pragmatism. One claims that "talk is cheap." There is a rush to "cash out" ideas, to determine their application, and this application is considered to be what justifies having taken the time to reflect on them. Implied in this pragmatism is the assumption that coming to an understanding of something is not good in and of itself. Rather, understanding derives its goodness wholly from the end it is meant to serve or the effect it is meant to bring about.[23] Thus, discussion gets cut short by the belief that some understanding has quickly been reached—at least as far as necessary to move on to the important stage: "Now what are we going to do about it?" Liberal arts colleges in general, and philosophy departments in particular, strain themselves to show that their subject matter is "useful" and "relevant"; emphasis is given in philosophy to courses in ethics, especially applied ethics, and the liberal arts are reduced to the teaching of certain skills, such as critical reasoning and articulate writing and speaking, which are considered necessary no matter what professional choices students eventually make.

Connected with this is a tendency to eliminate "depth" metaphors from our characterization of understanding, or at best making use of them in cases where the type of knowing would be better described in terms of breadth. Deep knowledge of a matter, so it is now believed, means having a lot of facts about it at one's fingertips, facts that are immediately graspable and (apparently) most immediately relevant to practical considerations. Because making pragmatic considerations determinative means breaking off inquiry the moment it ceases to produce some praxis, we may appropriately call this tendency a habit of intellectual impatience. Such intellectual impatience can often be oddly paired with an endless "moral patience":[24] one may be willing to give "all that it takes" in terms of time and energy to work out practical

---

23. It is interesting to note that Foucault opens the English translation of his book, *Les mots et les choses*, with the sentence, "This forward should perhaps be headed 'Directions for Use.'" *The Order of Things: An Archaeology of the Human Sciences* (New York: Vintage Books, 1994), ix.

24. The term is in quotations because, in reality, what may be thought to be the moral virtue of patience will invariably turn out to be a kind of vice to the extent that it excludes what we are calling intellectual patience. One cannot adequately respond to the whole without seeing it in its wholeness.

solutions, but one has no inclination to reflect on the nature of the problem simply for the sake of a comprehensive understanding.

Second, there is, moreover, a pervasive tendency in contemporary Western culture toward abstraction, understood in this context to mean the isolation of one aspect of an issue from others, and to treat that aspect as complete within itself. Christopher Alexander, for example, has suggested that the root cause of the crisis in contemporary architecture is the absolutization of individual desiderata in thinking about buildings, which results in a failure to integrate those desiderata into the larger, relativizing whole, leading to a general, ugly incoherence.[25]

Connected with this isolation of particular aspects is a disproportionate valuation of expertise and specialization and a subsequent fragmentation of thought in and about the public order. While "abstract" is an adjective colloquially reserved for intellectual matters, it properly applies to any consideration of a reality that fails to attend most fundamentally to the reality as a whole but instead reduces the significance of the reality to what is merely an aspect of it. Hegel was using the term in this proper sense when he made the charge that gossip is more abstract than speculative philosophy.[26] The assumption that a theoretical or philosophical consideration is necessarily abstract is itself due to an abstract notion of abstraction, which takes for granted that the *meaning* of a reality precisely in its wholeness—the *idea* of it, its *nature*, what it is—is not itself a fundamental part of the concretely real. Abstraction is thus also a form of intellectual impatience, which may again be coupled with a thoroughgoing moral patience: one may be willing to consult scores of experts to obtain precise information about some aspect of a question, and commit a decade or two to research in order to allow long-term tracking of data, and still not have a moment to spare to wonder how this particular aspect fits into a larger question concerning the whole.

Third, related to these first two points, and in a certain respect their practical synthesis, is a tendency to absolutize technology as a response to prob-

25. Alexander points to particular assumptions regarding truth (that it consists of "scientific" facts) and order (that it is essentially mechanistic) as the cause of this incoherence. See Christopher Alexander, *The Phenomenon of Life*, book one of *The Nature of Order: An Essay on the Art of Building and the Nature of the Universe* (Berkeley, Calif.: The Center for Environmental Structure, 2002), esp. 18–21.

26. See G. W. F. Hegel, "Who Thinks Abstractly?" in Walter Kaufmann, *Hegel: Texts and Commentary* (Notre Dame, Ind.: University of Notre Dame Press, 1986), 114–18.

lems. If, in fact, the solution is what really matters, then the meaning or nature of a problem in its philosophical dimension comes to represent an "abstraction" that is not immediately relevant—unless it happens to bear immediately on the solution. In this case, however, the value of reflection lies not in *understanding* the problem but in being a means to forget it; its aim cannot but be to bring about the solution in the most effective way possible through the establishment of a technique. It is the very nature of technology to disregard long-term or subtle effects to the extent that these lie beyond the scope of measurement and/or are not themselves amenable to additional technological responses, for the very same reason that it is the nature of technology to be ignorant of itself as merely technological: to recognize its partiality would be to see reality as a meaningful whole of which the manipulable is merely a relative part.

The first problem with a technological approach to solving a problem is not necessarily that it is a "bad" approach—it may not in fact be bad, as far as it goes—but that it is incapable of considering the nature of a problem in fundamental terms, so that it is essentially blind to all but a technological approach. In this respect, by its very nature, technology simultaneously *cannot* claim to be the "best" approach, since that would require a comparison with alternatives, and *cannot avoid* claiming (however implicitly) to be the best, since it presents itself as the only alternative.[27] To understand this point, we may consider Charles Williams's comment on a modern approach to the problem of overeating. If a drug could be invented, he suggests, which simply eliminated at one stroke all of the bad effects of overeating, technology would deem the problem solved, when in fact the problem has not yet even been considered. (Is gluttony merely a problem concerning the location of matter? Whatever the answer to this particular question, technology is incapable of raising it.) Technology is an expression of the stunted and fragmented conception of reason we have been calling intellectual impatience. Technology, too, is capable of coexisting with moral patience: Elizabeth Kübler-Ross, in a book describing her experience with dying persons, relates her observation that a terminal medical patient will receive an extraordinary amount of technical care—tests, measurements, procedures, drugs, thera-

27. This charge is, of course, analogous to the observation Socrates makes in the *Apology* (23d–e) regarding the ignorance peculiar to the craftsmen: an implicit claim to know the whole simply by virtue of expert mastery of a part.

peutic programs—but will often not succeed, in spite of persistent attempts, at getting a single one of the people busy on his behalf to pause for a moment to listen to and answer a question.[28] The attendants are certainly patient in their willingness to do yet another test, give yet another shot, and administer yet another pill, but it is nearly impossible for them to open their attention to what does not have relevance or admit of immediate resolution.

Fourth, finally, there is the tendency to reduce thinking to politics— meaning, for our purposes, the manipulation of and by opinion, rather than the study of the nature of human community. Hidden within the methodical resort to politics is the assumption that reason as reason possesses no goodness or persuasive force of its own and so must be supplemented by other means of persuasion. Related to this assumption is the reduction of knowledge to the fact of being persuaded. It is considered to be part of mature self-understanding to recognize that all of one's basic beliefs have been imposed on one by one's family, society, culture, and so forth. One is a "product"; from this perspective, to be conscious ultimately means to have been manipulated. It follows from this connection that while one may speak quite cynically about the ignorance, the depravity, or the superficiality of "society," one still grants authority to majority opinion, even with great conviction. The apparent inconsistency latent here may perhaps be explained by misology, which is characterized precisely by the absence of any need for consistency. It is no more necessary, within a misologist's understanding, for the view that the majority determines what is real to exclude the view that the majority tends to be wrong than it is necessary for a book defending one view to exclude from a misologist's bookshelf a book defending the other. These views come into conflict only with an effort to understand reality as an integrated whole. Or perhaps we may explain it by Tocqueville's classic argument that the absolutizing of individual minds, because it renders all views numerically equal, logically entails subservience to majority opinion: "The same equality that makes [democratic man] independent from each of his fellow citizens in particular, hands him over without support or defense to the action of the greater number."[29]

28. Elizabeth Kübler-Ross, *On Death and Dying* (New York: Scribner, 1969), 8.

29. Alexis de Tocqueville, *De la démocratie en Amérique,* vol. 2 (Paris: Garnier-Flammarion, 1981), 17.

There are two particular signs that philosophy is being reduced to politics and thus thinking to manipulation. One is the tendency to ignore the intrinsic meaning of a claim and attend instead primarily to its source—"*who* is making the argument, and *why* is he or she making it?"—or, in other words, to reduce all arguments to some *ad hominem* form. The other is a tendency to reduce communication—especially, but not merely, in the public sphere—to "sound bites." The point of a sound bite is not to articulate a meaning but to produce an effect. This intellectual impatience is compatible with moral patience: it can require a lot of time, energy, and reflection to produce just the right sound bite.

Each of these "misological habits" possesses an indispensable truth: as we will see over the course of this book, if thinking is not *practical, political, specialized,* and in some sense, capable of producing *technique,* it is insufficiently comprehensive. The point is not to reject any of these dimensions, but to refuse to allow them to stand for the whole of reason. The point, in other words, is to avoid as far as possible any form of reductionism.

What links these habits together in their fragmentary form, we suggest, is an impoverished notion of reason. We can point in summary fashion to three aspects of this impoverishment in particular, aspects that bear some relation to one another. (Each of these aspects will be taken up and developed at greater length over the course of the book.) First of all, these habits presuppose an essentially instrumentalist view of reason, a denial that reason has an absolute value in itself and beyond (though of course not exclusive of) any other considerations. Reason in this case derives its value from the nonrational end it serves; it must therefore continually be justified by the effects it produces or the changes it can bring about. As the young Marx wrote after reading Feuerbach, "The philosophers have only *interpreted* the world, in various ways; the point, however, is to *change* it."[30] If it is merely an instrument, reason does not have its own intrinsic end, which means it is not ordered simply to comprehensive and fundamental understanding. Second, lacking its own end means that reason cannot rest in itself—cannot rest simply in the act of knowing. In this case, reason cannot be the place, so to speak, wherein the human soul "communes" with the real. Third, reason thus becomes essentially manipulative in two respects. Reason as a mere in-

30. Karl Marx, "Theses on Feuerbach," in *The Marx-Engels Reader,* 2nd ed., edited by Robert Tucker (New York: Norton, 1978), 145.

strument will tend to instrumentalize in turn; a machine cannot "be" with its other, but can only "do" something to it. A purely mechanized reason will objectify, reduce, fragment, and alienate: it will be guilty, that is, of all the charges that postmodern thinkers lay on it and for which they understandably seek to put it away. Moreover, if reason does not have its own intrinsic goodness, then it will be simply a means of persuading and will at the same time lack any intrinsic power to persuade. To the extent that rationality is not *per se* good, it will have to appeal to something outside of itself in order to acquire any capacity to move. While the threat or use of physical force is an extreme option for this supplement to reason, other options ultimately differ from it merely in degree rather than in kind: manipulation is always, however subtly, a form of violence. The severance of reason from its natural *telos*, the comprehensive whole—ironically, an operation typically undertaken in order to make reason more modest (Kant, Vattimo)—necessarily entails the reduction of knowledge to power, so that reason becomes merely one among many other means of manipulation. The assumption that reason cannot have a *telos* proper to it unless that *telos* be the comprehensive whole may seem gratuitous at first. While the reading of the *Republic* offered here will attempt to show at greater length why reason must be set on wholeness if it is to be reason at all, the significance of the point warrants a comment. Understanding is essentially comprehensive: we do not understand a part until we understand the whole of which it is a part, and understanding of the whole requires a grasp of its differentiation into parts. But reason has no other *telos* than understanding. If there is an a priori limit to understanding, it cannot be set by reason itself without thereby transforming reason's nature. Notice, to say this is neither to affirm nor to deny that reason is capable of complete understanding; it is only to suggest that reason cannot aspire to less without being denatured, and, moreover, that if a limit *is* indeed set a priori, the source of that limit will be nonrational. The problem of reason's relationship to faith is admittedly a special case, which we cannot address here, but whatever solution one presents to that problem must respect the natural *telos* of reason if it is to avoid fideism. If reason is an empty instrument, appeal must be made to something nonrational in order to move us; bereft of such an appeal, reason is impotent. There would be no intrinsic reason in this case to follow reason: it would be irrational to do so.

The Significance of Plato

It should be clear that if reason is indeed in the sort of crisis we have been describing, it will not do simply to insist on the importance of reason or raise a moral exhortation to begin respecting the claims of reason once again. Instead, we must first recover a conception of reason that warrants this respect. To call for a rehabilitation of reason and a restoration of its aspiration to the comprehensive whole is *emphatically not* meant to imply that reason must attempt to "seize control" of the ground that is being taken from it and impose its order on the currents of irrationalism in the contemporary situation. The linking of knowledge and power in early modern rationalism has, for all of its productivity, been deeply destructive, and has engendered a spirit that clearly bears some responsibility for the political and cultural tragedies of the twentieth century. Moreover, as we hope to show, rationalism of this sort is by its very nature incapable of adequately grasping the whole, and this incapacity is not at all incidental to its destructive effects. Our proposal is that the tyrannical will to dominate in the rationalism that the critics of the Enlightenment desire to depose is not so much an instance of overexuberance and pride in reason as it is a symptom of its internal collapse. (Nietzsche's critique on this point is right on the mark.) We will try to show that reason cannot aspire to the whole except by renouncing its power over it. We thus agree with the postmodern thinkers who advocate the loosening of reason's grip, but we disagree with them in our conviction that a genuine modesty in rationality is possible only if we recover reason's natural ordering to the comprehensive whole.

One of the best sources for such a recovery—which offers an alternative to both rationalism and positivism, dogmatism and skepticism—is Plato's *Republic.* The key claim in the *Republic,* and it will be the central focus of this book, is that the idea of the good is the unhypothetical first principle of knowledge, just as it is the cause of being and truth. Reason, as reason, is therefore rooted most fundamentally in goodness. This means more than just that reason is good and that what is reasonable is also good (though of course it also means these things); as we will see, the claim means that reason is a kind of *desire* for goodness and thus has its proper end in the order governed by the good.

Plato points to the philosopher as the paradigm of reason, and defines him specifically as the *lover* of the *whole* of truth. To say that reason is ordered to the good implies, in clear contrast to the impoverished form of reason we described earlier, that it is by nature responsible for the whole beyond the fragmentation of its parts; that it, at the same time and ultimately for the same reason, is an end in itself and therefore essentially and intrinsically good (i.e., *desirable*); and finally that it therefore betrays itself if it seeks to compel by any means other than by simply being genuinely reasonable, which means simply allowing reality to show itself for what it is. To return to the questions posed at the beginning of this introduction, then, reason has a claim on us ultimately only because its *telos* is the whole, which is the same thing as saying it is founded in the good. Being ordered to the good, in other words, is convertible with comprehensiveness. The moment reason is cut off from this *telos,* the moment it is no longer understood as essentially philosophical, it will cease to be inherently compelling. But if it *is* founded in the good, this fact has implications for the nature of truth, the shape of understanding in general, and the proper mode of argumentation, implications that have not often received their due attention in the mainstream philosophical tradition. A systematic treatment of all such implications would be, of course, impossible in any single book. Our aim is to consider Plato's treatment of the issue in the *Republic* with these questions in mind. At the center of our interpretation, then, will be the connection between goodness and truth.

A host of objections could be raised at this point, perhaps most obviously the circularity of the diagnosis, the circularity of the proposed response to it, and the circularity of any attempt to give a rational argument in defense of reason. It is not possible to "preempt" these sorts of objections; an adequate response would require some sense of the nature of reason as Plato presents it in the *Republic.* It may be helpful, nevertheless, to point out that objections at this level cannot avoid a kind of circularity themselves: What sort of conception of reason is implied in the argument that a good argument in defense of reason cannot be in some basic respect circular? Is it possible to give a rational defense of *this* notion of reason without presupposing the very notion of reason one seeks to justify? The charge of circularity carries more weight if one's argument excludes it in principle. Our suggestion with respect to the book at hand is that Plato offers in the *Republic* not merely an argument in defense of reason, but a unique form of argumentation that is especially suited to this unique problem. Wittgenstein once said in a lecture on ethics (1929), "If a man could write a book on Ethics that was really a book on Ethics, this book would, with an explosion, destroy all the other books in the world."[31] The reason for the explosion? The intrinsically sublime matter of ethics lies beyond the sphere of words alone, and so expressing ethics in words would require a total transformation of the words themselves. The same thing could be said about a *real* book on reason, and the closest book I know to fitting this description is Plato's *Republic*.

To sharpen our sense of the distinctiveness of Plato's approach, it is instructive to reflect on Aristotle's grappling with the skeptic in *Metaphysics* IV. For Aristotle, to expect that one should be able to demonstrate everything is irrational. Every demonstration rests on assumptions, which cannot be demonstrated except with further assumptions that are in turn undemonstrated. The ultimate foundation of reason, then, will be a principle whose certainty stems from the very fact that it cannot be demonstrated, that is, because it lies at the basis of all other demonstrations.[32] This unhypothetical first principle, Aristotle says, using the very words Plato uses to characterize the good,[33] is what has become known as the "principle of contradiction": the same attribute cannot at the same time belong and not belong to the same subject and in the same respect.[34] What happens to this principle in Aristotle's confrontation with the skeptic? From a variety of angles, he shows that the skeptic inevitably ends up affirming and denying the same attribute of

31. www.galilean-library.org/witt_ethics.html.

32. To be sure, Aristotle claims it can be demonstrated "negatively," in the sense that one can show that even one's rejection of the principle presupposes it.

33. The ἀρχή must essentially be ἀνυπόθετον. See *Meta.* IV.3.1005b12–14; cf. Plato, *Rep.*, 510b. The reasons Kenneth Sayre offers for rejecting the identification of the unhypothetical first principle with the good (a position he previously said "the text could not have indicated much more clearly," in "Plato's Dialogues in Light of the *Seventh Letter*," in *Platonic Writings, Platonic Readings*, edited by Charles Griswold Jr. [New York: Routledge, 1988], 101) are not very convincing, and have not gained wide acceptance. See Sayre, *Plato's Literary Garden: How to Read a Platonic Dialogue* (Notre Dame, Ind.: University of Notre Dame Press, 1995), 173–81.

34. Plato mentions this principle, which seems to have been used often in sophistry, in the *Sophist* (230b) (cf. *Euthd.*, 293d) as an argument employed in elenchus to unsettle those who are content in their wisdom. He calls such argumentation "the principal and most important kind of cleansing" (230d), and clearly sees the "principle of contradiction" as fundamental. Nowhere, however, does he explicitly call it a "principle" or refer to it as the unhypothetical starting point of reason.

the same thing, etc. And then, as if recognizing the futility of this argument once he looks at it with the skeptic's own eyes, Aristotle concedes: "But perhaps they might say this was the very question at issue."[35] If reason is under attack, it does not do simply to reassert the principle. Instead, in order to deal with the more radical questioning—or better, calling into question—Aristotle turns to the sphere of action, showing that one cannot avoid making judgments in practice that rely in some respect on a *concern* for truth. In other words, in spite of what one may say, no one ultimately *desires* to be irrational, precisely because no one ultimately wants what he takes to be bad if something better is available.

What is crucial for our purposes (we are not claiming to do justice to what is admittedly a highly complicated problem in Aristotle), is the progression of Aristotle's argument: the problem of skepticism eventually compels Aristotle to go beyond the principle of contradiction in order to justify reason; he does not, of course, leave the scope of its applicability, but he enters into a larger, more concrete sphere in order to make its significance *evident*. His argument shifts from what we might call a merely logical register to what we might call an existential register—to the sphere ordered to and by the good. The question, then, is whether, in thus shifting his argument, he departs from the strictly rational order. Granted that it is clearly in no way *opposed* to the rational, we must still ask: In going beyond the principle of contradiction in his defense of reason, does Aristotle enter into a realm that is different from the rational in the strict sense? Modern Aristotleleans are wont to insist on a clear distinction between the orders of the true and the good and the corresponding orders of the intellect and the will/desire. Though Aristotle himself admits in one place that "the primary objects of desire and of thought are the same,"[36] he does not seem to make this fact a *principle* (except perhaps implicitly in the way he deals with skepticism). It is telling, for example, that the founding principle of reason for Aristotle seems to be *purely formal* in the sense of being absolutely without content.[37] It is

---

35. *Meta.* IV.3.1008b1–2.

36. *Meta.*, XII.7.1072a26–28.

37. To call it "purely formal" is not to imply it is simply a logical law. Joe Sachs is right to insist that, for Aristotle, the principle of contradiction governs logic only because it first governs reality; it is a logical principle *because* it is an ontological principle. (See *Aristotle's Metaphysics*, translated by Joe Sachs [Sante Fe, N.Mex.: Green Lion Press, 1999], 59n7.) Nevertheless, the

precisely this formality that makes it absolute in itself and at the same time true completely independent of any question of goodness. While Aristotle's foundation of reason is the contentless principle of contradiction, Plato's is the good, which is at once the root of all desire, reason, and being. As such, its being purely formal does not separate it in any way for Plato from questions of content. If the principle of contradiction were in fact the primary governing principle of thought, reason by its very nature would be indifferent to the question of the good, which would itself be only accidentally related to truth.

Aristotle does not draw this inference himself, and he seems, like the skeptic, to deny it in practice. But if it is true that reason is, by nature, at best accidentally related to the order of the good, we believe that one will not be able to prevent it from degenerating at some point into an empty instrument. As a result, any earnest form of fundamental argument will be merely a more or less subtle attempt at manipulation. Let us consider the contrast: when faced with a fundamental challenge to reason, one can appeal to the tiniest possible (and therefore perhaps easiest to defend) affirmation and move on from there, or one can appeal to the greatest and most comprehensive claim possible, and then reckon with the peculiar kind of defense it entails. The approach that seems more immediately effective, we suggest, will turn out in the long run to fail at the most decisive level. Logical consistency is a clear criterion, but there is nothing to say for it *logically* to justify it as a criterion for truth. But if *goodness* is the principle of reason, and at the very same time the ultimate object of desire, then the dialogical movement into the existential sphere becomes *an intrinsic part of argumentation itself.* As we will see in the *Republic,* the misologist can never adequately be answered by mere words alone, but only by words and deeds, by an argument that is itself an action. If reason *does* oblige us, its claims must be simultaneously *said* and *shown.*

Of course, even the clearest possible "saying and showing" of the claims of reason will not guarantee their efficacious communication to the "committed" misologist. But the point of this book is not to respond to the crisis of reason with an airtight argument against skepticism, or to derive a demonstration of what is referred to as "foundationalism" from Plato's *Republic.* Rather, the book seeks to make use of the radical challenge of misology

---

principle, even ontologically considered, is without content because it is the most minimal possible truth about things.

to bring to light something essential about the nature of being, truth, and knowledge—which is what we take Plato to be doing with Thrasymachus in the *Republic,* as well as with sophistry in other dialogues. The real strength of reason lies not in its success in securing clarity and distinctness through an infallible technique, but in its capacity to take what Plato calls the "noble risk" (καλὸς κίνδυνος)[38] with regard to ultimate meaning. This is not simply a virtuous employment of reason but constitutes its very essence, its most proper inner "shape."

These scattered observations, which are not intended to be systematic, seek primarily to illuminate the conviction behind the present book: namely, that the response to the impoverished conception of reason that afflicts our age requires above all the recovery of the intrinsic relation between the orders of goodness and intelligibility. The tendency toward abstract pragmatism, the tyranny of technology and politics, and the great difficulty of generating sustained and interesting discussion in the classroom—in short, the reduction of knowledge to power—are all due, we suggest, to the disjunction of these two orders, a problem that may equally be characterized by the "truncation" of reason, the undermining of its natural ordering to the whole. History is familiar with one-sided, partial responses to problems, and some will even say that it is in fact constituted by the exchange of one overreaction for another. But if the problem is one-sidedness itself, then a partial response is twice damned, and however urgent it may seem to exaggerate some neglected aspect to compensate for the prior exaggeration, such solutions merely serve to drive the problem deeper into our history and our institutions. The only adequate response to the crisis of reason is a comprehensive one, one that has a place for all conflicting claims precisely to the extent that the claims are legitimate—truly in accord with reason. The response to the crisis of reason must therefore be the sort of intellectual *patience*—the suffering (*patior,* πάσχω) of the claims of truth, the enduring necessary for serious understanding[39]—that Plato repeatedly urges in the *Republic:* reason is rooted in the good, and what is good or noble (τὸ καλόν), he consistently reminds us, is always difficult (χαλεπόν).[40]

---

38. *Phd.,* 114d.

39. One of the problems that Plato attributes to writing is its presumption to give rise to immediate understanding, which is as ridiculous as a farmer who expects his crop eight days after planting (*Phdr.,* 276b).

40. *Rep.,* 435c; cf. *Cra.,* 384b.

Plan and Method

Plato is the first philosopher to draw an explicit connection between goodness and intelligibility—unless we take Socrates' autobiographical speech in the *Phaedo* to be historically accurate and give this honor to Socrates.[41] Although Plato makes use of this connection in several dialogues, the *Republic* is where the issue takes center stage.[42] We intend here to examine the dialogue specifically in order to elucidate this connection and what it entails for the nature of reason. As we have already suggested, this examination is bound to take an equal interest in both *what* Plato says and the *manner* in which he says it. Making an argument for the good as the foundation of reason requires this in two respects: first, it is, in general, paradoxical to argue for what lies at the basis of argument, and one ought to expect that the object cannot have been achieved without being adequately reflected in the manner of the achievement. Such an argument will necessarily be characterized by a unity and reciprocity of form and content, in which the content determines the form and the form reflects the content. Second, insofar as it is specifically *the good* that lies at the foundation of intelligibility, and insofar as the good also represents the order of desire and action, the *method*, the path followed (μέθ᾽ ὁδός), will be an intrinsic aspect of the end sought: it is never simply a means.

Because of the unity of form and content, we cannot give a full account of methodology at the outset, prior to an elaboration of the substance of the idea. The method awaits the object, and cannot be explained to satisfaction until the object itself is seen. In a certain sense, we might say that this entire book is an account of methodology; in another sense, in addressing basic philosophical questions such as the nature of goodness and reason, full accounts of methodology always come either too late or too early.

Nevertheless, it is possible to make some general observations about the way we will be reading the *Republic*, both to characterize the method and to offer an *apologia* of sorts for it. First, this book is a philosophical interpreta-

---

41. The principle is, after all, a kind of mirror image of one of Socrates' most famous teachings, the identification of virtue with knowledge.

42. Rafael Ferber refers to the good as the "center of gravity" in Plato's philosophy in *Platos Idee des Guten*, 2nd ed. (Sankt Augustin: Academia Verlag Richarz, 1989), 49, and sees the *Republic* as the dialogue wherein that centrality comes most clearly to expression.

tion rather than a commentary. Thus, there will be no attempt to give a narrative account of the argument as it unfolds step by step from the beginning to the end. Many good commentaries of this type already exist. Instead, the point will be to bring to light what we take to be a basic theme—the relationship between knowledge and the good—and to address the other aspects of the *Republic* only insofar as they aid in illuminating this one. The theme becomes explicit only in the center of the *Republic,* although the implications of the connection between goodness and intelligibility are in play from the outset. We will be focusing on the basic "joints" of the dialogue's plot, the beginning, the middle, and the end, and we will draw out the significance of claims made at these junctures in relation to themes and scenes in other dialogues. Nevertheless, this will be a "whole" account of the *Republic,* insofar as the theme it addresses is fundamental to the dialogue. There is a difference between offering an interpretation of the whole and providing a commentary on and analysis of every part.

Because of the peculiarity of the dialogue form Plato employs—which has often enough been imitated in the history of philosophy but certainly never equaled—the question of how properly to read Plato has always been a significant part of studying him, especially since the general thematic turn to questions of philosophical style and genre in the nineteenth century. What is perhaps distinctive about the contemporary state of Platonic scholarship is the centrality the question of the dialogue form and Platonic authorship has acquired, which we witness in the growing number of works devoted primarily, if not wholly, to this theme.[43] In reaction to a tendency, particularly but not solely in analytic philosophy, to see what may be called the literary and dramatic elements of Plato's dialogues as so much dispos-

---

43. As an example, we might consider the number of anthologies collected around some aspect of this question published in the last decade or so: Frédéric Cossutta and Michel Narcy, eds., *La forme dialogue chez Platon: Évolution et réceptions* (Grenoble: Éditions Jérôme Millon, 2001); Gerald Press, ed., *Who Speaks for Plato? Studies in Platonic Anonymity* (Lanham, Md.: Rowman and Littlefield, 2000); Gerald Press, ed., *Plato's Dialogues: New Studies and Interpretations* (Lanham, Md.: Rowman and Littlefield, 1993); Christopher Gill and Mary Margaret McCabe, eds., *Form and Argument in Late Plato* (Oxford: Clarendon Press, 1996); Francisco Gonzalez, ed., *The Third Way: New Directions in Platonic Studies* (Lanham, Md.: Rowman and Littlefield, 1995); Anne Michelini, ed., *Plato as Author: The Rhetoric of Philosophy* (Leiden: Brill, 2003); Andrew Barker and Martin Warner, eds., *The Language of the Cave* (Edmonton, Alb.: Academic Printing and Publishing, 1992); James Klagge and Nicholas Smith, eds., *Methods of Interpreting Plato and His Dialogues, Oxford Studies in Ancient Philosophy* suppl. vol. (Oxford: Clarendon Press, 1992); Charles Griswold Jr., ed., *Platonic Writings, Platonic Readings* (New York: Routledge, 1988).

able casing for "Platonic doctrine,"[44] the dominant contemporary view insists that these elements have philosophical import or are otherwise directly relevant to Plato's purpose.[45] One of the most common inferences from an insistence on the intrinsic significance of the dialogue form is that Plato intended by his use of such form to invite his reader to take an active part in the dialogue, to enter into conversation with the interlocutors and thus to grapple himself with the ideas they propose. While this inference cannot be denied without ignoring not only a great deal of what Plato says in the dialogues but also the tangible effect they have always had on readers, a further inference is often drawn which is more debatable: namely, that in order to affirm the invitation to participate actively in the dialogue and come to insight for oneself, we must necessarily deny that Plato intends to communicate any particular insight himself.[46] It is said that Plato seeks not to teach us a particular philosophy but to train us or inspire us to philosophize for ourselves, and for this reason he tends to leave the dialogues open-ended and without resolution.[47]

Now, this inference has a certain validity, but in acknowledging it we have to avoid imposing conventional presuppositions regarding the nature of truth and freedom. It would be meaningless to encourage someone to philosophize unless one had (and offered) some positive view of what philosophy *is* and

44. Consider Richard Kraut's observation in his introduction to *The Cambridge Companion to Plato* (Cambridge: Cambridge University Press, 1992), 26: "The dialogue form of his works should not keep us from saying that they are vehicles for the articulation and defense of certain theses and the defeat of others. Though they are not philosophical treatises, many of them share these purposes with philosophical treatises." Kenneth Sayre has called this view the "proto-essay" approach. See "A Maieutic View of Five Late Dialogues," in Klagge and Smith, *Methods of Interpreting Plato and His Dialogues*, 221–43.

45. Griswold's blurb on the jacket of Press, *Plato's Dialogues,* states that "The general argument that Plato's dialogues are to be read as philosophical *dramas* has more or less won the day." There are far too many proponents of this argument in some form to name them all, but some of the better known or more recent are Arieti, Blondell, Brann, Clay, Desjardins, Ferber, Ferrari, Giuliani, Gonzalez, Gordon, Griswold, Howland, Hyland, Kahn, Klein, McCabe, Miller, Moes, Press, Randall, Roochnik, Rosen, Sallis, Sayre, and not to mention Derrida, Heidegger, Gadamer, Jaeger, Strauss, and Voegelin.

46. See Francisco Gonzalez's discussion of the literature and the relation between skeptical interpretations and the valorization of the literary elements of the dialogues. "Introduction: A Short History of Platonic Interpretation and the 'Third Way,'" in *The Third Way,* 1–22, here8–11.

47. Consider, for example, Jill Gordon, *Turning toward Philosophy* (University Park: Pennsylvania State University Press, 1999), 8–11; and Bernard Freydberg, *The Play of the Platonic Dialogues* (New York: Peter Lang, 1997), 11–22, esp. 14.

why it is good. Indeed, we cannot deny that, for Plato, philosophy is not just good but the ultimate human good. Such a conviction implies certain definite beliefs about the nature of reality and the human soul; the exhortation to philosophy would make little sense outside of beliefs of this sort. To say this is not necessarily to affirm that Plato has a doctrine that could adequately be translated into a set of propositions, but only to deny the claim that Plato has no view of the world or any wish to communicate a view and seeks simply to leave an empty space for the reader to fill in for himself. However much the more open-ended approach to Plato's dialogues is right to insist that philosophy demands firsthand participation, it cannot leave the concept of philosophy simply indeterminate (arguably, it never really does) without becoming at some point incoherent. The question will always be the *adequacy* of our understanding of Plato's own conception of philosophy, along with the nature of reality and the soul it implies, and what we ultimately make of that conception. There is no a priori reason, in any event, why a particular view of the nature of reality and the soul cannot encourage, or even in some sense *require*, rather than stifle or suppress, an active, firsthand engagement with reality and wonder over it. A lack of any clear conviction about the most important things is hardly the most effective intellectual tonic.

On the other hand, if Plato simply intended to express a definite philosophy, why would he employ a form laden with such resilient ambiguity?[48] The straightforward style of a treatise or even a monological poem would seem a more reliable route to this end. One of the most immediately obvious attributes of a dialogue is its inclusion of a plurality of voices.[49] Does this plu-

---

48. "Just before he died, we are told, Plato dreamed that he was changed into a swan and, flying from tree to tree, caused much trouble for the bird-catchers who vainly tried to take him. Simmias, the companion of Socrates, interpreted the dream to signify that all men would desire to catch the spirit of Plato, but none would succeed, for each would interpret him in his own fashion. It was a true dream, repeatedly fulfilled by admirers of Plato," Frederick J. E. Woodbridge, *The Son of Apollo* (Boston: Houghton Mifflin, 1929), 31.

49. Another is the "mimetic" aspect—the fact that the author does not speak in his own voice. Ruby Blondell has argued that the rejection of authoritative posturing this aspect implies is the only serious philosophical significance of Plato's use of a dramatic genre. See *The Play of Character in Plato's Dialogues* (Cambridge: Cambridge University Press, 2002). We will offer a different interpretation of Plato's "invisibility" as author in chapter 4. For the moment, it bears remarking that Blondell's concern that the dramatic interpretation may tend to reduce the dialogues to mere conflicts of ideas fails to acknowledge the possibility that such a conflict may indeed give rise to a comprehensive and unifying meaning, which is the possibility we seek to show in this book.

rality speak against the suggestion just made that Plato has "a" particular philosophy? One way to avoid this implication would be to insist that one of the
voices (most often Socrates') represents Plato's own, and the interlocutors
simply present occasions for him to articulate his position. While it is quite
evident that certain voices—and Socrates' above all—carry more weight than
others in the dialogues, if we accept the hypothesis that a single voice expresses what Plato intends, we cannot avoid reducing the dialogue form once again
to a disposable ornament. On the other hand, the assumption that a plurality of voices necessarily entails the rejection of any particular insight seems
to approach dialogue as nothing more than recorded conversations in which
various perspectives simply interact. But this assumption turns out to be sterile, leaving us with one of two problematic alternatives: either we assume that
one perspective "wins out" in the end, however much it may be modified
through the interaction, or we assume there simply is no resolution. In the
first case, we return to the question of why the dialogue itself has any intrinsic necessity if there is in the end a "right" perspective that could simply have
been articulated at the outset. In the second case, we are left with the monot-
ony of talk for its own sake that is not meant to go anywhere.[50]

An alternative way of taking the dialogue form, and the one we adopt
in the present book, is to look at the dialogues not as mere conversation or
aimless talk, but as *staged* discussion, to see the philosophical debate therein not as a "heap" of arguments, but as an enacted whole. According to this
view, the interaction of the various aspects of the dialogue—including not
only the multiplicity of perspectives, but also aspects such as concrete setting, the play of character, irony, the deliberately ordered arrangement of
arguments, the decisions and gestures made, and the like—gives rise to an
insight that would otherwise be unattainable. A number of contemporary
scholars have been proposing an approach of this sort, because it seems to
offer a sound alternative to both skeptical and dogmatic readings of Plato.
James Arieti is one of the best known for explicitly interpreting the dialogues
not just as including dramatic elements but as *dramas* in their own right.[51] In

50. John Herman Randall Jr. refers to Plato's dialogues as "Absolute Talk," and compares
them to the aimless, all-night conversations from which one emerges knowing perhaps less than
before, but having acquired a love of wisdom. *Plato: The Dramatist of the Life of Reason* (New
York: Columbia University Press, 1970), 4–5.

51. James Arieti, *Interpreting Plato: The Dialogues as Drama* (Lanham, Md.: Rowman and Littlefield, 1991).

Arieti's view, through the "plot" of the interwoven argument and action, the dialogues tend to offer a "dramatic" response to the question posed in the discussion, a response that would not fully have been achieved through discursive argument alone.[52] Though he does not often use the notion of drama explicitly, Francisco Gonzalez has shown that Platonic dialectic arrives at a kind of nonpropositional knowledge, which is quite determinate even if it exceeds definition, and that the literary and dramatic aspects of the dialogues serve to generate such knowledge.[53] Perhaps most closely related to the approach we take here is Gerald Press's notion of the Platonic dialogue as an "enactment" of philosophy, which is intended to introduce the reader, not to knowledge in the sense of, say, information, but into a *theoria,* that is, a *vision* of the world.[54] Common to these various ways of reading Plato is what we could call the "event-like" character they attribute in different ways to the insight the dialogues communicate. They allow us to take the philosophical content of the dialogues seriously while at the same time allotting a central role to their literary dimension. In other words, they do justice to the remarkable unity of form and content in Plato's philosophical artistry.

Though we affirm this "dramatic" approach to reading Plato, our own position is distinct from these other authors' in two respects. First, these authors tend to affirm in various ways that Plato ultimately seeks to communicate a kind of "knowledge" (or vision, inspiration, intuition, etc.) that is *nondiscursive.*[55] We prefer instead to suggest that the kind of knowledge Pla-

52. Rosemary Desjardins makes a similar observation in "Why Dialogues? Plato's Serious Play," in Griswold, *Platonic Writings, Platonic Readings,* 110–25, here 119–22.

53. Francisco Gonzalez, "Self-knowledge, Practical Knowledge, and Insight: Plato's Dialectic and the Dialogue Form," in *The Third Way,* 155–87; see also Gonzalez, *Dialectic and Dialogue: Plato's Practice of Philosophical Inquiry* (Evanston, Ill.: Northwestern University Press, 1998).

54. Gerald Press, "Plato's Dialogues as Enactments," in Gonzalez, *The Third Way,* 133–52; see also Press, "Principles of Dramatic and Non-dogmatic Plato Interpretation," in *Plato's Dialogues,* 107–27.

55. Arieti *opposes* the two: "Plato, like all great authors, has points to make. He simply makes them dramatically, not discursively," *Interpreting Plato,* 5. Why not say "both dramatically *and* discursively"? Though Press is generally concerned to overcome dichotomies in interpreting Plato, he seems to retain a certain exclusivity regarding the nondiscursive character of Plato's ultimate insights: "So a first point about Plato's philosophy is that it is a vision *rather than* a matter of doctrines." (Press, "Plato's Dialogues as Enactments," 147 [my emphasis]). Why not affirm simultaneously that Plato presents "doctrines" *and* vision, with each inseparable from and reciprocally supporting the other? For the most part, Gonzalez seems to do more justice to the logical and discursive aspects of the Platonic dialogues, even if he too ultimately affirms a kind of intuitive "insight" or inspiration in contrast to a describable theory. Ferber is surely right to claim that

to has in mind *is* discursive, but is never *merely* discursive. The "proposition-al" aspect is a necessary but insufficient condition of philosophy: according to Plato, we need to be able to say what we know even if our words will nev-er simply "contain" what we are trying to say. The point is not "nonproposi-tional" insight or inspiration, but rather "never-merely-propositional" knowl-edge. In other words, as we will elaborate further as we proceed, Plato aims at a kind of *comprehensive* knowledge that includes both a discursive and a nondiscursive element and does not simply exclude either. Second, we af-firm that Plato's use of the dramatic dialogue form arises specifically from the connection between goodness and intelligibility. As we have suggested, if goodness is the ground of knowledge, reason would depend in some in-trinsic way on the order governed by the good, namely, the order of action, in order for it to be reason in the fullest sense.[56] We propose that there is an essential link between Plato's claim that the good is the cause of being, truth, and the power to know, and the way in which he sought to commu-nicate that claim. He is not a philosopher who happens to have the talent for and inclination toward drama, but rather writes in a way that embodies methodologically the nature of what he means to show, the nature of reason itself. The *Republic* is not just a colorfully presented discussion of ideas and their possibilities, but a *dramatic argument* devised to bring to expression as decisively as possible a claim about the nature of reality. We will elaborate this statement further over the course of the book.

If it is indeed the case that Plato intends to use the whole of the dialogue, in the interrelation of its various (philosophical and literary) parts, to com-municate some insight, then it is legitimate to present the insight one at-tempts to discern in one's interpretation of the dialogue as belonging to Pla-to. Accordingly, we will often use expressions such as "Plato says" and "in Plato's view," in our discussion of the dialogue. If these expressions most fre-quently refer to claims coming out of Socrates' mouth—which is of course the source of nearly all of the words spoken in the body of the *Republic*—it is not because we are assuming that Socrates simply stands as Plato's mouth-

---

Plato intends a grasp of ideas that *precedes* the distinction between propositional and nonpropo-sitional knowledge. *Platos Idee des Guten,* 59.

56. There is a similarity between our position and that proposed by Wolfgang Wieland in *Platon und die Formen des Wissens* (Göttingen: Vandenhoeck und Ruprecht, 1982), namely, that knowledge of the good is essentially *practical* knowledge (222), but we would insist that it is si-multaneously practical and theoretical.

piece.[57] Rather, it is because Socrates represents the primary agent in the philosophical drama that Plato authored.

Finally, it is worth emphasizing again that we offer the following essay as a philosophical interpretation of the text rather than a historical study or analysis. Our interpretation takes for granted a basic unity in Plato's thought, and thus we will draw on other dialogues on occasion to illuminate an idea in the *Republic*.[58] If our purpose were primarily to record the history of Plato's intellectual growth, we would clearly have to attend especially to differences and make some judgment about relative dates. Since our interest, however, is more "constructive" or theme-oriented, and seeks above all to come to grips with the nature of reason as Plato presents it, too much comparison between treatments in various places and attention to the changes they betray would be inappropriate. Nevertheless, it bears remarking that a philosophical interpretation of a text has no less obligation to fidelity than what passes for a historical study. Any attempt to understand the unity of a text necessitates seeing more than what appears on the surface; the test of fidelity, then, is not whether an interpretation refuses to go beyond the surface—which means in fact a refusal to see the unity that ties the various appearances together, a refusal to interpret at all—but to what extent the unity does justice to what appears by offering an account of it and showing how the pieces fit together. Such an interpretation will invariably be guided by the interpreter's own horizon and sets of concerns; however one may wish to qualify details, the central argument of Gadamer's *Truth and Method* is incontestable.[59] One does best by being as forthright as possible about one's own presuppositions and concerns, which is one of the purposes of this introduction. If one's ultimately unique perspective on a text brings out a di-

---

57. On the problems with taking Socrates to be Plato's mouthpiece in the dialogues, see the various essays collected in Press, *Who Speaks for Plato?*

58. The assumption that there is a unity to Plato's thinking and therefore a fundamental consistency of philosophical understanding that runs through the various dialogues, such that they may be used to help illuminate one another, is of course controversial. It is not possible in the present context, however, to offer a complete argument on behalf of this approach, since that would require a book in itself. The most recent scholarship tends to favor a unitary approach (see Holger Thesleff, *Studies in Plato's Two-Level Model* [Helsinki: Societas Scientiarum Fennica, 1999], 2n2), in part because a number of major studies have shown the weakness of the developmentalist argument. We discuss this weakness in the coda of the book.

59. Hans-Georg Gadamer, *Truth and Method*, 2nd rev. ed. translated by Joel Weinsheimer, (New York: Continuum International Publishing Group, 2005).

mension that is not often noticed, it does not follow that this dimension has been "read into" the text, any more than the fact that certain friendships bring out different dimensions of a person's character implies that the person has no character. What is true about texts generally is particularly true in the case of Plato: as we said above, the dialogue form *intends* the reader's active participation because it presents ideas that are themselves still alive—or "ensouled," as Plato puts it in the *Phaedrus*.

In sum, if there is indeed some analogy between interpretation and friendship, perhaps it is true that the best and most faithful interpretation would come not from a critical (i.e., skeptical) objectivity, but from the best love of, or friendship for, Plato, even while this includes a willingness to criticize. Aristotle's well-known dictum, *amicus Plato, sed magis amica veritas*, rests on a fundamental misunderstanding (as Aristotle was of course fully aware). To the extent that Plato himself believes what he has Socrates say on several occasions, one is no more a friend of Plato's than when one disregards him for the sake of the truth he loved.

The first chapter of this book, "A Logic of Violence," will offer a reading of book I of the *Republic*. Plato gives indications that the discussion in this book takes place "in the cave"—i.e., within an inadequate horizon that cannot allow the "whole" truth to be seen. Paradoxically, we can recognize the inadequacy of this initial context only by anticipating what is to come, which means we can see it only from "outside" of the cave. Thus, an ability to read this first book properly implies already from the beginning a resolution to the central epistemological problem of the *Republic:* how to get outside a merely relative perspective. We will focus this chapter on Socrates' altercation with Thrasymachus and interpret it not merely as a play of character but as also a conflict between two views of reason. Our suggestion is that Thrasymachus's violence is a consequence of his relativistic epistemology, and he therefore shows himself to be a paradigm of the problem of "life in the cave." An adequate response to this problem, however, requires not just a good argument, but a shifting of the horizon in which understanding takes place. It requires, in other words, an essentially "dramatic" argument. In book I, Socrates therefore shows how Thrasymachus contradicts himself, but confesses at the end the inadequacy of his own response. His confession opens up the discussion to the movement of transcendence that the *Republic* will eventually describe in full.

Chapter 2, "With Good Reason," explores the relationship between good-ness and intelligibility as Plato expresses it in the *Republic*. Because this re-lationship is determined most fundamentally by the nature of the good, we take our bearings from the first point Plato makes about goodness in the main body of the discussion: the highest good is both good in itself *and* good in its effects. Our thesis is that this twofold characterization of the good as *both* absolute (good in itself) *and* relative (good for us) represents the interpre-tive key that unlocks the significance of the philosophical drama and prepares for the climax at the central part of the dialogue. To say that the good causes truth means that it establishes being in its nonrelativity, but also that it makes that nonrelativity accessible to the soul. The good, in other words, separates being from appearance, but it also bridges that separation, and thus makes truth and knowledge possible. But if intelligibility depends on goodness, un-derstanding will be an intimate relationship that requires the movement of the soul's transformation. Here we see why there is an intrinsic connection, for Plato, between *logos* and *eros*. The chapter thus includes a discussion of the ascent of love, from relative beauty to absolute beauty, as described in the *Symposium* and the *Phaedrus,* and argues for an analogy between this ascent and the ascent of reason Plato presents in the *Republic*.

Insofar as the good represents, for Plato, the principle of intelligibility, the possibility of knowledge depends on "immediate" access to the idea of the good. But this demand represents the most difficult paradox of the dia-logue, which is the subject of the book's third chapter, "Breaking In: Rever-sal and Reality": How is it possible to make intelligibly manifest that which lies beyond both appearance and intelligibility, as their ground? To disclose the nature of the good, Plato lays out three images in the central part of the *Republic:* the sun, the divided line, and the cave. Since Socrates admits that these are merely images, commentators tend to interpret the *Republic* as failing to carry through the method Plato outlines therein. Through a close reading of these central passages, this chapter claims, by contrast, that Plato intends to present the historical Socrates as the real image of the good. Not only does Socrates give an argument for the absolute priority of the good, but he also shows this priority in a lived commitment. By thus confirming the hypothesis of the good, he fulfills the epistemological conditions set forth in the divided line, and moreover responds in a direct way to the chal-lenges set forth by Glaucon and Adeimantus at the start of the discussion. The historical figure of Socrates, by standing both *in* and *beyond* the Platonic text, reflects the twofold nature of the good in a paradigmatic way. He himself is therefore the central "argument" of the *Republic*.

While the previous chapter showed how Socrates in principle satisfies the methodological requirements set forth in the *Republic,* chapter 4, "On Being Invisible," aims to lend substance to this claim in several ways. First, it suggests that Socrates' concrete "showing forth" of the good in an immediate way figures crucially in other dialogues, namely, the *Lysis* and the *Symposium.* Next, it argues that features of Socrates' character, as Plato presents it in his writing, play a metaphysical and epistemological role: for example, his refusal to accept money for his "teaching," his unconditional obedience to the good, his demonstration that it is better to suffer injustice than to commit it, are essential components to the task of bringing truth to light. Plato makes reference in many places to the "invisibility" of the philosopher; this chapter offers a philosophical interpretation of this image. An exclusive devotion to goodness makes the philosopher transparent to it, and by the same token allows things to manifest themselves in their intrinsic being. The chapter concludes with a reflection on the significance of Plato's own invisibility as an author.

Chapter 5, "The Truth Is Defenseless," addresses the question of justifying the view of reason presented in the *Republic* to one who does not take reasonability seriously. If defending something means appealing to something greater in order to justify it, then the good cannot be defended precisely because it is the ultimate foundation for reason. Through a comparison of the epistemologies in the *Republic* and in *Letter VII,* this chapter shows that the good being the cause of truth entails an "ecstatic" conception of reason: reason must come "out" of itself in order to reach the being of things, but by doing so it surrenders the capacity to defend itself. Such a view of reason provides a context for sketching out the basic contrast between the philosopher and the sophist. Sophistry is primarily concerned with defending a position and thus persuading one's hearers, while philosophy is concerned with discovering truth, even in spite of oneself. While sophistry seeks power, philosophy is essentially a renunciation of power. This understanding offers a new perspective for interpreting the apparently incommensurable dialogues Plato often depicts between philosophy and its enemies. If defenselessness characterizes the heart of the philosophical act, then the "failure" of dialogue, insofar as it provides an occasion for fidelity to the good, can become paradoxically a privileged locus for the manifestation of truth. Socrates' encounter with his accusers in the *Apology* is offered as a paradigm. The chapter concludes with a brief comment on the significance of Socrates' regular profession of ignorance in the light of the foregoing argument.

This book's interpretation of the twofold nature of the good sheds new light on the old controversy regarding Plato's simultaneous condemnation of poetry and his regular use of poetic images in his own work, especially in the *Republic*. The coda, entitled "Restoring Appearances," first discusses the problems that arise from the simple rejection of appearances and images that is typically associated with "Platonic" dualism. It then suggests that such a view of Plato is one-sided, first by showing the various self-contradictions and inconsistencies contained in the *Republic* in relation to this issue, and then by proposing a more comprehensive view that both preserves and overcomes the various tensions. Essentially, the absoluteness of the good both *distinguishes* being from appearance (thus requiring the elimination of appearances) and also *joins* them together (thus requiring the restoration of appearances). This twofold movement is reflected in the structure of the *Republic,* and seems also to be reflected in the trajectory of the dialogues in the Platonic corpus as a whole. Finally, the coda offers an interpretation of the concluding myth of Er: the dying and returning to life of Er is an image of the historical Socrates, who died but was brought back to life in Plato's writing. It concludes with a reflection on Plato's return to images in his writing of dialogues not as a compromise of philosophy's aims, but as a carrying through of the philosopher's obligation to return to the "cave."

CHAPTER ONE

A LOGIC OF VIOLENCE

Or, How the Impossibility of Knowledge Renders
All Communication Manipulation and
All Relation a Power Struggle

Where Do We Start?

The Republic begins (at least) twice; after the relatively independent and yet incomplete mini-dialogue of book I, book II starts with an explicit *da capo.* Even once the conversation is underway, restarts and revisions occur repeatedly.[1] The dialogue, it seems, runs into difficulty finding the right beginning, which is an unsettling difficulty if it is true that "the beginning is the most important part of every work" (337a). According to Socrates, "Everyone must therefore give great care to the beginning of any undertaking, to see whether his foundation is right or not."[2] Ironically, it is reported that Plato repeatedly revised the *Republic,* especially its opening lines.[3]

---

1. For example, in book I, Plato "tries out" several proposals for the meaning of justice and acknowledges that the procedure for adjudicating them is second best (348b); the ideal city undergoes more than one revision; Socrates insists that the method used to draw the analogy between city and soul is imprecise (436d); there are interruptions (419a, 449a) requiring aspects of the discussion to start again "from the beginning" (450a, 502e), and so forth.

2. *Cra.,* 436d (Loeb translation).

3. D. L., III.37, and Dionysius of Halicarnassus, *De compositione verborum* (New York: Classic Books, 1910), 25.209. See also Holger Thesleff, *Studies in Platonic Chronology* (Helsinki: Societas Scientiarum Fennica, 1982), 84–85, 107. Thesleff also describes the difference between modern publishing and the common ancient practice of repeated revision: 83–87. Cf. *Phdr.,* 278d–e: "On the other hand, if a man has nothing more valuable than what he has composed or written, spending long hours twisting it around, pasting parts together and taking them apart—wouldn't you be right to call him a poet or a speech writer or an author of laws?" See Alice Swift Riginos, *Platonica: The Anecdotes Concerning the Life and Writings of Plato* (Leiden: Brill, 1976), 185–86. Basil Mitchell and J. R. Lucas, *An Engagement with Plato's Republic: A Companion to the Republic*

The reasons for the difficulty of finding an adequate beginning become apparent when we consider the radical nature of the question the dialogue intends to explore: inseparably both *what* justice is—justice being not only one among the virtues, but in some sense "virtue-ness" itself[4]—and also whether it is good. As attempt follows attempt we eventually discover that such a fundamental question cannot be addressed without also addressing the more universal questions of what truth and goodness are, and these in turn require some apprehension of that which is ultimate in relation to all other things. In order to understand the initial question, then, we must already in some sense know what comes after it, and ultimately must know what comes last of all. In other words, we cannot truly begin until we have reached the end. Or as Plato puts it more commonly, all learning is a kind of recollection.[5] The notion of a "pure" or absolute beginning—which has been the aspiration in Enlightenment thought, German Idealism, and some forms of twentieth-century phenomenology—is foreign to Plato. Moving forward, for Plato, inevitably turns out to be in some respect a "catching up." When Socrates starts speaking in the opening scene of the dialogue, he reports something that occurred the previous day and in this report relates that he began already by coming from somewhere else: "I went down yesterday to the Piraeus." The natural question is: From where?

Literally, we know that the trek from Athens to its nearby port slopes downward. But more profoundly, if we begin from knowledge of the dialogue as a whole, we recognize that the first word of the *Republic,* κατέβην, signals one of its central philosophical themes, the ascent and descent through the levels of being and their corresponding powers of soul.[6] And if we consider the Greek mythical world more broadly, this philosophical theme resonates within another, that of the hero's (Odysseus, Heracles) journey to Hades and

---

(Burlington, Vt.: Ashgate, 2003), 1, refer to a legend that Plato revised the dialogue thirty-seven times. Hegel specifies that Plato revised it *seven* times, and then adds that, ideally, a major philosophical undertaking out to be revised seventy times seven times. Hegel, *Wissenschaft der Logik, erster Teil,* edited by Georg Lasson (Hamburg: Felix Meiner Verlag, 1967), 21-22.

4. So much so that Mitchell and Lucas translate τὸ δικαιόν and its variations as "morality," which they claim, with some justice, to be its rough equivalent in modern English. *Engagement with Plato's Republic,* x, 1–2.

5. "The narrative structure of the *Republic* suggests that the dialogue may provide the reader with a route to self-knowledge, to the extent that he is able to bring together or re-collect the *Republic* as a whole and grasp it in its philosophical integrity," Jacob Howland, *The Republic: The Odyssey of Philosophy* (New York: Twayne Publishers, 1993), 34.

6. See for example *Rep.,* 511a–b; cf. *Letter VII,* 343e.

back.[7] When Plato restarts the discussion in book II, the echo of the first beginning focuses more thematically the philosophical distinction that lies implicit already here: book II begins with Glaucon's compelling Socrates to
choose which he prefers, merely seeming (δοκεῖν) to persuade or truly (ἀληθῶς) to do so (i.e., to choose between appearance and reality). If philosophy
is, as Socrates will eventually say, an "ascent to what *is*" (521c) or an "upward
journey" (517a) to reality beyond appearances, then the first beginning would
seem to be an unphilosophical descent into appearances. The verb Plato uses
here is the same used in book VII (519d, 520c) to describe the philosopher's
going down from the vision of true being into the cave of unreal images.[8]

  Thus, the opening word of the dialogue places the scene of book I into
a particular context. Before considering how the philosophical context in
some sense determines the meaning of this scene, let us note its significance
for the question of finding a place to start, for the question prefigures the
problem that stands at the heart of the dialogue and therefore will present
the focus of our own study. It is, we suggested, impossible to find a fully adequate beginning, because doing so would require already having reached the
end. And yet one has to start somewhere. If we cannot explicitly presuppose
the conclusion as already having been concluded, we ought to begin in a way
that presupposes an openness to it. The best beginning would in this case
be one that recognizes its inadequacy, or to put it in other terms, its relativity to a further end. But even here, a certain paradox remains, and must not
be overlooked: if we as readers recognize that the beginning of the dialogue
is relative and provisional, and that the questions it initially addresses will be
revised within progressively developing contexts,[9] it is only because we are
already familiar with the dialogue as a whole and can anticipate where it is

7. On the rich philosophical and mythical significance of the theme of the ascent/descent
in the *Republic*, see Eric Voegelin, *Plato and Aristotle*, vol. 3 of *Order and History* (Baton Rouge:
Louisiana State University Press, 1985), 52–62; Eva Brann, "The Music of the *Republic*," St. John's
Review XXXIX: 1–2 (1989–1990): 1–103, here 1–12. On Plato's use of the mythological motif of the
descent to represent the way to attain truth, see Lars Albinus, "The Katabasis of Er: Plato's Use of
Myths, Exemplified by the Myth of Er," in *Essays on Plato's Republic*, edited by Erik Nis Ostenfeld
(Aarhus, Denmark: Aarhus University Press, 1998), 91–105.

8. On Socrates' going down as a descent into the cave, see George Rudebusch, "Dramatic
Prefiguration in Plato's *Republic*," *Philosophy and Literature* 26.1 (2002): 75–83, here 81; Joel War-
ren Lidz, "Reflections on and in Plato's Cave," *Interpretation* 21 (1993–1994): 115–34, here 117;
Stanley Rosen, *Plato's* Republic: *A Study* (New Haven, Conn.: Yale University Press, 2005), 19.

9. Oswald Utermöhlen, *Die Bedeutung der Ideenlehre für die platonische Politeia* (Heidelberg: Carl Winter-Universitätsverlag, 1967), 12–14. Utermöhlen cites a further observation from

going. Indeed, our sense of its relativity grows in proportion to the clarity of our perception of its eventual destination. At the same time, it is only when we know where the dialogue is going that we are able to enter into the beginning and appreciate its full significance.[10] While it is obviously true that we cannot get to the end except from the beginning, it is also, though more subtly, the case that we cannot get to the beginning properly except from the end. We have to be beyond it in order to see it for what it is. If we did not know that there was any destination beyond the place at which the dialogue starts, we would strictly speaking be without means for perceiving its relativity. We could not, in other words, keep from making the beginning in a certain sense absolute and thereby from falsifying it.

According to Heraclitus, "Unless the unhoped for is hoped for, it will not be discovered" (DK 18). To know where we are in the dialogue we already need to know in advance, however inchoately, where we are going. To see a part *as* a part requires a notion of the whole; to understand the significance of the first scene requires a knowledge of the entire plot. As general and abstract as these affirmations may be, we ought to note how directly they bear on both the form and content of the *Republic,* and thus on any endeavor to interpret the dialogue. The knowledge of justice Socrates seeks will depend on the capacity to relativize individual perspectives within a whole, which entails the capacity to transcend, at least in some respect, their inevitable relativity. The difficulty of meeting this requirement is not lost on Plato—indeed, he is so thoroughly aware of the difficulty that it comes to expression in his philosophical style itself. Many readers of Plato highlight what we could call the finitude—the situatedness, concreteness, particularity, and historicity of the dialogues, and the determinate limitations these imply—that characterizes the *dialogue* form in striking contrast to the omniscience and authority of a treatise or even epic narrative.[11] But a specifically dramat-

---

J. Stenzel (*Kleine Schriften: Zur griechischen Philosophie* [Darmstadt: Hermann Gentner Verlag, 1957], 42): "The *Republic* bursts open the form of a dialogue on justice, which is what it originally planned to be."

10. It is often the case that the prologue to a Platonic dialogue contains the significance of the whole implicitly in a concrete, dramatic form: consider Gonzalez's illustration of this point in the *Lysis* and his general reflections on the matter. "How to Read a Platonic Prologue: *Lysis* 203a–207d," in *Plato as Author,* 15–44. Press remarks on the pregnancy of opening words in particular. "Principles of Dramatic and Non-dogmatic Plato Interpretation," 107–27, here 123–24.

11. See, for example, Drew Hyland, *Finitude and Transcendence in the Platonic Dialogues* (Albany: SUNY Press, 1995), 7, 13–33; Blondell, *The Play of Character,* 48–52.

ic approach brings to light a dimension that is often overlooked even when the literary aspects of the dialogues are given their due.

Drama, by its form, entails a particular relationship between part and whole that is immediately relevant to the philosophical content of the *Republic,* insofar as the part/whole relationship is indeed one of its central themes.[12] A drama is not a random sequence of events but, as Aristotle observed, a proportioned whole with a beginning, a middle, and an end.[13] In the best drama, there is a moment of reversal (περιπέτεια), which brings about a "change from ignorance to knowledge," in other words, a "discovery" (ἀναγνώρισις). This moment, however, cannot arrive out of the blue, but must occur "in the probable or necessary sequence of events"—it must be prepared for, and anticipated by, what precedes it.[14] At the same time, precisely because it is a reversal, the moment introduces a *change,* it casts the whole in a new light, recasting the meaning of the moments that preceded it (and without simply eliminating their initial meaning, since doing so would make the reversal meaningless). It is for this reason that, for all of the surprise of the reversal, the spectators of a drama experience a sense of resolution: the arrival of what is most decisive gathers up all the parts into a compelling whole. The beginning of a good drama, from this perspective, must both anticipate the resolution by setting the scene through the establishment of a certain horizon of meaning, and await the resolution in order to receive its own final meaning. To read the *Republic* dramatically, in this sense, would mean that we refuse to isolate the particular arguments or scenes as "hermeneutically sealed" individual entities, and instead read them as dependent on what is to come, and thus in anticipation of the decisive reversal and the change it entails "from ignorance to knowledge." This change is the revelation of the idea of the good at the peak of the discussion.[15] Regarding the present context, if we fail to see the incompleteness of the opening scene as intrinsic to its meaning, then we imprison ourselves within the relative part by making it, in spite of ourselves, a *ne plus ultra.* Plato returned over and over to rewrite the beginning of the *Republic* in order, we might say, to make it perfectly incomplete.

12. David Lachterman lists it as the final of four central themes, but adds that "this fourth line of argument . . . is not really 'on a par' with the first three, but rather comprehends or is an ingredient in them all," "What Is 'the Good' of Plato's *Republic?*" *St. John's Review* 39.1–2 (1989–1990): 139–71, here 142.

13. Aristotle, *Poetics,* 7.1450b25.   14. Ibid., 11.1452a24.

15. A dramatic approach to the dialogue is particularly appropriate given that Plato presents it as a dramatic contest. On this, see note 77 below.

Plato resists the absolutization of any starting point, and thus effects the note of drama, precisely by repeatedly *starting over.* This gesture immediately relativizes the various points of departure, showing them to be exactly that. At the same time, each new beginning draws on a more comprehensive perspective, until we reach the most adequate starting point (ἀρχή), the most precise measure (504c), which is both an end and a beginning, and each new start in turn entails at least implicitly a revision of that which preceded.[16] Here, we note simply that the dialogue holds open a self-transcending intentionality from the beginning insofar as it is conducted by one who is in essence just visiting: having come from above, he is also on his way back home (327b).[17]

Shadows of Justice

To come back to the beginning: if we approach book I in anticipation of what is to come later, we pick up several clues that Plato intended this initial discussion, into which Socrates "descends," to be seen as taking place "in the cave."[18]

In the first place, we ought to consider why it would make sense for Plato to open the drama of the *Republic* in the cave. When Socrates introduces the

16. Referring to the approach as "dialectical" rather than "dramatic," David Roochnik makes a similar observation: "The *Republic,* conceived as a dialectical work, is a series of swellings. An early stage of the conversation is interrupted and then revised in an increasingly rich and more adequate manner," *Beautiful City: The Dialectical Character of Plato's* "Republic" (Ithaca, N.Y.: Cornell University Press, 2003), 5. Roochnik also observes that the form itself necessarily implies a certain content (2). William Chase Greene describes the evolution of the discussion as essential to its dramatic character, which builds up to an "anagnorisis," "The Paradoxes of the *Republic,*" *Harvard Studies in Classical Philology* 63 (1958): 199–216, here 201–2.

17. Diskin Clay notes the self-transcending structure of the dialogue: "By opening new frontiers of argument, and reopening arguments that had seemed settled by the agreement of the characters within the dialogue, the *Republic* is an open dialogue." "Reading the *Republic,*" in Griswold, *Platonic Writings, Platonic Readings,* 19–33, here 23. It eventually opens as a whole beyond itself to the reader: "And outermost is the group of readers Plato addresses through the argument, action, and structure of the *Republic,*" 24. The notion that the dialogue as a whole transcends itself in relation to its readers—and thus *enacts* the transition from the cave (writing) to the light of the sun (reality)—will become significant for us in chapter 3.

18. Kenneth Dorter offers twelve reasons to interpret book I as occurring at the level of *eikasia,* the lowest level of the divided line that is concerned with mere images of things and thus generally understood to correspond to existence in the cave. See "The Divided Line and the Structure of Plato's *Republic,*" *History of Philosophy Quarterly* 21.1 (2004): 1–20, here 3–8.

famous allegory at the start of book VII, the image seems utterly fantastical. Reacting to it, Glaucon immediately twice uses the word ἄτοπος, "strange, from another place," to describe the image itself and the prisoners depicted in it. But Socrates corrects him: the image is not something from a different world concerned with other people. Instead, he says, they are "like us" (515a). We will discuss the allegory at greater length in context in chapters 2 and 3, but we may observe here that Plato intends to represent with it the normal affairs of everyday human life when conducted within a community that is not founded on philosophical rule.[19] The arena into which Socrates enters at the start of book I is just such a community, and exhibits the sorts of things Socrates illustrates in the allegory. Those who are trapped in the cave are occupied wholly by appearances, cast by, if not a false light, at least by a derivative one that we may call false to the extent that its derivative character is overlooked. The prisoners compete with each other in identifying shadows in a manner Plato insinuates is like the arguments in court or political disputations (516e, 517d–e). The opening scene of the *Republic* takes place either around 421 or 411 BC,[20] in any event, during a period of great political instability for Athens. Between the date of the *Republic's* dramatic setting and the time of its composition, there occurred the establishment of the Thirty Tyrants (404 BC)—during whose brief reign Polemarchus was executed and his brother Lysias escaped into exile—and Socrates' own execution (399 BC) by the restored democracy. In Polemarchus's house, where the discussion of the *Republic* takes place, we have not only the (silent) Lysias, who was to become a well-regarded rhetorician,[21] but also the aggressive sophist Thrasymachus, and one often associated with these two figures, Cleitophon.[22] When Socrates enters the house, he is greeted by Polemarchus's father as one who occasionally (but not often enough) comes down to visit, bringing with him interesting intellectual discussion. Cephalus himself, unfortunately, no longer has the strength to make the journey up (328c–d). If the cave allegory aims to present the normal human condition within the dark periods of political dis-

19. Dale Hall, "Interpreting Plato's Cave as an Allegory of the Human Condition," *Apeiron* 14 (1980): 74–86, here 84.

20. For a discussion of the possible dates for the *Republic*, see Debra Nails, *The People of Plato: A Prosopography of Plato and Other Socratics* (Indianapolis, Ind.: Hackett, 2002), 324–26.

21. See *Phdr*, 228a.

22. *Cl.*, 406a, 410d. There is scholarly controversy over the authenticity of the *Cleitophon*; we briefly discuss this controversy in chapter 5, note 155.

order as the starting point for philosophy, the opening scene into which Socrates descends makes that condition quite concrete.

Moreover, the only thing to do in the cave is to gape; Socrates' primary motivation for visiting the Piraeus is, as it were, to "catch the show." A first-time festival and procession is to take place there, in honor of a goddess, Bendis, who is worshiped by the Thracians. Though Socrates desires to exercise his piety with respect to the goddess, he dwells in particular on the spectacle, calling it a beautiful procession, which he and his companions "look upon"— the verb here is θεᾶσασθαι, related to the English word "theater," and meaning to view something as a spectator. Later, at the end of book V, Glaucon alludes to those who love such spectacles, who "run around to every chorus at the Dionysia, missing none in the cities or the villages" (475d), as people who seem to be lovers of learning. But Socrates corrects him: they merely *seem* to be. In fact, philosophers are most decisively to be distinguished from the lovers of spectacle (φιλοθεάμενοι). The weight of this distinction becomes most evident only when Plato explicitly introduces the allegory of the cave, in which the prisoners are in a sense absolutely nothing but spectators.[23] Plato reinforces this foreshadowing of the cave by referring to a sunset horse race, a spectacle that will be illuminated by torchlight (328a), which of course calls to mind the fire that makes the shadow-watching possible in the cave.[24] While Socrates would prefer to return to the city, he is voted down by his companions, who are seduced by the desire to watch this novelty. Like those in the cave, they are held fast to the visual image. Quite significantly, the long conversation that ensues takes place through the night, and thus without the light of the sun.

Second, the opening scene is dominated by images of force and violence. When Socrates and his companions initially turn to head home, they are physically restrained: Polemarchus orders his slave to order them to wait,

23. It is interesting to note, however, that the verbs related to θεωρία tend to be reserved for a more noble contemplation, and do not occur *within* the cave image to describe the prisoners' activity. Plato introduces the verb in the allegory, in fact, only to describe the released prisoner's vision of the heavenly bodies (516a) and gazing at the sun (516b), preferring the more pedestrian ὁράω for the subterranean activity.

24. Kenneth Dorter observes that "just as in the allegory of the cave we move from the artificial firelight that illuminates the cave to the natural light that is the source of all being, so the dialogue itself moves from a goddess associated with the artificial firelight of torches to one [in the myth of Er] associated with the natural light of the heavens," *The Transformation of Plato's Republic* (Lanham, Md.: Lexington Books, 2006), 24.

and he carries out this order by grabbing Socrates' cloak and repeating the command (the verb κελεύω occurs three times in three Stephanus lines). At this stage, there is not yet any *reason* available to direct the action as a criterion for decision, and the only alternative seems to be physical force and command. When Socrates explains their intention to move on to town, Polemarchus simply increases the force, and in fact allows only force as a response: "Do you see how many of us there are? . . . Well, then . . . either prove stronger than these men or stay here" (327c). To Socrates' proposal to persuade them otherwise, Polemarchus simply retorts that discussion is useless with those who refuse to listen. Reason or discussion (λόγος), one might say, presupposes a willingness to reason. When Socrates and his companions hesitate to capitulate to force, Adeimantus attempts, instead, to entice them through the opportunity to watch the spectacle. It seems, as we will have occasion to explore further, that sensuous desire detached from reason is simply another form of force. What we ought to notice here, however this may be, is that Socrates is not given a choice. The dominance of force in this context foreshadows not only the violence that Socrates claims the cave-prisoners would wish to inflict on the visiting philosopher, but also, more directly, their own physical condition: they themselves are forcibly restrained. Plato ironically casts the decision to stay in the form of a political resolution (as opposed, for example, to a properly philosophical insight), to which Socrates—against his own wish—must give assent: "'Well, if it is so resolved,' I said, 'that's how we must act'" (328b).[25]

Finally, and perhaps most obviously, if the cave represents a place of insubstantial images of things rather than knowledge, the discussion of justice in book I is clearly subterranean. In each of the three conversations that transpire—with Cephalus, Polemarchus, and Thrasymachus—the same thing occurs: Socrates' interlocutor begins by proposing an opinion concerning the nature of justice, and this opinion proves, through Socrates' questioning, to be in some basic sense inadequate or unjustified. None of these proposals, then, can lay claim to being instances of knowledge: Cephalus is simply unable to respond to questions, Socrates brings Polemarchus to see, among

25. Allan Bloom's note to this passage is illuminating: "At the end of this scene, which is a dramatic prefiguration of the whole political problem, Socrates uses this word as it was used in the political assembly to announce that the sovereign authority had passed a law or decree. It is the expression with which the laws begin, 'It is resolved by [literally, "it seems to"] the Athenian people,'" Bloom, *The Republic of Plato* (New York: Basic Books, 1968), 441n6.

other things, the problems that arise when one defines justice in terms of the (apparent) relativity of friendship rather than the objectivity of genuine goodness,[26] and Thrasymachus shows that he in fact has no interest in what justice is, but relativizes all such questions to the project of acquisition. Though Socrates brings to light the inadequacies of the various proposals, he never offers a positive definition of justice himself. His explanation of his reluctance is illuminating: he claims (of course) not to have knowledge of such things himself,[27] and that even if he did, Thrasymachus would not allow him to communicate it (337e). Thus, Socrates finds himself in an impossible situation, being commanded to give his opinion about justice and at the same time forbidden to say what he sees as true. It is, in fact, the exact situation depicted in the allegory of the cave: the philosopher is compelled to dispute about shadows with those who have no experience of true justice (517e), and thus forced to speak within a context that excludes genuine communication.[28]

26. According to Leonardo Tarán, there is in fact a connection between the relativity implied in Polemarchus's interpretation of Simonides' definition of justice as helping friends and harming enemies and Thrasymachus's championing of *pleonexia*. "Platonism and Socratic Ignorance," in *Platonic Investigations,* edited by Dominic O'Meara (Washington, D.C.: The Catholic University of America Press, 1985), 85–110, here 103–4.

27. It is important to see, however, that Socrates' profession of ignorance here is not what we would generally call skepticism. As Norbert Blößner has observed, Socrates takes for granted the absolute goodness of justice and never once calls this into question. *Dialogform und Argument: Studien zu Platons "Politeia"* (Stuttgart: Franz Steiner Verlag, 1997), 32–33. Interestingly, Thrasymachus is the one who claims knowledge in book I, and he is at the same time the one we would more naturally associate with skepticism. We will discuss the relationship between Socrates' ignorance and his certainty in chapter 4.

28. There is an analogy between this true "aporia," and the problem of writing, the resolution of which is already presupposed, we ought to note, before Plato begins to compose the *Republic.* (We will discuss this issue at length in the coda.) By reading Socrates' reticence as a function of his being in the cave of appearances, we take a position quite different from Strauss's well-known expression of the tensions between philosophy and politics in, for example, *The City and Man* (Chicago: Rand McNally and Company, 1964), and the necessity for indirection they impose on the philosophical writer. Leon Harold Craig presents the strategic significance of writing for philosophy in the political realm succinctly in *The War Lover: A Study of Plato's Republic* (Toronto: University of Toronto Press, 1994), xviii–xxvi. Although political prudence is clearly important, it is just as clearly an insufficient explanation for the indirectness of Plato's dialogue form, for the simple reason that Plato uses this form universally, for every philosophical issue, and not just for the more obviously political dialogues upon which Strauss focuses. Our position is that political prudence is ultimately subordinate to metaphysical necessity in accounting for Plato's choice of the dialogue form and his ample use of irony and indirection. We hope to illustrate that such an approach to writing is in fact the best way to *say the whole* most clearly.

For all of the complexities of the discussions in this first book, there never appears a viable claim to knowledge or any reference point in relation to which the discussion could find its bearings and make some progress toward knowledge.[29] Paul Natorp observes that there is no hint of the ideas at all in book I, and while he suggests it is because this book is merely a "prologue" (*Vorspiel*) to the dialogue, the more compelling reason is that there are no ideas *as such* in the cave.[30] The absence of any truth, wisdom, or knowledge in this opening scene of the dialogue becomes particularly conspicuous in relation to two facts. In the first place, even with the attempts to formulate a definition for justice, the discussions tend toward the empirical and revolve entirely around the relative benefits that justice can bring, which is, as we shall see in the next chapter, precisely the sort of investigation that precludes making the *truth* of justice manifest.[31] Cephalus thinks of justice in terms of rewards and punishments. The attempt to discover a definition of justice with Polemarchus comes up short when it turns out to be "useful for useless things" (333e), in other words, lacking any extrinsic benefits specific to itself. This is an especially remarkable failure, given that the discussion restarts in book II with the assumption that a consideration of such benefits does not get us to the heart of the matter. When Thrasymachus explicitly reduces justice to its advantage to the stronger, and holds to this advantage even when it seems to require the embrace of injustice, he is following the logic of the cave, which governs the entire discussion of this book. There is as yet no contrast between truth and seeming, inasmuch as the capacity to draw the contrast requires a perspective that is not yet available at this point.[32] To adjudicate between positions, Socrates offers as alternatives either the tedious method of laying out their details and appointing judges

29. See Jörg Kube, *TEXNH und APETH: Sophistisches und Platonisches Tugendwissen* (Berlin: Walter de Gruyter, 1969), 186–96.

30. See Paul Natorp, *Platos Ideenlehre: Eine Einführung in den Idealismus,* 2nd ed. (Leipzig: F. Meiner, 1922), 182.

31. Kimon Lycos, *Plato on Justice and Power: Reading Book I of Plato's Republic* (Albany: SUNY Press, 1987), argues that book I intends to "turn the soul around" in order that one might see the "'realities' of justice . . . rather than merely considering its conventionally recognized 'appearances,'" and makes precisely the suggestion we are making here: namely, that "the relation of Book I to the rest of the work corresponds somewhat to the powerful and highly influential image of the Cave Plato describes in Book VII" (6).

32. To be sure, Socrates *does* allude to the need to make this distinction in his exchange with Polemarchus (334c), but it is merely recorded as a necessity, without exploration of its possibility or the means to realize it.

to count their respective benefits and thus to compare them, or the simpler, "dialectical"[33] method of agreeing to take certain things for granted without further justification, and proceeding on the basis of that agreement. Though Socrates presents the latter, which they adopt, as second best, even the former is a far cry from a genuinely philosophical approach to knowledge.[34] In short, the discussion of book I remains from start to finish within the realm of "seeming," the realm of the cave.

In the second place, and even more tellingly, Socrates raises a question here that he discusses at much greater length in books V–VII, namely, whether the act of ruling is something desirable. In the first mention, he explains that ruling, properly understood, is an act that renders a service like the other arts, and is therefore not desirable in itself, but must be joined with some extraneous benefit to become something worth doing (346e–347a). In this context, he lists three possible "wages": "money, honor, or punishment for not ruling" (347a), and names this latter as the only one that befits the "best," because "love of honor" and "love of money" have something ignoble about them. What is striking about this list is the absence of a third type of love, an absence all the more conspicuous for being the main theme of the much longer discussion of the same question in books V–VII (473d–521b), namely, the love of wisdom.[35] The present context does not allow for an explicit appeal to wisdom. If we understand the discussion of book I as occurring within the shadowy half-darkness of the cave, it is clear why it does not. Wisdom, we will see, depends on truth, and truth cannot show itself as such within the restricted horizon of appearance. An appeal to wisdom would be meaningless at this stage; the closest thing we find in book I is the brief mention that one needs to be able to distinguish between being and appearance in order to know who one's friends are (334c–335a). But the interlocutors are not permitted to pursue the significance of this distinction because of Thrasymachus's interruption.

33. The term "dialectical" is meant here not in the more rigorous sense Plato describes later in the dialogue, but in the Aristotelian sense of proceeding from received opinion, a method Aristotle distinguishes from the demonstration that renders knowledge.

34. Plato *does* in fact use the method indicated here at the end of the dialogue (book X), but he does so only after having passed through the properly philosophical method in the central books.

35. Of course, as he shows in the longer discussion, lovers of wisdom will still exhibit a reluctance to rule, and will have to become rulers by accident or be compelled by their educators to take office. We discuss this question at greater length in chapter 4.

We will turn to consider the discussion with Thrasymachus at greater length presently, but for now it is helpful to see the larger issue emerging. When Socrates goes down to the Piraeus, he is entering the realm of appearance in a certain sense *on appearance's terms*. He is there for the spectacle. There is no assessment, in book I, of relative opinions from some fundamental perspective that would serve to orient the discussion of the proposed definitions. Book I is thus essentially negative.[36] If this is the case, then it would be misguided not only to look for settled responses to the problem of justice—which is obvious and remarked upon by nearly all commentators on the dialogue—but also, more subtly, and perhaps more importantly, to look for an adequate formulation of the problem.[37] In these initial conversations, it may be possible to acquire a sense for the urgency of knowing what justice is and whether it is good, but to pose the question concerning justice in a serious and fruitful way will require a more ample starting point. The surprising breadth of themes that enter the discussion beginning in book II, and the surprising depth of the metaphysical and epistemological issues in the central books, ought thus to be seen as intrinsic to the initial concerns: *everything* is at stake in the beginning, even though it is not yet possible to see that at the beginning. In this respect, the first part of the *Republic* is more

36. See Julia Annas, *An Introduction to Plato's Republic* (Oxford: Clarendon Press, 1981), 16. According to Kenneth Dorter, "Book 1 illustrates this [the fact that *eikasia* looks only to images and not to forms] in the way Socrates, by his own admission, examines only words or images of justice, without attempting to discern justice itself. There were refutations but no affirmations," "The Divided Line and the Structure of Plato's *Republic*," 8.

37. In this respect, David Sachs's famous discovery of a "fallacy" in the *Republic* ("A Fallacy in Plato's *Republic*," in *Plato: A Collection of Critical Essays*, edited by Gregory Vlastos [Garden City, N.Y.: Anchor Books, 1971], 35–51) misses the deepest point, and is in fact an excellent example of the problem with a "nondramatic" reading of the dialogues that isolates arguments from their place in the whole. Sachs claims that the meaning of justice changes in different places in the dialogue, so that the notion of justice Socrates ends up defending is not the notion they begin with. But if the dialogue begins in the cave, it cannot establish the horizon for the rest of the discussion without undermining the very goal the argument seeks. To be sure, there must remain some continuity between the beginning and the end, in spite of the dramatic "reversal," but such a continuity is there even with the transformation of the terms. On this, see Timothy Mahoney, "Do Plato's Philosopher-rulers Sacrifice Self-interest to Justice?" *Phronesis* XXXVII.3 (1992): 265–82. According to Lewis Campbell, "The gradual evolution of the thought is not referable to the incoherence of an unformed thinker, but to the most deliberate literary and philosophical design" ("On the Structure of Plato's *Republic* and Its Relation to Other Dialogues," in *Plato's* Republic, *the Greek Text*, edited by Benjamin Jowett and Lew Campbell, 3 vols. [Oxford: Clarendon Press, 1894], cited in Greene, "The Paradoxes of the *Republic*," 201).

radically aporetic than we generally assume: it serves not merely to make us wonder about the typical answers given to the question of the meaning and worth of justice, but to make us wonder at the question itself and the way we pose it. It is impossible to look for something, as Plato famously proposes in the *Meno* (80e), unless one already has a sense of what it is one is seeking. Until we have that sense, we need to have the sense that we need it.

If in book I we are in fact within the cave of images, we might look at Socrates' three conversation partners as themselves images of a sort, representing the three parts of the soul, wisdom, spirit, and appetite, which become a theme later along with their corresponding ways of life: love of wisdom, love of honor, and love of gain. His first discussion with Cephalus (the "head"), reveals that the elderly gentleman is merely an image of the love of wisdom, the highest way of life.[38] He is, first of all, no lover, happy to have left eros behind, and second, he has no knowledge. He affirms a traditional story, which he fears might be true, and cannot respond to even the first question put to him, but instead hands the story down (331d) (παραδίδωμι, i.e., *tradere, traditio*) to his son, who inherits as well the obligation to defend it. The highest principle thus turns out to be empty, however respectable it may be on the surface.[39] Although Socrates seems to make progress with the lover of honor, Polemarchus (the "war leader"), he is violently interrupted by Thrasymachus (the "bold fighter"), who makes an unabashed appeal to the love of gain. Thus, we might say, in sum, that Socrates' descent to the Piraeus does not end at his host's house, but continues all the way to the bottom of the cave. What we find there is exposure to sheer power. The setting suggests— notably by images and without argumentation[40]—that if there *is* no real love of wisdom, and if knowledge is impossible, then the precipitation to Thrasymachus's view is inevitable.[41] As we will see, Plato seeks to show, particularly

38. In the *Timaeus,* Plato refers to the head as "the most divine part of us, and master of all our other parts" (44d) and makes it the seat of the soul (45b).

39. Howland refers to Cephalus as a "cave-dweller," *Odyssey of Philosophy,* 63.

40. Quoting Kierkegaard's observation that "Socrates begins most of his investigations not at the center but at the periphery" (*The Concept of Irony,* translated by Howard Hong and Edna Hong [Princeton, N.J.: Princeton, University Press, 1992]), Eva Brann points out that myth, rather than *logos,* occupies this initial periphery in the *Republic* (Brann, "Music of the *Republic,*" 7). It does so at the other end as well (myth of Er). We will nevertheless argue in the coda that myth turns out to be no less central for all that.

41. According to Annas, Plato means to show that the "void" of Cephalus and Polemarchus is "all too plausibly filled by [Thrasymachus's] skepticism," *Introduction,* 21. And we would add

in Socrates' exchange with Thrasymachus, that there is a logical connection between "unfoundable" opinion, submission to appearance, and the absolutization of power.

The Power of Appearance

We tend to think of violence most fundamentally as a moral issue; that is, violence is a way of characterizing behavior rather than, say, a person's understanding of the nature of reality and truth. From this perspective, we would interpret Thrasymachus's championing of power and oppression as independent of his epistemological presuppositions—what it means for him for something to be true. If we wanted to challenge him, we would urge him, for example, to respect others and develop a concern for the dignity of individuals.[42] We would not talk about the structure of reality. But Plato does. The attempt to give a response to the problem Thrasymachus presents gives rise to the longest dialogue in the Platonic corpus (next to the *Laws*), at the center of which lies an extensive discussion of the way things are and the way the soul accesses them. One of the words that appears frequently in the dialogue is the adverb ἱκανῶς, "adequately," "sufficiently." It arguably strikes the keynote: Plato seeks the most adequate answer possible to Thrasymachus's sophistry, and this aspiration leads him ultimately to the question of the relation between goodness, truth, and being. It is well known that Plato sees ethics, epistemology, and metaphysics as inseparably bound up with one another.[43] This interconnection, however, would mean that the ethico-political problem of violence, which Thrasymachus represents, is at root also an epis-

---

that it is also filled by the violence this skepticism necessarily entails and Thrasymachus so clearly represents.

42. Ruby Blondell, for example, claims that arguments are ineffective against someone so wedded to his passions as Thrasymachus, and thus Socrates must practice his *elenchus*, which Blondell interprets as "an intrinsically *ad hominem* form of argument" that works on his *character* rather than his reason. "Letting Plato Speak for Himself: Character and Method in the *Republic*," in Press, *Who Speaks For Plato?*, 127–46, here 128–30.

43. In his introduction to the Loeb edition of the second volume of the *Republic* (Cambridge, Mass.: Harvard University Press, reprint 1994), Paul Shorey claims that the discussion of the ideas in the central books of the dialogue is simply to illustrate how a philosopher would have to be trained, and serves no essential purpose at all in the predominantly ethical and political intentions of the dialogue (ix–lxxiii, esp. xviii). With an author like Plato, however, it makes far better sense to assume they are intrinsic to the dialogue's basic argument, since they occupy such a central place therein.

temological and metaphysical problem.[44] In order to do justice to the problem, it is essential to approach it from this root. We would do well, therefore, to reflect on the connection between Thrasymachus's violence and his sophistical epistemology.

Let us consider this point more closely. Plato explicitly introduces the idea of the good in book VI as offering the best possible vantage point for understanding what justice is,[45] but the account he gives of the good has primarily to do with the nature of reality and the soul's relationship to it, and above all with the problem of knowledge. Now, if Plato presents these central books of the dialogue as the core of his response to the problem introduced at the outset, it must be the case that he understands the problem of justice to concern, at its heart, the nature of the soul's relation to reality. To put it bluntly, the problem with Thrasymachus is not so much a problem of character as it is, more fundamentally, a problem with what he takes to be most real. We will propose in the next chapter that imprisonment in the cave represents the isolation of individual perception, or what we could call the fragmentariness of relativism, in contrast to the self-transcending commonality of knowledge. In anticipation of that discussion, we will try to show here that Thrasymachus makes manifest a particularly aggressive relativism that has a simultaneously epistemological and moral dimension. There is, in other words, an essential connection between violence and the sophistic epistemology. Because Plato does not make the epistemological issue explicitly thematic in this context, we will set the scene for our reflection on Thrasymachus by means of a brief look at Socrates' presentation of Protagoras in the *Theaetetus,* in which he sets forth the relativist epistemology and considers its implications.

In the attempt to discern the true nature of knowledge during a discussion with Socrates, Theaetetus proposes the hypothesis that knowledge is identical to perception (αἴσθησις) (151e).[46] Socrates immediately connects this view with Protagoras's statement, "Man is the measure of all things"

44. Lachterman, "What Is 'the Good'?" 145, makes a similar point.

45. Just before looking for the virtues in book IV, Socrates insists they first need an "adequate" (ἱκανόν) light (427d). After presenting the social virtues, Socrates affirms they would be the same in the soul, but claims they would need to follow a "longer and further road" to confirm that it is the case (435d). They arrive at this road the moment Socrates introduces the idea of the good (504b).

46. Ronald Polansky, *Philosophy and Knowledge: A Commentary on Plato's* Theaetetus (Lewisburg, Pa.: Bucknell University Press, 1992), is correct to point out that perception here does not

(152a), and suggests that it contains within it the "secret doctrine," which he attributes to Homer, Heraclitus, and others, of the universal flux in which all things are coming to be (152c–d).[47] What links these statements? To know something is to grasp what it is. If knowledge is identical with perception, then one's grasp of what something is is no different from the way it happens to appear to one: "As each thing appears to me, so it is for me, and as it appears to you, so it is for you" (152a). There is, in other words, nothing that would allow one to distinguish, in relation to oneself, between the being of something and its appearance (φαίνεται, 152a). But if being represents the reality of a thing as distinct from its being perceived, then eliminating the distinction implies that the criterion by which knowledge is determined lies with the perceiver alone. Indeed, Socrates affirms that perception is by its very nature something "private to the individual" (τι ἑκάστῳ ἴδιον) (154a). If knowledge is reduced to perception, and perception is ultimately relative to the individual, then the individual *qua* individual becomes the ultimate measure of knowledge. If the individual is a man, Socrates continues, then man is in fact the measure: Theaetetus's hypothesis thus entails Protagoras's dictum.[48] Moreover, it also necessarily implies the infallibility of perception (160d), insofar as knowledge, *as* knowledge, is infallible, and the hypothesis posits the identity between perception and knowledge (152c). We could not introduce the possibility of mistaken perception without affirming a reality to things beyond their appearance to us.[49]

[handwritten margin note: radical relativism]

---

necessarily mean sense-perception (67), even if Socrates tends to use sense-perception as his example. Nevertheless, Theodorus uses the term in 144a to refer to the *soul's* perception. What is most basically at issue here is not senses vs. intellect, as we will see, but relativity to the individual vs. commonality.

47. Of course, there is good reason to contest certain aspects of Plato's interpretation of Heraclitus, Homer, and even Protagoras. As far as we are concerned in the present context, however, the issue is not so much what these particular authors may in fact have meant, as it is the implications of a particular epistemological or metaphysical position that Plato takes them to represent.

48. Of course, as some commentators point out, Socrates gives the dictum a twist, interpreting "man" in the individual sense rather than the universal.

49. Socrates does not consider the "Kantian" position that things may have a completely inaccessible being in themselves, which would allow for a noumenon distinct from the phenomenon even if knowledge itself is limited to the phenomenal. But one may ask whether it is possible in the end to maintain Kant's position with consistency. Though we cannot discuss this problem in the present context, we would be inclined to side with Hegel's criticism: When Kant presents the categories of the understanding, for example, is he constituting them merely phenomenally? At some point, one must posit what *is* the case in order to posit anything else.

On the other hand, Socrates explains, through a rather complex argument, that the identification of knowledge and perception ultimately entails as well the Heracleitean dictum regarding continuous change. The heart of the argument is that universal flux represents a necessary condition of the infallibility of perception.[50] In a nutshell, if it is true that perception is essentially relative to the individual, that knowledge is essentially relative to perception, and that reality is essentially relative to knowledge, then the being of things is constituted by their being perceived. Socrates describes the reality of things as being essentially "tied to a partner" (160b) and generated at every moment through the interaction of perceiver and perceived (156a–b). Notice, the key to the flux is the *relativity* of the perception that is taken to be identical to the reality of things. In other words, there is no unity that transcends this relativity in some respect (153e). "And so," according to Socrates, "wherever you turn, there is nothing, as we said at the outset, which in itself is just one thing; all things become relatively to something. The verb 'to be' must be totally abolished—though indeed we have been led by habit and ignorance into using it ourselves more than once, even in what we have just been saying" (157a–b). After considering the logical implications of the three statements—that perception is knowledge, that man is measure, and that all is flux—Socrates concludes that they have "converged to the same thing" (160d).

But in fact Socrates quickly proceeds to point out that this convergence is in a significant sense illusory, insofar as it presupposes that the statements are not mere "wind eggs" (161a) but have some coherent meaning.[51] If the phrase means what Socrates has interpreted it to mean, namely, that things *are* just as they appear to us, then the very notion of a measure dissolves. Perception, as we have seen, is by its nature "private to the individual"; there is no way to tell, Socrates explains, whether any person perceives things the same way as any other: "[D]o you even feel sure that anything appears to another human being like it appears to you? Wouldn't you be much more dis-

50. On this, see David Sedley, *The Midwife of Platonism: Text and Subtext in Plato's* Theaetetus (Oxford: Clarendon Press, 2004), 40.

51. David Bostock complains that Socrates, inconsistently with the universal flux thesis, continues to speak of things as entities of a sort. *Plato's* Theaetetus (Oxford: Clarendon Press, 1988), 81–83. But Socrates is aware of the inconsistency, as we see here, and is simply trying to give the best argument he can muster for a position he does not accept. Bostock does show the radical implications of the theory, namely, that it implies the dissolution even of the integrity of any agent of perception.

posed to hold that it doesn't appear the same even to yourself because you never remain like yourself?" (154a). To be sure, to say this does not mean— as we would be tempted to infer from this quotation—that appearance is necessarily qualitatively different in every case, but only that it be at the very least "numerically" different.[52] In any event, the very nature of perception simply makes comparison impossible, insofar as the relativity that consti- tutes it precludes the commonality that would be necessary for comparison (and, if we wish to be radical, that includes even comparison with itself). Even if perceptions happen to be qualitatively the same, it does not—and indeed *cannot*—matter. While it would be anachronistic, no doubt, to think that Plato is operating with the modern psychological view of subjectivity as a sphere closed up within itself,[53] he nevertheless indicates that sense- experience lacks precisely trans-individuality; it is not *common*. In this re- spect, if we make perception the *measure* for things, there is no supraindivid- ual measure. No one person is in a "better" position to judge than any oth- er. More than that: there would be no reason to say that any human being is a better judge than any other "perceiver." Thus, Socrates claims, Protagoras ought to have begun his book more dramatically with the claim that "'Pig is the measure of all things' or 'Baboon' or some yet more out-of-the-way crea- ture with the power of perception" (161c).

In fact, it is not sufficient to say simply that each perceiver is the measure, for this affirmation assumes a commonness that transcends the moment of perception. Rather, one must say that each individual perception is its own measure—or as Socrates puts it, one judges truly "at every moment" (ἀεί, 170c). But to say that each individual moment is its own measure is to say that there *is* no measure, insofar as a standard, to be a standard, must be able to apply to more than one thing at one time. When Socrates develops his cri- tique, he shows that good judgment concerns not just the present moment, but must apply beyond a particular moment, and so most especially con- cerns the future (see 178a). In short, "man is the measure" means every man is a measure at every moment, with respect to that moment alone, which means in the end that there is no measure at all. The statement is therefore empty; it has no defensible meaning.

If the statement were nevertheless taken as "true," Socrates points out

---

52. Bostock, *Plato's* Theaetetus, 49.
53. See Sedley, *The Midwife of Platonism*, 41n3.

that it renders discussion pointless (161e). Clearly, discussion of any sort, even the most extreme of disagreements, presupposes the capacity to have the same thing in mind as another about which to agree or disagree.[54] As the Visitor in the *Sophist* explains, discussion requires not simply the same word, but having a common referent for that word.[55] Lacking any commonality, conversation would be nothing more than making noises at one another. The significance of what follows from this cannot be overstated: unless it is possible in some respect to reach a reality beyond individual perception, the only available mode of communicating is to impose one's relative perception on another from the outside. Even this is possible only in a loose sense, since it too depends on getting a person to see the *same* thing you do. Perhaps the best we could say is that one "communicates" by causing a change in another. A view would prevail, not because it has more claim to truth, but because it is able to effect a change in another. To persuade, accordingly, comes to mean to lend prevailing force to a particular appearance, or, as the historical Protagoras himself is supposed to have put it, to "make the weaker argument the stronger." Thus, knowledge comes to mean power in an even more direct way than we are accustomed to understanding it: not that knowing something gives one the ability to make changes, but that "knowledge" itself is *nothing more than* an ability to change. As Socrates' Protagoras puts it, "I certainly do not deny the existence of both wisdom and wise men: far from it. But the man I call wise is the man who can change the appearance" (166d). "Wisdom," in this respect, is something essentially *imposed* on others; animals, Protagoras insists, are not wise just because they can perceive. Instead, wise are the doctors that effect changes in animal bodies (167b). Again, this view of wisdom, we are proposing, follows necessarily from the reduction of knowledge to individual perception.

With a touch of irony, Socrates observes that, though he himself would never claim to be a measure, Protagoras's saying would force that obligation on him, willy nilly: "I, who am without knowledge, am not in the least obliged to become a measure, as the argument in [Protagoras's] behalf just now tried to oblige me to be, whether I would or no" (179b). There is a profound insight in this seemingly casual remark; the statement that there is no

---

54. In the *Phaedrus,* Socrates observes that a failure to grasp the nature of a subject in one's discussion invariably leads to conflict with oneself and others (237c).

55. *Soph.,* 218c.

measure for truth can *only* be imposed on a person from the outside—*even if one accepts it*, because in this case acceptance can mean nothing else but capitulation to an authority that derives its force from something other than intrinsic meaning, namely, the push of fear or the pull of desire. The paradox cannot be avoided: inasmuch as perceptions are always true, Protagoras makes each person an authority (170c); but in another respect, because the assertion does not *mean* anything, the basis for making each person an authority is simply his own impenetrable authority. Socrates compared his saying to an "oracle speaking in jest from the impenetrable sanctuary (ἐκ τοῦ ἀδύτου) of the book" (162a)—ἄδυτος, "sanctuary," means literally a place that cannot be entered (ἀ-δύω). It is not possible to "enter into" it, because that would imply its being an intrinsic meaning that one could understand and to which one could assent. If the idea cannot be "entered into," one can only be passively manipulated by it, even if one is manipulated into a similarly inviolable authority of one's own. In short, if we cannot distinguish between being and appearance, we have no resources for moving beyond our isolated relativity, and human beings have no alternative to forcing themselves in some form on one another. Unless there is a reality that transcends relativity in some respect, some unity that belongs to things *in* themselves (αὐτὸ κάθ' αὐτό) 157a, 182b), there can be nothing to connect people in any intrinsic manner. Indeed, if relativity is absolutized, which is the logical implication of the hypothesis, then individuals themselves have no intrinsic unity.

It is crucial to see that the difficulties created by the identification of knowledge with perception do *not* turn on the deficiencies of the senses *qua* bodily organs, as one might assume because of Plato's alleged contempt for the material world. The subtler thesis that the problem lies with the invariable changeableness, as it were, of the material world to which the senses are attached is likewise inadequate. As we pointed out, αἴσθησις need not refer merely to *sense* perception; Plato does not in fact feel it is necessary to justify treating αἴσθησις and the more intellectual power of δόξα as effectively the same in this context.[56] The essential problem is making the relative *qua* relative the criterion for knowledge, that is, absolutizing the relative,

---

56. See Michel Narcy, "Qu'est-ce que la science? Réponses dans le *Théétète*," in *Platon: L'amour du savoir*, edited by Michel Narcy (Paris: Presses Universitaires de France, 2001), 49–72, here 55–59.

which eliminates any grounds for distinguishing between the way things are and the way they appear.[57] In this case, as we see in the discussion of Protagoras and his doctrine, we encounter the odd simultaneity of sheer relativism and sheer authoritarian dogmatism. At the same time, and for the same reason, we have the simultaneity of complete mastery (man, as measure, becomes the final arbiter of "truth"),[58] and utterly helpless passivity. They are flip sides of the same coin.

The connection between sophistry and violence appears often in the dialogues, and seems to be one of Plato's most basic concerns. What lies implicit within this exchange on the nature of knowledge becomes more explicit in, for example, one of Socrates' most direct confrontations with sophistry, the *Gorgias,* a dialogue that begins with the words "war and battle." These words express the essence of conversation when sophistry sets the terms and thus the horizon for the exchange. If one wishes to find an alternative to violence, one has no alternative but to seek something that resists reduction to sheer relationality and the tendency of relativism to absolutize itself, which is an endeavor that lies at the heart of Plato's philosophy, and above all, at the heart of the *Republic.*

Before turning to see the dramatic expression of the epistemological "power struggle" in Socrates' discussion with Thrasymachus, we ought to note two further aspects of the passage in the *Theaetetus* that will find an echo in that confrontation. In the first place, Socrates and Theodorus indicate a fundamental difficulty in engaging with one who "holds the position" that there is no being beyond appearance, and thus beyond the relative: "You know, Socrates, these Heraclitean doctrines (or, as you say, Homeric or still more ancient)—you can't discuss them in person with any of the people at Ephesus who profess to be adepts, any more than you could with a maniac. They are just like the things they say in their books—always on the move" (179e). To discuss the issue of being and appearance is thus not merely to debate two different positions, but to confront the taking of a position— we might say that "being" has as its subjective correlate a kind of "taking-

---

57. See Sedley, *The Midwife of Platonism,* 40. Notice, this is *not* a critique of perception *per se,* but only its absolutization when it is abstracted from its relation to the whole soul in relation to the whole of reality, which is the critique, we will argue, that Plato intends to present in the *Republic.*

58. Robert E. Cushman, *Therapeia: Plato's Conception of Philosophy* (Chapel Hill: University of North Carolina Press, 1958), 40.

of-position-ness"—with the refusal to take any position at all.[59] Looked at in temporal terms, what *precisely* characterizes sheer appearance is infidelity or inconstancy. One cannot argue with a person who denies the difference between being and appearance; someone must substitute for the person to represent, adhere to, and defend the position. Of course, we have to acknowledge at the same time that to defend the position in such a way is already to betray it. Implied in the act of substitution for the sake of argument, nevertheless, is an affirmation of the integrity of the other, as far as possible, and beyond the integrity that he is able to claim for himself. It is an affirmation that, by respecting the difference of the other's position even in its op-position, becomes the opposite of the self-isolation implied in Protagoras's relativism. This act of substitution occurs often in Plato. In the *Theaetetus*, Socrates takes Protagoras's position; a similar move will take place in the *Republic* (357aff.).[60]

Second, when Socrates attempts, in his standing in for Protagoras, to give the best defense possible for Protagoras's position (165e), we see the shift from a logical to an existential register, just as we saw it in Aristotle's confrontation with the same position, and as we will see shortly in Socrates' discussion with Thrasymachus. The question of whether a position is truer than another is irrelevant, Socrates' Protagoras says; the issue is ultimately how to bring about better results:

Now what we have to do is not make one of these two wiser than the other—that is not even a possibility—nor is it our business to make accusations, calling the sick man ignorant for judging as he does, and the healthy man wise, because he judges differently. What we have to do is make a change from the one to the other, because the other state is *better*. In education, too, what we have to do is to change a worse state into a better state; only whereas the doctor brings about the change by the use of drugs, the professional teacher (ὁ...σοφιστής) does it by the use of words. What never happens is that a man who judges what is false is made to judge what is true. For it is impossible to judge what is not, or to judge anything other than what one is immediately experiencing; and what one is immediately experiencing is always true. This, in my opinion, is what really happens: when a man's soul is in a pernicious state, he judges things akin to it, but giving him a sound state of the soul causes him to think different things, things that are good. In the latter event, the things which ap-

---

59. Cf. *Euthydemus,* in which Socrates insists he will remain absolutely wedded to the statement he makes (283c) and associates the sophist, by contrast, with the ever-changing Proteus (288c) and the many-headed Hydra (297c).

60. Cf. also *Soph.,* 246a–d.

pear to him are what some people, who are still at a primitive stage, call "true"; my position, however, is that the one kind are *better* than the others, but in no way *truer*. (167a–b)

The elimination of any difference between being and appearance, in other words, entails a shift in the fundamental criterion. The question is no longer, "What is true?" but is now, "What is capable of bringing about the most desirable outcome?"[61] There is a total collapse here into effective power. Paul Feyerabend draws precisely the same conclusion in his defense of "Protagorean relativism": he calls it an "engineering approach," by which "'reality' (to speak the objectivists' language) is explored by attempts to satisfy human wishes in a more direct way."[62] The term "reality" is in scare quotes because the (necessarily inconsistent) use of the term is just that, a *use,* which exploits whatever one might mean by the term for the sake of a practical aim. At this point, it would be necessary to investigate the goodness of the good—as Socrates proceeds to do—which will eventually return us to the question of truth. When pushed to its limit, the epistemological question thus opens up the question of value, and vice versa; however distinct they may be, the issue of truth and that of goodness are not simply separate. A fundamental response to either question requires an exploration of both.

Thrasymachus: Relativism as Violence

The issues that we have highlighted in Socrates' imaginary discussion with Protagoras take on dramatic substance in his "real" confrontation with Thrasymachus. Here, we will see that the exchange is not just a debate over positions, but is itself simultaneously a kind of positioning. That Thrasymachus represents the presence of violence is unmistakable in Plato's description of his entry into the discussion: "Now Thrasymachus had many times started out to take over the argument in the midst of our discussion, but he had been restrained by the men sitting near him, who wanted to hear the ar-

---

61. We would naturally call this a turn toward pragmatism. Polansky, however, distinguishes Protagoras's position from modern pragmatism insofar as the former "completely suspends the question of truth" (*Philosophy and Knowledge*, 124n77), while pragmatism simply makes practical results the criterion for determining truth. One may ask whether this distinction can be sustained.

62. Paul Feyerabend, *Farewell to Reason* (New York: Verso, 1987), 52.

gument out. But when we paused and I said this, he could no longer keep quiet; hunched up like a wild beast, he flung himself at us as if to tear us to pieces" (336b). Contrary to one's expectations, he accuses the discussants of lacking an interest in getting to the truth of the matter and of preferring instead to defer to one another. Socrates responds by pointing out that a conviction about the goodness of truth would exclude such an approach. Doing so, he discloses at the outset what will remain his governing presupposition, namely, that the truth of justice has an absolute and unquestionable goodness.[63] He presupposes this without argument, as something to which all would agree—at least for the sake of appearance—and it represents the hypothesis that will undergird everything else he says. (We will not be able to address the question of whether the hypothetical character of this presupposition ever gets eliminated until chapter 3.)

Thrasymachus will of course eventually challenge this presupposition; he comes from a different perspective, and his own presupposition is revealed through the manner in which he engages both Socrates and the ideas they debate. He initially attributes to Socrates the sole motivations his position allows to human beings: he accuses him of asking questions rather than venturing an affirmation, because it is easier to do so (236c); moreover, he suggests that Socrates' motivation in doing so is to gratify his love of honor (336c, 337a) and that he seeks to take ideas from others rather than generously offering his own (338b); later, he suspects that Socrates is simply trying to harm him through argument (341a–b). He is presumably expressing the sorts of motivations that seem plausible to him. We are led to wonder what prevents Thrasymachus, given the frustration he expresses, from putting questions to Socrates, and, if Thrasymachus's charges are false, what presents Socrates from answering them. There seem to be three obstacles: first, Thrasymachus forbids certain answers from the outset—namely, "that it is the needful, or the helpful, or the profitable, or the gainful, or the advantageous" (336d)—while Socrates confesses his answer would likely have been something of the sort (337c). Socrates will not speak if he is not permitted to say what he believes to be true, that is, if the conditions do not allow the expression of truth. Second, Socrates makes his well-known claim that he "does not know and does not profess to know" (337e). And, third, Thrasymachus cannot in fact restrain himself from overriding Socrates and asserting his own

63. Blößner, *Dialogform und Argument,* 32–33.

view because he has an answer ready and expects it will impress the audience (338a).[64] Now, it would be possible to see in this initial interchange—as Thrasymachus does in fact—simply an expression of manipulative irony in Socrates; we might read it as Plato's attempt to make Thrasymachus look ridiculous because of his incontinence. But, as we know, even incontinence is for Plato and Socrates not a "moral" flaw but a failure of intelligence—it is due to a particular (mis)understanding about the nature of reality.[65] We receive more light on the exchange when we see it not simply as an interaction between two different moral characters but more fundamentally two different ways of knowing, different understandings of understanding, different views of what is most real. Socrates' reticence, and Thrasymachus's incapacity for it, are functions, we suggest, of two different ways of relating to ideas. Socrates professes no knowledge, and yet he remains throughout the dialogue a sort of *anchor* around which the discussion is ordered. Thrasymachus professes knowledge, and yet never seems to stick to a basic stance. How are we to make sense of this paradox?

We are not yet in a position to deal with this question adequately, but we can make a certain straightforward observation. While Socrates denies definitive possession of knowledge, here he suggests he has a certain idea, which Thrasymachus's strictures prevent him from proposing (376d). In other words, he does not yet reject the possibility of understanding a priori—for that would, indeed, depend on an insight it would be presumptuous to claim—but suggests that the activity of proposing and considering an idea does not depend on him alone. Instead, it requires the willing participation of others. For Socrates, an idea is essentially something that must be "inquired into." For Thrasymachus, by contrast, an idea is not something one explores, reflects on, penetrates, or tests, it is something one simply asserts and, if necessary, defends by further assertions. Positions, thus, have a kind of immediacy for Thrasymachus: they are, as it were, self-contained intellectual units, which are either presented or kept back; he thinks of ideas as *possessions*, things that can be extended to others only in terms of buying and selling.[66] It is this view of ideas that leads him to interpret the So-

---

64. See also 350e–351c: here, Thrasymachus again betrays an inability to keep silent; he cannot help but interject and desires, in particular, to make long speeches.

65. *Prt.*, 357b–e.

66. For a similar observation in relation to the *Phaedrus*, see Catherine Pickstock's discussion of the "trade of the sophists," in *After Writing: On the Liturgical Consummation of Philosophy*

cratic method as thievery; Socrates, he claims, will not sell his ideas, but always simply steals from others (338b), taking ideas without paying for them. When Thrasymachus finally presents his own view, he *immediately* demands recompense: "'Now listen,' he said, 'I say that the just is nothing other than the advantage of the stronger. Well, why don't you praise me? But you won't be willing'" (338c). Socrates, by contrast, wishes to sound it out before responding to it in order to understand what it *means*. Eventually, when Socrates allows the problems in Thrasymachus's position to become evident through questioning, he asks Thrasymachus to offer a better argument in order to persuade them, and Thrasymachus says that his only alternative is to ram the argument down their souls (345d). If ideas are merely immediate bits of content, they cannot be further unfolded but only asserted with more and more *force*. It is therefore not the case that Socrates and Thrasymachus have different ideas *and also* different dispositions—as Hegel observed, the phrase "und auch" signals an absence of philosophical penetration—but we will see that these are intrinsically bound up with one another. In what way are they connected?

Clearly, there is a link between Thrasymachus's view of the nature of an idea as expressed in his disposition toward understanding and the particular position he makes for the nature of justice: he seeks to *compel* the others to accept the notion that justice is what benefits the stronger and make them pay him for it, allowing him to benefit for having presented the most forceful idea. But we can uncover a deeper connection. Socrates immediately remarks (339a–b) that Thrasymachus's answer bears a strong resemblance to the one he himself would have given had Thrasymachus allowed him, namely, that justice is "the beneficial" (τὸ ξύμφερον) Thrasymachus claims that the difference is, indeed, slight, while Socrates states his intention to investigate it further. The difference turns out to be revealing.[67] One could say, initially, that what the phrase "for the stronger" adds to the definition Socrates would be willing to accept is *a relative condition*. To refuse the addition is to

---

(Oxford: Blackwell, 1998), 6–7. The capitalistic exchange represents a mode of interaction that leaves the parties involved extrinsically related to one another, that is, it leaves them individuals in the strict sense, rather than introducing them into community with one another. See part I of Lewis Hyde, *The Gift: Imagination and the Erotic Life of Property* (New York: Vintage Books, 1983), 3–140.

67. As bold an affirmation as it may seem, Lachterman is right to observe that the whole *Republic* is contained in the "rider" that Thrasymachus attaches to the definition of justice. Lachterman, "What Is 'the Good'?" 144.

make justice beneficial in an absolute and unqualified sense—not, of course, in a way that excludes relation, for it would make no sense for something to be beneficial without being beneficial *for* someone or something—but in a way that does not restrict that relation to one class, to the exclusion of others. Moreover, it does not seem to be accidental that the particular class to which Thrasymachus seeks to restrict the benefits of justice is that of the *stronger.* Notice, the word he uses here, κρείττων, is itself relative insofar as it is a *comparative:* he does not mean those that are strong (in an absolute sense), but specifically those that are strong in a *relative* way. What we see in this seemingly minor addition is a certain connection between relativity and power of a particular sort: the advantage of justice is made relative to strength, and this strength is in turn understood in a relative sense. Significantly, when Thrasymachus mentions it is a slight difference in *comparison* with Socrates' view, Socrates says "It isn't plain yet whether it is a big one. But it is plain that we must consider whether what you say is true" (339b). Thus, for Socrates, the primary concern is not in the first place how Thrasymachus's view compares with his own (i.e., its relativity), but how it is in itself (i.e., taken absolutely).

While it is true that Thrasymachus champions power in his view of justice, at the heart of this view lies a form of relativism. In our consideration of Protagoras in the *Theaetetus,* we saw that epistemological relativism leads to a reduction of relations to those of power. Is there any reason to suppose that Plato attributed an epistemological relativism to Thrasymachus? That Plato saw sophistry in general as characterized by such a relativism, broadly construed, needs no argument, and Thrasymachus is of course known as a sophist. It is not incidental that he displays some of the characteristics Plato attributes to the sophist in the dialogue of that name (i.e., being a wild beast, a business man in intellectual affairs, and one who gives the appearance of wisdom by playing with arguments).[68] We are not surprised, then, when Socrates introduces precisely the question he raised in relation to Protagoras's epistemological relativism, namely, whether he concedes the possibility of making a mistake. To concede this possibility is to admit the existence of a supraindividual measure, which is exactly what epistemological relativism excludes. But it is also what Thrasymachus's definition of justice excludes, insofar as it relativizes the criterion of justice to the individual and what in-

---

68. *Soph.* 231a, 224c–d, and 233bff., respectively. Cf. *Euthd.,* 304a–c.

creases the individual's strength. Socrates shows that Thrasymachus's definition will undermine itself the moment he allows a criterion of goodness independent of the individual, since it means that the stronger can be wrong
about what is to his advantage. At this point, other voices interrupt: Cleitophon sees the implications of Socrates' point, and immediately attempts to
come to Thrasymachus's rescue by eliminating the measure. What Thrasymachus *means,* he insists, is that justice is whatever *seems* to the stronger to
be beneficial (340c). Though Polemarchus protests that this was not Thrasymachus's original position, Socrates states that they ought to let him adopt
it, if he so chooses.

But Thrasymachus does not accept this option, and one must wonder why. It would seem that, if Thrasymachus is indeed a relativist, then he
should willingly take the path Cleitophon opened to him. After all, it would
have made his position much more difficult for Socrates to attack, at least on
one level. Instead, however, he chooses to insist on the effective power of the
stronger, and offers a response that has interesting implications in light of the
general project of the *Republic:* "'Do you suppose,' he asks Socrates, 'that I
call a man who makes mistakes "stronger" at the moment when he is making
mistakes?'" (340c). Rather than retreating to the security of sheer seeming,
Thrasymachus chooses to consider relative strength or power in its effective completion. He is thus absolutizing a kind of power, taking it in its most
ideal (i.e., most perfect and realized) sense. Alluding to a series of τέχναι —
medicine, logic, grammar, and eventually the production of crafts—he explains that the strictest meaning of the term applies only when the act is carried out perfectly. So too with the ruler: he is a ruler only when he is in fact
infallible and legislates in fact what is in his own interest. He thus links the
meaning of an art, too, to its effective realization. It is what it is when it is
successful; it is defined by its effective power.[69]

Thrasymachus's choice brings us before a question that is particularly
weighty in relation to the general argument we are making. We have been
suggesting that there is a logical link between relativism and recourse to
power. Is Thrasymachus, the champion of power, abandoning relativism
here? Some commentators contend, indeed, that Thrasymachus appears to

---

69. Interestingly, Socrates also defines arts relatively to the effects they serve to achieve
(346a), and thus in terms of a kind of power. The difference between them here turns on the
meaning of power in the two cases. Socrates explains that it is a capacity to serve, while for Thrasymachus it is the capacity to acquire.

be trying to navigate a position that avoids the radical relativism of Cleitophon. Allan Bloom, for example, suggests that Thrasymachus remains in the end attached to reason, and this is why Socrates is eventually able to win him over.[70] As a sophist, Bloom explains, Thrasymachus loves not only gain, but also knowledge, and this is why he is sufficiently tractable for Socrates to work out an ideal city in discussion with him. But where is the evidence for this suggestion? Socrates never wins Thrasymachus over, at least not in book I;[71] the "assent" he seems to give toward the end of the argument is not at all an indication of having been persuaded to Socrates' position, but as he explains himself it is simply because he no longer feels like arguing (350d–e). Ultimately, Glaucon and Adeimantus have to take over his position and defend it in order for Socrates to have an appropriate interlocutor. To suggest that Thrasymachus does not take up Cleitophon's proposal because he feels bound in some lingering way to the claims of reason requires that we interpret his insistence on the "precise meaning" of terms (κατὰ τὸν ἀκριβῆ λόγον, 340e) as arising from a concern for the truth of the matter. If we did, however, we would be at a loss to explain why he abandons this concern moments later in the argument, as Socrates points out (345c). It seems far more reasonable to suppose that he insists on the precise meaning of terms at this juncture because it promises to lend his argument greater force here. If this is true, we would have to acknowledge that the abandonment of the apparently relativist position at this point is not a compromise with some form of affirmation of objective reality, but is in fact a more extreme form of relativism. Relativism, and the skepticism it implies regarding the possibility of genuine knowledge, is less radical, as we argued in the introduction, when it remains consistent with itself than when it chucks concern for consistency in order to bring about desired results. Authentic relativism reduces "knowledge" to some form of power.

Let us consider Thrasymachus's decision in relation to the discussion of epistemological relativism in the *Theaetetus*. As we saw there, by denying the difference between perception and knowledge, epistemological relativism makes the individual perspective *infallible*. To admit the possibility of

70. Bloom, *The Republic of Plato*, 331.

71. Thrasymachus appears only once more (450a), at the start of the major digression of book V—when Socrates begins again, having been "arrested" in his discussion—to join the others in insisting that Socrates carry through the proposed argument. But desire to listen to arguments is by no means the same as docility to reason.

error is to concede the validity of an outside measure. If Cleitophon offers the possibility of disregarding an outside measure by claiming no more than the *perception* of advantage, Thrasymachus's insistence on the ruler's infallibility simply identifies that perception with knowledge, which is an essential implication of epistemological relativism. Though, superficially, Cleitophon and Thrasymachus seem to be pointing to two different options, in reality these options stem from the same position, which is presumably why it is natural for Cleitophon to assume he is giving an accurate representation of Thrasymachus's stance. Thrasymachus's affirmation that might quite literally *makes* right expresses the same logic by which Protagoras's relativism cannot help but impose itself as a doctrine for all. The key linking them together is the assertion that man is the measure—in one case of truth, in the other of justice. But they amount to the same.

Thus, it becomes clear why Thrasymachus's rejection of Cleitophon's proposal follows consistently from his real position—even if it will force him in a moment to reverse the surface content of his original claim and champion injustice rather than justice. What motivates his maneuver here, in fact, is the desire to affirm the supremacy of power. If Thrasymachus had accepted Cleitophon's amendment, he would in effect be asserting that the ruler has power, so to speak, only in his own mind. The impotence of this position is already evident in the way Socrates puts the question to Thrasymachus: "Are we to say that the just is to do merely what the ruler *thinks* is to his advantage, whether or not it is advantageous?" (340b–c). To say yes to this is to show oneself to be a fool, especially after the difference between being and appearance has already been in principle accepted by the audience that is now listening to the exchange (334c–d). Mitchell and Lucas show that accepting Cleitophon's amendment, while it would have saved Thrasymachus from refutation, would have done so "at the cost of making [his position] vacuous."[72] In other words, he would have given up power for the sake of intellectual consistency, and that is in fact the very opposite of what his position implies. Being consistent here would have been profoundly inconsistent.

To put it another way, if Cleitophon's position disregards the difference

---

72. Mitchell and Lucas, *Engagement with Plato's* Republic, 4. They explain the vacuity it would have entailed by pointing to the fact that it reduces to a kind of tautology, whereby whatever one happens to do is simply equivalent to an action done to promote self-interest.

between being and appearance, Thrasymachus attempts instead to overcome it. The significance of this attempt becomes clear in the light of Socrates' eventual project to do the same. Socrates, in the notion of the philosopher-king, seeks the coincidence of truth and power; so too does Thrasymachus.[73] But while Socrates seeks to reconcile them on the side of the absolute term, truth or being, Thrasymachus seeks the coincidence on the side of the relative term, appearance or power. We will discuss at greater length the implications of this difference in chapter 4. Here, we note that Thrasymachus affirms the ideal case in which the ruler rules perfectly—meaning that he makes decisions that truly benefit himself—and he thereby effectively absorbs truth into power. We can see in what respect Thrasymachus's relativism is far more radical than Cleitophon's: it is not a relativism that collapses into the isolation of subjectivism, but in fact *imposes* self-relation as a universal law, as "truth" itself. We have noted that such an imposition is necessarily entailed in epistemological relativism. In this respect, Thrasymachus's position simply makes explicit what would have been implicit in Cleitophon's; it is this latter's position brought to its end. If neither position is in the end defensible in logical terms, Thrasymachus's position nevertheless aspires to a practical effectiveness that is lacking in the other, an effectiveness that constitutes the essence of authentic relativism.

That power is in fact the point, the absolute to which all else is relative, becomes apparent in the exchange that immediately follows. Thrasymachus insisted on considering the τέχνη of ruling in itself and on its own terms. Socrates simply indicates the natural consequence of this step. No τέχνη aims at its own interest, he affirms, but is ordered to something beyond itself. Medicine serves the body, for example, it does not serve medicine itself. If it did, we would be led to an infinite regress: each art would be an art of an art, and would in turn require an art of that art, and so on (342a). Let us note the logic in Socrates' response: to consider an art on its own terms

73. Charles Kahn has also noticed this subtle foreshadowing of the philosopher-king in book 1. "Proleptic Composition in the *Republic,* or Why Book 1 Was Never a Separate Dialogue," *Classical Quarterly* 43 (1993): 131–42, here 137–38. Plato alludes to this peculiar coincidence between Socrates and Thrasymachus quite brilliantly in book VI. After Adeimantus observes that most people would object to Socrates' proposal regarding philosopher-kings, "beginning with Thrasymachus," Socrates replies: "Don't make a quarrel between Thrasymachus and me when we've just become friends, though we weren't enemies before" (498c–d). What is it that has just made them friends? Nothing else but their agreement in the coincidence of truth and power (even if they understand this coincidence in radically different ways).

is to understand it in terms of its purpose, which is another way of saying in terms of the precise sense in which it is beneficial or good. Further, to be beneficial is by its own intrinsic logic to be in some sense "other-regarding" rather than self-regarding.[74] We will have occasion in the next chapter to develop this connection further. Our point at the moment is to see how the exclusion of this sense of goodness ultimately ends in violence. Nevertheless it is worth remarking that one of the central insights of the *Republic* is already contained *in nuce* in this simple argument: namely, that *there is an essential connection between a thing's intrinsic meaning, its goodness, and its objectivity* or its having a "supraindividual" measure. In the particular case at hand, we see simply that the ruler, *qua* ruler, is at the service of the ruled (342e), and does not consider his own interest by definition.

Common Good or Good of Each?

Thrasymachus's response to this argument shows once again that his aim is the effective imposition of power. To carry this aim out initially seemed to require some claim to truth. But because this claim itself is wholly relative to the power sought, there is no longer any reason to remain faithful to the claim once it turns out that the claim does not produce the desired result. Abandoning any concern, then, for "truth," Thrasymachus turns the argument explicitly to the question of what is desirable. He seems to believe that what is most compelling is goodness rather than truth, and that truth is somehow a function of goodness. In this respect, Thrasymachus "reconnects" with the position that Protagoras represented, namely, that the important thing is not what is truer but what is "better." He concedes to Socrates that justice, in itself, is "other-regarding," "in reality someone else's good" (ἀλλότριον ἀγαθὸν τῷ ὄντι, 343c), and changes his position accordingly. Now he says that it is better to be as unjust as possible, that injustice leads to the service of one's "private advantage" (ξυμφέρει ἰδίᾳ αὐτῷ, 344a).[75] His position thus entails making all things relative to one's private

74. Lachterman insightfully observes that the discussion of τέχνη here offers the first possible experience of self-transcendence. Lachterman, "What Is 'the Good'?" 147.

75. Annas suggests that "The way [Thrasymachus] is driven from a partial and muddled to a clear formulation is no doubt meant to show, unsubtly, that he is an overhasty and confused thinker who needs lessons in rigour from Socrates," *Introduction*, 46. While this is no doubt correct, we wish to suggest, more strongly, that what Plato is in fact seeking (subtly) to show is the essential infidelity to a position that is entailed in radical relativism. Thus, it is not merely a

advantage, which is another way of saying he absolutizes the relative. What is *good*, from this perspective, is what benefits the self; injustice is *better* than justice precisely because it enables the individual to gain more than others (πλεονεξία, 344a). While it may seem that Thrasymachus is revising his initial position, in fact he reaffirms at least the same words—that "justice is the advantage of the stronger," meaning now that it serves "the other," and thus that the ruled is paradoxically stronger than the ruler—and simply becomes more explicit about his real aim: the "unjust is what is profitable and advantageous for oneself" (344c).

It is important to note that Thrasymachus is offering injustice as a *universal* good of a sort; he presents the *entirely* unjust man (the tyrant) as one who has nothing but admirers: "He gets called happy and blessed, not only by the citizens but also by whomever else hears that he has done injustice entire" (344b–c). Thrasymachus does not claim, to be sure, that injustice is good in itself (i.e., in an absolute sense), which is in fact impossible to do— for, indeed, there is no way to defend such a position insofar as the very hypothesis denies the relativity on which the purported desirability of justice depends. In fact, the arguments Socrates makes at the end of book I trade on this fact.[76] Nevertheless, by saying everyone would choose injustice if given the option, he is both giving it a merely relative justification (i.e., making it good *for the individual*), and extending that individualistic justification universally. It thus comes to represent a (perverse) kind of absolute, the "evil twin," one could say, of the idea of the good that Socrates will eventually introduce.

Crisis

It is at this moment that a crisis point is reached. Thrasymachus, after making this argument, like a "bathman" who has "poured a great shower of speech into our ears all at once" (344d), *turns to leave.* Here we have

comment on Thrasymachus's character or style of argument, but the manifestation of the "truth" of his position.

76. Note the premise from which the rest of these arguments proceed: "'Come now, Thrasymachus,' I said, 'answer us from the beginning. Do you assert that perfect injustice is more profitable than justice when it is perfect?'" (348b). The relativity has been removed; Socrates is not talking about its being more profitable for the stronger or for the individual *qua* individual, but "more profitable" *tout court.*

the concrete expression of self-contained relativism, both in the inward self-complacency it implies and in the very outward act of separating oneself off from the whole. His concluding gesture would in fact make sense if it is the nature of an idea simply to be violently imposed on others from the outside. But Socrates begs him to stay: "Thrasymachus, you demonic man, do you toss in such an argument, and have it in mind to go away before teaching us adequately (ἱκανῶς) or finding out whether it is so or not? Or do you suppose you are trying to determine a small matter and not a course of life on the basis of which each of us would have the most profitable existence?" (344d–e).

What is it about Thrasymachus's present position that marks such a momentous turn and reveals the stakes to include life as a whole? What began as a discussion of the meaning of justice has turned into a discussion of its goodness. But as we are beginning to see, this question cannot be answered, in turn, unless we have some notion about what "counts" as good. We therefore have to consider the goodness of the good, which is as fundamental a question as one could desire. In addition to this, Socrates raises the issue of reason's responsibility for and to this question, calling Thrasymachus to account for his willingness to depart without an adequate inquiry. The particular question of justice, when sufficiently challenged, opens to the universal and comprehensive questions of goodness in general and its relation to reason and truth. When the horizon opens up in such a way, a person cannot avoid making a decision (cf. 347e, 352d). While it is the case that such ultimate issues are implicit in *every* act of thought or desire, as the central books of the *Republic* will eventually affirm, most often this horizon does not itself come into question. But certain extreme moments introduce it, and when it appears, neutrality is no longer possible. A crisis is a decisive moment, because it is a moment of decision (κρίσις, κρίνειν) and it is so because it is here that foundations come into view. To see the *Republic* as concerned with foundations is to see it, dramatically, as a dialogue of crisis.[77]

77. Crisis is intrinsic to drama; drama presents a choice or judgment, not as an arbitrary act of the will, but as a response required by the meaning that imposes itself, a meaning that the judgment itself participates in determining. It is significant that the body of the whole *Republic* is set up in classic Greek style as a contest between two positions, taking place before judges who stand as it were outside the contest, in a place above the two. (See 360e, 361d, and 580a–b. Cf. 348b, where Socrates suggests a contest of this sort is essential for true judgment.) Appropriately, due prizes are awarded at the end, just as they would be for the public dramas or games (608cff.). We can

The specific form of the crisis in this confrontation between Socrates and Thrasymachus can be formulated thus: on the one hand, they *seem* to agree about the essential question, namely, what way of life is *best,* understood as "most desirable." Their disagreement apparently comes with the question of the criterion for what is best. Thrasymachus insists that there is no measure beyond the individual. If it is undesirable to suffer loss, "by stealth or by force" (344a), that is irrelevant to the fact that it is desirable to acquire by those means. Socrates, by contrast, will seek to affirm that the meaning of goodness cannot be reduced to its relativity to the individual, or even to the sum of all individuals. Instead, it has an essentially supraindividual measure. In the final part of book I, he presents three relatively brief arguments that point to this affirmation. Because the question of the absoluteness or relativity of the good will be a basic theme in the rest of the book, we will only indicate the gist of these arguments, in order to see that they reveal a common concern.

In the first place, the opposition implied in the individual's assertion of self over *all* others is incompatible with the notion of goodness, which, as Thrasymachus himself admits, seeks to overcome not all others but only the bad (348b–350c). Second, justice and goodness entail a unity or wholeness that necessarily runs counter to the absolutization of each individual (i.e., each relative part), which inevitably entails fragmentation (350e–352d). And third, if the soul, like all other things, has a purpose, it has the possibility of fulfilling or failing this purpose. Injustice represents this failure (352d–354a). Thus, once we think in terms of purpose, we must affirm both the existence and the value of a kind of objective excellence, i.e., virtue. Injustice, then, can be affirmed only at the price of the soul's integrity. The issue is not merely whether justice is better than injustice, but also whether it makes any sense to use the terms "good" or "better" in a coherent sense at all.

How much weight do these arguments carry? While they seem sounder than some commentators give them credit for,[78] we cannot measure

---

compare this to the *choice* of life that comes at the end, watched over and judged by the gods (cf. 619e–620a). Plato seems to associate decision with drama and judgment, and thus as taking place within an area embraced within a transcendent sphere. Consider, too, Plato's reference to the "men's drama" and the "women's drama" (*Rep.,* 451aff.). David Gallop refers to the *Republic* itself essentially as a "dramatic spectacle," "Image and Reality in Plato's *Republic,*" *Archiv für Geschichte der Philosophie* 47 (1965): 199–24, here 120.

78. Devin Stouffer, for example, in *Plato's Introduction to the Question of Justice* (Albany: SUNY Press, 2001), claims that the three arguments are all essentially flawed (103–14), though

their adequacy until we understand the problem to which they are responding. It is not, indeed, a problem, but a *crisis*. The different "understandings"
of what is best entail fundamentally different modes of relation. Thrasymachus is not, in the end, *making an argument* that injustice is best, since that
would imply establishing the very supraindividual measure that would in
effect undermine his position. Relativism cannot be argued for; it can only
be imposed through deception or violence. Instead of arguing for his position, Thrasymachus is in fact simply seeking to impose his injustice on others, and at the same time forcing others to attempt to do the same.[79] When
Socrates asks Thrasymachus to persuade them all of his position, he replies,
as we recall, that, if they don't automatically accept it, the only alternative is
to ram it down their souls (345b). The very act of adhering to a position and
making an argument on its behalf already entails a concern for others, an
"other-centeredness," and therefore in some respect a relation that possesses
a supraindividual measure. Socrates indicates this in his reaction to Thrasymachus's assertions, suggesting that Thrasymachus himself does not believe
the truth of his own position, "or else you have no care for us and aren't a
bit concerned whether we shall live worse or better as a result of our ignorance of what you say you know" (344e). But, again, this is just what Thrasymachus's position excludes a priori. When Socrates pleads with Thrasymachus to take a position, whatever one he wishes but only to be faithful to it
(345b), he is asking for a good deal more than is apparent on the surface; at
issue is the very possibility of allowing truth to show itself as true. It is necessary for him to assent to his own proposal in order for their discussion to
reach its end (ἵνα τι καὶ περαίνομεν, 346a). Clearly, adhering to a position is part of reaching the *completion* of an argument. This is why Socrates
is overjoyed when he catches Thrasymachus affirming something he really
seems to think is true (349a). But it is also why Thrasymachus dismisses this
as irrelevant, wanting Socrates instead to try to overpower it with his own

---

he admits difficulty in finding a flaw in the second (109), and ultimately says that the key flaw lies
in the analogy Socrates draws in the first argument between the wise and good, on the one hand,
and the just, on the other. But an argument from analogy, however weak one might think it is,
is not a *flawed* argument. Julia Annas is right to affirm that the three arguments are *not* formally flawed (*Introduction*, 55–56), even if they take too much for granted to be wholly convincing.
Wolfgang Kersting makes the same observation in *Platons "Staat"* (Darmstadt: Wissenschaftliche Buchgeselschaft, 1999), 38.

    79. Jacob Howland notes that Thrasymachus's *pleonexia* poses a threat not only to justice,
but to *logos*, to rationality itself. *Odyssey of Philosophy*, 69–72.

view: "'And what difference does it make to you,' he said, 'whether it seems so to me or not, and why don't you refute the argument?'"

When the tide undeniably begins to turn, Thrasymachus shifts from pure self-assertion to pure passivity: he states that he will henceforward merely nod—give the merely physical *appearance* of assent—to anything Socrates says (350e). This is not a change of position, but the flip side of precisely the same coin. Strauss is no doubt being overly optimistic when he affirms that Socrates has succeeded, by the end, in taming the "raving beast," since taming implies some genuine inward transformation.[80] Thrasymachus gives this superficial assent, he himself says, just to satisfy Socrates. In this respect, it is crucial to see that his very concession is a form of triumph, to the extent that it leaves power in place as the supreme criterion. In this case, he now simply hands the laurels to what he takes to be Socrates' selfish claim to impose himself.

Argument as Drama

The broader question that tacitly arises in the final pages of book I is how to engage an argument based not so much on a superiority of reasons as on a superiority of strength. Implied in the debate is the question of what properly constitutes an argument. *How* does one persuade, as Polemarchus asked at the very beginning of the *Republic,* if the rational means of persuasion—i.e., an openness to reason—are themselves called into question (cf. 327c)? What then does persuasion mean? As Barker and Warner put the question, "Does any vantage point exist from which Plato, and the *Republic*'s philosophers, can speak credibly and meaningfully inside the Cave?"[81] The question does not concern strategy first of all but the nature of *logos* as such in the world.

Plato's engagement with this question is essentially *dramatic*. Conventionally understood, argument is the confrontation of contrasting ideas (pieces of intellectual content). An argument becomes dramatic, by contrast, when form bears an intrinsic relation to content.[82] In this case, an argument turns into a more comprehensive kind of encounter; because the content on

---

80. "When Thrasymachus begins to speak, he behaves according to Socrates' lively description like a raving beast; by the end of the first book he has become completely tame," Strauss, *City and Man,* 84.

81. Barker and Warner, *Language of the Cave,* 6.

82. Richard McKim, from a related perspective, argues—referring specifically to the *Gorgias*—that "Plato presents Socrates as not even *trying* to meet the standards of logical proof,"

either side presents itself in a particular modality, we have an interaction be-tween ideas and modes of being. In other words, it is not a confrontation be-tween two mere contents, but between two form-content unities, and such a confrontation can take place only, as it were, within three-dimensional intel-lectual space. We must therefore, of course, attend to both form and content in reading Plato, but it is not enough to view the form as inspiring or provok-ing us to lay hold of the content in a more spontaneous way.[83] More radi-cally, we have to see that content and form mutually imply one another and that their mutual implication is an intrinsic part of the argument.[84] In a basic sense, a particular content necessarily entails a way of relating to that con-tent, and a particular mode of relating in turn discloses a horizon that deter-mines a content. Hence the drama: persuasion cannot occur unless there is a change in both one's understanding *and* one's mode of understanding simul-taneously. The most fundamental meanings can be grasped only through the transformation of one's way of relating to meaning in general.

If we wanted, in sum, to characterize the form-content unity that comes to expression in Thrasymachus, we could probably find no better notion than absolutized relativity. His *position* is the superiority of a single part over the whole, insofar as the desideratum he affirms is individual pleonexia; his

---

and instead uses a *psychological* rather than *logical* method of dealing with his interlocutors. See "Shame and Truth in Plato's *Gorgias*," in Griswold, *Platonic Writings, Platonic Readings,* 34–48. McKim's interpretation, however, simply reduces the form-content unity in the other direction. To say that logic is insufficient alone does *not* imply it is irrelevant. Our point is that Plato's ap-proach is *simultaneously* logical and existential, and not merely one or the other. Simply substitut-ing psychology for logic would ultimately be a concession to the collapse of reason that Thrasy-machus represents, regardless of the practical outcome of the interaction.

83. This is how Schleiermacher, who is the father in some sense of the literary bent in Plato scholarship in the modern era, put it. See his *Introductions to the Dialogues of Plato,* translated by William Dobson (New York: Arno Press, 1973), 36–38.

84. It has been observed that a kind of self-referentiality is typical of Plato, in that characters can seem to *embody* the position they argue for and that passages describing a method often fol-low the method they describe. See Robert S. Brumbaugh, "Digression and Dialogue: The *Sev-enth Letter* and Plato's Literary Form," in Griswold, *Platonic Writings, Platonic Readings,* 84–92. We wish to make the claim that this feature is not simply a matter of stylistic idiosyncrasy, but a function of Plato's notion of the fundamental nature of truth. It is the embodiment of Plato's po-sition. Cf. similar observations or arguments: Stanley Rosen, "The Role of Eros in Plato's *Repub-lic,*" *Review of Metaphysics* (March 1965): 451–75, here 452; Drew Hyland, "Why Plato Wrote Dia-logues," *Philosophy and Rhetoric* (1968): 38–50; Charles Griswold Jr., "Style and Philosophy: The Case of Plato's Dialogues," *The Monist* 63 (1980): 530–46; Mitch Miller Jr., *The Philosopher in Pla-to's Statesman* (The Hague: Nijhoff, 1980), ix; J. Gordon, *Turning Toward Philosophy,* 7–13.

positioning is precisely the same: the superiority of a partial perspective over the whole. If an individual is taken simply and exclusively on its own terms, as having its measure nowhere else but in itself, and thus as lacking any intrinsic relation to the whole, a relation that would necessarily subordinate it to something larger than itself, it *has no choice* but to relate to everything outside of itself in the mode of manipulation. Again, while we tend to associate dogmatism with authoritarian assertions of power, Thrasymachus shows us that "argument by violent imposition" is the final outcome of skepticism. There is, as we saw, a link between the epistemological position that being cannot be distinguished from appearance and the reduction of relation to reactionary demonstrations of power. Relativism, in short, betrays a logic of violence. Even if concessions are made from within this logic, if they occur without a corresponding transformation of the mode of relating, the concession remains merely apparent. The individual remains an utterly self-related identity. Thus, to say it once more, Thrasymachus can *only* pour his ideas over others' heads like so much bathwater; imposition from above or from outside follows the logic of his notion of truth.

What form-content unity does Socrates, then, present as a contrast to this? It is interesting to note that, at this point in the *Republic,* we have received only the barest hint of Socrates' position. Thrasymachus was correct: Socrates has so far shown a reluctance to present his thoughts. But this reluctance is already meaningful in light of the argument we have been making. From the beginning, we have not yet found a single instance wherein Socrates has imposed an idea of his own. His participation in the discussion has come at every turn at the (sometimes forcible) request of others.[85] Polemarchus, for example, forces him to stay at the outset, and the main discussion of the *Republic* is initiated through the insistence of Glaucon. As we saw, when the debate between Socrates and Thrasymachus begins, this latter initially asks Socrates for his view but cannot restrain himself from asserting his own. Restraint implies the very supraindividual measure that is denied by Thrasymachus's position. Significantly, while Thrasymachus never *asks* for anything from Socrates (see 341c)—unless one counts his demand to be paid for his first answer—but instead only makes accusations, Socrates himself constantly makes requests of Thrasymachus, and thereby makes himself in some respect *dependent* on him. He does not make an assertion without

85. Blößner, *Dialogform und Argument,* 36.

Thrasymachus's consent, he gives Thrasymachus freedom to choose whatever position he likes (340c), and his demand is only that Thrasymachus in fact like the position (346a). The conclusion can be reached only with Thrasymachus's real participation. Because he withholds precisely this, book I comes to an end without coming to a resolution. The mode Socrates presents is thus not imposition from above but cooperative participation in something else, a larger whole. We will eventually see that this mode is, in a way, the very point Socrates will make. The content is once again the form.

Shifting Horizons

Book II begins with Socrates' confession that the whole of book I was merely a "prelude" (προοίμιον, 352a). Glaucon claims Socrates has only *apparently* rather than *truly* persuaded, and thus the discussion starts all over again, this time on new ground. What is the difference between true and apparent persuasion? What is it, exactly, that was inadequate about the exchange between Thrasymachus and Socrates?

Socrates had said that they wished to reach a conclusion in the discussion (346a), using the verb περαίνειν, derived from the word πέρας, or "end." If the end of a discussion is not merely where it stops but where it reaches a kind of fulfillment, it can be only because reason finds therein a satisfactory object. It is illuminating to reflect on the ending of book I in terms of what it reveals about what constitutes the fulfillment of reason, meaning, about the very *nature* of reason.

In the first place, we might consider book I to be essentially complete within itself. In this case, because Socrates defeats the argument that Thrasymachus had proffered, we would say that the purpose of reason is to overpower, or to put it more gently, to bring about assent. If this is its purpose, it does not matter whether it makes good arguments—arguments that adequately convey an idea—but only that the interlocutors *think* that they are good or are otherwise unable to answer them. Presumably, it is just this notion of reason that Thrasymachus would "defend," insofar as he is ready to leave the moment he thinks he has made an overwhelming point. Indeed, our argument has been that, unless it is possible to achieve *truth* rather than simple conviction, reason cannot take any other form, regardless of its "user's" intentions. If this is the essence of reason, it is reduced to a mere tool that can be justified only by the effect it can bring about; the very notion of "understanding" is only itself a relatively convenient instrument. But the fact that Plato distinguishes between true and apparent persuasion, which would not make any sense unless genuine knowledge were somehow possible in principle, and the fact that Socrates opposes Thrasymachus's view, suggest quite plainly that Plato himself does not hold this view of reason.[86]

Another possibility is to suggest that book I is incomplete because there are certain holes in the arguments Socrates gives. We encounter the observation often in commentaries that it would be strange for the dialogue to continue if there were no flaws in the argument used to defeat Thrasymachus. A possible implication of this interpretation is that if Socrates had made a few more points in this context, or clarified his premises further, the rest of the *Republic* would have been unnecessary. Regarding the question of the nature of reason, this interpretation implies that reason seeks unflawed argumentation above all. While this view is undeniably true in part, it leaves open the question whether reason can be satisfied with partial truth. In other words, the question remains whether reason, as reason, possesses an inward need to raise ultimate questions. If it does not, and if partial truths are dependent on ultimate truth for their own truth, then it is not clear whether this view of reason is fundamentally any different from the previous one. Does reason seek *truth* or merely formal consistency? If consistency alone, then it governs a fairly tightly circumscribed kingdom and is in turn the servant of a more powerful ruler.

In any event, we know this is not Plato's view, not only because in the *Protagoras* he claims that knowledge is always and in every case the most powerful ruler,[87] and not only because he eventually shows the need to ask the question of ultimate foundations in order to answer the question raised so casually in the beginning, but also by Socrates' final comment at the end of book I. Thrasymachus assumes Socrates has "eaten his fill" (354a)—that his reason has found completion—in the discussion that just transpired. He assumes this because Socrates managed to overpower him. But Socrates remains unsatisfied, and whereas Thrasymachus had always laid responsibility on his interlocutor for his own frustrated desire, Socrates blames himself: "I have not had a fine banquet (οὐ ... καλῶς γε εἰστίαμαι), but it's my own fault, not yours. For in my opinion, I am just like the gluttons who grab at whatever is set before them to get a taste of it, before they have in proper

---

86. The contrast between mere persuasion and truth, and the implied question regarding the instrumentality of reason, is also a major theme of the *Gorgias* and the *Phaedrus*.

87. *Prt.,* 352b–e.

measure (μετρίως) enjoyed what went before" (354a–b). In other words, Socrates observes that their inquiry has been *fragmentary*, that it has failed to treat the parts in a measured way, which means as integrated into a complete or beautiful (καλός) whole. This is precisely why they did not get to the heart of the matter, however formally consistent their arguments may have been. Socrates has argued like one who is in the cave, that is, without any access to a transcendent whole, just like his interlocutors, but with this crucial difference: he is aware that he has.

Socrates' aim is more "gratuitous" than Thrasymachus's: he is disappointed because he showed the goodness of justice without having sufficiently considered its *meaning*. While Thrasymachus's point is not to understand injustice but to impose it, Socrates' aim is not simply the practical one of restoring justice, but also the more gratuitous one of *understanding* it. Thrasymachus seeks a particular result, namely, to get the better of his opponent; with an extraordinarily subtle gesture, Socrates breaks open the sophist's horizon by *simultaneously achieving and renouncing Thrasymachus's aim:* he defeats his interlocutor in a certain respect, but the outcome of the discussion for him is that he knows nothing (μοι νυνὶ γέγονεν ἐκ τοῦ διαλόγου μηδὲν εἰδέναι, 354b–c). Moreover, it is significant that the reasons he attributes to his failure to reach the desired understanding are precisely greed and lack of restraint. It is just these two things that characterize Thrasymachus and stem directly from his understanding of understanding. There is intimated here in Socrates' confession, by contrast, a connection between understanding the intrinsic meaning of justice, seeing it is as good, and setting oneself in order in relation to goodness.

Thus, to be content with the ending of book I is to fail to see that reason has a more comprehensive aspiration, an aspiration that, if it cannot be achieved, will leave us in the cave. Socrates defeats Thrasymachus, not primarily by defeating his arguments—since to do just this would have been to grant ultimate victory to Thrasymachus at a deep level—but by confessing his failure. The confession of inadequacy is itself already a shift of horizons. But it is crucial to see that the conclusion is not simply "left open" in an indeterminate sense, so that the following discussion would be only accidentally added on to it.[88] This interpretation would be looking at the in-

---

88. On the intrinsic connection of book I to what follows, see Annas, *Introduction,* 56–57; Blößner, *Dialogform und Argument,* 40; Kube, *TEXNH und APETH,* 187. For a contrasting view:

conclusiveness from the side of the cave, as it were; instead, we recognize the inadequacy only because we already know at least inchoately where the discussion must go. With this we return to the point made at the outset: we understand the partiality of this stage only in the light of the whole. We read the dialogue as a *drama* and not as an aimless series of conversations. Socrates breaks open this initial discussion beyond itself because he leaves us with little more than a gesture toward what transcends it—and we can see already it has something to do with the intersection of goodness and truth.

If it is impossible to get beyond mere appearances so as to be able to distinguish them from being, and thus impossible to discover a horizon more fundamental than that which Thrasymachus sought to impose, then Socrates' gesture of failure will turn out to be a particularly clever deception. There will then be no "cave," because there will be nothing but cave, and what we call philosophy will in the end be shadows and more shadows, bound by the logic of violence, vying against each other for domination.

H. Gauß, *Die Dialoge der literarischen Meisterschaft, vol. 2., part 2 of Philosophischer Handkommentar zu den Dialogen Platos* (Bern, 1958), 118–238. Thesleff (*Studies in Platonic Chronology, 107–10*) gathers evidence to suggest that book I was written separately but that Plato eventually reworked it into the rest of the material that would comprise the *Republic*.

CHAPTER TWO

WITH GOOD REASON

*Or, How the Idea of the Good Both Distinguishes
Being from Appearance and Provides
a Bridge between Them*

The First Sailing

The *Republic* stands out among all of Plato's dialogues, not merely because it seems to be the apex and flower of his mature period, not merely because it gathers together into a single dialogue many of the issues that appear
separately in other works,[1] but also because it sets for itself the most ambitious epistemological project in the Platonic corpus: namely, to find an adequate way of distinguishing being from appearance. If we see the connection
between this distinction and the corresponding distinctions between forms
and images, knowledge and opinion, we will not have any trouble claiming
that this distinction is the foundation upon which Plato's philosophy stands.
In most dialogues, however, Plato makes use of the distinction without explaining how it is possible to make the distinction in the first place.[2] Indeed, apart from the *Timaeus*, where he concedes understanding to a "small
group,"[3] he generally gives the impression that making such a distinction lies
beyond human capacity. In the *Cratylus*, the reality of the forms is something

---

1. "The chief witness to the unity of Plato's thought is the *Republic*, the great work of his maturity and the most complete synthesis of his teaching," Paul Shorey, *The Unity of Plato's Thought*
(Chicago: University of Chicago Press, 1903), 78. Cf. Natorp, *Platos Ideenlehre*, 179–80.

2. See, for example, *Ti.,* 27d–28a, where the distinction between "being" and "becoming,"
and its corresponding distinction between "knowledge" and "opinion," is asserted as a basic
premise for argument, rather than as something to be argued for itself. Cf. Harold F. Cherniss,
"The Philosophical Economy of the Theory of Ideas," in *Plato: A Collection of Critical Essays,* edited by Gregory Vlastos (Garden City, N.Y.: Anchor Books, 1971), 16–27.

3. *Ti.,* 51d.

Socrates says he often "dreams about."[4] The *Meno* ends with the suggestion that the best we can generally hope for in matters of virtue is true opinion;[5] the *Theaetetus* likewise brings the attempt to discern what knowledge really is to a fruitless close.[6] Famously, in the *Phaedo*, Socrates alludes to the reality of the forms as too bright to be stared at directly, and simply "hypothesizes" the existence of these realities, rather than bringing that existence itself to evidence.[7] He calls this approach a "second sailing" (δεύτερος πλοῦς, 99d), referring to sailors' recourse to the use of oars if a strong wind is not available to propel a ship.[8] The *Republic* is the only place in this great ocean where Plato seems to have caught the desired breeze.[9] And as Socrates says, "wherever the argument, like a wind, tends, thither must we go" (394d).

This claim hangs on the idea of the good, the central point around which the *Republic* turns. Over the course of the digression that occupies the dialogue's middle books,[10] Plato makes a series of basic statements regarding the nature of the good: it is not only the foundation of truth (508e), but it is also the cause of the existence of all things (509b) and the goal of all human action (505d–e). Two factors, however, threaten to obstruct whatever wind Plato claims to discover, and these have generated enough controversy to forestall any facile assumptions that the *Republic* simply resolves the epistemological problem. On the one hand, while Plato does state that nothing can be sufficiently known unless we first know the good, he resists, even here, speaking about the good directly but resorts to indirect images and thus seems to take up the same oars he did in the *Phaedo*.[11] Is he confessing, once again, that there is no accessible foundation for distinguishing knowledge and opinion?[12] On the other hand, though Plato affirms the good as fi-

---

4. *Cra.*, 439c–d.   5. *Meno*, 99aff.

6. *Tht.*, 210aff.   7. *Phd.*, 100a–b.

8. David Gallop, *Phaedo* (Oxford: Clarendon Press, 1975), 176. Cf. Giovanni Reale, *Toward a New Interpretation of Plato* (Washington, D.C.: The Catholic University Press of America, 1997), 95–101. Reale cites a classical reference for this metaphor. Eustachius, *In Odyss.*, 1453.20.

9. Utermöhlen, *Die Bedeutung der Ideenlehre*, 53, says that the *Republic* is the only dialogue to elaborate the method of the forms.

10. According to Robert Brumbaugh, "Digression and Dialogue," 84–92, here 85–86, the essential point for Plato is often expressed in what seem to be digressions. The *Republic* is certainly no exception, as we will see.

11. Glenn Rawson, "Knowledge and Desire of the Good in Plato's *Republic*," *Southwest Philosophy Review* 12.1 (1996): 103.

12. On the *Republic*'s apparent failure to get beyond the *Phaedo*'s hypothetical method, see Henry Jackson, "On Plato's *Republic* VI 509d sqq.," *Journal of Philology* 10 (1882): 132–50, here 149.

nal end, as cause of all being, and as foundation of truth, he does not make explicit how the good in fact plays this comprehensive role.[13] Even if the claim is accepted, the task still falls to the interpreter to explain it, and there has been a great variety of proposals in this regard. The first factor will form the matter of our next chapter; here, we will attempt to offer an explanation of how the claims regarding the good fit together, with particular attention to the good's epistemological function.

Because Plato says so little in explicit terms about the epistemological function of the good, one cannot avoid being somewhat speculative in attempts to make this function manifest. It is, indeed, not at all obvious how goodness has any relation, for example, to the sophisticated and somewhat abstract distinction between types of objects and powers of soul in the divided line, or why the good should illuminate the intelligible realm in such a manner, analogous to the sun's irradiation into the visible realm. Attempts to elucidate this issue often make the problem even more difficult by isolating this particular question from the dialogue as a whole rather than approaching it specifically in relation to the terms of the challenge Plato dramatized in books I and II.[14] It is no wonder, then, that those who thus isolate it are often left with either inventing explanations that, however plausible in themselves, seem to touch Plato's own presentation only tangentially,[15] or deriving an epistemology that draws on explicit aspects of Plato's theory of knowledge as expressed in the *Republic,* but that has in turn only an accidental relation to the idea of the good as it appears in this particular dialogue.[16] If we approach

Richard Robinson claims that the *Republic* is the one dialogue in which Plato insists on getting beyond a merely hypothetical method but that even here he does not manage to do so. "Hypothesis in the *Republic,*" chap. 10 of *Plato's Earlier Dialectic,* 2nd corrected ed. (Oxford: Clarendon Press, 1966). Drew Hyland observes that the forms are *always* assumed, and never "deduced": *Finitude and Transcendence,* 178.

13. R. C. Cross and A. D. Woozley claim we cannot find any explanation in the *Republic* for the good as cause of intelligibility. *Plato's Republic: A Philosophical Commentary* (New York: Palgrave Macmillan, 1979), 260–61. Hans Joachim Krämer catalogues an impressive list of similar claims in "Über den Zusammenhang von Prinzipienlehre und Dialektik bei Platon: Zur Definition des Dialektikers *Politeia* 534b–c," *Philologus* 110 (1966): 35–70, here 43n3.

14. A counterexample is Utermöhlen, *Die Bedeutung der Ideenlehre,* 11.

15. See, for example, Kenneth Sayre's explanation of the good's cause of intelligibility by interpreting goodness as "rightness," *Plato's Literary Garden,* 181–88.

16. David Hitchcock argues, in "The Good in Plato's *Republic*" (*Apeiron* 19 [1985[: 65–92), that the functions ascribed to the good make sense once we interpret the good as the One, but he does not show why the identification ought to be made in this particular dialogue, or why

the broader epistemological issue, by contrast, from the problem introduced in book I, and attend to the terms of the problem set out by Glaucon and Adeimantus at the very start of the main discussion, we will see that Plato's claims about the good's role as the foundation of rationality appear quite natural, and in fact turn out to be essentially related to the ontological and axiological claims. Moreover, as soon as these connections become apparent, we will see that the entire dialogue suddenly crystallizes into a concrete whole, with dramatic brilliance, existential weight, and philosophical integrity.

The Twofold Nature of Goodness

Socrates' discussion with Thrasymachus in book I, as we saw, becomes a crisis the moment it touches on the question of what is "better," and thus the question of the nature of goodness itself. It is not surprising, then, that book II, which initiates the main conversation of the *Republic* that follows upon the prologue of book I, begins with a distinction between the various ways something can be said to be good. In other words, the *very first point* made in the *Republic*'s main discussion concerns the nature of goodness. This point, we propose, will be determinative for everything else that follows. Glaucon suggests (357b–d), with Socrates' consent, that goodness appears in three forms (εἴδη): 1) there is a good we choose simply for its own sake (αὐτὸ αὐτοῦ ἕνεκα) and not for the sake of its "results" (τῶν ἀποβαινόντων, literally, the "things that issue or depart from it"); 2) a good we love both for its own sake *and* for what comes from it (ὃ αὐτό τε αὐτοῦ χάριν ἀγαπῶμεν καὶ τῶν ἀπ᾽ αὐτοῦ γιγνομένων); and 3) goods we would not choose to have for themselves, but simply for the reward they bring or other consequences that follow from them (τῶν δὲ μισθῶν τε χάριν καὶ τῶν ἄλλων ὅσα γίγνεται ἀπ᾽ αὐτων). To the question of into which category justice would fall, Socrates points to the second. Most people, according to Glaucon, would by contrast place it in the third category, because they consider it a burden to be endured only because of its benefits.

Plato would not simply have called it the One if this claim is true. We are left to wonder, in other words, whether goodness *qua* goodness has any relation to intelligibility. Because of the difficulties in understanding how *goodness* itself could be the cause of intelligiblity, Francis M. Cornford suggests that there is another form, Unity, alongside the good, at the top of the divided line. See "Mathematics and Dialectic in the *Republic* VI–VII (II)" *Mind* 41.162 (April 1932): 173–90, here 178–81.

goodness begets
good beyond 89
itself.

It is crucial to explore the significance of Socrates' decision. He places justice in the second category because this is the most noble (κάλλιστος, 358a).
That which is good in the supreme sense, in other words, is to be loved *both* for
itself *and* for the things that arise from it. As an illuminating point of contrast,
let us consider Aristotle's judgment about the meaning of goodness in the
Nichomachean Ethics. To be good in the highest sense (τὸ ἄριστον), he says,
is to be something that warrants being chosen always for its own sake and never for the sake of something else (ἀεὶ δι' αὐτὴν καὶ οὐδέποτε δι' ἄλλο).[17]
Accordingly, Aristotle recognizes only two senses of good—"1) things good
in themselves and 2) things good as a means to those"[18]—compared to Plato's three categories. Aristotle's view effectively separates the senses of goodness into a sharp dichotomy: we choose a thing either because it is intrinsically good or because it is instrumentally good. Though he affirms this difference,
Plato at the very same time refuses to make the dichotomy absolute and allows a third possibility, a "both/and." Hayden Ausland has observed that this
particular way of distinguishing goods seems unique to Plato in the classical
philosophical tradition.[19] This central class of good clearly represents the most
comprehensive form, which simultaneously allows and overcomes a distinction between an intrinsic good and its extrinsic benefits. To put the issue in
more technical terms, we could say that both Plato and Aristotle distinguish
between goodness in an absolute sense (in itself), and in a relative sense (in
relation to an extraneous benefit), but that Plato goes on to designate a third
sense of goodness that is absolute in a manner *inclusive of* rather than *exclusive*
of the relative.

Precisely because this most comprehensive sense of goodness includes
the relative, however, it becomes particularly difficult to distinguish from
Glaucon's third category, which reduces goodness to its extraneous benefits. If we admit that the benefits due to a thing are sufficiently desirable that
we would choose something for the benefits alone, how are we to discern
whether the thing is also desirable in itself? An adequate response to this
question demands a serious and rigorous method suited specifically to the

17. *Nich. Eth.,* I.7.1097b1.

18. Ibid., I.6.1096b14–15.

19. Hayden Ausland, "Socrates' Argumentative Burden in the *Republic*," in Michelini, *Plato
as Author,* 123–43, here 125. Ausland cites a passage from Cicero, which seems to be the only echo
of the distinction Plato makes, and suggests that Cicero may have been influenced by the Stoics,
who were in turn influenced by Plato.

problem it presents. Though the interlocutors adopt a particular approach here, the issue of methodology is not a thematic concern in this context; it does not become one until books V–VII. Is there any connection between the discussion of method in these later books regarding the distinction between forms and images and the way Glaucon sets the terms of the problem already here? This question, of course, concerns the unity of the *Republic* and whether the method specifically outlined in the central books is also reflected in the dialogue's general plot. Is the *Republic*, in other words, a good drama in Aristotle's sense? If we disregard this question, we will isolate the specifically philosophical moment of the dialogue and fail to see its essential relation to the discussion of goodness here in book II. But we can open up a deeper insight into both parts if we interpret them in connection to one another. Anticipating the discussion in the later books, we propose that the approach introduced at the outset for discussing the meaning and value of justice concerns the relation between being and appearance in the light of the nature of goodness just as it does in the later books, and that, in turn, the discussion in books V–VII depends on the various modes of desirability elaborated in book II. When Plato enters into the discussion of the nature of philosophy in book V (475eff.), he begins by talking about the difference between loving a thing in an extrinsic way (i.e., in terms of its appearances or opinions about it) and loving its being, its reality in itself.[20] The distinction is in fact an echo of the discussion here in book II, in which Plato first presents the love of something, not only for the rewards of opinion, but also for its own reality (358a). These two pivotal sections of the dialogue, we suggest, reciprocally illuminate one another, and in doing so present the basic joints in the unified structure of the dialogue.

Following the articulation of the three types of good, the discussion sets out with an agreement that Socrates will attempt to produce the *best possible* argument on behalf of justice. To this end, Glaucon and Adeimantus devise the best possible argument against it, one that intends to show that justice is a matter of appearances and extraneous benefits alone. It *is* nothing in itself because it has no value in itself. Glaucon mounts three steps in his elabora-

---

20. "'Won't we assert that these men [the philosophers] delight in and love that on which knowledge depends, and the others that on which opinion depends? Or don't we remember that we were saying that they love and look at fair sounds and colors and such things but can't even endure the fact that the fair itself is something? ... Must we, therefore, call philosophers rather than lovers of opinion those who delight in each thing that is itself?'" (479e–480b).

tion of the argument. First, he explains that justice is not natural, but merely conventional, and arises only as a compromise that protects one's natural inclination to injustice, since the badness of suffering the injustice of others far outweighs the badness of being just oneself (358e–359b). He then strengthens this suggestion by relating, as a kind of thought experiment, the story of the ring found by Gyges' ancestor (359c–360d), a ring that renders its wearer invisible. Anyone possessing this ring, he proposes, would obviously act unjustly, which is another way of saying that since justice is merely the relative good that everyone takes it to be, it follows that *if we eliminate appearances* (by becoming invisible), *there will be no justice.* This outcome serves, in effect, to link the relativism espoused by Thrasymachus (and Protagoras) with the twofold nature of goodness. To say that justice is desirable only for its benefits is to say that its entire "reality" consists in seeming, that it has no "in-itself" essence or nature of its own but is wholly relativized and therefore subject to manipulation.

Third, in order to clarify the point, Glaucon proposes a further thought experiment that aims at introducing the most complete disjunction possible between being and appearance. For the sake of argument, he says, "we must take away the seeming" (ἀφαιρετέον δὴ τὸ δοκεῖν, 361c). On the one hand, we will assume a perfectly (τελέως) unjust man, who, though being unjust "in himself" (absolutely), appears "for others" (relatively) to be perfectly just, and we will place next to him a man who has been "stripped of everything except justice" (361c) so that he appears unjust in spite of being just. The rewards and punishments each receives are accordingly extreme. The unjust man is wealthy, powerful, honored by all, and loved by the gods (362b–c), while the just man is universally reviled, tortured like a criminal, and even abandoned by the gods. Glaucon thus lays a challenge at Socrates' feet: if he can show that it is preferable to be this perfectly just man in spite of all the consequences and appearances, he will have shown that justice is good absolutely, that is, in itself.

Let us note that the thought experiment Glaucon sketches here draws an implicit connection between the *reality* of a thing independent of appearances and its possessing its own goodness. Moreover, he characterizes injustice specifically as the capacity to manipulate appearances, or in other words, he suggests that its "intrinsic goodness" consists of the total power it wields over extraneous benefits, i.e., its intrinsic quality is in fact wholly extrinsic, while the intrinsic goodness of justice stands as a certain independence from extraneous benefits. It is not an accident that the issue of being and appearance is raised in connection with the issue of justice and injustice. We begin to see even at this early stage in the argument that, for Plato, the nature of the relation between being and appearance lies at the very heart of the question of justice.[21] It is important also to note the way Glaucon lays out his challenge, which is meant to bring the truth of the matter to light, for, as we will see, Socrates will adopt a similar approach in his response in books VI and VII. Glaucon contrasts the two positions with one another by idealizing them in their most extreme form: "As to the judgment itself about the life of these two of whom we are speaking, we'll be able to make it correctly if we set the most just man and the most unjust in opposition; if we do not, we won't be able to do so" (360e). Rather than taking empirical instances of one or the other, Glaucon posits the complete paradigm in each case and infers the implications. Perfect injustice is shown to receive all honor, while perfect justice appears to have no claim to goodness at all. If appearances are neutralized in the manner Glaucon's argument demands, then nothing remains; there is thus, in spite of appearances, no such thing as justice.

When Glaucon finishes, it is Adeimantus's turn, and he says that the argument against justice has not yet been "adequately" stated (362d). To Socrates' insistence that the brothers stand by one another so that nothing be left out, Adeimantus responds by bringing forth the various speeches in the past that have been made in praise of justice, in both poetry and prose. His claim is straightforward: no one, he says, has ever explained how justice is good except in terms of its appearances, so there is nothing to prevent one from reducing justice's goodness wholly to its extraneous benefits: "There is not one who has ever blamed injustice or praised justice other than for the reputations, honors, and gifts that come from them" (366e). He therefore maintains, like Glaucon, that in order to make manifest the intrinsic goodness of justice, Socrates must take away the appearances (τὰς δὲ δόξας ἀφαίρει, 367b), and he concludes by reiterating twice in identical language.

---

21. L. A. Kosman expresses the essentially metaphysical significance of justice for Plato quite well. As he explains in a passing observation regarding the *Republic,* justice is the "principle by which the good distributes itself properly into forms and then into particulars, and thus perhaps the fundamental metaphysical principle according to which each thing is itself in conformity to its true nature. The ultimate justice is thus the justice of appearance to being, i.e., of the 'lower' to the 'higher' world," "Platonic Love," in *Facets of Plato's Philosophy* (Amsterdam: Van Gorcum, 1976), 53–69, here 54. We will see how Kosman's observation is borne out through the analysis of the causal import of goodness in the present chapter.

Socrates must not only "show by argument" (or "by speech": ἐνδείξῃ τῷ λόγῳ) that justice is better than injustice, but he must also show how justice and injustice each *in itself* affects the soul of the one who has it (367b, 367e). There are two things to note in this: first, implied in Adeimantus's argument seems to be that speech (λόγος) is in some respect bound to the extrinsic qualities of a thing. In other words, to give a speech in praise of something *is* to extol the "wages and reputations" it entails; speech concerns the realm of appearance. To manifest the intrinsic goodness of something requires a manner of showing *in addition to* the demonstration that words provide.[22] Secondly, Adeimantus points to Socrates in particular as the one to show this: "Leave wages and reputations to others to praise. I could endure other men's praising justice and blaming injustice in this way, extolling and abusing them in terms of reputations and wages; but *from you* I couldn't" (367d, emphasis added). If it is possible to bring to light the being of justice beyond its mere appearance, it will depend on the possibility of distinguishing philosophy from poetry or other forms of speech-making. The relation between poetry and philosophy, we know, is the primary concern of the dialogue's epilogue in book X. Again, we see an underlying unity to the various themes the *Republic* takes up, and an awareness of the unity will shed a decisive light on each of these themes.

Forms, Likenesses, and the Souls That Love Them

Plato first introduces the term "philosophy" in book II when Socrates indicates the need for education. The guardians of the city, to guard properly, must be able to tell friend from foe, and so require training. Plato follows this

22. In the *Cratylus*, Plato shows that the proper use of words (i.e., names) presupposes a more originary contact with things; he makes a similar point in the *Phaedrus*. We will address the question of the relationship between words, appearances, and knowledge more fully in chapter 5 and the coda. For an excellent account of Plato's view, see Francisco Gonzalez, "Nonpropositional Knowledge in Plato," *Apeiron* 31.3 (1998): 25–84. In this essay, Gonzalez shows, primarily through a study of *Letter VII*, that for Plato language is "weak," able to describe the qualities of a thing but not its *being*. For a similar observation, see Rosemary Desjardins, *Plato and the Good: Illuminating the Darkling Vision* (Leiden: Brill, 2004), 164–65, 224–27. Desjardins demonstrates the need for an integration of *ergon* and *logon* for true knowledge, an integration Plato offers in the dramatic-discursive dialogues. Moreover, what Wolfgang Wieland says about written words in his essay "La crítica de Platón a la escritura y los límites de la communicabilidad" (*Méthexis* 4 [1991]: 19–37, here 26–28), namely, that they serve to transmit opinions but not the intimacy with reality implied by knowledge, holds as well for spoken words.

observation with a critique of the conventional form of education, which was founded on what Socrates claims to be the false tales that the poets tell about the gods (376d–392c). Although the distinctiveness of philosophy is present implicitly in this critique, philosophy itself disappears as an explicit theme until the end of book V, when Socrates brings up, apparently unrelated to the specific issue at hand,[23] the notion of the philosopher-king, and is forced to defend it by explaining the nature of the philosopher. Not incidentally, it is also here that the distinction between being and appearance is addressed thematically for the first time. At this moment, Plato picks up the point made briefly in book II and expands it. In the challenge laid down by Glaucon and Adeimantus, the "in-itself" character of justice is related to its having a worth beyond its extraneous benefits. At the end of book V, Plato broadens this view in two respects. First of all, and most fundamentally, he connects the "in-itself" character explicitly to the question of the possibility of knowledge by way of the themes of love and being. Secondly, in doing so, he universalizes the scope of the inquiry. No longer is the discussion simply about justice, but now it concerns the relationship between being and appearance as such, and therefore the question of the possibility of knowledge *tout court*, of "all the forms" (πάντων τῶν εἰδῶν, 476a). Let us consider in more detail how the discussion expands in this way.

As a means of introducing the nature of philosophy, Plato quite surprisingly, and significantly, begins by discussing the nature of love or desire. Love is not love, he says, unless it wants the *whole* of what it loves, and is not content with a mere part (475b). A philosopher is one, therefore, who desires the whole of wisdom and possesses in this respect an insatiable love of learning.[24] Glaucon misinterprets this assertion, however, and forces a further

23. Socrates raises the issue in what seems to be a digression within a digression. Once they attain the "peak" of their search for the virtues (445c), Socrates is interrupted (449b) and asked to clarify what he has said about women and children being held in common. He thus has to "go back again and say what perhaps should have been said then in its turn" (451b–c). After he clarifies his statement regarding women and children, he is interrupted again with the question whether such a city could ever come to be, and it is at this point that he introduces, directly at the center of the dialogue, the notion of the philosopher-king (473d). If this entire discussion is a digression from the ascent of the argument that reached its peak at the end of book IV, we could say that it stands above the line of argument just as the good stands above the divided line, as we will show in the next chapter.

24. Cf. also book VI (486a), in which Socrates insists that a genuinely philosophical nature must be free, meaning that it strives after the *whole* of all that is divine and human. The love that characterizes philosophy is specifically a love that aspires to exclude nothing: "'And you too must

clarification from Socrates. What Glaucon first has in mind are the "lovers of sights" (φιλοθεάμονες) and "lovers of hearing" (φιλήκοοι), those who are driven to see and hear as much as they can (475d). But Socrates points out that there is a difference between these lovers and philosophers, insofar as the philosopher's desire is not set, in the first place, on sense-experience, but rather on truth (475e). Note that this distinction is meaningless unless there is something "there" in the object that is not reducible to sense-experience. It is precisely to elaborate this difference that the theme of forms arises, and in its train, the well-known central discussions of sun, line, and cave in books VI–VII.[25]

To grasp the significance of the move Plato makes here in book V, we ought to reflect for a moment on the relationship between the love of sense-experience and the love of truth, though to do so we must again anticipate some of the discussion that follows. These do not represent simply two different kinds of love set over two different kinds of objects, for what they are set on are actually, as Plato already intimates here, two different "modes of being" of the same object.[26] On one hand, there is the sensible appear-

---

of course also consider something else when you're going to judge whether a nature is philosophic or not.' 'What?' 'You mustn't let its partaking in illiberality get by you unnoticed. For petty speech is of course most opposite to a soul that is always going to reach out for the whole and for everything divine and human.'"

25. One of the immediate implications of raising the issue of the forms in the context of the difference between loving the whole and loving just sense-experience is that forms come to represent a kind of *whole* to which images are related as so many parts or aspects. Robert B. Williamson elaborates this implication quite convincingly in "Eidos and Agathon in Plato's *Republic*," *St. John's Review* 39.1–2 (1989–90): 105–37. Our own analysis follows a similar line.

26. See G. Vlastos's well-known discussion of the "degrees of reality" in *New Essays in Plato and Aristotle*, edited by R. Bambrough (London: Routledge, 1965), 1–19. Gail Fine likewise argues against the simplistic "Two Worlds" thesis, which claims that what makes the difference between belief and knowledge are two different types of objects, sensible things and suprasensible forms. She suggests instead that the distinction rests on different types of propositions (i.e., knowledge rests on true propositions, while belief rests on true and false propositions). See "Knowledge and Belief in *Republic* 5–7," in Fine, *Plato 1*, 215–46, here, 221. The argument we offer in this chapter agrees with Fine's critique of a "Two Worlds" thesis, but proposes that the powers are distinguished *not* by different objects, but by different "presentational modes," one might say, of the same object. Our proposal would seem to do more justice to the clear "object-centeredness" in Socrates' characterization of the powers. As we will see, this view does not exclude relation to the soul but in fact depends on it in some sense, even while it does not reduce to that relation. For a clear presentation of the different "modes of being" in Plato, see Eric Perl, "The Presence of the Paradigm: Immanence and Transcendence in Plato's Theory of Forms," *Review of Metaphysics* 53 (December 1999): 339–62, and Perl, "Sense-perception and Intellect in Plato," *Revue de*

ance of a thing, and on the other, there is the thing as it is in itself. The sensible appearance, Plato goes on to say, is not the thing itself but a *likeness* of it (476c). But a likeness cannot be the whole of a thing; it is, instead, literally an "aspect" *(ad-specere)* or relative part.[27] Love that is ordered to the sense-experience of a thing is the love of an aspect of a thing rather than the whole. But if love is not love unless it desires the *whole* of a thing (474c), then it follows that we cannot consider "philotheamonists" or "philekoists" (lovers of sights and sounds) lovers at all in the strict sense of the word. Instead, they can only be *likenesses* of lovers, since their desire for a mere aspect of a thing is only the "likeness" of love. Indeed, Plato refers to them as "like philosophers" (ὁμοίους μὲν φιλοσόφοις, 475e),[28] that is, imitators of what philosophers are in reality. Philosophers, by implication, are true lovers because they are lovers of truth, and to love truth is to love the whole of a thing rather than a mere aspect.[29]

But we must inquire further into the meaning of Plato's distinction between being and appearance, which forms the ontological foundation for the distinction between true love, set on the whole, and its partial likeness. It is at this point in the dialogue that Plato first makes explicit reference to the "forms" in a technical sense:[30] "The same argument also applies then to justice and injustice, good and bad, and all the forms; each is itself one, but, by

---

philosophie ancienne 15.1 (1997): 15–34. See also C. J. de Vogel, *Rethinking Plato and Platonism* (Leiden: Brill, 1988), 162; Ferber, *Platos Idee des Guten*, 25ff.; and Desjardins, *Plato and the Good*, 65. According to H. Jackson, "On Plato's *Republic* VI," image and reality are not two distinct existences, but one existence viewed either directly or indirectly (135). Thesleff concludes, after a thorough study of the Platonic corpus, that "there is no distinct gap of difference between the two levels in Plato's vision, no pointed χωρίς, no deep separation of the 'immanent' from the 'transcendent,'" *Studies in Plato's Two-Level Model*, 63. For a contrasting perspective, see N. Murphy, *The Interpretation of Plato's Republic* (Oxford: Clarendon Press, 1951), 197–200.

27. Without explicitly drawing the inference that the appearance or likeness is an aspect of the whole, Plato lays out the following string of analogies in 475b–e: form : likeness :: whole : part :: wisdom (truth) : sounds and sights.

28. An alternate version has "φιλοσόφους"; the difference does not affect the point being made.

29. John Sallis makes a similar observation, but at the same time immediately problematizes it with the claim that the love of truth seems to be a *restricted* form of love, so that "the philosopher, it appears, loves only a part of a part" (*Being and Logos: Reading the Platonic Dialogues*, 3rd ed. [Bloomington: Indiana University Press, 1996] 382). Nevertheless, he goes on to say that Plato eventually "revokes" this restriction.

30. Unless one counts the allusion in book II (369a). When Plato raises the issue in the present context, he does so as a theory familiar to his readers.

showing up everywhere in a community with actions, bodies, and one another, each is an apparitional many" (476a). Each of the forms exists in itself,
in relation to itself, and in this sense *is* "one." But each also exists in *communion* with (i.e., in relation with), other things, and in this sense *appears* many.
Plato specifically adverts to what we would call the physical and concrete aspects of bodies and actions, but generalizes to include any type of relation
with something other than itself (καὶ ἀλλήλων κοινωνίᾳ, 476a).[31] We
ought to recognize here the point made in a negative manner in the *Theaetetus:* if something does not exist beyond mere relativity to another, the verb
"to be" no longer has any meaning.[32] Being thus in some sense corresponds
to things in distinction from their relation, while appearance corresponds to
things as relative to others. Plato goes on to connect the "oneness" of things
with their sameness, which is their being and what makes them an object of
knowledge in the proper sense. Correspondingly, it is in relation to others
that things present different aspects, they undergo change, possess an ambiguity (ἐπαμφοτερίζειν, 479c), and thus qualify as objects of opinion at best
(479a–d). This does not make appearance simply *nothing*, however. It is not

31. We may wish to ask whether this relation to another includes interformal relations (i.e.,
the forms' relationships among themselves, such as those described in the *Sophist*). If it does,
then it would seem to follow that interformal relations belong to the sphere of appearance rather
than being. In this case, formal difference would apparently not, in the end, be "really real," an inference that would seem to run counter to Plato's customary ascription of reality to the formal.
While Plato doesn't address the issue of interformal difference in the *Republic,* his account of the
relationship between being and appearance here—as we will unfold it—provides a response in
principle to this problem. Forms *must* have an identity that is in some sense independent from
even their relations to other forms, but this requirement cannot make difference "unreal." As we
will argue in this chapter (and elaborate in the coda when we return to the positivity of difference), positing the *same principle* (i.e., the good) as the cause of both being in itself and relation
to others makes both, as it were, equiprimordial in a nonreductive fashion. This response to the
problem of being and appearance could be applied equally to the problem of interformal difference. To do so, however, would require a further differentiation of some of the vocabulary Plato
uses here, though the *Republic* also supplies resources for this: Plato claims that the spheres of
relation can be apprehended only by "opinion" (479a–d). But opinion, which corresponds to
physical manifestation, would obviously not be appropriate for interformal relations. For these
relations, we would need something higher than opinion, but lower than *nous.* The best candidate would seem to be *dianoia:* "Out of habit we called them kinds of knowledge several times,
but they require another name, one that is brighter than opinion but dimmer than knowledge.
Thought *[dianoia]* was, I believe, the word by which we previously distinguished it. But, in my
opinion, there is no place for dispute about a name when a consideration is about things so great
as those lying before us" (533d–e).

32. *Tht.,* 157a–b.

an illusion. It is quite real, even if it is not reality itself. Plato assigns it a place *between* being and non-being (479c). What he means here, as many commentators have pointed out, is not being in the existential sense, since Plato admits that appearances exist in a factual manner. Rather, being here means what we might call "in-itselfness" or absoluteness. In contrast to the in-itselfness that being represents, according to this account, Plato claims that relatedness always entails change and ambiguity. It is not difficult to understand why. There is no limit to the number of things something can be relative to, and each of these things is different from the others. It follows that what something is in relation to others, *qua* relative, will be in *some respect* different in each case.[33] It is this relativity that places appearance or manifestation—which is being's showing itself *to* another—between being and not-being. Things taken absolutely, in themselves, *are* what they are, which is a single thing, and taken relatively, they appear in various and thus changing ways. Their appearance is not simply different from the reality—because it is the appearance of the reality, which is why Plato calls it a *likeness*—but *as* appearance it is not identical to the reality, because this identity would be the reality *simpliciter*, as absolute and in itself rather than as relative to another. Again, appearance lies *between* reality and unreality.

It is this threefold ontological distinction—being, non-being, and the "between"—that gives rise in turn to the distinction in the soul's powers (δυνάμεις). According to J. G. Gosling, we ought not to read the distinction between *powers* here as a distinction between separate *faculties*: "They are not different faculties, but, if anything, different abilities that result from different applications of the same faculty."[34] As Plato explains, the powers of the soul are not beings in themselves juxtaposed to other beings in the world, but are wholly "relative" beings, in the sense that they are defined entirely by that to which they are directed:

In a power I see no color or shape or anything of the sort such as I see in many other things to which I look when I distinguish one thing from another for myself. With a power I look only to this—on what it depends and what it accomplishes (ἐφ᾽ ᾧ

33. Plato, as we saw, makes precisely the same argument in relation to the essential relativity of perception in *Tht.*, 153e–157c.

34. J. G. Gosling, "Δόξα and Δύναμις in Plato's *Republic*," *Phronesis* 12 (1968): 119–30, here 129. Gosling's conclusion corresponds exactly to the point we have made, namely, that the difference between forms and sensibles is *not* a difference between (separate) objects but between modes of presentation of one reality.

τε ἔστι καὶ ὃ ἀπεργάζεται); and it is on this basis that I come to call each of the powers a power; and that which depends on the same thing and accomplishes the same thing, I call the same power, and that which depends on something else and accomplishes something else, I call a different power. (477c–d)

To use modern language, which, though completely foreign to Plato, helps set in relief significant features of this text, we would say Plato has an *intentional* view of consciousness. As this passage attests, he posits a reciprocal relationship between reality and the soul. The soul is, on the one hand, *receptive* to its object, insofar as its very "being" consists in its relatedness to reality, and thus the nature of its "object" determines the power of the soul: if the "power" of knowing exists in the soul, it is because there exists in reality something beyond mere appearance. On the other hand, however, the soul is also *spontaneous* with respect to its object, insofar as it at the very same time brings about the mode of the object by which it is determined. Plato uses the verb ἀπεργάζομαι—the soul acts on and *effects* its object in some respect. In other words, to connect the two aspects, the object presents itself in a particular mode according to the quality of the soul's power that is ordered to it, even as it simultaneously determines that power. Neither comes before the other; the presentation of the object occurs as an "event," we could say, in the relation to the soul. This interpretation alone allows us to make sense of Plato's description of *both* understanding *and* truth being the fruit of the soul's "consorting and mixing," or as Bloom translates it, "coupling" with reality, in 490b: πλησιάγας καὶ μιγεὶς τῷ ὄντι ὄντως, γεννήσας, νοῦν καὶ ἀλήθειαν. It is not that truth is simply "there" and then it is received by the soul to give rise to understanding. Instead, truth, along with the understanding, "happens" as something the soul co-generates (γεννήσας) in the coupling.

This view of the powers of the soul as constituting the presentational mode of its object corresponds, moreover, with Plato's "extramissive" account of vision, which he claims to be analogous to the act of the soul's relation to the really real. The eye, which Plato calls the most "sunlike" of the organs, does not simply passively receive its image of the object, but rather sends forth its own beam of light which literally commingles with what we might call the "objective" illumination coming from the sun (508b).[35] This view of the powers of

---

35. Cf. the more elaborate presentation of the same view in *Ti.,* 45b–46a. Notice that the eyes were the first sense organs created, after the head, which is the most divine part (44d).

the soul implies that, in order to see the "whole picture" of Plato's understanding of knowledge, we will have to attend not only to the metaphysical issues
regarding the nature of reality, but also to the soul's dispositive character, the
subjective quality of the soul that pursues reality. To use contemporary language, it will turn out to be this "intentional" view of the soul that makes ethics, in the broad sense, intrinsic to both ontology and epistemology.

Most immediately in this section of the *Republic*, Plato characterizes the
soul's powers in terms of the nature of the object to which they are directed. Thus, knowledge represents the soul's relation to being: "Knowledge is
presumably dependent on what *is*, to know what *is*, that it is and how it is"
(478a). Ignorance, in turn, is the soul's relation to nothing (477a). Finally,
opinion, being "brighter than ignorance and darker than knowledge," is set
on that which both *is* and *is not* at the same time (478d), in other words, the
multiplicity of appearance. Non-being, in this context, clearly means not
the contrary but the relative opposite of the being that designates the "in-
itselfness" of things, and thus means relativity itself.[36] In this respect, opinion
is by nature essentially relative, lacking the absoluteness of knowledge (and
ignorance) because its object lacks the absoluteness of being (or non-being).
We can have only opinions about appearances because our sense-experience
of things is an ever-changing mixture of qualities. To recall the passage we
discussed in the last chapter, perception, like opinion, is defined precisely by
its relativity. A person who has never had any contact with things beyond
sense-experience has no basis for distinguishing between things as they really are and things as he happens to experience them in a particular moment.

Plato likens a person in this situation to a dreamer who is unable to tell
reality from likeness:

"Is the man who holds that there are fair things but doesn't hold that there is beauty
itself and who, if someone leads him to the knowledge of it, isn't able to follow—is
he, in your opinion, living in a dream or is he awake? Consider it. Doesn't dreaming,
whether one is asleep or awake, consist in believing a likeness of something to be not
a likeness, but rather the thing itself to which it is like? . . . And what about the man
who, contrary to this, believes that there is something fair itself and is able to catch
sight both of it and of what participates in it, and doesn't believe that what participates is it itself, nor that it itself is what participates—is he, in your opinion, living in
a dream or is he awake?" "He's quite awake," he said. (476c–d)

---

36. For distinction between absolute and relative non-being, see *Soph.*, 257b.

As this passage indicates, the knower is not someone who has simply gotten beyond likenesses and left them behind, but rather one who sees *both* forms and likenesses *and* the difference between the two.[37] In book III, Socrates similarly insists on seeking the virtues in *both* their forms *and* their images. The point in this earlier discussion regarding the virtues is that a genuinely educated (or "musical") soul would want virtue wherever it may be found; it would desire the *whole* of virtue. As Socrates puts it, we will never be musical "before we recognize the forms [of virtues] . . . everywhere they turn up, and notice that they are in whatever they are in, both themselves and their images, despising them neither in little nor in big things" (402c).

Though Plato remarks casually in these two passages on the "both/and" of forms and images, the point has vast implications and so warrants our careful attention. It recalls the analogous point made at the outset of book II, namely, that the noblest good is good *both* in itself *and* in its effects. If we are justified in taking appearance as *caused* by being and therefore as the relative effect of what exists in itself, the analogy becomes quite illuminating. Just as the highest goodness is not simply goodness-in-itself *as opposed to* goodness relative to something else, but is both together in their differences, so too we do not have here a dismissal of appearance but a cognitive grasp of both appearances and reality, as well as their difference. It is significant that Socrates more generally refuses to identify the good with either pleasure (which corresponds to sense-experience and therefore to images) or with knowledge (which corresponds to intelligible forms), because it transcends them both so as to include both (see 506b, 509a).[38] We have to keep this inclusiveness in mind as we enter further into the question of knowledge. The *being* of things is their in-itself reality, which would *seem* to exclude relation by definition. We would be inclined thus to separate being, in a dualistic fashion, from the relativity implied by appearance. In his articulation of types of goods, we recall, Aristotle proposed just such a dichotomy: *either* good in an absolute sense, *or* good in relative sense. But Plato is not satisfied with this dichotomy. Goodness in its truest form is both absolute and relative. If love, by definition, desires the whole of something rather than an aspect, it will seek this most inclusive form. The love of wisdom, from this perspective, wants the whole truth of a thing. It is not surprising, then, that Plato de-

37. Cf. Sallis, Being and Logos, 386–87.
38. Cf. *Phlb.*, 67a–b.

picts knowledge in this inclusive, rather than exclusive, sense.[39] His doing so reflects what we might call the general *ethos* of the *Republic,* the striving after the most adequate (i.e., most comprehensive), whole.

Love desires the whole of a thing rather than a mere aspect, which we have interpreted to mean that it desires the being or reality of a thing rather than its appearance alone. Being, we also saw, is that which transcends relativity. But love is itself a relation. The difference between the (apparent) love of appearance and the (true) love of being is not a difference between a relation and a nonrelation but between two different kinds of relation. The philosopher is one who loves a thing not only in its relative appearances but in its being beyond appearances. Being, or the in-itself nature of things, is that which discloses itself to a love ordered to the whole of a thing. We will still have to unfold further what this means, but we note three things in passing that indicate where we are headed. First, to the extent that appearances *are* indeed an aspect of a thing, they would seem to be included rather than excluded from the love of the thing as a whole, even as such a love is not limited to the appearances. Second, if powers of the soul are defined by that upon which they are set, and if the whole of something is its being, then, for Plato, there will be reason to think that love and reason are essentially the same: "That which depends on the same thing and accomplishes the same thing I call the same power" (477d). Third, insofar as there is a connection between love and goodness, the question of the intelligible essence of a thing will therefore turn out to be inseparable from its goodness.

But to maintain that love and reason are inclusive of, rather than exclusive of, relativity does not solve the problem posed by the claim that being stands for the "nonrelative" essence of things. So far, Plato has merely asserted a difference between love of the whole and love of a part, between reason and opinion, between being and appearance. He has not yet shown that such a distinction is *possible* or how we can in fact bring it to evidence. It is crucial to see the enormous difficulty this issue poses. Even if we insist on *both* being and appearance, rather than dualistically separating them, we must be able to have some access to reality as it is in itself, *as distinct from* as it is "for us." To put it in the terms of our discussion so far, to say that we can relate

---

39. Fine argues that the need for forms in order to have knowledge does not exclude sensibles. "Knowledge and Belief in *Republic* 5–7," in *Plato 1,* 216–17. This view follows naturally from a rejection of the division of sensibles and intelligibles into two worlds and seeing instead that sensibles are an aspect of the whole designated by the form.

[margin note: Plato cannot be a dualist. A philosopher is a lover of the whole.]

to something as it is beyond its appearances, beyond its manifestations, i.e., as it is in itself, is to say that we can relate to something beyond its *relativity*. Charles Kahn refers to the essentially "non-perspectival" character of the forms.[40] How is it possible to see anything except from within a particular perspective? Isn't knowledge just as bound to a perspective as perception? Another way to state the problem: if the powers of the soul are relative to reality, and vice versa, then *knowledge is relative to that which is not itself relative*—and vice versa. The paradoxical nature of this problem needs to be felt in all of its weight. How is this not a simple contradiction? How can we grasp something differently from the way we grasp it? How is it possible to distinguish knowledge from opinion?

This paradox is, of course, what prompted Kant's absolute distinction between phenomena and noumena.[41] To the extent that we gain access to a thing, we would seem to remain within the realm of "phenomena," and therefore precisely outside of the "in-itself" reality of a thing, which, lying beyond its appearance to us, remains by definition unknowable. Whatever light may seem to be coming into the closed room of our experience is passing through a window that has been locked and painted shut by the scholastic dictum, *quidquid recipitur in modo recipientis recipitur*—whatever is received is received according to the mode of the recipient. We have no way of knowing whether the window is refracting the light that passes through or what the light looks like outside. If it is true that, for Plato, that which discloses itself to the soul depends in some respect on the power to which it discloses itself, passage to the thing in itself would seem forever barred.

And yet this apparent contradiction must be resolved in some manner if there is to be a foundation for knowledge, which ultimately means if knowledge is to be possible at all *qua* knowledge. It is the obvious difficulty of this challenge that no doubt led Plato, in other dialogues, to adopt the "second sailing," that is, to take the distinction for granted or to content him-

40. Charles Kahn, *Plato and the Socratic Dialogue* (Cambridge: Cambridge University Press, 1996), 347.

41. Kant, *Prolegomena zu einer jeden künftigen Metaphysik, die als Wissenschaft wird auftreten können*, in *Werke in Sechs Bänden*, vol. 3: *Schriften zur Metaphysik und Logik* (Darmstadt: Wissenschaftliche Buchgesellschaft, 1998), A165 (and passim). David McNeill claims that Kant represents the best expression of Plato's views. "Human Discourse, Eros, and Madness in Plato's *Republic*," *Review of Metaphysics* 55.2 (2001): 245. His interpretation, however, fails to see the transcendence that Plato not only discusses but, as we will argue especially in the next chapter, seeks to *enact*.

self with showing that such a distinction is indispensable by means of problems that would result from denying it. Cherniss claims that the dialogues are so many "indirect arguments" showing how "separate ideas" must simply be "assumed" in order to "save the phenomena" in the three spheres of ontology, epistemology, and ethics.[42] But there is a fundamental difference between assuming that things exist in themselves, or even proving that they *have* to have an "in-itself" existence, and actually having access to them as existing in themselves. The *Republic* is the sole dialogue in the Platonic corpus to face this particular question squarely, making it a central preoccupation of the discussion between Socrates and his friends. We can, and perhaps must, assume that we know; but is it possible to *know* that we know? This problem is, as Aristotle remarks, one of the most difficult in all of philosophy. The present section is only the beginning of a response; the later chapters of this book will continue with other aspects.

The Good as Cause of Truth

It is no accident that the dialogue that confronts this particular problem happens to be the only dialogue that thematizes the idea of the good as supreme over other forms.[43] If the *Republic* has many times restarted in order to seek an increasingly adequate vantage from which to engage the question of justice, it reaches its highest point in the section stretching from the last part of book VI to the first part of book VII, 502d–521b.[44] The good will turn

42. Cherniss, "The Philosophical Economy of the Theory of Ideas," 16–27.

43. Though there are indications, of course, in many other dialogues. The beautiful, which Plato more or less explicitly identifies with the good (see A. E. Taylor, *Plato: The Man and His Work* [New York: Meridian Books, 1959], 287; cf. Kahn, *Plato and the Socratic Dialogue*, 267–71), is supreme in the *Symposium* and the *Phaedrus*; the *Cratylus* speaks of the good that permeates all things (417b); the *Philebus* distinguishes the good from everything else because of its perfection and self-sufficiency (60c); the *Lysis* presents the good as that which is loved in all that is loved (219d–220b); the *Timaeus* makes the perfectly good Demiurge the first principle of the cosmos (29a, 29e); the *Phaedo* makes goodness the principle of intelligibility of all things (97c–98b), and so forth.

44. After the discussion reaches a sort of peak at the end of book IV (445b–c), Polemarchus interrupts Socrates once again to give a more adequate explanation of the common life of the city—which drives them up to a higher vantage point; in the course of this digression, Socrates himself introduces the "biggest wave," the theme of the philosopher—up another level; the section we are now addressing represents the "loftiest study" (up once more) for the philosophers, at the very pinnacle of which is the idea of the good. Just as they enter into this part of the

out to be the key to the problem we are addressing because it is what "gives truth to the things known and the power to know to the knower" (508d); in other words, it *both* establishes the knowability of the thing *and* offers the way to reach it—which means that it governs the entire event of reciprocity between reality and the soul. If the difficulty in coming to knowledge lies in the apparent impossibility of transcending the relativity of perspective, Plato suggests that a response to this difficulty lies in finding the "best possible perspective on things" (ὡς μὲν δυνατὸν ἦν κάλλιστα αὐτὰ κατιδεῖν, 504b),[45] so that they can show themselves "most clearly" (καταφανῆ). Similarly, the problem of sophistry has arisen in part from making the perceiver the measure of what is perceived. For Plato, the good presents an alternative; it is the *most precise* measure, because it does not fall short in any way in being, which is the object of knowledge: "a measure which in any way falls short of that which *is* in such things is no measure at all. For nothing incomplete is the measure of anything" (504c).[46] Only something "τέλειος" in an absolute sense can be a measure. Although we still need to unfold what this means exactly, we can at least begin to see why Plato insists that our grasp of things—*all* things whatsoever, and not just, say, the virtues[47]—will always remain inadequate to the extent that we fail to know the good (504b-c). If knowledge, after all, depends upon the being of things rather than on their

---

discussion, Glaucon urges Socrates not to desist at the very moment they are crossing the threshold to the destination (506d).

45. An alternative version has "ὡς εσμὲν . . ."

46. On the good as measure, see Werner Jaeger, *Paideia: The Ideals of Greek Culture,* 2nd ed., vol. 2 (Oxford: Oxford University Press, 1986), 286; Rafael Ferber, "Did Plato Ever Reply to Those Critics, Who Reproached Him for 'the Emptiness of the Platonic Idea or Form of the Good'?" in *Essays on Plato's Republic,* edited by Erik Nis Ostenfeld (Aarhus, Denmark: Aarhus University Press, 1998), 53–58. It is true, as Desjardins claims (*Plato and the Good,* 53), that Plato doesn't *explicitly* identify the good with measure, but the identification is certainly implicit in his insistence that what is most complete ought to be taken as measure and his then immediately pointing to the good as the highest form.

47. Cf. Richard Hackforth, "Plato's Divided Line and Dialectic," *Classical Quarterly* 36.1–2 (January–April 1942): 1–9. Hackforth claims that the good is the source of intelligibility for "primarily moral εἴδη, though . . . not exclusively" (2), and similarly—as we will also propose later and develop in the next chapter—that the third section of the line contains not just "mathematicals" as intermediate entities between forms and sensibles but rather forms understood in a particular way, viz., as hypothesized. Mathematical objects illustrate this intermediate status without exhausting this class of objects. In other words, in the central analogies of the *Republic,* Plato intends to present the good as a universal principle of intelligibility and does not intend to limit its epistemological function to one class of objects or another.

appearance, the good would seem to play a role in the attainment of knowledge, because lying "beyond appearances" is, Plato tells us, part of what goodness means. In the first substantial claim he makes about the good in the section of book VI in which it becomes the focus, Plato makes precisely this point: "When it comes to good things, no one is satisfied with what is opined to be so but each seeks the things that *are,* and from here on out everyone despises the opinion" (505d).

But we have to wonder *why* lying beyond appearances or "opinion" and "reputation" is essential to the nature of the good. Indeed, what is it about goodness that earns it the role of the "highest object of study" in Plato's philosophy, and the status of being in some respect beyond being and truth? There is a temptation, here, to suggest that Plato holds it in such regard because the goal of philosophizing is to lead the "good life," and the nature of the good is quite obviously central to ethics. There are, in fact, some commentators who consider the more "metaphysical" claims Plato seems to make as so much "poetic vesture" that needs to be stripped away.[48] But any interpretation that is forced to disregard what are clearly central claims in order to remain consistent cannot be taken seriously. In this central moment of the *Republic,* wherein the dialogue's drama comes to a head, Plato has Socrates say that the good is responsible (as the ἄτιον and ἀρχή) for the being of things and their being known; whatever role it may have in ethics, that role is inseparable from its ontological and epistemological function. As we saw above, in Plato's understanding, the themes of being, love, and knowledge are intertwined in a basic way. Plato doesn't address the difference between forms and likenesses without first raising the question of the nature of love, and he cannot shed light on either of these themes without a discussion of the nature of being itself. What accounts for one theme will have immediate implications for the others. Because the explanation Socrates gives concerns especially the epistemological function of the good, and points to its ontological status as if by implication, we will enter this issue of the nature of the good by way of the question: What does goodness have to do with truth and knowledge? Our discussion of this question, which is the central theme of the present book, will overflow into the next chapter, in which we will address the three central analogies of the sun, the line, and the cave in more

---

48. Lachterman discusses the problem of one-sided interpretations of the significance of the good: "What Is 'the Good'?" 139–41. The expression "poetic vesture" he cites from Paul Shorey.

detail. In the present context, our goal is to explore how the good, in principle, both generates and resolves the problem of the distinction between being and appearance and thereby knowledge and opinion.

Approaches to the Good

The most obvious point to make about the connection between goodness and intelligibility in the *Republic* is that the connection is not at all obvious. Strangely, though this question is arguably the most fundamental in all of Plato's questioning—insofar as it seems to underlie in some respect nearly every aspect of his philosophy—when he finally addresses it directly, he actually refuses to address it directly. Rather than provide any explicit statement of the connection, Plato communicates his point through open suggestions, metaphors, and imagery. Indeed, he does so precisely at the moment when he says images are least wanted. The greatest study requires a precision that surpasses the precision in other studies, Socrates claims (504d–e), but then balks at the suggestion that he present that statement with the same precision he accorded the others (506d). He insists that a "real man" despises appearances or opinions in this regard (505d; 506b), and yet proceeds to offer nothing but an image for the good instead of the thing itself (506e–507a). It is not surprising, therefore, that there have been, and likely always will be, a great variety of explanations of what this connection precisely is. If we take Plato's reticence seriously, it is no doubt best to leave the explanation as open as possible without leaving it simply indeterminate and empty. In the following, we will list a number of different interpretations, which represent common or interesting possible approaches to the question of how the good makes the world intelligible. The list is by no means meant to be an exhaustive overview of the scholarship; instead, we intend to give a general sense of the broad spectrum of interpretations and then to offer an interpretation that can account for the main features of these approaches within a single view rooted squarely in the trajectory that Plato opened by the way he framed the problem in books I and II. Without explicit texts in Plato that would allow us to judge the fidelity of any particular interpretation with complete assurance, the "second-best" option is to affirm the variety of interpretations (assuming of course a certain internal coherence and plausibility), and to seek a comprehensive view that reveals their interconnection. This seems, in any event, most faithful to the spirit of the *Republic* itself.

The approaches tend to fall into certain basic groups. One of the more common explanations identifies *teleology* as what connects intelligibility and goodness.[49] We understand a thing when we see what purpose it fulfills or in what way it is useful or desirable, i.e., "good." This interpretation can point to the teleological account of causality that Plato introduces in the *Phaedo*'s second sailing, which is where he presents a version of his theory of forms.[50] Gail Fine specifies the teleological view further by identifying the good with the formal and final causality that the forms represent.[51] Interpreting goodness as perfection, we could also read the forms as intelligible because paradigmatic, and paradigmatic because they share in the good, which is perfection itself. Nicholas White, along these lines, proposes that "to understand what it is to be the Form of F, then, is to understand what it is to be an unqualified, and thus nondefective, and thus perfect, and thus good, specimen of an F."[52] A further well-known view proposes that the good grants the "ideal" attributes—the permanence, stability, universality, and so forth, that make a form a form—to the forms, which renders them reliable objects of

49. Shorey, in the footnote to 508e4–5 in his translation (Loeb ed., 104), says "We really understand anything only when we apprehend its purpose, the aspect of the good that it reveals." See also Eric Perl, "The Living Image: Forms and the Erotic Intellect in Plato," *American Catholic Philosophical Quarterly* 69 (1995): 194–95; Herman L. Sinaiko, *Love, Knowledge, and Discourse in Plato: Dialogue and Dialectic in* Phaedrus, Republic, Parmenides (Chicago: University of Chicago Press, 1965), 137; H. W. B. Joseph, *Knowledge and the Good in Plato's Republic* (Oxford: Oxford University Press, 1948), 17–19; David Evans explains, in "'Beyond Reality': Plato's Good Revisited," *Philosophy: The Journal of the Royal Institute of Philosophy* 47 (2000, suppl.): 105–18, that he moved from a "paradigmatic" interpretation (i.e., for "*F*" to participate in goodness is to be a "good species of *F*") to a more teleological one, because such an interpretation shows the essential reference to *value* in understanding, which is clearly important in Plato (see esp. 114–17). Murphy (*The Interpretation of Plato's Republic*, 153) *rejects* (unconvincingly) purposiveness or teleology as an adequate explanation for ideal forms.

50. *Phd.*, 97c–99d; cf. also *Ti.*, 46d.

51. Fine, "Knowledge and Belief," 228. Glenn Rawson likewise refers to the role of goodness in knowledge in terms of its being the final cause ("Knowledge and Desire for the good in Plato's *Republic*," 106), but emphasizes the more dynamic aspect: the good drives us to desire to know and guides us by means of the degrees of satisfaction of this desire. Rawson's explanation, however, does not make goodness genuinely *intrinsic* to knowledge *qua* knowledge.

52. Nicholas White, *A Companion to Plato's* Republic, 2nd ed. (Indianapolis: Hackett Publishing Company, 1978), 101 Cf. Ferber, *Platos Idee des Guten*, 30; R. M. Hare, "Plato and the Mathematicians," in *New Essays on Plato and Aristotle*, edited by R. Bambrough (London: Routledge, 1965), 21–38, here 36; Mitch Miller Jr., "Platonic Provocations: Reflections on the Soul and the Good in the *Republic*," in *Platonic Investigations*, edited by D. J. O'Meara (Washington, D.C.: The Catholic University of America Press, 1985), 163–93, here 182.

the mind.[53] Francisco Gonzales combines the "idealizing" function of the good (good as object of knowledge) with its being the cause of our knowing (good as *way* of knowing).[54]

A number of interpretations are founded on identifying the good with unity in some sense. Hans Joachim Krämer suggests that all of the difficulties of discovering the relation between goodness, knowledge, and being disappear once we substitute the One of Plato's oral teachings for goodness in the *Republic*.[55] Another view maintains that the identification of the good with the One is able to reconcile the "ideality" of the forms in general—their remaining uniform in time and in being—and also allows us to see how the good could be the foundation of mathematics.[56] Eva Brann, also with an eye on the One, sees

53. Gerasimos Santas, "The Form of the Good in Plato's *Republic*." Cf. Ferber, *Platos Idee des Guten*, 25ff., 98–99, who explains that goodness gives things perdurance, truth (i.e., *Echtheit*), and evidence, and that is how, for example, it makes mathematicals intelligible. Rosen proposes a very similar interpretation in his recent book, *Plato's Republic: A Study*. According to him, the good is not a separate idea but rather "a property or set of properties of Platonic Ideas, namely, intelligiblity, stability, and eternity" (262). Francisco Gonzalez offers a careful critique of Santas's position in *Dialectic and Dialogue*, 359n9, in which he indicates the problems that arise once one separates the ideal attributes (due to the good) from the proper attributes that constitute the form as such. This critique is a compelling one, but it seems we could save Santas's essential point simply by insisting on a radical difference of orders between the two "sorts" of attributes, saying that goodness expresses not a set of attributes but a *way of possessing* whatever attributes a form possesses, and more specifically, the *best* way of possessing proper attributes. In this respect, the qualities of goodness would not be juxtaposed to the qualities proper to the forms, but would present their own intrinsic fulfillment.

54. Gonzales, *Dialectic and Dialogue*, 213–18. Cf. his mention of the issue in "Self-knowledge, Practical Knowledge, and Insight," in *The Third Way*, 174.

55. Krämer, "Über den Zusammenhang von Prinzipienlehre und Dialektik bei Platon," 36. Mario Veggetti, in "L'Idea del Bene nella *Repubblica* di Platone," *Discipline filosofiche* 1 (1995): 207–30, rejects the proposal that the good and the One are identical in Plato (210). (For a brief account of the esoteric-systematic school—generally known as the Tübingen school—and a criticism, see 209n1.) Ferber likewise denies that the identity between goodness and unity is expressed in the dialogues. *Platos Idee des Guten*, 77–78.

56. Hitchcock, "The Good in Plato's *Republic*," 65–92. Hitchcock rejects the need to understand things in relation to goodness *qua* good through a *reductio ad absurdum* argument (70), which compels us to interpret goodness as unity instead. Cross and Woozley likewise deny that goodness can be the cause of intelligibility, at least for mathematicals. *Plato's Republic*, 260–61. David Evans, in "'Beyond Reality,'" affirms that it is ultimately the unifying function of goodness that enables it to grant intelligibility. See also Samuel Wheeler, who argues, in "Plato's Enlightenment: The Good as the Sun," *History of Philosophy Quarterly* 14 (1997): 171–88, for the identity of goodness and unity in terms of the mathematical structure implied in "complete" knowledge (i.e., knowledge of all aspects of a thing).

the good as cause of truth because it yokes together or unifies the knower and the known.[57] David Lachterman interprets the unity of the good as the *community* of forms, each harmonizing with the others by performing the work proper to it. In this sense, the good *is* the συμπλοκή of the forms which gives each its meaning.[58] As Utermöhlen puts it, one has to see a thing's interconnectedness with all other things in order to understand *what* it is, and such an integrated vision belongs specifically to the dialectician.[59]

Moreover, some authors approach the question of the connection between goodness and intelligibility from a more practical than theoretical angle, or else see the good not as a metaphysical principle of knowledge and truth, but rather as a regulative principle of some sort. In his classic study, Paul Natorp offers what is considered a "neo-Kantian" view. He suggests that we think of the good primarily as a regulating principle for both being and thinking. For Natorp, the good is less a metaphysical reality than a law preserving the being of things and governing the mind's intercourse with them—not, to be sure, merely as a logical principle, but as the principle of logic itself.[60] One of the better-known expressions of the practical interpretation is that of Wolfgang Wieland. According to Wieland, the good is not an "object" of knowledge; instead, it has the function of motivating and regulating particular activities.[61] It thus concerns primarily practical knowledge. As Wolfgang Kersting puts it, knowledge of the good is not a *"was-wissen"* but a *"wie-wissen,"* not a particular "what" that is known, but rather knowledge of how to treat everything else.[62]

Finally, there are more unique proposals that seem to stretch the text to some extent. Crombie connects goodness and intelligibility by positing *or-*

---

57. Brann, "The Music of the *Republic,*" 64; cf. 70–71.

58. Lachterman, "What Is 'the Good'?" 157–61.

59. Utermöhlen, *Die Bedeutung der Ideenlehre,* 107. See also Murphy (*The Interpretation of Plato's Republic*), who speaks of goodness as the "belonging of things to a coherent system" (155). Though he thinks this is what Plato means by goodness, Murphy suggests that in the end it is not a good account (185–86).

60. Natorp, *Platos Ideenlehre,* 194. Natorp does, however, say that, as the principle of both being and thought, the good is in some sense the "being-est" of things and an object of knowledge (191). For a succinct presentation of Natorp's view of the good, see Ferber, *Platos Idee des Guten,* 256–61. For a brief criticism of the phenomenological/neo-Kantian view of the good, see Veggetti, "L'Idea del Bene," 215.

61. Wieland, *Formen des Wissens,* 180. Cf. M. Veggetti, "L'Idea del Bene," 213n3; Gonzalez, "Self-knowledge, Practical Knowledge, and Insight," in *The Third Way,* 177–78.

62. Kersting, *Platos "Staat,"* 239.

der as a mediating third that unites them: order is good and it is also intelligible.[63] Kenneth Dorter proposes that the nature of reality, in Plato's view, is good, and that we do not understand the forms until we see them as possibilities in accordance with the nature of reality.[64] Rosemary Desjardins similarly maintains that the good gives order and in that sense provides a measure.[65] Kenneth Sayre suggests reading the good as the "right," which seems to reflect much of the polyvalence of the Greek term. When we know something, we are "right" about it, which presumably means we have a "good" grasp of it.[66] We also have Heidegger's famous interpretation of the radiance of the good as that which brings the manifestation of appearance to evidence, i.e., "das Scheinen seines Aussehens zum Erscheinen."[67]

It is evident that the elusive texts from the *Republic,* particularly viewed within the complex array of the other Platonic dialogues, allow a great variety of interpretations. But it should also be evident that these interpretations do not simply exclude one another, and in some cases that they are variations on a similar theme. Is it possible to find a point of reference that would enable us to order them in relation to each other? Something all of these interpretations have in common is that they read the texts regarding goodness and intelligibility in books VI and VII independently of the rest of the dialogue, rather than viewing this central part of the book specifically as a response to the problem raised by Thrasymachus and then amplified by Glaucon and Adeimantus. The key to these central texts in relation to the original problem, we have been suggesting, lies in the twofold nature of goodness, which is the very first statement about the good made in the main body of the dialogue. We must see the connection between this twofold nature and the distinction between being and appearance, which is the fundamental distinction in Plato's discussion of the forms in the *Republic* and essential to the nature of intelligibility.

---

63. I. M. Crombie, *Plato on Knowledge and Reality,* vol. II of *An Examination of Plato's Doctrines* (New York: The Humanities Press, 1963), 180–81. Mary Margaret McCabe offers a similar explanation in *Plato and His Predecessors: The Dramatisation of Reason* (Cambridge: Cambridge University Press, 2000), 227. Jim Robinson cites Patterson as affirming that participation in the good is a thing's place in intelligible order. "A Change in Plato's Conception of the Good," *Journal of Philosophical Research* 18 (1993): 231–41, here 231.

64. Dorter, *Transformation of Plato's* Republic, 187–88.

65. Desjardins, *Plato and the Good,* 106.   66. Sayre, *Plato's Literary Garden,* 185–88.

67. Heidegger, *Platons Lehre von der Wahrheit,* 4th printing (Frankfurt: Vittorio Klostermann, 1997), 31.

What is able to be *known*, rather than merely perceived or opined, is the *being* of things. As we saw, a thing *is*, in the most precise sense, in itself as distinct from (though not separate from) its relation to another. It is not an accident that this distinction between a thing's being in itself and its "appearing" in relation to an other echoes the modes of goodness: something can be good in itself, i.e., absolutely, or good in relation to something else, i.e., relatively, and although it is possible—and indeed *best*—to be both at once, these aspects are not reducible to one another. Now, the most *fundamental* mode of goodness is goodness in itself; "fundamental" is the appropriate word because unless something is good in itself, it cannot be good in relation to something else. As Plato says elsewhere, and as Aristotle has shown, relative goodness is always derivative of fundamental goodness.⁶⁸

Let us return to the question of justice and the challenge proposed by Glaucon and Adeimantus, which we investigated at the outset. We saw there that if justice had no *intrinsic goodness* of its own, there in fact would be no such thing as justice; it would have no intrinsic, or we might say "objective," reality, but would turn out to be whatever anyone wanted to make of it. If we acknowledge that something is intrinsically good, rather than merely instrumentally good, we take it as representing a *terminus* of relation; our relation to it comes to an end *in* it. In the *Lysis*, Socrates observes that things loved instrumentally find their completion and end (τελευτῶσιν) in that which is loved for its own sake (220b). This means a thing worthy of being loved as an end has its own, irreducible being. By contrast, if a thing were merely instrumentally good, it would form no terminus of relation but would be wholly a pathway to something beyond itself, and thus in this respect unreal: there would be no "there" there. Goodness would so far seem to be connected with the intrinsic reality of a thing. For something to be good in itself means for it to have its own being, to exist in itself and not merely in relation to something else. In other words, the intrinsic goodness of a thing just *is* its "in-itself" character. Socrates implies such a sense of goodness in the *Philebus*: "[T]he difference between the nature of the good and everything else is this. . . . Any creature that was in permanent possession of it entirely and in every way, would never be in need of anything else, but would live in perfect self-sufficiency."⁶⁹

---

68. *Lysis*, 220a–b. See *Nich. Eth.*, 1096b14–15.

69. *Phlb.*, 60b–c. Plato also characterizes the "good person" in the *Lysis* as essentially self-sufficient: "Isn't a good person, insofar as he is good, sufficient to himself?" (215a).

If we interpret this self-sufficiency ontologically, to be *absolutely* good, in the strict sense of having a goodness of its own that cannot finally be reduced to anything else, means to have being in itself that, however much it may exist in relation to other things, is ultimately irreducible to that relativity. To be good in this sense is to have precisely the sort of intrinsic unity that the Protagorean relativism in the *Theaetetus* excludes in principle. Plato regularly refers to the forms as representing a thing in relation to itself, a thing taken in its own regard: αὐτὸ καθ᾽ αὐτό. Notice: this expression connects the essential identity of things with a kind of measured relation, the self *as* or *according to* itself. Goodness, we could say, *binds* a thing to itself and thus makes it be what it is. The same notion can be found in another expression Plato uses to characterize real beings, namely, that they "remain forever according to themselves and as themselves" (ἀεὶ κατὰ ταυτὰ ὡσαύτως).[70] If goodness is a measure, or indeed, *the* measure, insofar as it is what is perfect and complete (cf. 504c), to share in goodness would be *to be* in a complete way. It would thus make sense to characterize the good as Plato does in the *Republic* specifically as what "preserves and benefits" in contrast to the bad that corrupts and dissolves (608e). In the *Phaedo*, goodness is, so to speak, the "glue" that binds things together,[71] while badness entails disintegration because it renders a thing an enemy to itself (cf. *Republic* 351e–357a).[72]

But it is crucial to keep in mind that, though "in-itselfness" is the most fundamental mode of goodness, *it is not the sole mode*. To be good "merely" in itself can in fact be the lowest form of goodness if we recall the three categories originally set forth by Glaucon: he puts in this lowest form only delight and harmless pleasures, i.e., relatively trivial things. Goodness in its most *complete* form, of course, includes relativity in its absoluteness. In the present context we could say that the most complete instance of being includes relation to others. The goodness for others is *not* in this sense simply separate from, but rather is the most complete form of, goodness in itself, insofar as it is the same goodness that makes something both self- and

70. See *Rep.*, 484b, *Phd.*, 78c, *Soph.*, 248a, *Ti.*, 41d and 82b, and *Epin.*, 982b and e.

71. *Phd.*, 99c.

72. Interestingly, the Platonic definitions, presumably from the middle Academy, describe the good in a manner that brings together its ontological function, as what holds a thing together and makes it self-referential, with its role as representing the final object of love: it is "that which is for its own sake" (413a), "what causes the preservation of beings; the cause toward which everything tends, from which is derived what should be chosen" (414e).

other-related. There is a certain paradox here, but if the paradox is denied, the structure of the *Republic* would collapse under the weight of contradiction, as we will see:[73] absolute goodness is not absolute unless it is also relative. Indeed, absoluteness and relativity cannot be simply juxtaposed to one another without making the absolute relative to the relative and therefore no longer absolute. Logically, while the relative is in some sense opposed to the absolute, the absolute is not in turn opposed to the relative, but inclusive of it. Likewise, then, if being represents the intrinsic goodness of a thing, then appearance is its relative goodness, its goodness "for others." And by the same token, while appearance is in some respect opposed to being, being is not opposed to, but rather inclusive of, appearance. The κοινωνία with others is *part* of being, taken as a whole, just as the relative goodness is part of a thing's absolute goodness, and as we shall see, this implies that appearance is in some sense intrinsic to the intelligibility of a thing, even as it does not account for the whole of that intelligibility.

On the basis of these considerations, we receive what seems to be a novel way of reading Plato's remarkable statement that the good "supplies truth to the thing known" (508e). In the section of book VI prior to this assertion, Plato uses the term "truth" specifically in relation to the philosopher (485c and d), drawing on the first definition of the philosopher he gives towards the end of book V as a contrast to the lover of merely sensible images: he is the "lover of the sight of truth" (475e). When Glaucon asks Socrates "what exactly" he means by this, Socrates answers by distinguishing the forms of things from their appearance. We infer that this difference is constitutive of the truth of a thing; truth means, at least in part, the difference between being and appearance. If this inference is justified, then to say that the good bestows truth on things therefore means that *it is precisely the good that establishes the difference between being and appearance.* It is goodness, in the absolute sense, that makes something nonreducible to its relations, that is, intrinsically good in itself and therefore *real.* If there were no goodness in this absolute sense, a thing would have no in-itselfness but would become a function of its relations and therefore a pure instrument to be manipulated.

73. The most obvious contradiction is Plato's use and condemnation of images, which we will discuss at length in the coda. But there are more subtle problems in the dialogue's "plot" that rely on the simultaneity of absoluteness and relativity to make sense, such as the rewards for justice that Plato distributes at the end, the philosopher's need to return to the cave, and the happiness of the "relative" individual who lives for the "absolute" goodness of the whole.

But this is not the only benefit of the good; it also grants to the knower the power to know. We will have to develop the meaning of this claim further in relation to the meaning of *eros;* but at the very least we can see that a thing's goodness opens it up, so to speak, beyond its in-itselfness to others: it makes it not only absolute but also relational. In other words, goodness is what makes things *manifest,* and therefore also accessible to others. Thus, to say that goodness gives things truth and gives the knower the ability to know means that there is *one thing* that simultaneously "anchors" things in themselves as real *and* opens them up to others. Because it is a single thing that does both, these two aspects cannot simply be opposed to one another. It is illuminating, in the light of the argument we are making, to compare the fundamental aporia Parmenides introduces to the young Socrates in the dialogue named after him at 133b. Parmenides defines forms specifically as things that "have their being in relation to themselves but not in relation to things that belong to us," that is, the things of our material world (133c–d). Taking for granted that their "in-itself" (absolute) character *is opposed to* their "for-us" (relative) character, Parmenides shows that they cannot be known by us. Lacking here is precisely the "highest" sense of goodness that comprehends absoluteness and relativity at once.[74] In a word, the good *simultaneously* opens an absolute distinction between being and appearance *and* bridges that gap. It therefore unifies being and appearance without reducing them to one another, and can be said at the same time (and for the same reason) to be the proper "measure" of the relationship.

Now it becomes apparent how this interpretation of the connection between goodness and intelligibility might be developed to bring together aspects of the various interpretations we have mentioned. Here, we simply indicate general relations and make no claim at all to reconcile whatever tensions may exist among them. To understand a thing teleologically is to understand it in light of the purpose it serves; purpose points to the good that results from a thing, as its effect, so to speak. Thus, a teleological explanation provides what we could call the "relative" intelligibility of a thing.[75]

74. Cf. the *Sophist*'s suggestion that the philosopher must, like a child, insist on *both* the absolute and the relative, i.e., both being and becoming, no matter how exclusive of one another they may seem. 249c–d.

75. This is not to say that a teleological account of something apprehends only what is extrinsic to the thing. To understand a thing's purpose requires, of course, an understanding of the thing's *inner* dispositions—i.e., qualities and virtues—that make it apt to fulfill that purpose.

As we have seen above, the relative goodness is an indispensable part of the meaning of things. But our proposal suggests that, as necessary as it is, teleology does not suffice alone to account for the intelligibility provided by goodness. The more fundamental aspect is the absolute goodness of a thing, or its "in-itselfness." Insofar as a thing's intrinsic goodness refers to its self-sufficiency or self-relatedness, it is clear that to be good is to be complete, and therefore there is a connection between a thing's in-itself being and its perfection. "Justice itself" represents justice in its perfection, and therefore the paradigm of justice, that which all things express precisely to the extent that they are just. If "to know F is to know what it means to be a good F," then the self-completed form of F, which is the perfection of F, presents the intelligible paradigm. Furthermore, insofar as the intrinsic being of a thing is its absoluteness or transcendence of relation, we also have no difficulty seeing how it accounts for the "ideal attributes" of the form, its permanence, stability, and universality; to be *intrinsically* good is to be in some sense absolute, i.e., not reducible to the constant shifting and inevitable particularity of relation. (See 484b, 485b.)

Along similar lines, once we see the connection between goodness and "in-itself" being, the identity of goodness and unity becomes quite natural and requires no appeal to outside sources, whether they be unwritten doctrines or even other dialogues, for its justification. There can be no doubt that a general theme appearing repeatedly in various contexts in the *Republic* is goodness as what brings a comprehensive unity to a complex whole. When Plato, in a summary fashion at the end of the dialogue, contrasts goodness with the badness that dis-integrates (ἀπολύον, 608e), he is referring to the integral wholeness goodness implies. Such a reference echoes the unity associated with virtue that Socrates highlights right at the start (351e–352a), and also the unity of the perfectly good city described in book IV (427dff.). The dialogue intends an analogy between this macrocosmic schema and the microcosm of individual beings in themselves (368c–369a), an analogy that sets in relief the shared term.[76] The unity of the city as a whole,

---

Nevertheless, a teleological account, if it is not extrinsicist in terms of the content of its account, remains extrinsicist in terms of the *mode* of its understanding unless more is said. The crucial point for Plato, at least in the *Republic*, is the mode of knowing that relates to a thing *as* it is in itself, not merely a grasp of *what* it is in itself.

76. "Then, we'll also go on to consider it in individuals, considering the likeness of the bigger in the *idea* of the littler" (369a).

we could say, illuminates the unity of each thing, and thus the good, which concerns itself with the unity of the whole, is itself what unifies. Goodness, as what relates things most properly to themselves (and to others), *is* therefore perfective unity. If this is true, it becomes possible to affirm all of what Hitchcock and others say about uniformity across time and space and even the nature of mathematics,[77] but to do so in a way that bears an immediate relation to the narrative of the *Republic* itself. The dialogue begins, essentially, with the question of whether justice has an intrinsic goodness in addition to its relative goodness, and the interpretation we are proposing furthers the inquiry in basically the same terms, even as it affirms the identity between goodness and unity that these scholars claim. As we follow it forward, moreover, we will see how this interpretation responds even more fundamentally to the problem posed by Thrasymachus.

If there is a connection between goodness and unity in this sense, we can also accommodate Eva Brann's proposal that the good is what *unifies* the knower and the known—as the one "thing" that simultaneously establishes knowable reality in itself and opens it to others. Likewise, the good can appear as a principle governing both thought and being, as Natorp described it, without entailing any sort of reduction to a purely formal "rule" in a (neo-) Kantian sense. The proposal we make even lends substance Sayre's otherwise quite odd proposal of the good as "right," insofar as the good, as the *tertium quid* mediating the relation between knower and known, represents the true "measure" of that relation and thus determines when the relation "succeeds." And Heidegger's reading of the good as giving radiance to the forms highlights the good's role as that which makes manifest, i.e., opens being to accessibility. Finally, if the relative goodness of things represents their relation to one another, and thus their measured inter-ordering, this view also gives place in different ways to the proposals of Crombie and Lachterman. We will see in the next chapter why knowledge of the good is *necessarily* practical (Wieland, Kersting) but is so in a manner that does not exclude its theoretical dimension and, in fact, requires it.

77. We only mention the possibility in principle. It would require far more time and space to work out the details than we have in the present context.

Intimate Knowledge

Interpreting the good's epistemological function from the perspective of its twofold nature, furthermore, provides a reason for the peculiar manner in which Plato characterizes the act of knowing in the *Republic*. He considers it a ὁμιλία, a "being together," which is probably best translated as "intercourse," insofar as the Greek term, like the English, immediately connotes the sexual relation. Plato also uses the verbs ἅπτεσθαι and ἐφάπτεσθαι "to bind onto," which have a military as well as a sexual meaning.[78] The connection between physical eros and philosophical eros may be hinted at in other dialogues, and may be presented at length in the *Phaedrus*, but none makes the analogy between sex and knowledge as explicit as the *Republic* does. It is perhaps a key analogy for knowing in the *Republic*, and our interpretation suggests that the reason for this is precisely the centrality of the good.[79]

Plato uses the term ὁμιλία in book X to describe the object of the philosophical soul's longing (611e), and this usage itself is but an echo of a note struck in the most sustained discussion of the nature of the philosopher in book VI, a discussion that makes constant reference to desire (ἐπιθυμία), eros, and the erotic in relation to truth and wisdom. (See, e.g., 484a–485d.) The description of the philosopher no doubt reaches its climax in the following summary passage:

So then, won't we make a sensible apology in saying that it is the nature of the real lover of learning to strive for what *is*; and he does not tarry by each of the many things opined to *be* but goes forward and does not lose the keenness of his passionate love nor cease from it before he grasps (ἅψασθαι) the nature itself of each thing which *is* with the part of the soul fit to grasp (ἐφάπτεσθαι) a thing of that sort; and it is the part akin to it that is fit. And once near it and coupled with what really is, having begotten intelligence and truth, he knows and lives truly, is nourished and so ceases from his labor pains, but not before. (490a–b)

78. Veggetti, "L'Idea del Bene," 220–21.

79. Illuminating in this context is Rafael Ferber's suggestion that Socrates' hesitation to disclose the good in discussion with Glaucon is precisely an *erotic modesty*. Comparing this theme in the *Republic* to H. Kelsen's interpretation of the *Symposium*, Ferber says that Glaucon's "mocking tone" when he receives a glimpse of the good (509c) results from the fact that Socrates is, in a sense, baring his nakedness. The good, Ferber claims, is so to speak the "genitalia" of Plato's philosophy, and is not meant to be exposed to others: "'Da sagte Glaukon in sehr lächerlichem Ton . . .' (R. 509c1–2): Ein obszöner Witz Platos?," *Archiv für Geschichte der Philosophie* 75.2 (1993): 211–12.

If it were the case that the intelligibility granted to things by the good consisted merely in their teleological aspect or their relation to an ideal form, as a great many interpretations propose, Plato's description of the act of knowing as an erotic coupling would serve no obvious purpose and therefore (precisely according to the teleological account) would make little sense. It is possible to understand a thing's purpose or grasp its ideal without an intimate relation. Notice too: there would be no inherent difficulties in communicating such an understanding with words or images, since one can describe a purpose as well as one can describe anything. Didn't the poets that Adeimantus summoned in book II enumerate the many purposes of justice? And didn't the interlocutors find these exhortations defective in presenting its genuine reality? Furthermore, any such description can be grasped as so much "information," which demands no corresponding transformation of the soul, no shift in one's mode of relating to reality, for its registration.[80] But the *Republic*, as we have seen, has asked for more than words, and has introduced its questioning from the beginning in the context of a drama concerning one's understanding and mode of relating at the very same time.

The problem from the beginning was to see if justice had a reality beyond its appearances. It turns out to be specifically the good that causes the transcendence of appearance: Plato *distinguishes* the good from both justice and beauty/nobility on precisely this score (505d). In this respect, the truth of justice comes to it from the good; it is true *because it is good* in the strict sense of having its own intrinsic and irreducible reality. That reality cannot, however, simply be described for the very same reason it cannot be reduced to its manifestations, insofar as description depends on manifestation. Thus, knowing that something is good is one thing—and here one can enumerate all of a thing's benefits. But knowing the goodness of something *in itself* is something else, and this knowledge requires a direct contact (ἅπτεσθαι), an intimacy, an "entry into" its goodness. For knowledge of this sort to occur, it must be possible in some (yet to be described) sense to identify oneself with a thing's inner being, its intrinsic goodness. "In-itself" goodness cannot be comprehended from the outside. To be sure, this

---

80. Francisco Gonzalez also notes that the good's being both the object of knowledge and also cause of our knowing implies a sort of knowledge that cannot be had without the transformation of the soul and cannot simply be passed on to others (at least, we might add, not without their own intimate participation). "Self-knowledge, Practical Knowledge, and Insight," 175–76.

intimate knowledge beyond description need not be interpreted *"schwärmerisch"* as a mystical event that leaves all words dismissively behind, because it remains the case that the absoluteness of the good cannot be detached from its relativity.[81] To detach it thus, if we recall Glaucon's initial distinction, would be to trivialize it. Instead, it simply implies that at the root of any statement about what something is lies an immediate, "internal," and nonanalyzable grasp of the thing itself,[82] insofar as a thing's truth ultimately entails a simple unity.[83]

Now, if it is the case that Plato views the essential moment of knowledge in the intimate terms we describe, then we run into a serious question given our discussion in the previous chapter: Does this not make knowledge something essentially *private*? If so, does this conception of knowledge bring us back, in spite of everything, to a sort of Protagorean relativism, whereby the individual measure, *qua* individual, becomes the final criterion of truth? It is worth noting that those who interpret Plato not as passing on a body of knowledge but as encouraging his readers to see things for themselves typically shy away from the more "universalist" expressions in Plato's thought. We will give a fuller response to this issue in the fifth chapter, in which we take up the transcendence of knowledge beyond what can be articulated verbally, as Plato describes this especially in *Letter VII*. For now we can see that, if intelligibility is founded on goodness, and goodness in its most complete sense exhibits no opposition between its absoluteness and relativity, the most complete knowledge will likewise lack an opposition between its "private" (in-itself) and "public" (for others) dimensions, that is, between its intuitive dimension and its discursive or "sayable" dimension, even while it maintains an irreducible difference between these.[84]

81. Yvon Lafrance (*La théorie de la doxa* [Montreal: Bellarmin, 1981], 39–45) describes this point in the *Republic* as a "rational intuition" rather than a mystical one in the usual sense. His emphasis is crucial if we are to guard the fundamentally rational aim of Plato's presentation. Nevertheless, Lafrance may go too far in divorcing the rationality of this intuition from the transcending movement of love that is indispensable to it, as we shall see shortly.

82. On forms as essentially noncomposite unities, see *Phd.*, 78c.

83. See *Phdr.*, 249b–c. What Plato indicates here may be fruitfully compared to Aristotle's description of the rational grasp of simples as a "contact" (θίγειν), or "non-contact" (μὴ θιγγάνειν), *Meta.*, IX.9.1051b24–26.

84. Paul Friedländer observes, along these lines, that Plato never eliminates the difference between the I and its object in knowledge as, for example, (in Friedländer's view) Plotinus does. *Plato: An Introduction*, 2nd ed., vol. 1 (Princeton, N.J.: Princeton University Press, 1969), 82. The immediacy of intimate knowing does not exclude the mediation of difference.

The immediate grasp of the unity of truth is not merely an intellectual act. While Plato often characterizes the grasp of forms as achieved by νοῦς alone, he means to distinguish it from a grasp by perception, and not from the striving for the whole inherent in eros. Indeed, the "intimate" view of knowledge described here begins to shed more light on the philosophical significance of Plato's associating reason with love. The basis for this association, as we saw, is the fact that the powers of the soul are determined by what the soul depends on and at the same time brings about, and both reason and love are set on and seek to achieve union with the unified whole of a being. To say that the good is the principle of reason means that, however much they might be distinguished at one level, reason is at its core one with (true) love.[85] The *Phaedrus* presents love not as a mere appetite, but in fact as the "philosopher's thinking in flight."[86] This association reveals reason to be more than a passive recipient of ideas but instead to have an inherent dimension of outward striving, a desire to get to the core of reality. Such a sense of reason echoes throughout book VI in Socrates' description of philosophers, who "are always in love with that learning which discloses to them something of the being that *is* always and does not wander about, driven by generation and decay" (485a–b). "Therefore the man who is really a lover of learning must from youth on strive as intensely as possible for every kind of truth" (485d).

But we must nonetheless keep in view the paradoxical nature of what Plato seems to assert here. As Plato shows quite clearly in the *Sophist* and the *Parmenides,* to be *known* is to be πρὸς ἄλλον: knowledge is itself a kind of relation.[87] The expression "the learning that *manifests* the *being* of things" seems to be a direct contradiction to the distinction that Plato had drawn just a few pages earlier, which implied that being is characterized *precisely* as

---

85. Rosen refers to eros as "a striving for wholeness and perfection," "The Role of Eros," 453. But he emphasizes a basic tension between the "erotic" and "mathematical" aspects of philosophy, which we could see as a tension between love and reason. Though it is true that Plato points to the "tyrannical" tendencies of eros, this eros seems much more akin to the false eros Plato depicts (and then corrects) in the *Phaedrus,* and also to the *false* aspiration to totality we find in Thrasymachus. If eros could *legitimately* be described as tyrannical, on what basis could we call it a striving for wholeness and perfection? When Thrasymachus seeks the effective domination of pleonexia, he is precisely *not* striving for wholeness and perfection but rather for fragmentation and corruption. Consider, in this regard, Plato's contrast between the ὀρθὸς ἔρως set on the orderly and beautiful and the manic pleasure of Aphrodite in 403a.

86. πτεροῦται ἡ τοῦ φιλοσόφου διάνοια, Phdr., 249c.

87. See *Soph.* 248e; *Prm.,* 133b–d.

what is not manifest, i.e., set in relation to another. If knowledge is going to be possible, it will require a kind of relation that is at the same time a non-relation, or the manifestation of what is non-manifest, *as* non-manifest. We can put the problem in yet another way once we recall that what disqualifies perception as knowledge is its link with a relative measure. In this case, for knowledge to be possible, it must be possible to have a relation that is in some respect *wholly measured* by the object of the relation. Let us note the qualifier: "in some respect." To resolve this apparent contradiction will require the paradoxical reversal that forms the subject of the next chapter. Here, we must first see the need to "transcend" relativity, which means to move beyond appearances to the being of things. It will turn out to be its essential connection with love that allows reason to get beyond itself, i.e., to transcend its own perspective in some respect, which is the response to the problem of knowledge we have been discussing.

Knowledge and Love as Ascent

There is almost no end to the philosophical insights that can be drawn from the images of the divided line and the cave,[88] but we will content ourselves in the present context with highlighting a single motif. If we consider them in the light of reason's connection with love, and thus in the light of the movement of love that Plato presents in the so-called erotic dialogues, they prove to map the itinerary of that movement in specifically epistemological terms. They bring into view the fact that the essence of the problem of knowledge is the transcendence of the relativity of perspective, and that goodness is what makes such transcendence possible. Interpreted in this way, the line and the cave provide a direct response to the problem raised by Thrasymachus in the opening book of the dialogue.

The Divided Line

Coming between the sun and the cave images—and thus in a sense dividing them[89]—the divided line, true to what we have called Plato's inten-

---

88. For a comprehensive overview of the literature on the divided line, see Yvon Lafrance, *Pour interpréter Platon: la ligne en République VI, 509d–511e: Bilan analytique des études (1804–1984)* (Montreal: Editions Bellarmin, 1986), and Lafrance, *Pour interpréter Platon: la ligne en République VI, 509d–511e: Le texte et son histoire*, vol. 2 (Montreal: Editions Bellarmin, 1994).

89. According to Rosen, "In the dramatic structure of the *Republic*, the divided line is itself

tional view of consciousness, presents in a somewhat abstract and technical manner the "levels" of being and their corresponding "powers" of the soul.[90] It provides an interpretive key for the analogy that follows, offering a technical description of what the cave enacts in the more dramatic terms of ethics and politics. Moreover, it further differentiates the realm that the sun image has characterized. The well-known sun image describes an analogy between the two distinct realms, the invisible and the visible, echoing the distinction Plato makes between being (which is *essentially* nonappearing) and appearance at the end of the book V. But the divided line carries the distinction a step further, subdividing each of these two realms. Socrates first distinguishes visibles (physical things), from their appearances in water and shiny objects, calling these appearances "images" (εἰκόνες, 509e) of the visible. This distinction is bound to seem strange, insofar as reflections of things in water represent a fairly insignificant class of objects,[91] but it serves two essential purposes: first, it establishes an analogy for understanding the relation between visible image and intelligible reality (which we will discuss in the next chapter), and second, it allows Plato to isolate the phenomenon of appearance in order to better distinguish it from being. It is clear that Plato has

the dividing line between the icons of sun and cave. . . . [W]ith all due caution, I believe it is helpful to think of the divided line as a sort of ladder suspended between noetic and political existence. In modern terminology, the divided line is an epistemological icon, intermediate between noetic vision and political praxis, hence pointing in both directions, and therefore indeterminate (if not altogether meaningless) in isolation from the sun and cave," *Nihilism: A Philosophical Essay*, 2nd ed. (South Bend, Ind.; St. Augustine's Press, 2000), 157. Rosen's suggestion accords well with the interpretation we mean to offer here: the line represents the intentional relationship between reality and the soul, and thus connects them. If this is true, there will be in principle a connection between the noetic/metaphysical on the one hand (i.e., the sun analogy), and the moral/political on the other (i.e., the cave analogy). Just as the line distinguishes the two from each other without separating them, so too it distinguishes the sun and the cave—without separating them. In fact, it precisely *links* them. As Jaeger puts it, "the image of the sun and the image of the cave . . . are linked into a unity by the simile of the divided line," *Paideia*, vol. 2, 294.

90. Desjardins provides a good account of the line in both metaphysical and epistemological terms. *Plato and the Good*, 55–90.

91. When read in light of the analogy of the cave, which Socrates calls an "image of education" (514a), and in light of the general theme of education in the *Republic*, especially as recounted in books II and III, it seems likely that the "images of images" in this lowest segment of the line represent the poetic tradition of Homer and Hesiod through the tragedians, which formed the basis of the Attic education Plato intends in some sense to criticize. On this, see Eric Havelock, *Preface to Plato* (New York: Grosset and Dunlap, 1967), 11–15. Of course, Plato was at the same time critical of the pure rationalization of education by the sophists—given what form reason took in their endeavors. See Jaeger, *Paideia*, vol. 2, 205–30, and vol. 1, 286–331.

in mind here art objects; this becomes explicit in book X, when Plato characterizes art objects in precisely the same terms (596d–e). In book X's discussion, Plato defines art as an imitation of appearance that aims "at the appearance of the appearing thing *as* appearing": πρὸς τὸ φαινόμενον, ὡς φαίνεται, φαντάσματος (598b).[92] In other words, the lowest level of the divided line depicts not just the physical appearance of things but appearance-ness *as such,* the very phenomenality of things considered in their phenomenality, as distinct from the object of which it is the appearance. The lowest level, we might say, presents the *perfection* of appearance.

In a parallel fashion, Plato subdivides the intellectual realm. He classifies the lower of the two subdivisions as "hypothesized" intelligible objects, which are understood on the basis of assumptions for the sake of forming certain conclusions. While commentators tend to assume Plato is speaking of "mathematicals" here, it is clear that he offers mathematical objects simply as an example.[93] In fact, what characterizes the levels of the line are not particular sets of objects but the particular *modes* of understanding and the modes of being they disclose. More specifically, the line designates a particular relation between the soul and reality, a relation with both a "subjective" and an "objective" component. Plato explicitly states that the segments of the line represent varying degrees of *manifestness* (509d).[94] In this third segment of the line, then, lie *any* intelligible objects, not as known in themselves, but rather as "hypothesized" for the sake of further conclusions. We

92. To speak of art objects as sheer appearance hardly does justice to the complex reality of art. We will discuss the relationship between art and philosophy at greater length in the coda. Our intention here is to see not what Plato thinks of art but what he specifically means by *appearance.*

93. Hackforth makes a compelling case that it is, in fact, *forms* that lie on this third segment, rather than some intermediate objects (i.e., mathematicals) between forms and sensibles. See Hackforth, "Plato's Divided Line and Dialectic," 1–4. The view of this segment as representing mathematicals, however, is so common as to be treated generally as a given. Part of the confusion, it seems, would lie in a failure to recognize the intentional nature of the soul's relation to reality, so that one has to posit a class of objects to mark the distinction in the line. Another part is the failure to recognize how the good fulfills its epistemological function in relation to the general methodology of the dialogue, so that one lays little emphasis on the difference between forms seen by themselves and forms seen in the light of the good.

94. When Plato thus speaks of the difference in truth of the levels (510a), he obviously does not mean truth in the sense of the correctness of propositions, but in the sense of degrees of reality. On this crucial point in Plato, see Walter Bröcker, "Platons ontologischer Komparativ," *Hermes* 87.4 (1959): 415–25.

see that this segment includes more than just mathematicals once we recognize that this "hypothetical" mode of understanding characterizes the forms as Plato presents them in every dialogue other than the *Republic*. When Cherniss, for example, says that Plato generally *assumes* his theory of forms in order to "save appearances," i.e., to justify certain conclusions, he fails to consider the highest level of the divided line that Plato offers in the *Republic* alone (although a reference can arguably also be found in *Letter VII*).[95] The highest section, though it begins by "hypothesizing" its intelligible objects, proceeds to confirm these hypotheses and thus eliminate their hypothetical character (533c),[96] by grasping them in relation to what Plato calls the "unhypothetical first principle of everything" (511b), the good.[97] By representing "knowability" in its most complete mode, this section isolates the phenomenon of the forms and presents intelligible objects *in* their intelligibility. Thus, just as the lowest level represents appearance in its most complete sense, the highest level represents form in its most complete sense. The line recapitulates the method we saw in both books I and II, namely, the drawing of a distinction by representing the two differentiated terms in their most perfect form, and thus in their greatest opposition to, or furthest extremity from, each other (see 360e). The line divides not only the sensible and the intelligible, but more specifically phenomenality and intelligibility as such. This further specified division allows us to see more clearly what, in particular, characterizes appearance and being in the cave on the one hand, and in the real world outside on the other.

The Cave

Those at the bottom of the cave are the spectators of the images of images, which means they view things *as severed from all contact with reality*. In this sense, the content of their experience is purely conventional, without roots—as far as they can possibly be aware—in φύσις. Plato depicts them as *prisoners* (514a–515c). They are bound in such a way that they are incapable

---

95. See *Letter VII*, 342a–b. Cf. Gonzales's interpretation, "Non-propositional Knowledge in Plato," 243–53.

96. Robinson interprets Plato's talk of "destroying the hypotheses" in this passage not as refuting them but as destroying their hypothetical character through the transformation of our relation to them. *Plato's Earlier Dialectic*, 160–62. Cf. Cross and Woozely, *Plato's Republic*, 248–49.

97. We will address further what it means to grasp forms in relation to the good in the next chapter.

of the slightest movement, even of turning their heads. Nothing with which they make contact has any direct relation to reality: their *backs* are to the real; what they see are appearances separated from their sources. The voices they hear—even their own—come to them not directly from the mouths of others, but only in a disembodied form, as reflected off of the "screen" at the bottom of the cave, which we might refer to as the "wall of phenomenality." This analogy shows us what appearance looks like considered wholly in itself; it is sheer relativism, the imaginative depiction of Thrasymachus's view of the world. If Plato were to give a title to the "movie" these prisoners are forced to watch, it would no doubt be "Man Is the Measure."[98]

Why does Plato present sheer phenomenality—appearance as severed from its relation to being—as imprisonment? If appearance, taking it as we did in our discussion of the *Theaetetus* in the last chapter, represents a thing insofar as it is given "to me," then appearance absolutized would be sheer "self"-relation.[99] Sheer "self"-relation, in turn, implies the complete lack of movement: It is impossible to move without getting somewhere, and thus moving beyond where one was, beyond one's mere "self." Movement depends on the sort of otherness that sheer "self"-relation excludes in principle. At the bottom of the cave, a person has contact with things only insofar as *they* move into immediate relation to the "self," which is not in any way turned toward things. Their reality is perfectly reduced to their "for me" significance. Sensible images, received not as images *of* a reality beyond them but only as absolutized in themselves,[100] thus represent a relation of pure

---

98. The eerie similarity between Plato's cave and the phenomenon of television is of course often remarked upon. ("But in the *Republic* we can *see* the willing prisoners in the cave, their eyes glued to the wall, as if it were a television screen running a never-ending series of *Dallas*, and no more willing to be moved than they would by the announcement of a lecture on metaphysics in the next room, without slides," Gerard Watson, "Plato and the Story," in *Platonic Investigations*, edited by Dominic O'Meara [Washington, D.C.: The Catholic University of America Press, 1985], 41; cf. John O'Neill, *Plato's Cave: Desire, Power, and the Specular Functions of the Media* [Norwood, N.J.: Ablex Publishing Corp., 1991]). However, it still constantly surprises one how deep the likeness goes. Just moments ago, a promotional ad from a cable company arrived in the mail at my home: "Make Your TV Revolve Around You!" Plato could put it no better.

99. Or more precisely, it *approximates* sheer "self"-relation. Sheer self-relation, as exclusive of all otherness, is strictly speaking not possible insofar as relation requires some otherness. Plato is presenting an idealized mode in order to show it for what it is. Note, incidentally, that we put "self" in quotation marks here: it represents a wholly *reduced* notion of the self, a mere part of the self, as we saw in Socrates' discussion of Protagoras in the *Theaetetus*.

100. Heidegger elaborates this distinction beautifully in his discussion of the cave allegory

immediacy in which the perceiver on a moment-by-moment basis presents the sole measure for the meaning of the thing perceived. We have once again encountered Protagoras.

Once we see the immediacy of sense-perception, taken merely in itself, we understand what it is that binds the prisoners at this level. What is implicit here becomes explicit when Plato discusses the tyrant, Thrasymachus's model of sheer relativity, in book IX. As Plato shows there, the tyrant, who has *no* measure for his desires outside of himself, is for that very reason perfectly enslaved (576a, 577c–e). What binds us, in other words, is desire that has no ordering to reality. This is not the desire for the *whole,* which Plato describes in book V as philosophical love; it is not desire for things *in themselves.* Instead, it is desire for a mere aspect, namely, a thing in its appearance-ness, which means solely in its goodness "for me." To desire something *merely* in its appearing, to put it most decisively, is to desire it precisely as *not* transcending me, or better, it is to desire myself *by means of* the thing. It is to treat the thing as having nothing but instrumental goodness. In fact, it is already too much to say that the meaning of things gets reduced to the "self," since the movement of reduction implies a fragmentation that undermines even the unity of the self. When the "self" instrumentalizes reality, i.e., deprives it of any "in-itself" quality, the "self" invariably becomes an instrument in turn. We saw the peculiar simultaneity of sheer power and sheer helplessness that logically follows from relativism in the *Theaetetus.* There is a clear connection between that paradox and the fact that the prisoners in the *Republic*'s cave, wholly "self"-absorbed as they are, are at the same time the utterly impotent victims of whatever shadows happen to be cast down, as it were, for their benefit.

Desire normally entails movement, but in the cave the movement is frustrated insofar as it does not lead to any "beyond."[101] We see, thus, the aptness of Plato's saying that the tyrant lives in a "dream" world (576b; cf. 534c).

---

in *The Essence of Truth,* translated by Ted Sadler (New York: Continuum, 2002), 36–39. As Heidegger points out, even sense-perception, *qua* perception, requires a movement beyond mere sense data.

101. Iris Murdoch expresses Plato's criticism of art objects—which, we have seen, Plato takes to represent appearance as such—in just these terms: "Art objects are not real unities but pseudo-objects completed by the mind in its escape from reality. The pull of the transcendent as reality and good is confused and mimicked," *The Fire and the Sun: Why Plato Banished the Artists* (Oxford: Clarendon Press, 1977), 66.

When we dream, Plato explains, we act on our desires without the capacity to restrain ourselves (571c–d). We lack the restraint that we claimed in the last chapter requires some self-transcending measure. At the same time, in a dream one has no means of recognizing the images one sees as images only, and not reality itself. In the analogy Plato draws between the tyrant and the person caught up in dreaming, the epistemological and axiological aspects of the problem converge: the tyrant is both incapable of distinguishing appearance from reality and unable to restrain the attempt to find *immediate* satisfaction of desires. It is for this reason that Plato, in the *Phaedo,* describes the person caught up in superficial desires as his own jailor, locked in himself by himself: "It is through desire that the prisoner himself collaborates most of all in his own imprisonment."[102] As Plato observes in the *Cratylus,* the strongest shackles for a living being is not force but desire.[103] Being trapped in this cave means being totally isolated, even from oneself, because one is caught up in the tyranny of the tiniest of vicious circles. According to Nalin Ranasinghe, "The cave is nothing more or less than the absence of a certain generosity in one's disposition toward reality and grace."[104]

If it is desire for a mere aspect of a thing divorced from its reality that implies imprisonment, the way through the bars becomes immediately apparent: an expansion of desire beyond partiality to the *whole.* This expansion entails a shift of focus, which Plato presents as the soul's περιαγωγή (518c), its *conversio,* from sheer phenomenality to the *good.* Liberation, in other words, is the movement from a sheer "self"-centered view of reality to a *bonocentric* view. To put it another way, it is a movement from the reduction of a thing to its relation to me, to seeing it as existing in its own right, as good in an absolute sense (which, to say it yet again, *includes* its being good for me without being limited to that mode of goodness). What brings about this movement? If the good in its twofold nature is what establishes the difference between being and appearance, it is also the *bridge* between them. But the good, as Plato says elsewhere, is the essential object of love (505e).[105] Love of goodness, then, is precisely what brings about, or in fact *is,* this move-

---

102. δι' ἐπιθυμίας ἐστιν, ὡς ἄν μάλιστα αὐτὸς ὁ δεδεμένος ξυλλήπτηρ εἴη τοῦ δεδέσθαι, *Phd.,* 82d.

103. *Cra.,* 403c.

104. Ranasinghe, *The Soul of Socrates* (Ithaca, N.Y.: Cornell University Press, 2000), 154.

105. Cf. *Symp.,* 206a.

ment. Love thus proves to be an indispensable aspect of coming to true knowledge.[106]

The Ladder of Love

Two aspects of Plato's view of love are important in relation to the present issue, namely the possibility of knowing the real. First, as the erotic dialogues—the *Phaedrus* and the *Symposium,* but especially the latter—show, love implies a kind of *growth,* a pedagogical movement Plato depicts as an ascent. We wish to suggest that *love grows precisely because it is set on a single object that has a twofold nature.* Since the *very same form* causes a thing's goodness in relation to me and its goodness in relation to itself, it is the same love that carries the soul from the relative to the absolute (and back again, as we will see in the next chapter and in the coda).[107] It would be impossible to get from one "side" to the other if they were simply separate.[108] But for Plato the good lies on both sides, because in its excessive transcendence, it is beyond each; and this very good elicits the love that enables "self"-transcendence. What the soul loves, when it loves truly, is thus more than it initially thinks it loves, and so it must constantly make the effort to catch up. The *Republic* begins, we recall, with attraction to the vision of a torch-bearing horse race, i.e., with the firelight of the cave, but this original desire eventually gives way to the desire for the good, of which the cave's fire is an image, to the extent that the torch race is forgotten.[109] The movement *beyond* the visible image nevertheless draws on the first impulse toward the image—

106. In this precise sense, we could affirm with Glenn Rawson ("Knowledge and Desire of the Good") a certain priority of desire to reason in making the ascent, insofar as Plato maintains the impossibility of desiring something other than goodness while affirming the capacity to be mistaken about what one desires.

107. Herman Sinaiko expresses this point well in *Love, Knowledge, and Discourse in Plato.* For him, love is "necessarily a grower of wings" (97). This is so because "[i]nherent in [a person's] desire for this unique individual thing he loves, whatever it may be, is the ultimate desire to attain transcendence again and to behold the 'realities'" (86). There is therefore "a fusion of the selfish interest of the lover with a selfless devotion to his beloved . . . and as such it is characteristic of all men from the best to the worst" (95).

108. Annas claims that Plato has no means of reconciling the absolute and relative aspects of goodness. *Introduction,* 266–71. She would be correct if it were not the very nature of the absolute to include the relative, which we are suggesting is Plato's view.

109. Indeed, we could follow the progression of desire in the *Republic* more closely: first, after the attraction to the spectacle there is a desire for intellectual discussion, then a more focused desire for the meaning of justice, which leads at its peak to a desire to know what philosophy and

because it is one and the same good that is its source. Beauty (which Plato identifies in some respect with the good) is so (intelligibly) radiant, he says in the *Phaedrus* (250d–e), that it is also physically visible—it possesses the same twofold character we have been associating with goodness in general.[110] And this is why love is essentially connected with the role of mediation (*Symp.* 202e–203a).[111] The "ladder of love" that Plato describes in the *Symposium,* a movement from the relative beauty of appearance to absolute beauty in itself,[112] thus depicts a movement from reception in the mode of the recipient to reception in the mode of that which is received. The soul's final object is the thing, not merely as one wishes to determine it according to one's own measure, but altogether *as* itself: αὐτὸ καθ' αὐτὸ μεθ' αὐτοῦ. One of the senses lurking behind Plato's repeated refrain that the beautiful/good is difficult (435c, 479d),[113] is no doubt the pangs the soul suffers in adapting itself to the measure of its beloved object. As Iris Murdoch once put it, "Love is the difficult realization that something other than oneself is real." In the *Sophist,* Plato suggests that the life experience one endures as one gets older aids in grasping reality beyond appearances and words.[114] This is why Plato describes the philosopher's education not merely in terms of purely intellectual subjects to be learned, but also as the radical discipline of an ordered way of life, which involves an unstinting love of the whole. He insists on the comprehensive love of labor that is required for its success (535d).

---

the good are. Though this desire was implicit in the first desire for spectacle, it was obviously not consciously *intended.*

110. See Hans-Georg Gadamer, *The Idea of the Good in Platonic-Aristotelian Philosophy* (New Haven, Conn.: Yale University Press, 1988), 115–16; cf. Gadamer, *The Relevance of the Beautiful and Other Essays,* translated by Nicholas Walker (Cambridge: Cambridge University Press, 1986), 15. In this latter work, Gadamer states that the "ontological function of the beautiful is to bridge the chasm between the ideal and the real," or as we would put it, between the absolute and the relative.

111. Léon Robin, in *La théorie Platonicienne de l'amour,* 2nd ed. (Paris: Librairie Félix Alcan, 1964), draws the same conclusion: "L'Amour établit une liason entre les deux sphères que Platon avait tout d'abord si profondément séparées l'une de l'autre, la sphère sensible et la sphère intelligible" (173). He thus reports that love is for Plato simultaneously a principle of movement and knowledge (179). It would have to be both if our characterization of the problem of knowledge is just. Thesleff remarks on the same function of *eros* in mediating between the "two worlds". *Studies in Plato's Two-Level Model,* 31, 62.

112. *Symp.,* 211b.

113. The refrain also appears in *Hp. mai.,* 304e, *Cra.,* 384b, *Soph.,* 259c, and in a variant form in *Phdr.,* 274a–b.

114. *Soph.,* 234d–e; cf. a similar point made at 251a–c.

Second, and along the same lines, Plato espouses what might be called an *ecstatic*, rather than merely "natural," understanding of love.[115] Love is *self-transcending* of its very nature, because it aims at what lies beyond mere relativity to the self.[116] Some interpret Platonic love as reducible to self-love.[117] But to do so fails to grasp the significance of the twofold nature of the good toward which this love aims. While Aristophanes, in the *Symposium*, portrays love in the immanent, and thus merely physical, sense of seeking wholeness in relation to one's body, Diotima insists that the whole to which love is ordered transcends mere relativity to the self precisely because it is absolute:

"Now there is a certain story," [Diotima] said, "according to which lovers are those people who seek their other halves. But according to my story, a lover does not seek the half or the whole, unless, my friend, it turns out to be good as well. I say this because people are even willing to cut off their own arms and legs if they think they are diseased. I don't think an individual takes joy in what belongs to him personally (τὸ ἑαυτῶν) unless by 'belonging to me' he means 'good' and by 'belonging to another' he means 'bad.' That's because what everyone loves is really nothing other than the good."[118]

115. For a further account of this point, see D. C. Schindler, "Plato and the Problem of Love," *Apeiron* (forthcoming). This distinction is drawn from Pierre Rousselot's classic work, *The Problem of Love in the Middle Ages*, translated by Alan Vincelette (Milwaukee, Wis.: Marquette University Press, 2001). Rousselot, however, leaves in place a basic dualism between natural love (based on self-love) and ecstatic love (based on love of the other), which we argue Plato's notion of the good as twofold succeeds in overcoming. Thus, when we speak of "ecstatic" love here, we do not mean to oppose it to self-love, but rather to root self-love in the transcendence toward the other that goodness implies. We are speaking, in other words, of a "bonocentrism," which is neither self-centeredness nor other-centeredness, but rather asymmetrically both at once.

116. Ferber, *Platos Idee des Guten*, 37.

117. See, e.g., Gregory Vlastos, "The Individual as Object of Love in Plato," in *Platonic Studies*, 2nd ed. (Princeton, N.J.: Princeton University Press, 1981), 3–42, here 30–31. To be sure, Vlastos does say that ideas can be loved "for their own sake" in Plato. A full assessment of the position Vlastos takes in this essay is not possible in the present context.

118. *Symp.*, 205e–206a. Kosman interprets Diotima's "correction" of Aristophanes as showing that what is essentially at issue is not simply one's "other half," but one's "*better* half," i.e., the "good" half. "Platonic Love," 63. But such a reading fails to see the nonreducibility of goodness to the self, which is essential to Plato's view *however much it remains always also relative*. A more paradoxical understanding of the good would have allowed Kosman to affirm the *intentional nature* of love, as he does (58), without having to force an ultimately inadequate reconciliation with "autoeroticism," which is what he ends up proposing (54). For Kosman, self-love is ecstatic because of the difference between the real and ideal self. It would be much more adequate, we propose, to say that love is ecstatic because it is set on the *kalon, simpliciter,* and that, precisely for this reason, it always also represents the fulfillment of the self.

Whereas Aristotle affirms that self-love is the paradigm of love, so that the union of self with self offers the ideal toward which all other loves strive,[119] Plato defines love precisely in terms of its lack, and thus in terms of its dependence on what is other than itself. Eros in this sense is constituted by a movement "beyond." Moreover, as we see in this passage from the *Symposium*, the lack is defined not in the first place relative to the lover, but rather in terms of the absoluteness of the object of love, which includes, but is not defined by, reference to the lover's partiality. Instead of calling whatever belongs to the self good and whatever belongs to the other bad (as, for example, Thrasymachus does in his final definition of justice), Socrates reverses the perspective and gives the name "one's own" to what is simply in itself *good*.[120] In this respect, the primary measure of love is not the capacity of the lover, but rather the absoluteness of the goodness toward which the love aims. To be sure, there is a paradox in this, insofar as it is not clear how it is possible to love something unless it is good for oneself.[121] A fuller response to this paradox awaits the next chapter. But it bears remarking that this is the very same paradox that arises in the consideration of the possibility of knowledge: how is it possible to know something as it is *in itself*? The coincidence is of course no accident: since they are both rooted in goodness, love and reason possess an essential unity.

The *ecstatic* character of Platonic love is specifically what qualifies it as a *divine madness*. It is by nature a "gift from the gods" (*Phdr.*, 244a), precisely because it is elicited from beyond the merely relative, that is, it breaks in on one essentially from "the beyond."[122] And it is a *madness* because, rooted

119. See *Nich. Eth.*, IX, 8, 1168bff.

120. Francisco Gonzalez illustrates precisely the same change from a relative to an absolute notion of philia in the *Lysis*. "Socrates on Loving One's Own: A Traditional Conception of ΦΙΛΙΑ Radically Transformed," *Classical Philology* 95 (2000): 379–98.

121. See Terry Penner's insistence that goodness that is not good for oneself in some respect is meaningless. "The Forms, The Form of the Good, and the Desire for the Good," *Modern Schoolman* 80 (2002–2003): 191–233, here 192–95. We do not deny this point, but rather claim that it likewise becomes meaningless to eliminate from goodness any transcendence of mere relativity to the self. In a word, the good is always good for the self *and more than* good for the self.

122. Óscar González-Castín records the crucial observation that an ultimate object, *qua* ultimate, can be attained only by that object's *revelation* of itself. It would not be ultimate if the soul could simply work its way up to the object on its own, but in that case would be essentially relative to the soul. See his essay, "The Erotic Soul and Its Movement towards the Beautiful and the Good," *Δαίμων: Revista de Filosofía* 21 (2000): 75–86. González-Castín suggests, however, that

in the absolute and in-itself goodness of things, it cannot ultimately be justified, and thus explained, by anything beyond itself. (See chapter 5.) If it were
not a "madness" in this precise sense, it would not be divine but would be essentially relative to the human (μέτρον ὁ ἄνθρωπον), nor would it present
the means to the in-itself reality of things. The seemingly Romantic description of love in the *Phaedrus* thus proves to have a rational place in Plato's philosophy: it provides the precise contrast to the absolutization of relativity
and the epistemological corollary to it, namely, that knowledge cannot be
differentiated from perception.

Plato characterizes the "place" to which love brings the soul as a realm lying "beyond the visible heavens" (*Phdr.,* 247c). What lies in this realm cannot be related by poets, but must be attempted by Socrates insofar as his
theme is about truth (περὶ ἀληθείας). We see here the very same contrast
drawn by Adeimantus in book II of the *Republic* between the poets and Socrates the philosopher, but we are now in a better position to understand its
philosophical significance. As we suggested in the previous chapter, any description of something is by definition limited to the describable qualities
of a thing; words can only say something *about* a thing, they cannot say *the
thing itself.*[123] They concern being as it appears rather than being as it is beyond any manifestation. And yet, as we have seen, truth requires precisely
this: a grasp of the reality itself, which is beyond relation and thus beyond
description. To communicate such a truth will require more than words.
What lies in this realm, the *telos* of love, is "really real reality" (οὐσία ὄντως
οὖσα),[124] which is "colorless, figureless, and non-appearing" (ἀχρωματός
τε καὶ ἀσχημάτιστος καὶ ἀναφής). Plato says the same things about it,
in other words, that he says of being in book V, and reiterates that it is precisely this really real reality that forms the object of true knowledge (περὶ
ἥν τὸ τῆς ἀληθοῦς ἐπιστήμης γένος, 247c–d). The strange phrase οὐσία

---

while we see this revelation in the *Symposium,* we do not see it in the *Republic* (85). We will show
in the next chapter, by contrast, that the revelation in the *Republic* is far more radical than in the
Symposium, or indeed in any other dialogue, and that this is fitting because it is precisely in the
Republic that Plato emphasizes the radical *transcendence* of the "ultimate object."

123. In the coda, we will attempt to show, in light of this book's arguments in general, that
there *is* a sense in which words—and therefore speeches, images, and poetry—have a necessary
role in disclosing things in themselves.

124. According to Friedländer (*Plato: An Introduction,* vol. 1, 221), the adverb ὄντως, or
τῷ ὄντι, had been recently coined in Greek (e.g., used by the sophists and found in Aristophanes
and Euripides) to distinguish between being and seeming. Plato clearly amplifies this usage.

ὄντως οὐσα, "being which is beingly being," in its triplex unity, provides a perfect contrast to the phenomenality of art objects at the lowest segment of the line, "the appearance of the appearing thing *as* appearing." Here, being is at once the noun, adverb, and verbal predicate; it thus represents a perfect unity which can nevertheless be differentiated into various aspects, designating not only the thing itself (being), but what it does (being), and how it is doing it (beingly). If this is the final object of love, we would say that love in its most perfect form no longer takes its measure from the relative self that loves, but rather wholly from the object to which the love relates once it sees it as good in itself. It is precisely *this* that Plato meant by saying that the good is the most precise measure: it allows an "objective" perspective because it demands a transcendence of all partiality.

Love and reason thus essentially coincide, insofar as both entail an *identification* of the self with its object in some respect. Falling in love, an experience in which one is literally driven outside of oneself through the encounter with what lies beyond one's comprehension,[125] is the mirror of the shift from opinion to knowledge. It involves a renunciation of the Protagorean measure, because it is a consent to be measured by what is other than the self. Knowledge means taking something, not merely as it is for me, but "non-perspectivally" as it is in itself, and this requires the essentially ascetic movement of inserting oneself into *its* goodness. To be sure, we must keep in mind that the twofold nature of goodness is never lost; the "absolute" identification with the beloved object does not eliminate a "relative" difference from it.[126] The self-transcendence of eros is thus not the *loss* of the self, but rather a forgetting of the self in a focus on what is good, even while that goodness, if it *is* good, will always necessarily include a goodness for the self.

In the *Republic,* and specifically in its central analogies, Plato depicts this movement from a kind of "self"-centeredness to a bonocentrism explicitly in epistemological terms. We may, at this point, summarize the basic argument regarding the connection between intelligibility and goodness and its

---

125. *Phdr.,* 250a–b.

126. In *Alc. I,* 133a, Socrates remarks on the fact that when lovers look at one another, each is reflected in the pupil of the other's eye: the "highest part" of the person, the organ of sight (knowledge), is also where that person becomes the "other." On the depth of the significance of this image, see Sergio Benvenuto, "'Lo Specchio della Potenza': Eros e Volontà di Potenza in Platone," *Il Cannochiale* 2 (2002): 3–27. Most scholars dispute Plato's authorship of this dialogue, but the image nevertheless provides a nice illustration of the point we are making.

implications for the relationship between being and appearance. The object of knowledge, Socrates says, is being; to know something in the most fundamental sense is to attain to the in-itself reality of it, which is not only to see its goodness but in fact to enter into its goodness. But to do so is to grasp it in its difference from me, that is, to grasp it in its difference from appearance, which is the thing taken in relation to me. This requires a movement beyond relative goodness to goodness itself, which includes *both* the other as absolutely different from me *and* the other as identical to me. This movement is the essence of *eros* in its true form, which we might call the subjective correlate of goodness. The movement up, through, and out of the cave (which is also a movement up the divided line) from phenomenality to the forms in and by themselves is thus not a movement of abstraction, at least not as we conventionally understand the term. Nor is it simply a movement from one set of "things" to another set of "things." Rather, for Plato, the movement is an ever-greater penetration into the reality of things, a movement drawn by love. The reason this movement represents increasing intelligibility is that we come closer to things as they are in themselves, and therefore to that which presents the foundation of knowledge. It would therefore be true to say that the more "objective," i.e., bonocentric, one's love becomes, the more things disclose themselves in their truth, and also the more beautiful and desirable they become—precisely because the goodness that is at the root of all of this becomes more manifest. For this reason, in the *Republic*, Plato defines philosophy in terms reminiscent of the erotic dialogues, which speak of the ladder of love; philosophy is an "upward journey" (517c–d), the "ascent to what really is" (521c). Reason, for Plato, is not merely an instrument for registering truth, but designates a *journey* because it has a destination, even if that destination continues to lie on the other side of the perceivable horizon.

Surprised by Truth

If the previous chapter was right to conclude that the absolutization of the relative entails the submission of all things to effective power (Thrasymachus), then the way out, the outmaneuvering of power, will require vigilant and steadfast insistence on its relativity. This can be something other than the replacement of one relative position by another only if it is possible to get *beyond* what is relative, i.e., somehow to reach what is absolute. The outmaneuvering of power will thus turn out to be the same as coming to knowledge of things in themselves, and we have now seen that knowledge itself is possible only in the context of the ecstasis of love. Reason outside of love will fail to be reason insofar as reason is ordered to being beyond appearances.[127] But, while we have begun to see the relationship between ecstasis and reason, we must avoid affirming it in a facile manner that would miss the great paradox that lies at its center. Before turning to face this paradox head on in the next chapter, we will conclude the present one with an indication of where this paradox seems to be heading.

Plato famously refers to the good as beyond knowledge and truth in its beauty, and by the same token "beyond being, exceeding it in knowledge and power" (509a–b). While we must still elaborate the meaning of these assertions, let us take note of how they illuminate the ethos of the *Republic*. If reason is drawn on by the good, which is in some respect beyond the *knowledge* that presents reason's proper object, then it follows that reason is by its very nature drawn beyond itself. In this respect, just as love loves more than it initially thinks it does, reason too will be brought to know more than it can anticipate. In other words, reason will necessarily be taken by surprise by its insights precisely to the extent that it remains true to itself. At every step, it always implicitly knows more than it knows—or as Plato puts it, it has a pre-awareness (the verb is ἀπομαντεύομαι, which literally means it "prophesies") about what its ultimate object is, but is "confusedly unable to get a sufficient grasp (ἱκανῶς) of its precise nature" (505e).[128] As we have seen in the dialogue, what seems to be an end in one respect always turns out to be a call to go further.[129] The problem with both Protagoras and Thrasymachus

127. At 518c–d, it may seem that Plato is describing the mind as a mere instrument, which can be turned in one way or another, indifferently toward or away from being as illuminated by the good. But in fact, though it may be turned one way or the other, the "present argument" he alludes to in this passage in order to make his point, namely, the allegory of the cave in relation to the sun and line, shows clearly that the mind is not at all indifferent to reality. Plato calls reason here a power, which, as we saw, is defined by that upon which it is set, and an "instrument." The word for instrument he uses is ὄργανον, derived from ἔργω, "to work," and just as every work has a proper end (see 352dff) in which it finds its fulfillment and perfection, so too does reason find its defining fulfillment in being illuminated by goodness.

128. According to Ferber (*Platos Idee des Guten*, 51), the good cannot be an entirely *new* discovery. But Ferber goes on to say that Socrates thus *feigns* ignorance in order to get the better of his opponent. It seems more adequate to suggest that the good always remains in some decisive respect *beyond* knowledge even while it is immanent to the soul, and therefore that Socrates is not merely lying about ignorance. We will discuss this point at greater length in chapter 5.

129. Kenneth Sayre has observed that the "open-ended" quality of some of Plato's dialogues

was essentially a refusal to consent to this movement beyond, instead allowing a partial point of reference to be the determining measure. Socrates evidently has this perspective in mind when he says that "nothing incomplete is the measure of anything. But certain men are sometimes of the opinion that this question has adequately (ἰκανῶς) been disposed of and that there is no need to go further" (504c).

If, by contrast, we follow this need, where will it take us? If love for the good, in which reason has its proper place, *is* love *only* if it is love for the whole of its object, and if the whole of the good is not only the good in itself but necessarily also in its consequences, then love and reason can be what they are only by aiming comprehensively at both aspects. And what are the consequences of the good? "Therefore say that not only being known is present in the things known as a consequence of the good, but also existence and being are in them besides as a result of it" (509b). But there is more to add. By virtue of the twofold nature of goodness, things themselves are good not only in themselves, but also in their relations, that is, in their appearances and images. One cannot say one loves a thing, Socrates pointed out, unless one loves it wherever it appears, no matter how imperfect its appearance. It follows that one cannot have adequate knowledge of anything at all without an ultimate desire for knowledge of everything. Being cannot disclose itself as being in any particular instance except to a reason seeking the whole of it. Reason cannot *rationally* establish for itself any proximate end as ultimate, but can have for its end only *the* ultimate, and therefore the comprehensive. Anything less becomes irrational the moment it absolutizes itself.

We remarked that the analogies of the cave and the divided line present the *itinerary* of reason's journey, but that is quite different from making the journey itself. Indeed, the possibility of making this journey depends on catching sight of the good in some direct manner. But we have yet to discover whether the good can in fact become visible *as* good, and not merely as yet another relative image. Until we do so, we remain trapped in the rela-

---

is consistent with his view that learning is recollection: knowledge does not need to be put into the soul, but rather the main thing is to remove obstacles ("Plato's Dialogues in Light of the *Seventh Letter*," 103). Similarly, Kelley Ross suggests that the truest knowledge for Plato, knowledge of forms, ultimately does not need to be verified but is always already "there" for us. "Non-intuitive Immediate Knowledge," *Ratio* 29 (December 1987): 163–79, here 173. In the terms we are using in the present context, the soul is always already beyond itself at the deepest level, and so surprises itself with the discovery of what it already knows. For a dramatic portrayal of just such a discovery, see 432d.

tivity of perspectives. It would be too much to believe that a progressive approach would suffice, insofar as the relative distinctions in the order of being depend, as we have seen, on the possibility of an *absolute* distinction. The *very first* movement in the cave is not a gradual backing-up toward the light, but a complete reversal to face the good. Only after this turn is progress made. The way out of the cave thus depends on making the good visible as a relative image (i.e., *within* the cave), without compromising its absoluteness. Robinson claims that "[n]owhere in the dialogues is any proposition put forward as an anhypotheton or a beginning."[130] We have to wonder whether a genuinely "unhypothetical" proposition, *qua* proposition, is possible, and indeed whether this sort of thing is what Plato has in mind in his search for the proper place to start. In any event, we discussed in the first chapter the difficulty of finding an adequate beginning, and suggested that the possibility might come, oddly enough, only a further distance along the way. It is to this possibility that we turn in the next chapter.

130. R. Robinson, *Plato's Earlier Dialectic,* 159.

CHAPTER THREE

BREAKING IN

Reversal and Reality, Or, How Socrates,
as the Real Image of the Good, Fulfills the Sun,
the Line, and the Cave Images
by Overturning Them

The Overburdened Image

An image is volatile by nature. It is not simply a thing lying next to other things, because its own reality does not simply belong to it but lies in part elsewhere. We look *through* a photograph of a loved one as much as we look *at* it, in the sense that our attention moves to the *person* that we know and doesn't come to a stop at the colored shapes on the surface. An image *is* in a decisive way what it is *not*. In this respect, we ought to think of an image not primarily as an object, but as a task to be accomplished: it has a goal beyond itself that must be reached, and it is itself constituted by the movement toward this goal. Plato captures precisely this inner tension of images in the *Phaedo*, where he describes them not primarily as things but as *actions*, using the verbs ὀρέγεται and προθύμεται, meaning "to reach out toward" and "to be eager for" (*Phd.*, 75b). Images are a kind of movement, or better, a striving, since this movement is quite indeterminate. But if images are a movement or a task, we must at once acknowledge that the task is, at least in one respect, an impossible one. What images strive for and long to be is something that they necessarily, constitutionally, "fall short of" (ἔστιν δὲ αὐτοῦ φαυλότερα), for if they did not they would thereby cease to be images.[1]

---

1. To be sure, it is also the case that if they *merely* fell short of their goal, they would *also* cease to be images. They are thus not *merely* movement, we might say, but at the same time possess an inherent rest. In this they display a paradox similar to that of reason or love, the poverty and fullness of mediation. We will develop this point in the coda.

Now, if images in general are an impossible task, this is much more the case for those meant to represent the *good,* the "reality" of which lies not only beyond images, but beyond everything at all. It is no surprise, then, that Plato's idiom becomes especially elusive the moment he enters upon this core problem in the *Republic.* As is well known, Socrates shows a profound reserve regarding the idea of the good, which lies "beyond being" (509b). Gadamer points out that Plato never refers to the good in the neuter form *eidos,* but only in the feminine form *idea,* which emphasizes more the *looking* toward it than the *look* of the thing itself.[2] Indeed, Socrates balks at talking "about things one doesn't know as if one does know" (506c), and refuses to attempt the sort of definition for goodness that he has given for the virtues (506d). Such reticence is not merely rhetorical, but seems to be compelled by the very nature of the good.[3] As Rafael Ferber observes, that which makes intentionality (i.e., the relation between the mind and being), possible, must necessarily be itself "atentional," or else we would fall into an infinite regress.[4] Transcendence, as we have seen, is the very essence of the good, because of its connection with the "in-itself" being of things. As Voegelin puts it, "concerning the content of the Agathon, nothing can be said at all. . . . The transcendence of the Agathon makes immanent propositions concerning its content impossible."[5] At the same time, however, Socrates does not simply abandon the good to sheer inaccessibility, but speaks of it as an object

2. Gadamer, *The Idea of the Good,* 27–28. Friedländer makes a similar observation. *Plato: An Introduction,* 16–18. Cf. Jaeger, *Paideia,* vol. 3, 24, and vol. 2, 283. Jaeger suggests that *"eidos"* refers to "types," whereas *"idea"* points to the unity underlying a multiplicity. Monique Dixsaut claims that Plato uses the term *"idea"* precisely when he wants to avoid the term *"eidos,"* which seems in these cases to represent a definable essence. *Platon et la question de la pensée,* vol. 1 of *Études Platoniciennes* (Paris: Vrin, 2000), 126–27.

3. There are some—particularly the Tübingen school—who insist that nothing but prudence kept Plato from discoursing directly on the nature of the good. For a recent representation of this view, see Thomas Alexander Szlezák, *Die Idee des Guten in Platons Politea: Beobachtungen zu den mittleren Büchern* (Sankt Augustin: Academia Verlag, 2003), 47–53. In his essay "L'Idea del Bene," Mario Veggetti offers a survey of the interpretations that argue that Plato did, in fact, hold the essence of the good to be something one could present in discourse, but insists that the view of the good presented in the text itself philosophically precludes this possibility. Though we cannot enter into the controversy here, we agree on this point with Veggetti. For a thorough treatment, see Rafael Ferber, *Die Unwissenheit des Philosophen oder Warum hat Plato die "ungeschriebene Lehre" nicht geschrieben?* (St. Augustin: Academia Verlag, 1991).

4. Ferber, *Platos Idee des Guten,* 277–78. Dixsaut makes a similar observation: *Platon et la question de la pensée,* 147.

5. Voegelin, *Plato and Aristotle,* 112. See also Pickstock, *After Writing,* 11.

of vision and as something that can be grasped intellectually.[6] It is quite frequently assumed that Plato means to imply we never have access to the good in itself, that is, never a "direct" vision, but only ever see it through images.[7] However, Plato explicitly insists on the necessity of grasping what the good itself is by means of reason, the same language he uses for the understanding of forms generally.[8] Indeed, when he begins to present the images of the good, rather than the good itself, he says merely that he is putting off a "quest for the good itself . . . for the time being."[9] If one were to insist that Plato denies the possibility of knowing the good, moreover, one would have the burden of explaining why he vigorously objects to opinions *without knowledge* in matters of such importance (506c). If opinion is the subjective correlate of image, he is objecting to the very method he is about to present, and this is the case even if the images happen to be true, or "second best," or inevitable. Images simply do not suffice; it is, in short, impossible to provide an adequate image of the good.

At the same time, the project of the *Republic* makes it impossible to accept such an impossibility. Again, the crux of the problem from the beginning has been to discover a ground for judgment beyond the relativity of appearances. To make such a ground "appear" requires a "perfect image," failing which the dialogue as a whole would necessarily founder.[10] This challenge of finding a perfect image of the good thus itself contains a twofold demand: on the one hand, genuinely to *show forth* the good so that it is made in principle accessible (rather than, say, merely gesturing, *faute de mieux*, in the direction of the

6. See, for example, *Rep.*, 516b, 517b, 526d. On the good as known in some sense, even while remaining "beyond" knowledge, see Natorp, *Platons Ideenlehre*, 191–92.

7. Sallis, *Being and Logos*, 412: "The good always shows itself *as it is not . . . . The good shows itself only through images.*"

8. αὐτὸ ὃ ἔστιν ἀγαθὸν αὐτῇ νοήσει λάβῃ, 532b. Cf. Utermöhlen, *Die Bedeutung der Ideenlehre*, 99. Notice, however, how Plato puts it here: the person grasps what the good *is*, which is not the same as grasping the good itself.

9. *Rep.*, 506d. Shorey claims that Plato often leaves expressions like these unfulfilled (see p. 95 of his Loeb translation, fn. f). However, this possibility ought to be accepted only if we fail to find an attempt to provide an answer. We propose in this essay that the reason for Plato's ironic delay is that the good cannot be presented in itself the way other things can, but demands a fundamentally new stance that is brought on *through* the dialogue rather than merely *in* it.

10. Andrew Barker and Martin Warner suggest that even language in the cave must be defective unless there is some possibility of a "'perfect' image," and then go on to show that there cannot be, and that there is thus no "direct access to the nature of [the] Forms," *Language of the Cave*, 3.

vacant space of transcendence), and, on the other hand, doing so in a way that does not compromise its transcendence. Indeed, this twofold demand is itself an expression of the highest form of goodness that Plato described in the beginning of book II: what is truly absolute must *also* be relative; what is truly transcendent must *also* be immanent. Insofar as the central analogies in the *Republic* deal with the nature of reality and its intelligible structure in the light of the good, we can see this core section of the dialogue as a response to the question that Shorey says Plato tackles in the later dialogue, the *Parmenides:* "How can we bring the absolute into intelligible relation with the relative?"[11] This is not just *a* question but is rather *the* question of knowledge, intelligibility, and truth, as we have sought to show from the beginning.

The present chapter will propose that the three analogies—the sun, the line, and the cave—work together to respond to this question. If Plato rejects *both* knowledge *and* opinion with regard to the good, and nevertheless insists on an intellectual *grasp* of it, we can assume that he envisions a grasp of a unique sort and that he has in mind a singular "methodology." The images that Plato presents here in the *Republic,* we will suggest, participate in this methodology by bringing about a real relationship to the good as an intrinsic part of the same gesture by which they describe it, and thus will mediate an immediate relation. We will first make an argument for why the three images need to be read together, as parts of a whole that is more than any one of them can communicate in isolation. Next, we will show that each reflects in its own way the twofold nature of the good, insofar as each displays both the "ascent" of transcendence and the "descent" of immanence. In other words, each contains a movement of striving that is interrupted by a reversal. The reversals in these images, which have a different significance in each case, culminate in the reversal in the cave, where the philosopher is sent down. At this moment, the very expression of reversal by means of images is, as a whole, reversed, and the historical Socrates steps forth himself as the "perfect" image. In this, as the image is enacted in reality, we have an argument that is both *said* and *shown* (which is what Adeimantus required), we have a man who is just, beyond and in spite of all appearances (as Glaucon required), and we have a hypothesis confirmed (which is the ultimate step in the divided line). It is Socrates who makes the good manifest without compromising its absoluteness.

11. Shorey, *Unity of Plato's Thought,* 36.

Keeping the Parts Together

It is significant that Plato makes use of *three* images, all of them quite different from one another, so different that commentators occasionally suggest they might not be related at all.[12] It would have been possible, in principle, for Plato to say much of what he says through the elaboration of a single, sophisticated image: perhaps a cave under the sun separating the visible and the intellectual realms constructed according to strict mathematical proportions. The multiplicity of images has implications from the first for the significance of each. Had there been a single image, the temptation would be great to absolutize it as the definitive and conclusive presentation of Plato's meaning. But we have seen that Plato has made a point, from the beginning, to restart and revise each step along the way. His approach is no different here. The three images immediately relativize one another, and thus the simple fact of their multiplicity prompts the mind to acknowledge that the reality they articulate lies beyond each one of them, and thus beyond all of them together. There is such an abundance of significant aspects and relations in the conglomeration of these images that, as Julia Annas says, they force us to look in too many directions at once.[13] The point may be simply to make sure we look away. Indeed, Plato frequently points out in his dialogues that one need not take so much care regarding particular words once one grasps that which the words mean to express; here, Plato underscores this notion by insisting in as direct a manner as could be wished that he is presenting an *image* rather than the reality itself, and that we ought not allow ourselves to be deceived by losing this fact from view (cf. 507a). The very number of images invites us to consider them—to anticipate Plato's expression in the divided line—as so many "hypotheses" from which to spring, to grasp what is more ultimate than they.

12. See, for example, J. R. S. Wilson, "The Contents of the Cave," in *New Essays on Plato and the Pre-Socratics*, edited by R. Shiner and J. King-Farlow (Guelph: Canadian Association for Publishing in Philosophy, 1976), 117–27. On the question of whether the three images are connected, see Jackson, "On Plato's Republic VI," 132–50; J. Ferguson, "Sun, Line, and Cave Again," *Philosophical Quarterly* (1963): 188–93; J. Malcolm, "The Line and the Cave," *Phronesis* 7 (1962): 38–45; J. Malcolm, "The Cave Revisited," *Classical Quarterly* 31 (1981): 60–68; J. E. Raven, "Sun, Divided Line, and Cave," *Classical Quarterly* 3 (1953): 22–32; R. G. Tanner, "Dianoia and Plato's Cave," *Classical Quarterly* 20 (1970): 81–91; Lidz, "Reflections on and in Plato's Cave," 115–34; Dorter, *Transformation of Plato's* Republic, 202–3.

13. Annas, *Introduction*, 256.

Now, many people have disputed the notion that Plato intended a correspondence between these images, most often between the divided line and the cave.[14] They do so in spite of the great evidence to the contrary: not only are the images presented in continuous succession,[15] as a whole in response to the single question of knowing the good in relation to everything else, and not only does Socrates explicitly instruct Glaucon to read the cave in relation to "everything that was said before," i.e., the line and the sun (517a–b), but all three depict a hierarchy of being and intelligibility in relation to an ultimate.[16] The attempt to isolate these images seems prompted by the difficulties of establishing a one-to-one correspondence between the levels of the cave and the line and of seeing how the political-psychological situation described by the cave could have epistemological significance. We proposed a way of connecting the contexts of the line and the cave in the last chapter. The moment we recognize that each image aims at the same thing from a *different* perspective, with different concerns that set different things into relief regarding the reality depicted, there is no need to make them simple duplicates of one another in order to suppose they are intrinsically related. We need only recognize the abstract character of the divided line if isolated from its context (and therefore from the *Republic* generally), or the unresolved hermeneutical problems the cave would present when simply detached from the line.[17] It is best, by contrast, to read the images as Plato straightforwardly presents them, namely, as occupied with essentially the same reality from a

14. Influential examples are Joseph, *Knowledge and the Good in Plato's* Republic, 31–45, and R. Robinson, *Plato's Earlier Dialectic*. See the discussion of this interpretation in Hall, "Interpreting Plato's Cave," 74–86.

15. We recall that the break between books VI and VII that divides the line from the cave was introduced by a later editor.

16. Cross and Woozely provide a clear account of objections to reading the line and cave together, and then a sober defense of the "traditional" view (*Plato's* Republic, 196–228). Their sole remaining difficulty is understanding *how* the good is meant to be the ground of intelligibility for things like mathematics (260–61), though they have no doubt that Plato means to imply that it is. We have suggested in the previous chapter a way of accounting for this.

17. To illuminate the potential problems, we could consider the essay by David McNeill, "Human Discourse, Eros, and Madness in Plato's *Republic*," 235ff. Because he does not read the allegory in light of the line that precedes it, he observes, for example, that we have no way of knowing whether the images below correspond at all to the realities above. He thus posits a complete disjunction between the sensible and intelligible, and moreover makes the startling suggestion that there is no "transcendence" in the *Republic*. The problems with this interpretation would have been avoided had he considered the allegory within the broader context of the dialogue.

different perspective and thus as reciprocally illuminating.[18] Again, they are offered altogether as a response to Glaucon's request that Socrates tell them about the good. When we read them specifically as a response to this request and keep in mind the connection between goodness and intelligibility, we discover a pattern in them that has a decisive significance for the basic problem of knowledge underlying the *Republic*.

Bringing Forth the Good

The Sun

Let us first consider the sun analogy. Although Socrates admits he would prefer to present the good in itself, he is prevented by two things: his capacity to "pay" or "render" (ἀποδύναι) and Glaucon's capacity to "receive" or "bear" it (κομίσασθαι). The good surpasses, in other words, both terms of the relation. As usual, Socrates hesitates to speak about something he does not claim to have adequate knowledge of, but Glaucon persuades him to present his supposition *as* a supposition (506c). He consents to Glaucon's proposal, and yet, considered closely, what he offers is not exactly what Glaucon requested. While he does indeed provide an image of the good rather than articulating it as it is in itself, he presents it, not as a metaphor he has produced—which is how one would characterize a normal conjecture or supposition—but as something the good itself has produced: the sun, he says, is the "interest and child" of the good (507a). The difference will turn out to be quite significant.

Drawing on the everyday experience of his interlocutors, Socrates indicates the essential role that the sun plays in allowing visible things to be seen and eyes to see.[19] This role has several important aspects. First of all, Socrates insists that the sun is *different* from both the eye and its vision (508a–b). This difference allows it to be a mediating third that joins the eye to its object. Moreover, its being the mediating third makes it the specific cause (αἴτιος) of sight.[20] And Socrates observes that, as the cause, it can be said to be *pres-*

18. Raven gives perhaps the best brief account of how the three analogies complement each other without being strictly parallel. See *Plato's Thought in the Making*, 131–87. Cf. also Utermöhlen, *Die Bedeutung der Ideenlehre*, 47–49, and Wieland, *Formen des Wissens*, 197.

19. Utermöhlen makes the interesting observation in this regard that the sun image is the only elaborate image in the entire Platonic corpus that Plato did not "invent" himself. *Die Bedeutung der Ideenlehre*, 34.

20. See Ferber's excellent observations in this regard. *Platos Idee des Guten*, 60–66. Cf. Dixsaut, *Platon et la question de la pensée*, 133–36.

ent in vision: "'And the sun isn't sight either, is it, but as its cause is seen by sight itself.' 'That's so'" (508b). Finally, the power that the eye has to see is *not* separate from the sun's power to make things visible.[21] It is for this reason that Plato calls the eyes "sunlike," that he refers to seeing as a sharing in the sun's rays, and that he insists that the eyes gain or lose their *own* power in proportion to the sun's presence. This implies the eyes share in some intrinsic manner in the sun's power, so that the more the sun is active, the more the eyes are active. The operation of sight, for Plato, is clearly not a purely "mechanical" act, but involves an intrinsic relation among the elements.[22] The sun, as the sovereign agent in this act, is simultaneously distinct from and present within the act itself, and this simultaneity is the condition of possibility for the act to take place.

Now, after his account of the operation of seeing, Socrates "springs" to the analogue of the good's causal presence in the act of knowing: "'Well, then,' I said, 'say that the sun is the offspring of the good I mean—an offspring the good begot in proportion (ἀνάλογον) with itself: as the good is in the intelligible region with respect to intelligence and what is intellected, so the sun is in the visible region with respect to sight and what is seen'" (508b–c). Socrates thus appears to be drawing what would later be called an analogy of proportion, which illuminates one set of terms by another, in spite of their difference in nature, by virtue of an identity of relation between the terms in each set. Such an analogy reveals a similar formal structure by comparing proportions.[23] In this case, we would understand the good as the mediating third that makes knowledge possible, as the *cause* of knowledge and truth, by being simultaneously distinct from and present within the knower and the known. If we therefore understand the act of sight properly, we will receive a proper understanding of the act of knowledge: the two sets are different, but still *parallel* to one another, and this allows us to move intelligibly from the set of terms that are known to those that are unknown. In this way, the image mediates an understanding of something that would otherwise remain obscure.

21. To the ancient mind, there would not be such a sharp contrast between illuminating and seeing. Notice, for example, how Homer describes the sun as having the most penetrating vision, precisely because it has the most penetrating rays. *Iliad* 14.344–45. For an elaboration of this view of seeing, see D. C. Schindler, "Homer's Truth: The Rise of Radiant Form," *Existentia: An International Journal of Philosophy* 16: 3–4 (2006): 161–82.

22. See Raven, *Plato's Thought in the Making*, 134–35.

23. Which is how some incorrectly interpret the sun analogy, as Sinaiko explains. *Love, Knowledge, and Discourse in Plato*, 300n4.

But things are more complex than they initially seem. As Socrates elaborates the analogy, it becomes clear that our initial understanding of the act of sight requires significant revision. After indicating the parallel between the sun and the good, Socrates makes a further distinction between seeing by day, which we could call proper vision, and seeing by night, which we could call "defective" vision (508c). The latter is a lesser form of the former, and can be understood only as such—in other words, it is not a different kind of seeing, but an inferior modality of the one kind of seeing. Next, Socrates explains that a similar distinction holds in relation to the intelligible and the good. When we grasp things, as it were, in the light of the good, we have knowledge (proper intellection). On the other hand, if we grasp them apart from the good, we have mere opinion:

> Well, then, think that the soul is also characterized in this way. When it fixes itself on that which is illumined by truth and that which *is*, it intellects, knows, and appears to possess intelligence. But when it fixes itself on that which is mixed with darkness, on coming into being and passing away, it opines and is dimmed, changing opinions up and down, and seems at such times not to possess intelligence. (508d)

Note that the "realm" to which opinion is ordered is that of "coming into being and passing away." Plato refers to the "many" beautiful and good *things* we perceive with the senses as opposed to the forms perceived by the mind. Recalling the end of book V, we would say he is referring here to the relative aspect of reality, which is manifest to the senses, in contrast to the absolute aspect accessible to the mind. This relative aspect is the realm indicated on the divided line as that of the physical as opposed to the intelligible. These are the things that make up the visible realm. But this means Plato is characterizing physical vision as a "dim" or "derivative" form of intellection. If this is the case, then, insofar as what is derived gets its meaning from that from which it is derived, we can in fact understand sight *only on the basis* of that which it had purported, itself, to disclose through analogy. As Herman Sinaiko puts it:

> [I]t now appears that the sun and the visible realm, which were to be the basis of the exposition because they were already known to the audience, are not understood by them at all! Insofar as the objects of the visible realm are among the privative objects of intelligence, they can only be understood by reference to their state of perfection, that is, to the ideas, and ultimately this means by reference to the good. The argument, as initially set up by Socrates, purports to explain the good in relation to the intelligible realm by analogy with the sun in relation to the visible realm. Now, how-

ever, it is clear that the entire visible realm can only be understood as part of the intelligible realm.[24]

That which provides the "ground" for understanding in this moment becomes the "grounded," and the direction of the mind gets reversed. All of a sudden, the analogy becomes a "katology." Rather than grasping the good by ascending analogously from the physical sun, we must understand the sun through downward thought, katalogically, from the good. A reversal of this sort is inevitable when it is a question of understanding something absolute. Because the good is the transcendent principle of understanding, it *cannot* in fact be understood "in terms of" anything but itself. Whatever is therefore used as a means for understanding the good must therefore be revised or relativized in the very moment it completes its service precisely to the extent that it performs this service successfully. The "transformation" of the relative that occurs through this reversal does *not* destroy "the very foundations of the analogy," as Sallis suggests.[25] While it is true that we lose what we thought was the "ground," so to speak, the similarity and the causality that founds it remains. It is just that, now, the order has been reversed and the relationship between the terms fundamentally recast. To say that the analogy is destroyed implies that the insight it offers undermines itself; but it is more accurate to say that the insight, though taken by surprise, is nevertheless deepened.

Let us follow the mind's movement in this reversal carefully to see how this is so. We begin with an image, as we must. We intend first to understand this image, and then move from there upward to the good of which it is the image. However, if it is the case that the good is the foundation of knowledge and that we cannot understand anything adequately until we have understood *it* (505a), it follows that we *cannot* come to a complete understanding of the image until *after* we have understood the reality to which it points.[26] We ought to recall that this is the very problem we faced at the outset in trying to find an adequate beginning. The reversal does not imply, however, that we can dispense with images. Because of the transcendent nature of the good, we have no direct access to it, but can grasp it only in terms

24. Ibid., 130.
25. Sallis, *Being and Logos*, 407.
26. Mary Margaret McCabe describes images as "cognitively incomplete". "Myth, Allegory, and Argument in Plato," *Apeiron* 25.4 (1992): 47–67, here 61.

of relative images. It therefore follows that, while we must aim to understand the image, the act that attempts to grasp the image must be "broken into" from above by the reality that gives it its intelligibility. The ascent of thought here can come to completion as an ascent *only by being interrupted* by a descent from above. To put it another way, in an ordinary analogy of proportion, understood as a comparison between two proportions, the two items being compared are set up as two separate but parallel items bearing a certain formal relation in common. Such a form of analogy allows one to "survey" the meaning of the analogatum from a distance or from the outside. With respect to the absolute, *qua* absolute, there can in fact be no "outside" perspective from which to achieve a grasp, insofar as any "foundation" one would stand on other than the absolute cannot but itself be founded upon, and therefore essentially relative to, something beyond it.

The analogy that Socrates presents to us here is thus not simply a logical structure that traces out the shape of thought in abstraction from the real, but rather a *dramatic* structure.[27] While logic, at least as conventionally understood,[28] proceeds in a linear fashion from one term to the next, the intelligibility of a drama proceeds through a decision or event that both surprises and fulfills by "retroactively" revising the meaning of the precedent unfolding of the plot: we do not fully understand the beginning until we get to the end, though we cannot get to the end but by working toward it from the beginning. Now, such a dramatic view of understanding follows from the twofold nature of the good at its foundation. The good is good in itself, and thus

---

27. We recall once again Gerald Press's proposal that Plato's dialogues present a whole new *kind* of document: they are not treatises, nor are they simply the "miming" of doctrine, but they are *enactments* of ideas, or as Press puts it, of a "vision" of reality. The Platonic dialogue gives rise to a concrete experience, into which the reader is invited. We are suggesting that the analogy of the sun is just such a dramatic enactment (though to be sure it is specifically a *philosophical* drama, which is different from a play in the normal sense). Monique Dixsaut argues, in a similar way, that the good cannot be grasped as an object of science because it is precisely the principle of the difference between knowledge and opinion, which is what every science presupposes at its base. Instead, it can be grasped only *within* the *actualization* of this difference, which means through the real *act* of being intelligent. *Platon et la question de la pensée*, 144–46. Again, we see that the good cannot be known abstractly, but only concretely through the en-acting of a relationship to it, precisely because of its role as principle of intelligibility.

28. The conventional view is no doubt flawed. Hegel's dialectical view of logic, for example, is far richer on this particular point. There is, however, an essential difference between a dialectical and a dramatic view of logic, but the exploration of that difference awaits a future project.

absolutely different from its appearances, and yet it is by the very same token good in its consequences, and thus present in its appearances. In the analogy of the sun, the mind that pursues the good must begin with and *ascend from* a relative image in order to grasp the good's absoluteness and therefore transcendence, but it must simultaneously descend from the good to its image, and thus perceive its relativity. These movements, as distinct as they are, cannot be simply separated from one another without undermining both of them. Instead, they form a complex whole in the flash of the paradoxical "moment" (ἐξαίφνης) that Plato describes at the length in the *Parmenides,* which connects contraries and thus lies at once within and beyond time.[29]

This moment, in which the dramatic structure of the analogy presents itself in its full significance, entails in fact a different relationship between the knower and what he is attempting to grasp.[30] The transformation of this relationship will become most evident with the allegory of the cave, but it is already implicit here and worth remarking upon. To say that there is no "outside" perspective from which to grasp the absolute means that we can grasp it, as it were, only from "inside" of it. In other words, if something is genuinely comprehensive, as the absolute is by definition, one cannot grasp it simply by seeing that it is comprehensive; one can grasp it *only by being actually comprehended by it.* This means—as we will elaborate further in this and the next chapter—that it is impossible to "understand" the good except from within a real, and not merely "imagined," relationship to it. Plato would say that an image *as* a mere image, in this case, does not suffice.

Socrates in fact praises Glaucon at the threshold of this discussion for not being content with other people's opinions about the good (506b). When Socrates first begins to lay out the sun analogy, we are inclined to take it as an extrinsic metaphor, as a commonly known reality that happens to bear a resemblance to something that transcends it. It is natural that we do so, since an analogy points away from itself by nature; it is founded on the distance it has from that which it expresses. However, the moment Socrates characterizes vision as a derivative form of intellection, just as night vision is a deriva-

---

29. *Prm.,* 155e–157b. Incidentally, the discussion in the *Parmenides* is thematically similar to this central part of the *Republic,* inasmuch as both are concerned with how the absolute relates to the relative. The philosophical significance of the dramatic "moment" is connected specifically with this problem.

30. According to Shorey, Plato's dramatic form is not merely a vehicle intended to deliver an idea in a colorful way, but *effects* the ideas themselves. *Unity of Plato's Thought,* 6.

tive form of day vision, we understand that the sun is what it is by virtue of participation in the good. We then realize that Socrates meant the words he used to introduce the sun quite literally: it is the *offspring* of the good, and it is similar to the good precisely because the good is its cause.[31] There is a dramatic insistence when Socrates repeats the comparison: *this* is what I meant (τούτον τοίνυν), and states that the good quite literally *generates* the sun as an analogy to itself (508b). Indeed, if we have any doubt about Socrates' meaning, his claim in the allegory of the cave makes it abundantly clear that the source of light in the visible realm is not the sun but the *good*—even if we would want to say that the good exercises its agency in this regard *by means of* the sun: "But once [the idea of the good is] seen, it must be concluded that this is in fact the cause of all that is right and fair in everything— in the visible it gave birth to light and its sovereign" (517b). As the wording suggests, it is the good that "gives birth" to visible light because it gives birth to the light's proximate cause. At 516c he likewise makes the good the "cause, in a way" (τρόπον τινὰ... αἴτιος) of all the things the prisoners had seen. The good is thus always already present in a real way even to the pure lover of sights, though this presence becomes manifest only through the reversal of the image in its relativization by the absolute.

The Divided Line

The most explicit account of reversal occurs in the image of the divided line. It is essential that we bear in mind the context of this image in order to interpret it correctly. The line differs from the sun and the cave by its abstract character and its discussion of mathematical objects, which are not mentioned or apparently even alluded to by those other images. It is therefore not surprising that the commentators who interpret it in isolation from its context and the basic purpose it is meant to serve express bafflement in finding a way to relate it back to the *Republic* once they have finished. It is worth insisting, again, that the point of the line image is *not* to delineate different kinds of objects of perception and intellection—i.e., physical objects, mathematical objects, etc.—and the powers of soul that correspond to them. Rather, it shares the same purpose as the other two images that enclose it on both sides, namely, *to offer an account of the good.* Socrates enters into his elabora-

---

31. Crombie also calls attention to the literalness Plato intended with this affirmation. *Plato and the Knowledge of Reality,* 178.

tion of the line without skipping a beat after he finishes the sun analogy, and all of this, we must remember, comes as a response to Glaucon's request that he tell them about the good. The distinction between the levels of truth and manifestness, which is what Socrates states the line presents (511e), is therefore undertaken for the sake of showing forth the significance of the good. In other words, the difference between the various segments of the line ought to reveal something about the nature of the good if this analogy is to warrant the place Plato gives it in the discussion.

Keeping this purpose in mind allows us to avoid a lot of unnecessary confusion. We are thus prompted to consider the segments of the line principally as designating the various modes of relation that hold between the soul and reality, modes that are given their ultimate measure in the good, as we saw in the previous chapter. The line presents these modes in terms of that aspect of things upon which the soul depends in its relating to reality, a dependence that is always for Plato simultaneously moral and epistemological. It is significant that the greater part of the image is taken up with elaborating the different states of hypotheses—that upon which the mind stands, as it were, in its reasoning—in the third and fourth sections of the line, a difference that exists only by virtue of what he calls here the "unhypothetical first principle." We may thus read the line as a response to the question, How does our grasp of the good affect our grasp of everything else? This is, indeed, the very issue Socrates raises when he first begins to speak about the good (505a). Those who ignore its context tend to fixate on the nature of geometry and other branches of mathematics, and then wonder what the good has to do with math and the kinds of deductive reasoning it implies.[32] If we read the line analogy primarily in terms of this question, we will be more inclined to understand that Socrates presents these areas of thought as an illus-

32. See Sayre, *Plato's Literary Garden,* 166: "Although it is commonly assumed that Plato intended the good and the nonhypothetical *archē* to be identical, however, it is not at all clear how the Form of the good could serve as the basis—nonhypothetical or otherwise—of any form of logical inference." Ferber presents the opposite view. *Platos Idee des Guten,* 97–98. J. Robinson, in "A Change in Plato's Conception of the Good," argues that Plato came to abandon the epistemology presented in the *Republic* because he could not manage to "deduce" the forms from the idea of the good (Murphy makes a similar observation: *Interpretation of Plato's* Republic, 181), but Robinson explicitly takes for granted a modern notion of formal deduction that is simply foreign to Plato (see p. 233) and does not consider any other mode of intellectual movement. The reasons for rejecting what is otherwise clearly implied in the text would be answered if it were shown what relationship obtains between goodness and intelligibility, which was the subject of chapter 2 of our book.

trative *example* of a way the mind relates to its object and not primarily to articulate the nature of mathematical objects.[33]

Approaching the image in its context provides illumination of the other images in this central part of the *Republic;* the line interprets in further detail the relation between the visible and the intelligible realms presented in the sun analogy and prepares for the dramatic reversal depicted in the allegory of the cave. Several aspects of the line analogy are significant in this regard.

1. The line spells out in greater detail than did the sun analogy the relationship between the lower (visible) and the higher (intelligible) realms. Let us note three details in particular.

a) Plato reveals in a fairly direct manner a causal relationship between the intelligible and the visible.[34] There is an identical proportion between the visible and the intelligible sections, and a subsequent subdivision within each of these. The resulting proportions clearly suggest comparison. The subdivision of the visible realm is between physical things—whether natural or artificial—and their shadows or reflections. A reflection is, of course, caused by the object of which it *is* the reflection; the whole of its reality, the whole of its perceptible content, comes to it from something that exists "at another level." We could thus call the reflection a lower-order manifestation of a particular reality.[35] Now, the visible realm as a whole exists in the same propor-

33. Of course, Plato's discussion illuminates interesting things about the nature of mathematical objects in comparison to philosophical objects, things that anticipate Hegel's observations that—despite what Cartesian rationalists may think—mathematics lacks the *rational necessity* of philosophy. (See Hegel, *Phenomenology of Spirit,* translated by A. V. Miller [Oxford: Oxford University Press, 1977], 25–26.) But Socrates brings in the example of mathematical objects only after presenting the essential point he wished to make, and does so because of Glaucon's initial comprehension. It is significant that Plato appends a phrase such as "and the like" whenever he refers to mathematical objects or mathematicians (510c, 511b, 511d) and refers to this same hypothetical mode of thinking as belonging to the arts more generally (511c). See Raven, *Plato's Thought in the Making,* 156–59; Dorter, *Transformation of Plato's* Republic, 152. Utermöhlen points out that mathematicals can be known in other ways than this hypothetical mode, which underscores the fact that what is at issue here is not a type of object but a mode of knowing. *Die Bedeutung der Ideenlehre,* 55ff. Gallop, in "Image and Reality in Plato's *Republic,*" 121–23, argues that Plato presents forms on both the third and fourth segments of the line and distinguishes between the two in terms of modes of approach.

34. Cf. Desjardins, *Plato and the Good,* 65. David Hitchcock affirms a link between likeness and causal dependency. "The Good in Plato's *Republic,*" 74. Utermöhlen describes the segments as representing objects related as "Ur und Abbilden," *Die Bedeutung der Ideenlehre,* 35.

35. It is in this respect that Findlay calls sensibles "parasitic upon" the forms. See his essay

tion to the intelligible as the reflections do to physical objects. Plato must thereby mean to indicate that the visible is likewise derivative of that which stands above it. A *drawn* square is thus a reflection of "square itself," he says explicitly at 510e, just as a mirror image of this drawn square is a reflection of the physical object. We can infer that the physically drawn square is likewise "caused" by square itself, in the sense that the whole of the intelligible content it possesses comes to it from the form it expresses.[36] Plato does *not*, on the other hand, make this causality explicit in the relationship between the subdivided segments of the intelligible portion of the line, even though these segments stand in the same mathematical proportion as do the others. The relationship between these highest levels is to be sure a much more subtle one; we recall that Plato does not elaborate the difference that constitutes them anywhere else in his written work. What could he mean to say by placing it in the same proportion as the other clearly causal relations? Do we have any reason to think that the fourth section *causes* the third? Indeed, we do, if we understand it properly. As we will explain (in section 'c' below), the difference between these sections amounts to a difference between forms known in themselves and forms known not in themselves but in their implications (once again a reflection of the twofold nature of the good). It is not difficult to understand the *intrinsic* meaning of a thing as the ground for, and thus the cause of, its significant implications. This interpretation justifies the proportions Plato establishes between the various sections of the line, and also justifies his speaking of them as varying degrees of *truth* that increase as one travels up the line.

b) Once we view the sections of the line as standing in a "cause-effect" relation to one another, we can better understand the point made in the previous chapter that the division of sections on the line does not simply represent different sets of objects that can be juxtaposed to one another within the same order. Instead, the sections represent varying derivative manifestations of one and the same "thing."[37] It is, after all, one and the same line

---

"Towards a Neo-Neo-Platonism," in *Ascent to the Absolute: Metaphysical Papers and Lectures* (New York: Allen and Unwin, 1970), 251. Sallis describes the "varying degrees of adequacy" in the manifestation of a thing, which constitutes the continuity of the line. See *Being and Logos*, 419–20.

36. We need to read "cause," of course, in the Greek sense of "that which accounts for or is responsible for" rather than in the mechanical sense of modern physics.

37. See Jackson, "On Plato's *Republic* VI," 133. A more detailed investigation would be required to show precisely *how* the effect is the "same" as the cause, though it is this "same" as mani-

that is divided: consider how different the effect of the image would have been had Plato described four different groups of objects.[38] Moreover, it is not a horizontal line, which places different objects next to one another, but is rather—as the movement up and down illustrates (cf. 511a–b)—a *vertical line*, wherein each segment designates the same line at a higher or lower "stage." We recognize an ontological dependence of each segment on the one above. Physical things and reflections of those things cannot be juxtaposed to one another as two things of the same order, because the dependence is nonreciprocal.[39] We can remove a reflection without affecting the physical thing at all, but we cannot remove the physical thing without eliminating the reflection. Similarly, the physical thing would not exist if its intelligible form did not exist, and so forth. Indeed, if it were not for the existence, ultimately, of the form in itself, there would not be shadows or reflections. In this sense, though the objects in the second segment are the proximate cause of those in the first, the objects in the highest segment are the more basic cause. Each thing, then, is *nothing other than* the one reality, but is this reality manifest in a particular (and relatively limited) mode to a particular (and relatively limited) mode of receptivity on the part of the perceiving soul. Here, then, we have a model for the way in which the good is the cause of the existence, truth, and essence of all things, which Plato asserted at the outset but did not elaborate in any detail. If it is the case that things receive from above the significant content of what they express in a manner specific to their own order, we can understand the basis for the affirmation that all things exist as modes of goodness in a relatively limited way, such that the whole of their intelligible content is ultimately accounted for by the good.[40]

---

fest within a different order. But to carry it out would take more space than is warranted in the present discussion. We take it to be, in any event, a common principle in classical metaphysics.

38. Cross and Woozely make a similar point. *Plato's Republic*, 258. Cf. R. Desjardins's proposal (echoing Klein and Howland) that the segments of the line are parts of a single whole, *Plato and the Good*, 69n13. Her interpretation confirms our reading of the relationships of appearance to reality offered in the previous chapter.

39. According to Eric Perl, "Since the form is the universal determination by which the instances are such, the instances can do nothing for the form, while the form does everything for the instance," "The Presence of the Paradigm," 352. This notion of nonreciprocal dependence will have to be revised once we recognize the reversal occasioned by the good, but that does not affect the present point.

40. In his analysis of the *Philebus*, "The Doctrine of the Good in the *Philebus*," *Apeiron* 11 (1977): 27–57, John McGinley argues that, for Plato, goodness is what makes a cause a cause (34–35). If everything exists by virtue of some cause, and the good is the cause of causality, then

c) The main aspect of the relation between the various sections that interests Plato, if length of exposition is any indication, is the difference between the third and fourth sections, between διάνοια and νόησις. This distinction is the most significant because it is precisely here that we see most clearly what the good has to do with our understanding of the world. This is, as we have been insisting, the very point for the elaboration of the image. The heart of the difference between the two is the nature of the soul's dependence on its objects, specifically, on the forms and their sensible images, and how this dependence is transformed in relation to the good. In the third segment, the soul takes as first *things that are not first by nature* (i.e., it absolutizes what is relative), and proceeds from these to certain conclusions (511a). This segment is unusual in relation to Plato's typical distinction between the intelligible and the sensible. Plato admits that the objects at this level are intelligible in themselves (καί τοι νοητῶν ὄντων), and that reason grasps them without the senses (διανοίᾳ ... ἀλλὰ μὴ αἰσθήσιν). Such a description fits the forms as he presents them elsewhere in his dialogues. However, in this particular case, he insists in rather strong language that the soul at this level is without intelligence (νοῦν οὐκ ἴσχειν). To have intelligence requires a kind of freedom from hypotheses, not in the sense that they are not used, but in the sense that they are immediately relativized in relation to what is genuinely absolute, what Plato calls the "unhypothetical first principle of everything" (511b). It is possible to be free from hypotheses in this sense only by inquiring into their foundations, which in turn is possible only in the determined view of what is ultimate.

We ought to note the paradox in this characterization of the difference. When the soul treats the forms themselves as absolutes, taking them for granted as obvious to everyone (ὡς παντὶ φανερῶν) without giving a justification (οὐδένα λόγον) (510c), the hypotheses do not have an absolute character but stand below true knowledge as things less real, true, and manifest. By contrast, when the soul relativizes them in relation to the absolute, it is precisely then that they become absolute in their own way, qualifying as perfectly real objects of knowledge. One could say that they become absolute only when they do not claim an absolute character for themselves—this point will be important when we discuss Socrates in the next chapter.

all things are due to the good. According to our own analysis of the *Republic* in the previous chapter, the good is what accounts for the "in-itself" reality of things and their manifestation.

Now, the nature of the difference between the third and fourth segments also stands out when we look at them in relation to the mind's movement. In the third segment, the soul treats its objects as starting points for a conclusion, while in the fourth segment it is the intelligible forms that are the goal of reasoning. In other words, the third segment contains forms whose significance lies in the conclusions they imply, while in the fourth the forms themselves are significant. Using our customary distinction, we could say that the third segment takes intelligible objects as significant for their consequences (relatively significant), while the fourth takes them as significant in themselves (absolutely significant). Along similar lines, we might consider Wieland's observation that an analogy stands out between sections two and four, and thus also between one and three, insofar as one and three represent objects grasped in terms of a fixed, determinate predicate, whereas sections two and four represent the "objects" that underlie these predicates.[41] Using Hegel's language, Wieland suggests that one and three represent a more abstract modality of their order (i.e., section one is an abstract mode of visibility, while section three is an abstract mode of intelligibility). To make the same point, we could employ the distinction Plato presents in *Letter VII* between the knowledge of how a thing is qualified, that is, what could be said about it (τὸ ποῖόν τι), and knowledge of the thing itself (τὸ τί).[42] Wieland does not notice, incidentally, that the parallel he draws between the second and fourth segments and the first and third could be drawn between the intelligible realm as a whole and the visible as a whole, since these share the same proportionality. Thus, the visible form would be a more abstract mode of the intelligible, since it presents a single profile, as it were, of the ground of all the profiles. This interpretation harmonizes well with the relation between being and appearance as Plato presents it in book V. In sum, the most perfect instance of the thing itself, beyond all relative predication or visible manifestation, is the form in itself, which is the form understood as not relative to anything at all except to that which is absolute *simpliciter*. If we begin with the various forms as our first principle, we do not understand them in relation to themselves but in relation to their implications. But if we begin with the forms as relative to the good, we are "freed" from hypotheses. Paradoxically, we grasp the forms by themselves only when we grasp them in relation to the good.

---

41. Wieland, *Formen des Wissens*, 218.   42. *Letter VII*, 343b–c.

2. It is important to note that while the divided line was elaborated in continuity with the sun analogy as a means of presenting the significance of the good, the good itself does not appear anywhere on the line. The highest level designates the forms as objects of true knowledge; they become such when the soul rises *above* them, taken as hypotheses, to the unhypothetical first principle, and then subsequently returns *down* to them (511a–b). What can be higher than the highest section? Only a "point" that is not itself a function of the line at all, that does not represent simply a further extension of the line. In other words, the good, as first principle, *transcends the line altogether*.[43] It is the ἀρχὴ τοῦ παντός (511b), the first principle of the figure as a whole, and in this respect is wholly outside the line, representing an altogether different order. It is precisely in reference to this transcendent point that the line is formed according to its designated structure. If there were no point outside the line, we would have no distinction between the third and fourth sections, because we would be able to move only from hypothesis to hypothesis, with nothing to confirm them. We might consider this movement as representing the purely *formal* scope of thought, which can display perfect consistency but can never by itself reach truth. Something "more" than conceptual connections and implications is necessary for an understanding of the real in itself. The good's transcendence in relation to the line stands out most sharply if we recall that the line displays the complex structure of reality in relation to the powers of the soul. As Socrates puts it at the end of the illustration, the levels of the line designate, on the one hand, varying levels of being and truth, and on the other hand, the varying degrees of clarity or manifestness, corresponding to particular passions occurring in the soul (511d–e). But Plato has said with all desired clarity in the sun analogy that the good is neither a power of the soul nor the object perceived (except as mediated by its effect), but transcends them both so as to make them possible; here, too, the unhypothetical first principle is what makes the divisions on the line possible by transcending it altogether.

3. Finally, it is precisely the transcendence of the good that occasions the mind's reversal in its apprehension of reality. There are, once again, three aspects to note in this.

---

43. Annas also notes that the good does not seem to fit on the line at all. *Introduction*, 250–51. For her, this is one among many of the "oddities" of Plato's image that has no solid explanation. Cf. Rosen, *Nihilism*, 158.

a) First, there is the reversal itself. For every other part of the line, greater understanding is achieved by going *up*: from reflections we move up to physical things, and these are taken as images for conclusions concerning objects grasped by reason alone. It is only the highest section that is constituted by a dual movement: first, an ascent *from* hypotheses to the first principle, and then a return to the very same hypotheses that depend on it (πάλιν αὖ ἐχόμενος τῶν ἐκείνης ἐχομένων) by means of a concluding *descent* (καταβαίνη).[44]

b) Second, it is interesting that the unhypothetical first principle *is not* itself a resting place for the mind. Plato does not characterize it as the *end* of the mind's movement. Instead, it is that by means of which the mind reaches an end by understanding the forms through themselves and by themselves: "Making no use of anything sensed in any way, but using forms themselves, going through forms to forms, it ends in forms too" (511c). Although he says elsewhere that the mind has to understand the good in itself in order to understand anything else, the absoluteness of the good is here shown to be immediately relative to our understanding of other things. There are certainly grounds to infer that, if the good became a straightforward object for the mind like the other forms, it would belong, as it were, to the fourth segment of the line. In other words, it would no longer be genuinely absolute but would be another relative form—which would then of course require something *beyond* itself as an absolute ground. Thus, we could say that it can be known *as* absolute not simply in itself in opposition to other things, but only as simultaneously distinct from and related to all other things. To put it another way, to reach the good as absolute requires *both* an ascent to it and a descent from it. Knowing the good would thus appear to be the same as transforming one's relationship to everything else one knows, and its absoluteness becomes manifest in the fact that it transforms this relationship.

c) Finally, we point out that there is a parallel between the effect of this reversal and that which we saw in the sun analogy. There, the sun changed from a mere metaphor to the real offspring of the good once we viewed the sun from the perspective of the good *as opposed to* viewing the good from the perspective of the sun. We could say that this is a transformation from a merely conceptual similarity to a real or ontological unity; or, using Pla-

---

44. Some texts omit the "αὖ." We note that the verb καταβαίνω is the same used at the very beginning of the dialogue, and also the same in the philosopher's return to the cave (519a).

to's language, we could say that the change is from a hypothesis as a starting point to one in which the hypothetical character has been "destroyed" or
eliminated, since it has been viewed in relation to that which is not hypothesized. As transformed, it is viewed in terms of its basis in reality. Here we see
how the divided line serves to interpret an important aspect of the sun analogy.

The Cave

The line's reversal also puts us in place to appreciate the allegory of the
cave. As the last of the three images, the cave represents a dramatic culmination of this central section, and the philosopher's return to the cave thus
forms the conclusion of the whole. It is the final answer that Socrates gives
to Glaucon's question concerning the good.[45] This last image differs from the
previous two by explicitly depicting an *action* rather than an established state
of affairs, and thus is a step closer to the movement of the actual world.[46] In
this, the sense of drama also becomes palpable. As we shall see, the dramatic swelling that occurs here is not a mere rhetorical ploy but plays an indispensable role in responding to the problem Plato is addressing.

If we set aside for a moment the reversals we have indicated in the two
previous images, we would have to acknowledge that Plato has described the
philosophical life, both in the rest of the *Republic* and in his other dialogues,
as an upward journey, or an ascent to reality. The ascent is also the dominant theme of the allegory of the cave, in which prisoners are set free and
dragged, somewhat forcefully, up and out of the darkness and into the light
of the sun. Following this motion, we expect that this "daylight" vision of reality should be the philosopher's destination, and that the journey should
come to an end at this peak. But it does not:

"Then our job as founders," I said, "is to compel the best natures to go to the study
which we were saying before is the greatest, to see the good and to go up that as-

---

45. Wieland, *Formen des Wissens*, 222. According to Wieland, the cave, in its dramatic action,
represents the climax of the point Plato meant to present with the other two, essentially static,
images (219).

46. In the *Timaeus*, Socrates says "I'd like to go on now and tell you what I've come to feel
about the political structure we've described. My feelings are like those of a man who gazes upon
magnificent looking animals, whether they're animals in a painting or even actually alive but
standing still, and who then finds himself longing to look at them in motion or engaged in some
struggle or conflict that seems to show off their distinctive physical qualities" (*Ti.*, 19b–c).

cent; and, when they have gone up and seen sufficiently, not to permit them what is now permitted." "What's that?" "To remain there," I said, "and not be willing to go down again among those prisoners or share their labors and honors, whether they be slighter or more serious." (519c–d)

When Socrates, at this crucial moment in the dialogue, says that remaining above and beyond the cave and enjoying the forms is deficient, we cannot help but be surprised. True eros has been the driving impulse of the philosopher thus far. If what the erotic soul had sought is the "really real," there would seem to be nothing else, nothing *more* real, to desire beyond the very "things in themselves" that one had loved in images. Though there is resistance at first in the scene Socrates describes, the liberated persons have a good reason for every step of the way along the ascent, and this no doubt becomes evident to them when they reach what seems to be their destination. But the reversal that sends them back into the cave appears to be without reason altogether.[47] One could even say it does a certain violence to the philosophical soul on the rise—which is precisely the gist of Glaucon's initial response: "What?" he interjected. "Are we to do them an injustice, and make them live a worse life when a better is possible for them?" (519d). Indeed, according to Plato, a soul that had reached the highest realm of forms would feel, "with Homer, that he'd much prefer to 'work the earth as a serf to another, one without possessions,' and go through any suffering, rather than share their opinions and live" as those in the cave (516d).[48] Though there has been an explicit descent in the divided line, this comes to an end in the pure intelligibility of the forms, and thus prepares us only distantly for this more radical return to the cave of transient things and shadows.[49] The only other dialogue to mention a "descent" in the philosophical life, the *Phaedrus*,[50] shows

47. Annas remarks that the reversal has always been recognized as problematic. *Introduction,* 269.

48. It is significant that here, at the place in the dialogue where the difference between the philosopher and poet is seemingly most extreme, Plato has Socrates, the philosopher, cite a passage from the poet, Homer.

49. Sayre takes this as evidence that the two images, and thus their two reversals, are unrelated. *Plato's Literary Garden,* 172.

50. Unless we consider the mention of the descent in *Letter VII* (343e) and Aristotle's mention of Plato's discussion of first principles in the *Nich. Eth.,* I.4, which seems to parallel in many ways the presentation in the divided line. Aristotle refers to Plato's raising of the question of moving *from* or *to* first principles, interestingly, specifically before he begins his own discussion of the nature of goodness.

it to be a fall, without any reason behind it, due only to distraction, disorder, or weakness of desire.[51] In the *Republic,* by sharp contrast, Plato suggests that there is a *reason* for going down.[52] The vision of the forms, which were previously the apparent goal, is suddenly transformed into a penultimate stage in the soul's development; the real end or the real good pursued, it turns out, lies even beyond the forms—and this "beyond the forms" turns out to lie, quite surprisingly, back in the cave. What could this mean philosophically?

The reversal in the previous two images was occasioned by the absoluteness of the good. Here, however, it does not appear to be the good that brings about the descent. The image portrays a cave illuminated by a fire, which is in turn an imitation of the sun giving light to the whole outside world. Now, the prisoners are released (by whom?), dragged up past the wall and flame, and taken out into the light. In this image, the good simply stands sovereignly unmoved over all of these events; it seems to have nothing to do with setting the liberation and subsequent obligation of return in motion. We might be able to say that this ultimate light is in a broad sense the cause of the ascent, insofar as it is that for the sake of which the prisoners are released. If there were no sunlight outside of the cave, there would be no point in leaving it. If we ask what specifically causes the descent, however, the answer is disorienting. It is nothing at all inside the cave allegory that causes the philosopher to go down. Rather, it is Socrates and his companions who bring it about, when they decide it is necessary for the good of the whole that they go down. There seems to be a great difference between this and the previous images; one wants to say that the reversals of the first two cases arise from the inner logic of the image itself and are caused by the absoluteness of the good, while here it seems to be a somewhat arbitrary decision imposed from the outside.

But, considered more profoundly, the reversal in the cave image is in fact analogous to the other two. Our thesis is that, as he makes Socrates here

51. *Phdr.,* 248a–b.

52. In his essay, "Der Logik des Rückstiegs," *Philosophisches Jahrbuch* 92 (1985): 316–34, Stefan Schenke offers several possible motives for the return. Though he says that none of them excludes the others, the motive he lends greatest weight in his own interpretation is the one he refers to as the "theological motive," according to which the philosopher imitates the good. Schenke interprets the good here in the light of the god of the *Timaeus,* who is not jealous but seeks to multiply goodness (325–26). Our own approach agrees with Schenke's, but we stress the importance of showing how this interpretation satisfies the dialogue's own methodological conditions.

the cause of the reversal, *Plato means to present Socrates himself as the effective image of the good.* What is the evidence for this proposal? We will lend substance to this claim in more general philosophical terms in the next chapter; here, we note the formal features of the dialogue that point in this direction. In the first place, we saw that the reversal in the divided line requires a point lying entirely outside the line. Here, it is the narrator, Socrates, who stands wholly outside the figure of the cave that he draws with Glaucon and the others, and does so in a far more radical way than the image of the sun, which is after all simply a part of the figure. He calls himself and the others the *founders* (οἰκίσται), which places him in the same relationship to the city in speech as the good is in relation to reality in general.[53] Indeed, Socrates is the *author* of the cave allegory, responsible for the being and essence, and for the intelligible content, of all within. In this respect, Socrates transcends the allegory as a whole in a much more radical way than the image of the sun inside the allegory. He embodies the essence of the good more directly than the sun can.

However, Socrates not only transcends the allegory, he also *breaks into it* "from above" and becomes present within it. The simultaneity of being "above" and "in" is a reflection of the twofold nature of the good. There is an echo here of the katological reversal in the sun image, by which the good "broke into" the analogy and became really present in it. We can see Socrates' presence in the cave allegory in two respects: first of all, he is the one who sends the philosopher back down into the cave, and in this sense directly intervenes in the "plot" of the allegory. As the founder of the image, he enters into it in order, as it were, to direct the action. There is no other image in the Platonic corpus in which the author intrudes in such a direct way; in fact, this rhetorical gesture appears to be unique in ancient literature. But at a more profound level, we see that the paradigm of the philosopher who returns to the cave is none other than Socrates himself. There can be no doubt

53. The *Anonymous Prolegomena to Platonic Philosophy*, translated by L. G. Westerink (Amsterdam: North-Holland Publishing Company, 1962), composed in the sixth century, proposes that the cosmos is like a dialogue, and Plato was imitating the demiurge's creation of the world in developing this particular genre for his philosophy (28). The analogy of author/creator works as well for Socrates, who is the origin, *within* the dialogue, of the cave allegory. Plato seems to be himself quite aware of this analogy, since he draws attention to it in Timeaus's "creation" of his own account of the cosmos. On this, see Catherine Osborne, "Space, Time, Shape, and Direction: Creative Discourse in the *Timeaus*," in Gill and McCabe, *Form and Argument in Late Plato*, 179–211.

that Plato intended this connection. Not only does he portray the philosopher who returned as one who cuts a ridiculous figure before others as he examines the meaning of justice before the courts (517d–e), but he also alludes to the idea that the one who comes to free the others would be killed if those others were able to get their hands on him (517a). Socrates' first word in the dialogue, after all, is "I went down," and the fact that this opening word echoes at precisely this most dramatic moment of the structure of the dialogue can hardly be seen as a coincidence.

This maneuver is striking in that it "explodes" the immanent space of the narrative structure, which is itself a rhetorical image of the springing from the cave, or the transcendence of the relativity of perception. The explosion gives the dialogue an immediate reality that surpasses even the dramatist's art. At 378e–379a, Socrates explicitly contrasts their founding of the city with the activity that occupies the poets. We recall that Plato presents a sophisticated account of the narrator's relation to his story and the dangers and limits of imitation in book III, and in fact has Socrates conclude that "when the sensible man comes in his narrative to some speech or deed of a good man, he will be willing to report it as though he himself were that man and won't be ashamed of such an imitation" (396c). If we view the return to the cave as such a "deed of a good man," we are led to consider Socrates as imitating in his person what he here describes. In other words, he appears as *the* "good man," as one who makes goodness real by living out its implications. A "two-dimensional" image becomes in this moment a flesh-and-blood reality.[54] When we reach the culmination of the images showing forth the good, we have a reversal that reverses the whole phenomenon of providing images of the good. It is only thus that the actual absoluteness of the good shows itself in the brilliant flash of Plato's and Socrates' philosophical genius.

A Good Turn

No matter how much of a surprise it is, the reversal in the cave allegory is in fact no less necessary than the reversal in the previous two images. There is, after all, a specific reason for the decision to send the philosopher down:

54. As Etienne Gilson puts it, "Socrates had no philosophy, he was it," *Being and Some Philosophers* (Toronto: Pontifical Institute of Mediaeval Studies, 1952), 146. Cf. Günter Figal's observation. "Bei Sokrates . . . ist das, was er sagt, immer zurückgebunden an sein philosophisches Leben, an seine Person," *Sokrates* (Munich: C. G. Beck'sche Verlagsbuchhandlung, 1995), 13.

it is for the good of the whole (519e–520a). Or in other words, the good, taken in its most comprehensive sense, demands this decision. In issuing these commands, then, Socrates is speaking for the good, or indeed, *as* the good. We see once again that the twofold nature of the good requires both the ascent and the descent. The philosophers would fall short in remaining above because they would never get beyond their own individual and therefore relative good; they would not be seeking the good in its absolute and most complete sense. The theme of Socrates' discussion of the philosopher's going down in 519d–521b is the relation between private goods and the common good. The common good, which both transcends and includes the private goods, is the cause of both the ascent and the reversal. In this respect, the reversal is not simply imposed from the outside, but in fact fulfills the meaning of the ascent.[55] If it is the case, as we recall from the previous chapter, that the only way to move beyond images is to attain to the goodness of things in an absolute sense, then it is impossible to reach the ultimate goodness of any particular thing except from within a desire for ultimate goodness *tout court*. But this ultimate good is *more than relative,* and so the final expression of the desire for goodness is the "dispossession" of self for the sake of the good of the whole. We may resist the notion that an existential and dramatic event of this sort of sacrifice should have an epistemological function, but if we do, we are in fact resisting a fairly common basic theme in Plato's philosophy; a kind of freedom from immediate pleasures is invariably, for him, a part of clear intellectual vision,[56] and we are simply seeing in this case its full "practical" implications.

But let us consider the relation between public and private interests more closely. We are here returning to a theme introduced in Socrates' initial interchange with Thrasymachus. There, Socrates strives to show the inner incoherence of an absolutized relative good, which is captured in the notion of *pleonexia*. Dwelling on this helps us to avoid some common misinterpretations. There is a regular debate over the question of whether Plato, in the *Re-*

55. Cf. Schenke, "Der Logik des Rückstiegs," 332–35. Schenke shows that the descent must be understood as a *function* of the ascent, and that going down thus turns out to be a logical outcome of the dialectic.

56. The *Phaedo* is the most obvious place to find this. see for example 82d–83c. Being fixed to sense-experience is for Plato not a moral problem but an intellectual one; or perhaps it is best to say the problem is always both at once. We refer back to our discussion of this issue in the previous chapter.

public, is proposing a *eudaimonistic* concept of justice: the dialogue ultimately justifies justice by showing it to be self-serving.[57] The problem with the very question at the heart of this debate is that it presupposes an opposition between the good taken absolutely and the good viewed in a relative sense.[58] But we have seen that the overcoming of this opposition is one of the principles of this dialogue. There *is,* in fact, an opposition between the relative and the absolute, but only *from the perspective* of the relative. The absolute is *not* in turn opposed to the relative (since this would make it in fact relative and no longer absolute). This metaphysical fact is what accounts for the complexity of the dialogue's structure, and why there are always opposed interpretations of it. Moreover, this complexity requires a dramatic resolution, which is precisely what Plato gives it. On the one hand, if there is an absolute difference between the absolute and the relative, it is essential that the common good represent a kind of imposition on the relative seeker of goodness. Glaucon calls it an "injustice" (519d), and Socrates responds that the individual or relative good is *not* what is being aimed at. Nevertheless, it turns out that this renunciation of one's own best good in fact results in a greater fulfillment than one would have otherwise possessed; the ones who take up the task laid, somewhat forcefully, upon them by the good are the really rich (οἱ τῷ ὄντι πλούσιοι), since they possess the "riches required by the happy man, rich in a good and prudent life." In contrast to them, those who pursue their own good fail even that, since doing so gives rise to a disorder that harms both the whole and themselves (521a). In sum, it is crucial that philosophers not want to rule (521b)—because this negation of their individual desire indicates that the whole is not reducible to the part—but then this re-

57. For varying treatments of this problem, see the essays by David Sachs, Raphael Demos, J. D. Mabbot, and Gregory Vlastos in *Ethics, Politics, and Philosophy of Art and Religion,* vol. 2 of *Plato: A Collection of Critical Essays,* edited by Gregory Vlastos (Garden City, N.Y.: Anchor Books, 1971), 35–95.

58. Julia Annas interprets the *Republic* as proposing a completely impersonal, nonrelative notion of goodness, and rightly objects that such a good would no longer have any intelligible relation to an individual's desire. But she sees only one "side" of the good. *Introduction,* 266–67. Terry Penner, too, sees only one "side," but his is the other. As we mentioned in the previous chapter, in his essay, "The Forms, the Form of the Good, and the Desire for the Good," 191–233, Penner offers a lively argument that the good in the *Republic* is always relative, always "good for me" (192–95). They are both (relatively) right. The best view, of course, would affirm both, and see the good as always both relative and absolute—and only relative *because* it is absolute. Timothy Mahoney suggests a solution along these lines. See his essay, "Do Plato's Philosopher-rulers Sacrifice Self-interest to Justice?" 265–82.

nunciation must entail the greatest fulfillment, because an absolute that was not also relative would not in fact be genuinely absolute.[59]

There are, then, three moments required for the dramatic resolution of the absoluteness of the good. There is, first, the positive movement of the ascent driven by desire for what is good; here we have the continuity of an ascent. Second, there is the interruption of the ascent by the appearance of the good in its more than relative character, which means that it cannot fall on the line of ascent but must disrupt this ascent with a discontinuous intrusion, a genuine surprise of expectations and anticipations. And, third, if this irruption is truly of the good, and therefore of that which was in fact the goal of the original striving, then for all of its discontinuity and perhaps even violence, it will necessarily be a fulfillment of the original desire. This is implied in the very logic of desire. Desire seeks what is good absolutely, but it can understand this at first only in relation to itself. As we said before, love loves more than it thinks it loves, whenever it loves. If one stays true to this love, it will necessarily at some point face a reversal, which will come in the form of a demand imposed from what is truly other than the self. There will necessarily be a moment in its ascent when one is presented with something one does not want, precisely because it is *more* than what one wants, and its consent to this more will in turn result in a greater happiness than could originally be conceived. The good that the philosopher relentlessly pursues to the extent that he is a philosopher is a good that belongs to more than himself alone, and it will belong to him only if he makes himself a servant of the whole of which he is an individual part. If he does not, the good he attains will turn out to be merely an image of what he truly wants. It will not be goodness itself.

The "Perfect" Image

The interruption from outside could not have been more directly presented than by Socrates' breaking into the image he had been drawing. We could say that this dramatic event offers a more perfect image of the good

---

59. Rosen misses the paradoxical relationship between absoluteness and relativity in the *Republic*, and thus interprets the "imposition" of justice on the philosopher-kings as a vindication of Glaucon's initial argument, namely, that no one *wants* to be just. See *Plato's* Republic, 282. This conclusion regarding such a central aspect of the *Republic*, to my mind, calls Rosen's general interpretation into question in a fundamental way.

than we could have anticipated. And yet this is precisely what the dialogue requires. As we suggested at the beginning of this chapter, the inner tension that constitutes an image results from the fact that it *is* not what it expresses or professes to be. We could specify this tension further by saying that a disjunction exists in the image between form and content: the content of the image is the reality that is present *through* it while remaining *other than* it, and this abiding otherness entails a discrepancy between the expression and the way it is expressed, its mode of manifestation. In this moment of the *Republic*, however, wherein Socrates breaks open the cave allegory and descends into it, form and content converge in an extraordinary manner, with almost endless implications. Socrates *says* that the philosopher must go down, but he in fact *is the very philosopher who goes down*. Socrates is known as one whose words and deeds "match up."[60] As we noted in the introduction, many modern readers of Plato emphasize the unity of form and content in his dialogues. But they do not often point to the connection between this philosophical "style" and the figure of Socrates himself, who embodied philosophy for Plato. Once we recognize the significance of the historical Socrates for the cave allegory he creates, the expression and mode of expression, the content and the form, become in a certain respect identical. And if this "going down" is a result of the absoluteness of the good, then the philosopher who knowingly goes down (the convergence of form and content), becomes an immediate presentation of goodness itself. Socrates simultaneously explains and enacts a meaning; he is the embodiment of the truth he communicates.[61] In this respect, then, he represents a real image of the good.[62] As such, he is an image of an altogether different order from the other three: the sun, the line, and the cave. But that is just what we should expect given the very singularity of the demand for an image of the good. The image Plato most intends to offer in his presentation of these is an image that transcends the other images. The absoluteness of the good here bursts forth in a way that overturns the discussion and by the very same gesture fulfills it.

The fulfillment extends even further than we have been suggesting. If we recall the structure of the first two images, the sun and the line, we see

60. *La.,* 188e.

61. See Desjardins, *Plato and the Good,* 164–65.

62. With reference to 500c, Mitch Miller suggests that "keeping company with the good" makes the philosopher—and specifically here, Socrates—analogous to it. "Platonic Provocations," 188.

that they start with a relative perspective that is presented as a hypothesis. In order for the image to manifest itself in its truth, it must be reversed and viewed in the light of the absoluteness of the good. When it is, its hypothetical character is "destroyed," and it makes manifest its ontological grounding. In the dramatic moment of the return to the cave, we have Socrates describing what a philosopher ought to do. In other words, he is speaking in the formal terms of a general assertion. But as a general assertion, it remains hypothetical and in need of real confirmation, in much the same way, for example, as an axiom in geometry would: i.e., we are here in the third section of the divided line. To reach the fourth, the good must enter the picture. While Socrates speaks of the duties of a philosopher, he also carries out these duties in reality. He confirms, in his person, the hypothesis he articulates. In this respect, compared to the guardians he is training in his hypothetical city-in-speech, he is the *unhypothetical philosopher,* the unconditional image of the good. This interpretation of Socrates' relation to the cave allegory therefore confirms the methodology presented in the divided line in an unsuspected way.[63]

Not only does it carry through the methodology of these central books, but it responds to the challenge in book II that sets the whole *Republic* in motion in the first place. When Glaucon takes up Thrasymachus's original argument against justice in order to give it the strongest possible articulation and thus to provoke the best possible defense, he ends with a challenge to Socrates: in order to show that justice has an intrinsic and not merely extrinsic goodness and therefore reality, Socrates would have to present a man who is willing to be stripped of all the honors of justice and be left with nothing but the thing itself. In spite of the reality of his justice, he must be regarded by the many as unjust and executed for it. He must in fact prefer to be executed rather than be rewarded and praised for seeming but not being just. It is, of course, transparent that Plato is fingering the historical Socrates here, who claims in the *Apology* (see 30c–e) to be happier in his condemna-

---

63. Dorter interprets the structure of the *Republic* in terms of the divided line but has difficulty distinguishing *dianoia* and *noesis,* because, while they both refer to intelligibles, what characterizes the highest level—*noesis*—depends on seeing the good in itself rather than hypothetically in an image. But, according to Dorter, the *Republic* provides only an indirect indication of the good. See his essay "The Divided Line and the Structure of Plato's *Republic,*" 16–17. Our interpretation removes this difficulty by showing that the *Republic* intends to present Socrates as the real image of the good.

tion than the men who condemned him, the victors in that particular contest for public opinion. Unless we interpret this central reversal of the *Republic* in the manner proposed, Glaucon's challenge would go unanswered in the
dialogue, except in the most general of terms.[64]

Moreover, we recall that Adeimantus had added a challenge to his brother's. The whole of ancient literature, poetry and prose, he claims, "beginning
with the heroes at the beginning (those who left speeches) up to the human
beings at present" (366e), has justified justice only in terms of its good consequences. As we proposed in the previous chapter, the fact to which Adeimantus points is not true simply *de facto* but also *de jure:* it is precisely the relative goodness of a thing that can be defined and described with mere words.
An argument for the intrinsic goodness of something must necessarily be
more than a mere argument: it must be an argument that springs from the
wholeness of a *life*. The wording of Adeimantus's challenge is crucial, insofar
as it associates discourse with relative goodness and insists on more immediate evidence for intrinsic goodness: "Now, don't only show us by argument
(τῷ λόγῳ) but show what each in itself does to the man who has it" (367b).
We have here an allusion to the more intimate form of knowledge we have
argued lies at the heart of the epistemology of the *Republic* and distinguishes it from Plato's other dialogues. There is no better way to show the effect
of something that inheres in the soul than to live out its effect; indeed, anything else can be feigned. It is in this sense that Plato points to philosophy
as supplanting poetry as the foundation of social order: not in the first place
because he takes philosophy to be a superior mode of discourse (an affirmation that will need to be significantly qualified, as we shall see in the coda),
but because philosophy is in fact a *life* if it is philosophy at all, while poetry
need never be more than words.[65]

---

64. To be sure, book IX makes the argument, to Glaucon's satisfaction, that the just man
is the happiest of all, but no mention is made of the original thought-experiment he laid out in
book II and its apparently dire implications. Drew Hyland claims that Socrates never takes up
Glaucon's challenge. But Hyland does not look *through* the *Republic* to the historical figure of Socrates to whom the dialogue explicitly points. See his *Finitude and Transcendence,* 38.

65. As Eva Brann has shown, at the center of the *Republic* there is more than a *logon,* there is
an *ergon,* a *deed.* "The Music of the *Republic*," 7; cf. Sallis, Being and Logos, 401.

The Dramatic Structure of Knowledge

The foregoing interpretation of the three central images of the *Republic* reveals the complexity of the act that "grasps" the absolute. If the divided line represents the intentional relationship between the soul and reality, the good's not lying on this line implies that it is not the simple object of an intentional act.[66] But this is just what allows it to "break through" the cave, i.e., to overturn the strictly immanentist epistemology that can never dissociate itself from relativism. An intentional perception is appropriated by the perceiver, and thus will necessarily be measured in some respect by the mode of reception. Even after Socrates elaborates the cave allegory, Glaucon responds that he understands "in the way that I am able" (517c). As the absolute—or, better, as absoluteness itself, since it is the good that supplies everything else that is real with that thing's own absolute quality, its truth—the good is not appropriated by the receiver *except by first expropriating him;* the relativity of the good follows from its absoluteness. The mode of reception is in this case first measured by that which is received before it is in turn measured by the recipient, which is simply another way of expressing the fact that the continuity of fulfillment comes only with the discontinuity of ecstasis. In the wake of this fundamental act of intellectual expropriation, all other things stand out before one in their being and truth.

There are necessarily several moments to the single act of "grasping" the good—which is in fact more a "being grasped" than a "grasping." It is this complexity that makes it a "supra-" intentional object. It becomes immediately manifest only through the articulation of an ordered sequence—desire, expropriation, and fulfillment—a unified sequence we could describe as a plot, with a beginning, middle, and end as Aristotle prescribed.[67] Indeed, for Aristotle, the very best plots possess a reversal that brings about a resolution. The dramatic character of philosophical thinking reveals the need to read the central section of the *Republic* in relation to the general structure of the dialogue, and thus to avoid isolating the pieces as so many unsolvable intellectual puzzles. Perhaps this explains the frustration Richard Robinson experiences in

---

66. See Ferber's discussion of this point cited earlier (Platos *Idee des Guten,* 277–78). Cf. Francisco Gonzalez's interpretation of knowledge of the good as identical to reflexive, and thus nonobjectifiable self-knowledge, in "Self-knowledge, Practical Knowledge, and Insight," 155–87, and in his discussion of the *Laches* and the *Charmides* in *Dialectic and Dialogue,* 19–61.

67. Aristotle, *Poetics* 1450b26.

his well-known analysis of the central part of the dialogue. Plato promises here, he says, a kind of knowledge that surpasses the hypothetical method of other dialogues, but fails insofar as he is unable to provide a new methodology adequate to this end.[68] Robinson focuses on the divided line, which he interprets in a primarily mathematical sense, and does not see the "methodology" that not only embraces the whole of the *Republic* but transcends it in the direction of the historical Socrates. In this case, as Plato would no doubt insist, the comprehensive view must provide the measure for the particular aspect, and not the other way around. The method adequate to the good cannot be derived simply from the divided line alone,[69] but would *have* to be as existential as it is intelligible, to the extent that the good itself is comprehensive of both realms. Gabriel Marcel once spoke of the difficulty in detecting the melody in Debussy's compositions, until he realized that they were *all* melody. The most comprehensive method is always the hardest to see.

Several aspects of the dramatic knowledge of goodness are worth remarking upon in conclusion. First, we note that the very comprehensiveness of the good is what makes the act of apprehending it simultaneously immanent and transcendent. If it were merely immanent, we would not be able to get beyond a relative perspective. On the other hand, if it were "merely" transcendent (and therefore falsely transcendent), it would be imposed simply from the outside as an epistemological violence, with no relation whatsoever to the soul's power to know or to the things that form its objects of intelligibility; we would have either a continuity without discontinuity or a discontinuity without continuity. But it is not absoluteness as such that entails violence. As we saw in chapter 1, violence arises from the absolutization of what is in fact relative, and this results the moment the absolute as such is not taken as the ultimate aim. For Plato, by contrast, the good is so absolute that it is also relative. This means that the capacity for the good never has to be introduced from the outside but is always already present in every soul from the beginning (518c–e).[70] At the same time, this capacity needs to be

68. See chapter 10 of R. Robinson's *Plato's Earlier Dialectic*. In a section called "Translation of passages on method in the 'Republic,'" Robinson provides only the two passages devoted to the divided line (509d–511e, and 533b–535a), as if it is only here that method is an issue. Such a restricted starting point is bound to lead to the failure Robinson attributes in conclusion to Plato.

69. Instead, the line ought to be read in the light of the more comprehensive approach to the good, as we have been arguing in this chapter.

70. Note, the "a priori" presence of what Plato here refers to as the virtue of exercising

realized by something that lies beyond the soul's inner capacity. It cannot occur simply as a function of one's own aspiration. If it could, we would never
get beyond a relative perspective. We must understand that, in Socrates' image of the cave, the prisoners cannot release themselves. This impossibility
is not just an implication of the image, but makes good philosophical sense.
The prisoners cannot possibly know "from within" that what they see is not
most real, but must be solicited to this insight "from without"; the movement beyond the private measure (which our first chapter suggested is a
fundamental epistemological issue for Plato) requires the breaking in from
beyond that measure, the reversal that allows things to show their truth. The
distance between the self and other must therefore be crossed first by the
other. For this reason education, for Plato, consists of both desire and compulsion; only both at once can bring the soul to see the very thing that it desires more than it can possibly realize.

Second, the very way Plato brings forth the good reveals it to be a unique
sort of knowledge, which we would do best by characterizing as simultaneously *contemplative* and *active*.[71] We noted in the last chapter that certain recent interpretations of the *Republic* have argued powerfully that knowledge
of the good is essentially a practical sort of knowledge.[72] Such an interpreta-

---

prudence (which is the soul's relation to the good) is due precisely to the good's being more divine than other things. In other words, it is the transcendence of the good that makes it incipi-
ently present everywhere.

71. Plato explains in the *Statesman* 258eff. that the most complete knowledge is both theoretical and practical. Julia Annas claims that the theoretical and practical versions of the philosopher are incompatible, that Plato gratuitously introduced the contemplative view here after giving justification in the *Republic* only for the practical understanding, and that he thus ends up
undermining his argument. See her *Introduction*, 260ff. But Annas separates these two aspects,
as we observed, rather than seeing the intrinsic relation between them that follows once we understand the comprehensiveness of the good at which the intellectual soul aims. In this respect,
though the contemplative and practical dimensions are radically different from one another, the
practical is *essential* to the contemplative: "Despite the attraction which Plato and Aristotle give
to the life of pure contemplation, it was always meant ideally to culminate in action; and action
is what justifies it," Jaeger, *Paideia*, vol. 2, 300. But while Plato and Aristotle might agree on the
necessity of action, for Plato it follows from the ultimacy of the good (cf. A. J. Festugière, *Contemplation et vie contemplative selon Platon* [Paris: Vrin, 1967], 454, who claims that, for Plato,
contemplation "is fulfilled and perfected in action"), while Aristotle views it as a sort of compromise with what is in fact the highest form of life, namely, the life of contemplation. Friedländer
is therefore right to say that Plato is "anything but a 'theoretical man' in Aristotle's sense". *Plato:
An Introduction*, 104.

72. See Wieland, *Formen des Wissens*, 222, and Kersting, *Platons "Staat,"* 239. Borrowing

tion could account for the inability to define it in a straightforward manner, and it makes sense that goodness would properly govern the practical rather than the conceptual realm. As Wieland has suggested, the fact that the discussion of the good concludes with the descent into the cave—which is, after all, a return to the active life of human affairs—shows that the ultimate form of knowing the good is a *doing* of it. This interpretation, however, is quite literally "one-sided," insofar as it restricts knowledge of the good to the inside of the cave: it affirms the descent only by eliminating the ascent. Not only does Socrates speak at several key points of an intellectual apprehension of the good, he also makes it the climax of the philosopher's ascent, which is undeniably more "theoretical" than "practical." Instead of saying that knowledge of the good is practical *rather than* theoretical, we would characterize it most adequately by saying that it is *necessarily both*. It requires both words and deeds. Only thus would we do justice to its true nature, since the absoluteness of the good makes it simultaneously something in itself (and thus to be grasped—theoretically—with the purest of thought) and always relative to others (and therefore to be grasped—practically—through its "communion with actions and bodies," 476a). Socrates makes it clear that the good is present in the cave (of action) but that this becomes manifest only as a result of one's (contemplative) grasping of the good in itself (517b–c). In short, the good, in its excessive transcendence, pours over (without eliminating) the distinction between the theoretical and the practical, and thus can be known only in the reciprocal illumination of words and deeds.[73]

Finally, the simultaneity of the immanent and the transcendent, the practical and the theoretical, offers a reason for the persistence of ambiguity regarding knowledge of the good: Do we ever have explicit, definitive knowl-

---

from Wieland, Kersting contrasts theoretical knowledge of an object *(Was-wissen)* with practical "know-how" *(Wie-wissen)*, and claims that only the latter characterizes knowing the good.

73. Jacob Howland expresses this point very well in *The Odyssey of Philosophy*. According to Howland, eros is "sufficiently complex and comprehensive to attempt to encompass both the outer world and the cave," and it is so because the good, or as he puts it, the Whole to which it aspires, "consists of originals *and* images" (145). The key to understanding the paradox of the philosopher's destination being both inside and outside of the cave is, as Howland sees, the comprehensiveness of goodness. Mahoney makes a similar argument: "The preeminent aim of the ideal human life is to satisfy reason's desire for the actualization of the good of everything and anything," a desire he refers to as "the desire for the unrestricted good". See "Do Plato's Philosopher-rulers Sacrifice Self-interest to Justice?" 280. It is important to see that reason thus desires more than reason alone can achieve, but requires the movement into the practical sphere in order to achieve its specifically intellectual ends.

edge of this supreme idea, or don't we? The ambiguity here explains the traditions of both skeptical and dogmatic readings of Plato. Our analysis to this point implies a need to frustrate both traditions by refusing the dichotomy each presupposes: that either we have immediate access to the nature of the good in itself or we do not and are left with the onion skin of layers of mediation. But the foregoing suggests that the good can in fact become immediately present, manifest in its absoluteness, though only through the mediation of a real image. This paradox will eventually allow us to see that the task of coming to know the good can never reach a conclusive end, while at the same time rejecting the aimless straying of uncertainty.[74] But to understand how this is possible requires that we understand exactly how an image can be become wholly transparent to the reality to which it points. This is the theme of our next chapter.

74. Ferber also suggests that the good is somehow simultaneously known and unknowable. *Platos Idee des Guten,* 149.

CHAPTER FOUR

ON BEING INVISIBLE

*Or, How an Exclusive Love of the Good Makes
the Philosopher Transparent to It*

An Altogether Different Level

"So I turned around, and Socrates was nowhere to be seen."[1] Plato often refers to the realm of being, in contrast to the realm of becoming, as invisible, beyond manifestation to the physical senses.[2] At the same time, however, Plato will affirm that the higher realm of being is the one that is the brightest or most visible. The end of book V of the *Republic* contrasts being to becoming as the invisible to the visible (see 476a–b). But then the three analogies of books VI and VII all present the intelligible realm as superior to the sensible realm in clarity, manifestation, and brightness (508d; 511e; 515e). The higher realm is thus somehow at once closed and open to our gaze. Now, Plato also asserts that a person will become like what he loves (500c) and that there is a correspondence between the character of the object of love and the character of the soul that loves it.[3] If this is the case, and it is also true that the philosopher is defined precisely by an insatiable desire for the "really real," then it would follow that the philosopher would take on some of the characteristics of this real reality. In other words, he would be both supremely bright and invisible. And this happens to be exactly what Plato says of him:

"And you'll assign this dialectical activity only to someone who has a pure and just love of wisdom." "You certainly couldn't assign it to anyone else." "We'll find that the philosopher will always be in a location like this if we look for him. He's hard to see clearly too, but not in the same way as the sophist." "Why not?" "The sophist runs off into the darkness of *that which is not*, which he's had practice dealing with, and

---

1. *Symp.*, 174e. 2. *Phd.*, 78c–79b.
3. *Phdr.*, 252d–e.

he's hard to see because the place is so dark. Isn't that right?" "It seems to be." "But the philosopher always uses reasoning to stay near the form, *being*. He isn't at all easy to see because that area is so bright and the eyes of most people's souls can't bear to look at what's divine."[4]

While philosophers dwell in a place *above* the world of ordinary affairs—and here we may think of the line and the cave, and also of the "ladder of love" described in the erotic dialogues, or we may consider Cleitophon's image of Socrates as a "god suspended above the tragic stage"[5]—they are also present, according to the *Sophist,* in various disguises among people below.[6] In loving, and thus imitating, reality, the philosopher somehow both stands beyond and within the ordinary run of the world. It is this that makes him appear insane in one respect,[7] perfectly free in another,[8] and in general the sole person in a position to render judgment.

But as we saw in chapter 2 especially, even more than loving being (τὸ ὄν), the philosopher, in Plato's view, is meant to love goodness. To do so faithfully is to undergo a radical shifting of horizons that opens the soul in a definitive way to "the whole." We have seen that knowledge of the good extends beyond the particularity of the immanent and the transcendent orders considered separately, beyond the partiality of the practical or the theoretical realm alone; the good in a fundamental sense is beyond definition because it is *sui generis,*[9] even if it nevertheless offers a kind of access to the intelligence. As an "embodiment" of the love of goodness, the philosopher will likewise display an essentially elusive character[10] and will turn up in surprising places, invariably introducing a kind of turmoil which is the precondition for a deeper and more comprehensive order.[11] As Plato depicts it in the dialogues, the philosopher's presence, however unwanted or even unnoticed, tends to upset situations, interrupts people in carrying through their intended plans, and turns them around, if not to gain a new and deeper insight into the matter they thought they had in hand, then at least to acknowledge, even for a moment, the need for such insight.[12]

---

4. *Soph.,* 253e–254b.

5. *Cl.,* 407a.

6. *Soph.,* 216d–e.

7. *Soph.,* 216d.

8. *Tht.,* 172c–d.

9. Cf. Veggetti, "L'Idea del Bene," 211.

10. Socrates confesses the difficulty of finding an image to depict the philosopher's relationship to his city, which he says cannot be compared to anything else (488a).

11. Cf. Lachterman, "What Is 'the Good'?" 141–42.

12. For example, in the *Alcibiades,* Socrates gives Alcibiades a moment's pause in the pursuit

The previous chapter suggested that it is necessary to "see" the historical figure of Socrates as a real image of the good in order for the *Republic* to fulfill its promise to disclose a true method of attaining truth. Our aim in the present chapter is to flesh out this claim and what it reveals about the nature of philosophy by drawing on Plato's description of Socrates in other dialogues, especially in the *Symposium* and the *Apology*. We will first strengthen the plausibility of our suggestion that Plato intends to present Socrates as a real image of the good by showing how Socrates plays that role in the *Lysis* and the *Symposium*. Next, we will propose that the dramatic situations in which Socrates appears make manifest a single-hearted devotion to the good, which is what allows Socrates to *mediate* to others an *immediate* relationship to it. This devotion will thus be developed in light of the themes of justice and obedience in the *Republic*. Finally, we will suggest that the "invisibility" Socrates displays lies at the heart of the philosophical life. Such a view of philosophy offers a reason for Plato's elusiveness in presenting the nature of the philosopher and also for his own anonymity as a philosophical author.

It is important to insist that the following is not intended in the least as an edifying hagiography of Socrates. Moreover, we will not attempt to distill the "historical" Socrates from Plato's literary and philosophical portrait (by comparing Plato's Socrates, for example, to Xenophon's or Aristophanes'), nor do we intend to elaborate a complete "character study" of the figure that Plato presents.[13] Our purpose, instead, is more philosophical than directly biographical: we seek to read Socrates as the interpretive key to Plato's *Republic*. What we hope to show is that the idealized character Socrates displays in Plato's dialogues has a strict epistemological and metaphysical import and purpose; it is, if you wish, a particular method—which can claim to be scientifically rigorous precisely to the extent that a rigorous method is one determined by the nature of its object—that allows things to manifest themselves in their truth. As such it presents just that philosophical method that Plato calls for in the *Republic*.

---

of his " great ambitions" by showing him he does not know the meaning of excellence. In the *Euthyphro,* Socrates at least manages to slow down Euthyphro on his way to prosecute his father by revealing to him his ignorance regarding piety.

13. A full character study would of course have to explore the more difficult features of Socrates' personality, such as his dismissive treatment of his wife, his occasional use of irony that is unnecessarily brutal, and so forth.

Socrates as a Stand-in for the Good

The *Republic* is not the only dialogue that presents Socrates in some sense as the real image of the good; the *Lysis* and the *Symposium* furnish two other examples. While we do not have the space to explore how they do so in every detail, it is helpful to consider Plato's portrayal of Socrates in general terms in these two dialogues, because it repeats a pattern we have sketched in the *Republic*. Socrates' emerging as a figure of the good is, in all of these cases, coincident with a *dramatic* resolution of a philosophical problem.

In the *Lysis*, first of all, Socrates engages in a discussion of the nature of friendship and love with two boys who are in fact friends with one another. The discussion is thoroughly aporetic, and as many people claim, it comes to an end, like the early dialogues, without coming to a conclusion.[14] Francisco Gonzalez has recently argued, however, that the dialogue in fact acts out a solution that is left implicit in the conversation.[15] Among the conundrums surrounding the question of the nature of love, Socrates affirms that the perfectly like and perfectly unlike are unable to love one another, and that the only true object of love seems to be the "first friend," the absolute good. But this must necessarily be a nonreciprocal love, though according to Gonzalez love would seem to need to be mutual by nature. Gonzalez weaves the strands of the problem into an integral whole by proposing a reciprocal love among "intermediates" that is rooted in our universal "kinship" with the good, a kinship that essentially supplants the traditional limitation of kinship to blood relations: "This view of course makes all human beings akin, but it can also explain more local kinship: two people who explicitly recognize their mutual kinship with the good and therefore pursue the good together will be οἰκεῖοι in the strictest sense."[16] He then shows that this solution, while left unspoken, is dramatically portrayed in the closing scene of the dialogue: the boys are called home by foreign slaves to join their families (i.e., "their own" in the traditional sense), and instead choose to stay in the company of Socrates and pursue conversation with him.[17] What Gonzalez does not make explicit in his account, however, is that this dramatic resolution presents *Socrates himself*, not simply as a part of the boys' relationship, but as

14. Socrates is the first to make this claim. *Lysis*, 222e.
15. Gonzalez, "Socrates on Loving One's Own," 379–98.
16. Ibid., 395.   17. *Lysis*, 223a.

the *first friend* (the good), in the common pursuit of whom the boys enjoy a deeper mutual friendship. Socrates essentially turns them around.

What is gained by acting out this solution to the problem rather than simply stating it? Among other explanations, we can suggest that it does greater justice to the problem it addresses. Friendship is, of course, not merely an intellectual problem—though Plato is wont to insist, perhaps contrary to our general assumptions, that it is in every case *also* an intellectual problem. But to say this does not mean only that, when dealing with something like friendship, we need both to understand what it is, *and* we *also* need to live our understanding. Plato would certainly agree with Hegel that the "and also" is the bane of philosophy, insofar as philosophy aims at a more integrative and comprehensive truth that such an "additive" mode of combination only imitates. By resolving the conceptual aporia dramatically, Plato shows that a real and properly ordered relationship to goodness is intrinsic to the very understanding of whatever includes goodness in its concept. In this respect, we do not have an intellectual account of friendship juxtaposed to an admonition to live it out. Instead, we have a dramatic whole enacting the insight that something more than a definition is necessary *even for a proper intellectual understanding*. Notice how such an approach overcomes a dualism between truth and reality: if it is the case that one can attain to the truth of something without reaching a concrete relation to its reality, then these two occupy separate "planes" that can at best parallel one another.[18] Now, it is not difficult to see with a thing like friendship, which is so directly bound up with goodness for its meaning, that something more than a conceptual grasp is necessary for a real understanding.[19] But the *Republic* makes the claim that the intelligibility of all things is bound up with the good. As we recall, to acknowledge the in-itself integrity of a thing, indeed to *real*-ize this acknowledgment, is essential for proper understanding, and this realization is simultaneously a movement of love and reason, both caused and measured by the good. This implies that a dramatic resolution of some form is necessary in an analogous form to everything we wish to understand.

18. It is clear that Plato had precisely this problem in mind in writing the *Parmenides* (see 133bff), but one sees it also reflected in the *Sophist*. (It is arguably the essence of the "battle of gods and giants over being" [246a–c].) Moreover, the separation between the "ideal" and the "real" is also a different way of articulating the problem we have been exploring in the *Republic*.

19. As G. Tindale puts it, friendship "will always be something that cannot be 'said,'" "Plato's *Lysis*: A Reconsideration," *Apeiron* 18 (1984): 102–9, here 107, cited in Gonzalez, " Plato's *Lysis*: An Enactment of Philosophical Kinship," *Ancient Philosophy* 15 (1995): 69–90, here 86n36.

Plato's presentation of Socrates as the real image of the good takes on a more evident, though more complex, form in the *Symposium*. While the *Lysis* used the aporia to open the argument to a more-than-conceptual resolution, the *Symposium* uses the image of layers of images that must, so to speak, be peeled away or otherwise transcended in order to get to the really real reality. The dialogue's prologue opens *in medias res*: "In fact," Apollodorus says, "your question does not find me unprepared."[20] Apollodorus is responding to a question that *the reader* apparently put to him about the symposium once held at Agathon's house, a question arising from the reader's presumed desire to get as close a connection to the actual reality as possible. Apollodorus says he just had the same question from another person (Glaucon), who after having received a faulty account thirdhand, wanted to hear the real story. But Apollodorus reports to the reader that he told this person that he himself was not present, but had heard the story from Aristodemus, who *was* there. There are therefore many intermediaries, and Plato emphasizes that they are all mad with love for Socrates.[21] The dialogue is, of course, about love, and about dialogues about love, and it explains that love must pass through images, or intermediaries, to find its real object of desire, the beautiful and good.[22] But note: there is not an endless series of intermediaries here. Rather, on the one end is the actual historical event of the conversation at Agathon's house,[23] and at the other is, not one of the characters in the dialogue, but "you," the reader.

It has often been pointed out that the description of love Socrates reports from Diotima in the *Symposium*, when his turn comes to speak, bears a striking resemblance to Socrates himself.[24] There is, of course, a physical

20. *Symp.*, 172a.

21. See, e.g., *Symp.*, 173b, d.

22. Although the primary object of love in this dialogue is the beautiful, Plato does not seem too concerned to distinguish it in this dialogue from the good (which represents the primary object of love in all the other dialogues apart from the *Phaedrus*). In fact, Diotima simply substitutes the good for the beautiful when her questioning of Socrates stalls, and does so without apology, as if to say the difference in relation to love is not essential (*Symp.*, 204e).

23. Though the conversation as recorded is no doubt fictitious, the main characters are historical and the occasion for the celebration is as well. See Nails, *People of Plato*, 314–15. In this respect, the *Symposium* is distinct from most other dialogues (apart, perhaps, for the group surrounding Socrates' trial and execution) which tend not to be set in relation to a very precise event.

24. Stanley Rosen explains that the resemblance has been noted from "at least the time of Ficino," *Plato's* Symposium, Carthage Reprint (South Bend, Ind.: St. Augustine's Press, 1999), 233.

similarity: love is "always poor, and he's far from being delicate and beautiful (as ordinary people think he is); instead, he is tough and shriveled and shoeless and homeless, always lying on the dirt without a bed, sleeping at people's doorsteps and in roadsides under the sky."[25] But the similarity lies even deeper. Diotima says that love is essentially a philosopher, constantly chasing after beauty, and goodness, and truth. While the gods *possess* wisdom, love desires it, which means love is different in some respect from both wisdom and ignorance. Significantly, the reason love cannot be *pure* ignorance is that ignorance is ignorant of its ignorance, and thus has no desire for wisdom. Love, by contrast, knows that it doesn't know.[26] It is impossible to overlook the allusion here. The identification of Socrates with love is reinforced, moreover, by the very structure of the dialogue. Socrates does not present the divine doctrine about love as something he possesses, but reports it as coming from the divine priestess, Diotima. In other words, he shows himself to be a lover of wisdom, just as love itself is, rather than as one who possesses wisdom like the gods. But the structure of the dialogue points most emphatically to Socrates at the end, with Alcibiades' raucous crashing of the party. Alcibiades gives the evening's last speech. While everyone else provided a discourse on love, Alcibiades presents instead a discourse on Socrates.[27]

The complexity of these allusions and the suggestive resonance they produce certainly bring us to admire Plato's rhetorical skill. But they lead us to astonishment at his display of philosophy when we begin to unfold their significance.[28] While the speakers before Socrates spoke *about* love, Socrates embodies what he says. The rhetorical figure of self-illustration occurs often in Plato,[29] but in this case, there is more going on than a simple illustration

25. *Symp.,* 203c–d.

26. *Symp.,* 204a–b.

27. *Symp.,* 214c–e. As Günther Figal puts it, when Alcibiades praises Socrates in the *Symposium*, the latter "wird zur Eros". *Sokrates*, 97.

28. For a more thorough exposition of the interpretation of the Symposium presented here, see D. C. Schindler, "Plato and the Problem of Love: On the Nature of Eros in the *Symposium*" in *Apeiron* (forthcoming).

29. Robert Brumbaugh suggests it is "a device other classical philosophers do not use; it is almost as distinctively Platonic as a fingerprint or trademark". "Digression and Dialogue," 86. (One could point to Heraclitus, however, as preceding Plato in this device. See David Valiulis, "Style and Significance: A Note on Heraclitus, Fr. 62," in *Studies*, vol. 1 of *Atti del Symposium Heracliteum 1981*, edited by Livio Rossetti (Chieti: Università di Chieti, n.d.), 163–68.

of a philosophical concept. The first point Socrates makes when it is his turn to speak is that love is not itself beautiful but is a desire for beauty; in other words, it is not the *object* of the soul's aspiration, but is the act of aspiring itself.[30] But this means that love is, as it were, essentially "intentional": it is always *of* something,[31] which is another way of saying it *points beyond itself rather than to itself.* The problem with the earlier speeches is that they made love, as it were, its own end. The effect of this inversion of love is to produce an essentially sterile image, for it fails to offer anything but itself alone. An intentional reality like love, by contrast, because it is desire, makes present a reality other than what it itself is. It opens up to something beyond itself. Immediately after adverting to its essentially "intermediate" status, Diotima reverses the previous image of love as identical with beauty, and thus as a *"being loved,"* insisting that love is a *lover,* and thus dynamically ordered to what is greater than itself.[32] By not speaking *about* love as a self-enclosed "thing," but instead embodying the very intentionality he is presenting, Socrates thus becomes *in person* a pointer to this greater reality. There is a paradox, then, in the *Symposium:* while all of the speakers in some sense forge (meant in both senses) eros in their own image,[33] and at the same time make eros something loved for its own sake (which we see most clearly in Agathon's presentation), Socrates does the reverse: he makes *himself* an image of eros, which, because eros is essentially what points beyond itself, *actually* gets embodied in Socrates. As Kosman insightfully observes, Socrates does not, like the others, praise *love,* which would contradict love's essentially intentional nature through its introversion, but instead praises the *object* of love, namely, the beautiful and good. His speech thus indirectly *becomes* a praise of love, not λόγῳ but ἔργῳ.[34]

This transparency has important implications. Alcibiades senses what they are, and expresses this with an appealing naiveté: "He has deceived us all: he presents himself as your lover, and, before you know it, you're in love with him yourself!"[35] The other speakers had mistakenly thought of love as a *beloved* rather than as a *lover;* but Socrates presented love properly, indeed,

30. *Symp.,* 198d–201c.   31. *Symp.,* 199d.

32. *Symp.,* 204c.

33. Arieti makes this point well (*Interpreting Plato,* 107) but fails to see the radical difference in Socrates' manner of imitating eros.

34. Kosman, "Platonic Love," 58.

35. *Symp.,* 222b.

became that love, and for that very reason makes present through his presence the genuine object of love. In other words, by embodying love, he becomes by the very same token a *real* image of the good.[36]

While commentators have often seen Socrates' resemblance to love, they have less often seen the indications scattered through the dialogue that Plato meant to show Socrates as goodness itself. The *Symposium* makes ample use of the happy accident presented by the name of the drinking party's host; *Agathon,* "of the good," is often portrayed in this dialogue as an *image* of that which Socrates represents in a more direct and more real manner. Agathon is like the good in name, which is a kind of image or likeness.[37] Moreover, he also happens to be a dramatic poet, which makes him in Plato's eyes a professional imitator, so to speak. The play between the reality of the good and its image is signaled early on in the dialogue. Aristodemus encounters Socrates on his way to the dinner. At Aristodemus's expression of surprise that he is so unusually well-groomed, Socrates explains: "I'm going to the house of a good-looking man; I had to look my best,"[38] or more literally, "I adorned myself so that I might go beautiful to the beautiful" (ἵνα καλὸς παρὰ καλὸν ἴω). Inviting Aristodemus to accompany him, he then repeats this figure with a pun, altering a proverb: We are coming as good men (ἀγαθοί) to the good (Ἀγάθων'), i.e., to Agathon's. In the series of speeches on the nature of love at the dinner, the last two to speak are Agathon and Socrates, and Agathon seems to present the best possible speech . . . until Socrates gives his.[39] The reality, as it were, once again transcends the image. Socrates does not appear simply as one in an ascending series, but seems to introduce a wholly different order. Significantly, he insists that his speech is not to be compared to the others'.[40]

In his speech, Socrates describes the stages of a journey by which one

36. See the same changing of roles in *Alc. I,* 135d. According to Walter Bröcker, Socrates' transformation from lover to beloved occurs precisely because he represents the place wherein the good and beautiful become accessible to the one following him. See *Platos Gespräche,* 2nd printing (Frankfurt am Main: Vittorio Klostermann, 1967), 166. Similarly, Nalin Ranasinghe explains that Socrates' identification with eros has to be reinterpreted once we see that eros is essentially a mediator, and thus points essentially beyond itself. *Soul of Socrates,* 147–48.

37. Cf. *Plt.,* 258a, where Socrates comments on the fact that the student present bears his name: "As for the other, he is called and designated by the same name as I am, and that produces a certain relatedness."

38. *Symp.,* 174a.　　　　　　　　39. *Symp.,* 198a.

40. *Symp.,* 199b.

ascends to the good/beautiful by learning to see through images—which would presumably include even the image Socrates himself presents, his own mythical-poetic account of love—until one reaches the ultimate revelation of the reality itself. Just as he finishes his speech, another surprise occurs: Alcibiades comes pouring into the room. This interruption repeats the discontinuity of Socrates' speech in relation to the others that preceded it, and also the discontinuity of the ultimate object of love that he speaks about, but it does so in the concrete order. And Alcibiades, in fact, acts out the drama of the journey Socrates has just described; in his drunkenly unrestrained eros he aims directly for the image of the good, Agathon, but is then *taken by surprise* by the real presence of the good: "As he [spoke], he *turned around,* and it was only then that he saw Socrates. No sooner had he seen him than he leaped up and cried: 'good lord, what's going on here? It's Socrates! You've trapped me again! You always do this to me—all of a sudden you'll turn up out of nowhere where I least expect you!'"[41] He thus finds himself on a couch *between* Agathon and Socrates, a dramatic situation that characterizes the real life choice he faced growing up as an extremely talented, fortunate, but not necessarily faithful follower of Socrates.[42] Plato has him confess his struggle between responding to the claim of the good he experiences in Socrates and his desire for images of the good, and he acts out this confession in his attempt to supplant Socrates' place next to Agathon.[43]

Like the *Lysis,* and, we propose, like the *Republic,* the *Symposium* takes on a dramatic form the moment it endeavors to communicate a reality beyond description, and it does so because it requires a "breaking through" of the horizontal mode of mere narration or argumentation. The *Lysis* finishes its argument in the mutual friendship with Socrates, the *Symposium*'s final speech is a love play that Alcibiades acts out between Agathon and Socrates, and the *Republic* transcends the images describing transcendence toward the historical life of Socrates. We see that the *Republic,* while perhaps not as tangibly dramatic as the other two dialogues (no doubt in part because of its length), nevertheless presents a more radical transcendence insofar as it breaks out beyond the dialogue altogether.[44] In any event, what is required

---

41. *Symp.,* 213b–c, emphasis mine.   42. Cf. *Alc. I,* 135d–e.

43. *Symp.,* 222d–e.

44. Ranasinghe interprets the dramatic reversal of the scene with Alcibiades in the *Symposium* like us in terms of the descent into the cave, but claims that the *Symposium* offers us the *reality* of what was only an *image* in the *Republic.* See *Soul of Socrates,* 145 (cf. also 101). We have

in each case for the resolution of the problem it engages (and especially the latter two) is a more-than-figurative image.

But both aspects of this affirmation are necessary: it must be "more than figurative" and it must nevertheless be an image. If in fact the reality at issue is transcendent, as it quite clearly is in the *Symposium* and the *Republic,* that reality cannot be presented in a merely immanent manner; it requires a mediator present in the immanent order but open to the transcendent. At the same time, however, the mediation cannot direct attention to itself without undermining its function. Here we see why love is the key. It is other-regarding by its very nature; this is what desire means. Pure love, in its most ideal sense, is completely set on the good, and is thus transparent to it. By *becoming* love, Socrates becomes wholly transparent to the good, in the sense that every aspect of his being "points" to the object of his desire. When Socrates attempts to place himself between Alcibiades and Agathon,[45] he is attempting to become for Alcibiades just such a mediator. Playing again on Agathon's name, Plato has Socrates insist on the exclusiveness of his love for the good: "Agathon, my friend . . . let no one come between us!"[46] This exclusiveness makes Socrates, then, the perfect mediator, which is what Plato needs to communicate the incommunicable: an intermediary that mediates an immediate relationship. By embodying love for the good, in short, Socrates makes the good immediately apparent.

The ambiguity of Socrates as an image of love and an image of the good thus stands at the center of the *Symposium.* It is what makes Socrates in a sense *be* more than he *is.* We can thus understand the significance of the "more" that Alcibiades points to as he sums up his description of Socrates with an increasingly unrestrained excitement. He first explains that Socrates cannot be compared with anyone else.[47] Like the good itself, we might say, Socrates does not surpass others in a relative way (as the heroes do, who though great can be compared among themselves), but represents an altogether different order:

---

shown that the reality is already *in* the *Republic* but expressed more subtly here precisely because of the radical character of the transcendence it communicates.

45. *Symp.,* 222e.

46. *Symp.,* 222d.

47. Jaeger observes that Socrates cannot be defined, but only known (*Paideia,* vol. 2, 36)—just like, we might add, the good itself.

You could say many other marvelous things in praise of Socrates. Perhaps he shares some of his specific accomplishments with others. But, as a whole, he is unique; he is like no one else in the past and no one in the present—this is by far the most amazing thing about him. For we might be able to form an idea of what Achilles was like by comparing him to Brasidas or some other great warrior, or we might compare Pericles with Nestor or Antenor or one of the other great orators. There is a parallel for everyone—everyone else, that is. But this man here is so bizarre, his ways and his ideas are so unusual, that, search as you might, you'll never find anyone else, alive or dead, who's even remotely like him.[48]

This unique radiance, Alcibiades continues, passes over into his very words. Referring to an image he used earlier, that of the statue of Silenus, Alcibiades says his words seem simple and banal on the outside, but open up to reveal divine depths of an unspeakable beauty. And it is just this that makes them compelling:

If you were to listen to his arguments, at first they'd strike you as totally ridiculous; they're clothed in words as coarse as the hides worn by the most vulgar satyrs. He's always going on about pack asses, or blacksmiths, or cobblers, or tanners; he's always making the same tired old points in the same tired old words. If you are foolish, or simply unfamiliar with him, you'd find it impossible not to laugh at his arguments. But if you see them when they open up like the statues, if you go behind their surface, you'll realize that no other arguments make any sense. They're truly worthy of a god, bursting with figures of virtue inside. They're of great—no, of the greatest—importance for anyone who wants to become a truly good man.[49]

Socrates' words carry a greater power because he speaks them, as it were, from a different place. At the same time, this "difference" is not at all a separation (as it would be if we forgot the twofold nature of the good). The transcendent radiance of his words is present, as Alcibiades observes, in the humblest, most ordinary aspects of everyday life. The good comes *into* the cave and transforms whatever is inside. As we have been arguing, a genuinely philosophical argument in Plato's sense presents words that are more than words, insofar as they radiate the light of an absolute good that alone makes truth possible as truth. It could be said that Socrates' devotion to the good gives his speech a truth "beyond images," which is just what the *Republic* requires. We now turn to further develop the epistemological significance of his devotion to the truth.

48. *Symp.,* 221c–d.   49. *Symp.,* 221e–222a.

Seeing Through

For Plato, what best determines the character of a person is what he most loves. We see this view in the *Phaedrus,* where Plato ranks souls according to the pursuits around which they ordered their existence.[50] Similarly, in the *Republic,* Plato distinguishes three classes of people according to which "part" of the soul dominates in them, whether the desiring part, the spirited part (θυμός), or reason, each of which relates to reality under a particular aspect. This is another way of saying people are distinguished according to what they most supremely love. Thus, we have lovers of gain, lovers of honor, and lovers of wisdom (580d–581a).

Now, recalling what Plato says at the end of book V and in the discussion of the divided line, we may affirm that these types of love do not merely reveal the character of a particular person, but they also make manifest an aspect of the reality to which a person relates. In line with this, we propose to compare Socrates as Plato presents him with these three classes of souls, and to do so with the metaphysical and epistemological issue in view, as well as the more obvious ethical issue. As we will see, love of gain tends to reduce things to the self, love of honor expresses a false dependence on others, which implies a reduction to appearance, and only the third love (which includes self and other) brings to light the true being of things. This love, which Socrates most clearly exhibits, is a love of wisdom and truth only because it is a love of the good. Once again, we find a suggestive echo here of the three types of good: simple pleasures and delights (which tend to reduce to the self), merely instrumental goods (which tend toward a disordered dependence on appearances), and, finally, genuine goods, the really real.

Let us start by comparing Socrates to the first class of souls. Not only does he display a singular freedom with respect to the body's needs, as Alcibiades reported with some frustration,[51] but he also manifestly has little concern with money,[52] which Socrates says is the primary object of pursuit for the lover of immediate pleasure (581a). Socrates' poverty is well-attested. Just as he confesses his inability to pay a fine in his trial,[53] so too he claims

50. *Phdr.,* 248d–e.
51. *Symp.,* 219e–220d.
52. "I knew very well that money meant much less to him than enemy weapons ever meant to Ajax," *Symp.,* 219e.
53. *Ap.,* 38b.

that he has no money to pay his "fine" to Thrasymachus for not having offered a better definition of justice than he (338b). But Socrates' poverty has a deeper significance than is immediately apparent. In the *Apology*, he points specifically to his poverty as evidence confirming his defense of the life of philosophy he has chosen to lead: "I, on the other hand, have a convincing witness that I speak the truth, my poverty."[54] What is the connection between poverty and truth? In this particular context, Socrates is defending himself against the unspoken charge that he is a sophist, by pointing out that while the sophists receive money for their teaching, he receives none.[55] Ranasinghe remarks that Socrates confounds sophistic logic, not only by *giving* his "nonwisdom" for free, but also by throwing *himself* into the bargain.[56] But it is illuminating to dwell on the significance of what distinguishes Socrates' activity from that of the sophists. The difference between the two implies a difference in the *telos* of an activity, which is another way of saying the ultimate locus of the act's goodness. As Socrates explains in the *Republic*, the earning of wages for an activity, insofar as this "money-making" art comprehends and so governs that activity, transforms the practice of the activity in a fundamental way because it changes the particular good at which the acting aims (345c). Rather than being ordered to its *intrinsic* ends, the activity becomes ordered to an extrinsic end. While the shepherd's art as such, for example, "surely cares for nothing but providing the best for what it has been set over" (345b), its aim becomes the personal wealth of the agent once wages are introduced. Thus, when an act is governed by its relation to wages, the final good that determines the basic nature of the act becomes the individual's private benefit, and thus *ceases* to be what the act itself aims at by nature.[57]

54. *Ap.*, 31a.

55. See D. L., II.27. The second definition the Visitor offers of the sophist in the dialogue of that name, after the private, money-earning hunter of human beings (*Soph.*, 223b), is the following: "We'll say that the expertise of the part of acquisition, exchange, selling, wholesaling, and soul-wholesaling, dealing in words and learning that have to do with virtue—that's sophistry in its second appearance" (*Soph.*, 224c–d).

56. Ranasinghe, *Soul of Socrates*, 153.

57. In the *Euthydemus*, Socrates ironically recommends that the two sophists in the dialogue ought never to offer their wisdom to the community as such, but only make it available in private, and says: "If you must have an audience, then let no one come unless he gives you money" (*Euthd.*, 304a–b). The reason is that precious things tend to be rare, even though, he adds with yet more irony, the very best things, like water, are cheapest.

If we were to imagine, for a moment, that love of gain were the highest possible form of love, we would at one stroke undermine the intelligible integrity of all human activities and the meaning and value of their ends. We are now in a better position to see why Socrates views Thrasymachus's arguments as calling into question the meaning of life in general. The absolutization of love of gain and the reduction of activities to the money they produce are thus *structural* and *institutional* forms of the epistemological relativism at which Plato's philosophy as a whole takes aim. Socrates' renunciation of monetary benefit for his philosophical life breaks open the purely immanent web of exchange values;[58] it reveals that there are things "more important than business,"[59] and this brings to evidence the "more than relative" character of things. We might say that Socrates' poverty lets in a transcendent light that makes everything else look different: it brings to light the *objectivity*, the wholeness and integrity, of human activity.[60] If he were to benefit financially from what he does, it would not be evident whether he or the activity was the final end, which means that he might seem to be himself the final good in a reductive sense, the absolute to which the activity was relative. As it is, his poverty becomes, so to speak, a manifest sign that the good lies beyond his individual person. In other words, he makes himself *essentially relative,* an image that underscores its character as an image, and thereby makes present the reality to which it points. The absence of possessions implied by poverty is a clearing away of anything that would obstruct this manifestation. This is what makes Socrates' poverty a witness to the truth of what he says; or, in

58. In her discussion of the *Phaedrus,* Pickstock observes: "Thus the sophistic consciousness is positioned in relation to the object as capital, of which it sees nothing but infinite variations of an equivalent measure. Such instrumentalized 'seeing' is presented as a parodic version of the philosophic gaze. . . . While the sophistic assessment is fastened to oscillations of value and opinion, and remains entirely alien from its object, the philosophic gaze, in its exercise of *Mnēmē* (recollection), is a penetrative, essential recognition which links the seer to the seen without abolishing the distance of the 'object' from the 'subject.' In this way, the Socratic 'object' acquires a transcendent quality before which the philosopher abases himself," *After Writing,* 7.

59. *Phdr.,* 227b.

60. In his series of essays entitled *Unto This Last,* John Ruskin compares the radical difference in the nature of activities carried out by the "so-called liberal professions," which are not ordered simply to profit, and those performed by the merchant who is " presumed to act always selfishly," *Unto This Last and Other Writings* (London: Penguin Books, 1997), 176–77. Ruskin adds, in complete sympathy with Socrates' remarks in book I of the *Republic,* that in the precise meaning of the reality, those that act for self-serving reasons cannot truly be called merchants but represent a decadent form of the same.

other words, his poverty is what makes him a self-transcending instrument of what is highest, and such an instrument is indispensable to the truth of truth. Poverty that is the result of a single-hearted devotion is thus a tangible expression of "bonocenteredness": it is not an accident that poverty represents one of the defining characteristics of love, the essence of which lies in a longing for the good that it itself *is not*.[61] Socrates lives in reality the poverty that essentially constitutes eros.[62]

It is also clear that Socrates is not a lover of honor: "You can't imagine how little he cares whether a person is beautiful, or rich, or famous in any other way that most people admire. He considers all these possessions beneath contempt."[63] Socrates claims, of course, that his trial was occasioned by his generating slander and hostility for pursuing an activity that cuts against public currents (πράττειν ἀλλοῖον ἢ οἱ πολλοί, *Ap.*, 20c). A lover of honor, Aristotle says, is essentially dependent on others.[64] If honor is necessarily associated with the opinions (δόξαι) of others, then, to the extent that one makes honor the supreme end of one's activity in a way that trumps intrinsic goodness, one must necessarily become a servant of opinion. One would therefore have to rank appearance over being; from the perspective of honor, there could be no benefit in *being* something that would not already come from *seeming* so.[65]

The *Apology*'s account of classes of people in the city, interestingly, can be read as presenting an inverse relationship between being and appearance in relation to wisdom: the more a class claims to have wisdom, i.e., gives the appearance of being wise, the less wisdom it has in reality.[66] Thus, the politicians who have the greatest reputation for wisdom prove to be the most vacuous; the poets, who certainly communicate a kind of wisdom, are incapable themselves of accounting for it; and the craftsmen, who would seem to be the lowest in rank, while they do indeed possess the knowledge of their

61. *Symp.*, 203c–e.

62. On poverty as essential to eros and therefore to philosophy, see Benvenuto, "Lo Specchio della Potenza," 8.

63. *Symp.*, 216d–e.

64. Aristotle, *Nich. Eth.*, 1.5.1095b23–28.

65. And this was *precisely* what Glaucon's challenge claimed. 361b–362c.

66. "And by the dog, gentlemen of the jury—for I must tell you the truth—I experienced something like this: in my investigation in the service of the god I found that those who had the highest reputation were nearly the most deficient, while those who were thought to be inferior were more knowledgeable," *Ap.*, 22a.

craft, are still mistaken in their presumption to have knowledge of the whole. Now, in his speech, Socrates does not rank himself among these classes. Instead, he merely insists that he has no wisdom at all. Once again, he represents something that cannot be compared to the different classes, with their relative claims of wisdom. His stance is incommensurate with theirs; his renunciation of claims to wisdom has an absolute, i.e., a nonrelative, character. But, seen in relation to this ordering of classes, making no claim at all for wisdom would make him the wisest. He does not *say* that he is wise, but for that very reason *shows* that he is: to make the claim explicit would be to undermine it.[67] It is suggestive that the claim regarding wisdom is not something he makes himself (in fact, he actively disputes it), or even something made by others in the city, but is, so to speak, decreed from above by the god.[68] Socrates manifests in his person the essentially "divine" mania described in the *Phaedrus,* which we discussed in chapter 2. In this, Socrates does not aim to project an appearance, which is what a lover of honor must do, but instead aims at being and allows the appearance to arise as a (natural) consequence: as he puts it, "Throughout my life, in any public activity I may have engaged in, I am the same man as I am in private life."[69] The single-hearted devotion to the good simply overlooks (which does not mean eliminates) the distinction between public and private that formed the crux of the problem of justice Glaucon and Adeimantus elaborated in book II.

The difference between being and appearance, and its relation to the love of honor, shows through as well in the contrast the *Symposium* presents between Alcibiades and Socrates. Alcibiades characterizes himself as being almost wholly occupied with "pleasing the crowd,"[70] and thus as a quintessential lover of honor. The story he relates of a battle in which he and Socrates fought sets into dramatic relief the connection between being and appearance. Socrates, he affirms, showed an exemplary bravery in the battle,[71] and in fact saved Alcibiades' life. Ironically, however, it is Alcibiades who received the decoration for bravery (τἀριστεῖα, the prize for the *best,* ἄριστος). As

---

67. Sometimes a refusal to answer is the very best answer. Consider *Chrm.,* 158c–d.

68. *Ap.,* 20e–21a.

69. *Ap.,* 33a.

70. *Symp.,* 216b. Cf. also *Alc. I,* 105a–b, where Socrates says Alcibiades thinks he should be honored above even Pericles just by presenting himself (i.e., showing himself) before the Athenians.

71. Cf. Laches' similar report of Socrates' valor in battle, *Laches,* 181b.

Alcibiades explains, the generals decided to give it to him rather than Socrates because of Alcibiades' social position, and Socrates was "more eager than the generals for me to have it."[72] Socrates, in other words, possesses the reality—the bravery itself[73]—while Alcibiades receives the ornament, the appearance of bravery. Similarly, Alcibiades, in his amorous state, wants to give his body (i.e., his physical *appearance)*, to Socrates, claiming that being with Socrates makes him want to become a good person more than anything else. Socrates' response is excellent:

> If I really have in me the power to make you a better man, then you can see in me a beauty that is really beyond description (ἀμήχανον)[74] and makes your own remarkable good looks pale in comparison. But, then, is this a fair exchange that you propose? You seem to me to want more than your proper share: you offer me the merest appearance of beauty (δόξης . . . καλῶν), and in return you want the thing itself (ἀλείθειαν), "gold in exchange for bronze."[75]

We note that Socrates' love for a reality beyond appearances simultaneously makes him beautiful beyond appearances and makes a real goodness of the same sort accessible to others. In other words, he does not offer simply the manifestation of beauty, but rather what one might call an inner beauty of soul or an intrinsic nobility, though paradoxically this non-manifest beauty thereby becomes manifest in an almost blinding manner. Socrates' pointing away from himself to a deeper reality makes him the most "potent" image of that reality.

If we were to imagine that love of honor were the highest possible form of love, then being would dissolve without a trace into the play of appearances. In this case, as we saw in our first chapter, there would be no alternative to the manipulation of appearances, and power would become the ultimate criterion for determining the meaning of things. All relations would be forms of imposition from the outside, and thus forms of violence. Now, the only way to avoid such a reduction is if there does exist, *in fact,* a love that is higher than a love of honor.[76] It is not enough simply to say that there is a re-

---

72. *Symp.,* 220e.

73. ἀριστεία: notice the similarity to the *prize* for bravery: τἀριστεῖα.

74. More literally, "beyond our means or capacity," or "beyond what we can achieve by our own devices."

75. *Symp.,* 218e.

76. Note that at 521b, Plato suggests that the sole love *higher* than the love of honor which

ality beyond appearance, and thus things more important than the opinion of others, because words can always be means of manipulation. Instead, one must simply love what is other than appearance,[77] and this is possible only if there is an absolute goodness beyond the relativity of appearance. It is significant that Alcibiades' supreme love of honor gets called into question only in the actual presence of Socrates, who manifests such a goodness: something must break open the horizon of appearance from the other side, that is, from the side of reality. Alcibiades, of course, always knows *about* Socrates, but it is only the event of a concrete encounter with Socrates, in which the goodness of the good becomes actually manifest, that he turns around, or at least feels the need to do so.[78] Socrates is quite reticent to *speak* about the good, but shows no hesitation at all about ordering his life around it in a manifest way.

The transcendence of opinion implied by transcendence of the love of honor does not entail the rejection of judgment, as the conventional version of this transcendence ("I don't care what other people think") seems to. Indeed, it places one's life under judgment in a more radical sense than the judgment by public opinion. While the latter judgment, we might say, is made "horizontally" by one's peers, the former entails the "vertical" judgment of a transcendent measure. By the same token, while the horizontal judgment is extrinsic, the vertical one is essentially intrinsic. If we read Alcibiades' speech about Socrates as a concrete reflection of the drama of love

---

attaches to the pursuit of rule is the love of wisdom, i.e., philosophy itself, so that absolutization of the pursuit of rule can be called into question only by the actual existence of philosophers: "'Have you,' I said, 'any other life that despises political offices other than that of true philosophy?' 'No, by Zeus,' he said, 'I don't.'"

77. Because of our inherited intellectual habits, it is probably necessary to remind ourselves that this does not mean to *exclude* appearances. Rather, we are talking about a love that includes *but does not reduce to* appearances.

78. "Still, I swear to you, the moment he starts to speak, I am beside myself: my heart starts leaping in my chest, the tears come streaming down my face, even the frenzied Corybants seem sane compared to me" (*Symp.,* 215e). Notice the temporal precision: the effect occurs *when* (ὅταν) Socrates speaks; it is not *simply* the general content of Socrates' words (though of course it is always also that). Socrates tells Alcibiades in fact that it is impossible for his deepest desires to be brought to completion (τέλος ἐπιτεθῆναι) without Socrates (*Alc. I,* 105d). In the *Theages,* Aristoles claims that he makes more progress (in unlearning his pretensions, it seems) the closer he gets to Socrates, to the point of needing actually to *touch* him. *Theages,* 130d–e. Even if this dialogue was written by some member of the Academy other than Plato, as generally assumed, it nevertheless bears witness to the reputed effect Socrates had on students.

of the good, several aspects shed light on Socrates' own relation to the good. Alcibiades makes the impressive claim that "Socrates is the only man in the world who has made me feel shame."[79] While he normally possesses a desire to please the many, to win their admiration, the presence of Socrates makes him acutely aware of the *lack* of value of his own life. It does so because Socrates represents a greater good—indeed, as Alcibiades professes, a uniquely great good. Socrates is more than an impressive hero, he is the manifestation of something that has no other measure by virtue of his absolute relation to the good. When Alcibiades catches sight of Socrates, he both sees through his own political aspirations[80] and recognizes the triviality of his own life in comparison. It is significant that the *Symposium* opens with Apollodorus making precisely the same observation in his own case.[81] But we notice that encountering transcendent goodness entails an *intrinsic* measure. This is the essence of *shame* (αἰσχύνη);[82] it is also, of course, the heart of the σωφροσύνη, which is defined at one point in the *Charmides* as self-knowledge, i.e., self-judgment.[83] While according to the external measure of public opinion, Alcibiades has no equal, and thus no cause to experience his inferiority, he becomes *his own judge* in the presence of the good: "I have heard Pericles and many other great orators, and I have admired their speeches. But nothing like this ever happened to me: they never upset me so deeply that my very own soul started protesting that my life—*my* life!—was no better than the most miserable slave's."[84] Standing under judgment of an

---

79. *Symp.*, 216b.   80. *Symp.*, 216a.

81. *Symp.*, 173a.

82. The meaning of shame in relation to the locus of standards of judgment is much more complex than some make it out to be. Cf. E. R. Dodds, *The Greeks and the Irrational* (Berkeley: University of California Press, 1951), 28–63. The internalization of the standard of goodness is not necessarily a movement away from genuinely aesthetic categories, i.e., a moralization of transgression into a source of psychological guilt-feelings as opposed to the more publicly grounded phenomenon of shame. The capacity to experience shame *depends* on some internalization of judgment. Consider, e.g., Socrates' inner dialogue that we will cite from the *Greater Hippias* (304c–e).

83. *Chrm.*, 164dff. It is interesting that Socrates, at a particular moment in the dialogue, describes self-knowledge as a radically different form of knowing than all the others, since, as "knowing what one knows and doesn't know" (167a), it is a unifying measure for all knowledge. In this, it would resemble the good. There would thus seem to be a connection between knowledge of the good and the self-judging knowledge of self. For related observations, see Gonzalez, *Dialectic and Dialogue*, 41–60.

84. *Symp.*, 215e.

absolute, as opposed to a relative measure, is thus coincident with one's being one's own measure. Socrates, again, represents the paradigm of this self-
judgment by pointing to himself as his most persistent questioner.[85] For this
reason, Socrates' very presence is a call to judgment (which we would expect
if he is a real image of goodness).[86] There is, in this respect, a connection between being measured by the good and being absolute in one's own right,
which is analogous to the way chapter 2 articulated the good's being the cause
of truth. It is the soul's appropriation of the general metaphysical structure of
reality. Knowing the good, and thus becoming a self-knower/self-judger, is a
likeness of the αὐτὸ καθ᾽αὐτόν relation that constitutes the reality of being
(as we saw in chapter 2). By being measured by the absolute, a person *becomes
inwardly true,* and his becoming true allows the truth of things to become "apparent."

   If Socrates is not a lover of gain or a lover of honor, he must be essentially a lover of wisdom. We might think of Glaucon's challenge to Socrates
in book II as working under the assumption that a self-centered greed, i.e.,
a love of private gain, is the defining human desire, and Adeimantus's challenge as founded on the assumption of the supremacy of the love of honor.
Part of Socrates' response to these challenges entails becoming in his person
a defense of the life of reason by manifesting a freedom from these other objects of love (on this, see chapter 5). He "proves" the existence of an object
superior to these others, which is the same thing as saying he makes evident
the transcendence that enables the true being of things to disclose itself.

85. In *Greater Hippias* (2998b–c), we find the following exchange: "Hippias: Those things
might slip right past the man. Socrates: By Dog, Hippias, not past the person I'd be most ashamed
to babble at, or pretend to say something when I'm not saying anything. Hippias: Who's that?
Socrates: Sophroniscus' son [i.e., Socrates himself]. He wouldn't easily let me say those things
without testing them, any more than he'd let me talk as if I knew what I didn't know." See also
Hp.mai., 304c–e. The person who always refutes Socrates is Socrates himself: "But when I'm convinced by you and say what you say, that it's much the most excellent thing to be able to present
a speech well and finely, and get things done in court or any other gathering, I hear every insult
from that man (among others around here) who has always been refuting me. He happens to
be a close relative of mine, and he lives in the same house. So when I go home to my own place
and he hears me saying those things, he asks if I'm not ashamed that I dare discuss fine activities
when I've been so plainly refuted about the fine, and it's clear I don't even know at all what *that* is
itself!" Significantly, as negative as the insults he hears from "that man" are, he ends by suggesting
that they are *good* for him (304e).

86. In *Laches* 187c–188b, the fathers acknowledge that with Socrates present they will necessarily be put, as it were, to the test. On this, cf. Jörg Splett, *Denken vor Gott: Philosophie als Wahrheits-Liebe* (Frankfurt am Main: Verlag Josef Knecht, 1996), 140.

But it is essential to see that wisdom, as Plato understands it, can be an object of love *only if* the good itself is the highest end pursued. The divided line shows that apart from the transcendence of the good reason's objects can be no more than hypotheses, which are never grasped in themselves and for their own sake but simply as means to conclusions different from them. To be an end in themselves, they must be viewed as relative to "end-ness" itself—i.e., to the good. In this sense, *one must love more than ideas in order to love ideas properly.* It is significant that Socrates, as we saw in chapter 2, takes care to avoid identifying the good simply with knowledge (505b–c).[87] Moreover, in the *Greater Hippias* he explains that we love knowledge precisely because of the good it entails.[88] If knowledge were identical with the good, then not only would we no longer have a foundation for knowledge (which would mean that knowledge as such would ultimately be impossible), but Plato would in fact end up being guilty of the dualism he is often mistakenly accused of, as we will see at greater length in the coda. The distinction between the good and the other forms is what necessitates a descent back into the cave. Without this difference, the only "philosophical" movement would be the ascent beyond the sensible realm into the intelligible.[89] But this movement, understood unilaterally, implies a separation between being and appearance that is never reconciled. Making knowledge itself the good necessarily implies an unbridgeable dualism. But if the good is distinct from knowledge and thus able to comprehend the realm of appearance as well, then love of the good would be a love of the whole that both distinguishes *and* unites the two realms. If the *Parmenides* is any indication, Socrates may, in his youth, have tended toward a kind of dualism, which is expressed moreover in his reluctance to seek wisdom in what is "lower" and trivial. But Parmenides predicts: "That's because you are still young, Socrates . . . and philosophy has not yet gripped you as, in my opinion, it will in the future, once you begin to consider none of the cases beneath your notice."[90] Perhaps we may read this judgment as Socrates' not yet having reached the maturity of the descent.

87. For a similar distinction, cf. the *Phlb.,* 21d–22a.

88. *Hp.mai.,* 297b.

89. Sallis interprets, by contrast, the "descent" in the *Republic* in wholly negative terms, precisely, it seems, because he does not acknowledge the twofold nature of the good that makes images *themselves* good *as images.* See *Being and Logos,* 448–54.

90. *Prm.,* 130e. The problem that frames the *Parmenides,* in fact, is that of finding a way to reconcile the absolute and the relative without denying their difference.

On the other hand, Socrates is unequivocal about knowledge being the *highest good* (as distinct, that is, from goodness itself). The one who pursues knowledge is presented as enjoying the best life, exceeding the joys of the life of pleasure and honor by far. To be exact, it is 729 times (!) more pleasurable (*Rep.*, 587c).[91] Moreover, Plato repeatedly shows in the dialogues the necessity of knowledge for virtue. If virtue means being good, i.e., possessing goodness in an intrinsic way, then the life of reason is an indispensable part of a pursuit of goodness. In short, we may conclude that, in Plato's eyes, it is impossible to love the good unless one desires to know as much as possible, and at the same time, one cannot desire to know in the fullest sense without desiring more than knowledge. Doing, knowing, and having the good ultimately form a single whole. We saw that Plato characterizes philosophers as deficient if they remain simply on one side of the cave's threshold or the other (519c). The mature life of the philosopher, as Parmenides suggests in the dialogue named after him, is expressed in the philosopher who both ascends to the ideas and embraces the multiplicity of appearances. This life finds a paradigm once again in Socrates, who shows a willingness to share the labors of others—to accept the civil duties of political office and to go to war when necessary for his city—and who seeks wisdom as the greatest of all goods, not in the perfect solitude where Heraclitus apparently sought it,[92] but in the thick of the marketplace: "I went down."

This love of wisdom, which is founded on a love of the good that transcends the distinction between being and appearance, allows Socrates to bring to light the full truth of things. Moreover, as transcending the particular loves that characterize the other classes of people, the love of the good does not need to eliminate any of them, but can integrate them within an order proper to them. Thus, while Socrates is free from the love of honor, he is happy to receive praise from Alcibiades, once he has the assurance that Alcibiades will speak the truth.[93] And, though he is not dependent on mon-

---

91. Plato is no doubt having fun with this precise calculation of the varying degrees of pleasure. But the humor expresses the serious point that the difference in pleasure rests upon an "objective" quality, namely, on the very structure of reality.

92. See D. L., IX.3. The legend of Heraclitus's life of solitude may not stem from his actually living apart from his countrymen (which would be hard to reconcile, in fact, with his view of the essentially "common" nature of the *logos*; see DK 1, 2, 113, 114), but from his characterization of the wise as "set apart": DK 108.

93. *Symp.*, 214e.

ey or physical pleasures, he is able to drink copiously when the occasion requires it.[94] Indeed, he even asks for free meals at the Prytaneum for the rest
of his life as a just recompense for his service to the city.[95] An exclusive love
for the good is apparently the *only* love that has room for every other love,
and such a love is alone able to show reality for what it is.

Obedience unto Death

Two further aspects of Plato's Socrates make him transparent to the good
even more directly than poverty: indifference toward honor and pursuit of
wisdom. There is likely no more compelling manifestation of Socrates' total
commitment to the good than his willingness to die, as it were, for goodness'
sake. According to Diogenes Laertius, Socrates was "the first who discoursed
on the conduct of life, and the first philosopher who was tried and put to
death."[96] While a Kantian would interpret such a willingness in terms of a
pure sense of duty, a more properly Platonic approach would locate this paradoxical act of will in the ecstatic nature of eros. It is not, in the first place, a
moralistic determination to do what is right even if it entails sacrifice that inspires this otherwise nonsensical act, but rather the desire to embrace a good
that lies altogether beyond one's own horizons.[97] We suggested in chapter 2
that true eros, set as it is on an object that exceeds one's own capacities, is
self-forgetting of its very nature. Plato always emphasizes this dimension in
his explanation of love; it is precisely what makes eros the proper response
to the appearance of the transcendent form of beauty. As he depicts it in the
Phaedrus, a glimpse of beauty is the in-breaking of the transcendent. When
the soul catches such a glimpse, "it forgets mother and brothers and friends
entirely and doesn't care at all if it loses its wealth through neglect. And for
proper and decorous behavior, in which it used to take pride, the soul despises the whole business. Why, it is even willing to sleep like a slave, anywhere,
as near to the object of its longing as it is allowed to get!"[98] Socrates is un-

---

94. *Symp.,* 220a.   95. *Ap.,* 36c–37a.

96. D. L., II.5.20.

97. "Sokrates ist sowenig wie ein Prophet ein Moralist, der etwa altruistisches Wohltun predigt," Splett, *Denken vor Gott,* 143. On p. 136, Splett implies that the nonmoralistic character of
Socrates' eros distinguishes him from the proto-gnosticism in Plato. But this is a one-sided interpretation of Plato, as we will show in the coda.

98. *Phdr.,* 252a.

deniably present in these words. Only such an ecstatic view of eros explains why the *Phaedrus* depicts the peak of love's ascent not as a final possession of the beloved, but rather as a reverent distance from the beloved, so that the soul remains always relative to an absolute that exceeds it.[99] Thus, love depends on the "ever greater" character of its object. The *Symposium* presents a similar picture, insofar as it emphasizes the lack of possession as an intrinsic quality of love.[100]

Significantly, even the altogether self-seeking Alcibiades cannot help but speak first in the mode of ex-propriation in his encounter with the good present in Socrates: "Well, here's how I look at it. It would be really stupid not to give you anything you want: you can have me, my belongings, anything my friends might have. Nothing is more important to me than becoming the best I can be, and no one can help me more than you to reach that aim" (218d). Alcibiades will surrender what belongs to him in the most extensive sense— not only, literally, his *substance* (τῆς οὐσίας τῆς ἐμῆς), but also that of his friends—in order to share intrinsically in genuine goodness. Love of goodness, we might say, involves an exchange of substance.[101] It becomes clear, however, that Alcibiades intends ultimately to *take possession* of the good for himself, and thus falls prey to the critique Socrates makes of seeking goodness for the sake of merely immanent fulfillment. But if it is the case that the pursuit of goodness in an absolute sense necessarily entails the relativization of everything else, the perfection of desire is the perfection of expropriation.

Such a view of the nature of eros casts some light on Socrates' disconcerting poise as he faced the jury in 399 B.C.[102] What motivated him, as he

99. *Phdr.*, 252a; 256a–b. The notion that desire is essentially "egocentric" (rather than, say, "bonocentric," with all that this implies), has been one of the most poisonous in modern thinking. Such a view of desire lies behind Anders Nygren's "desire" to separate purely selfless love (agape) from the Hellenistic eros in his influential book *Agape and Eros*, translated by Philip Watson (Philadelphia: Westminster Press, 1953). His interpretation of eros as essentially ego-centered, and his pointing to Plato as the primary representative of this form of love, shows a misunderstanding. As we have already suggested, beginning with the "best" good allows us to avoid *both* the problems of egocentrism and altruism. For a good account of the problem of altruism, see Max Scheler, "Ressentiment and Modern Humanitarian Love," in *Ressentiment*, translated by W. Holdheim (New York: The Free Press of Glencoe, 1961), 114–36.

100. *Symp.*, 200e.

101. D. L., II.34, reports an exchange between Socrates and Aeschines: " Aeschines said to him, 'I am a poor man and have nothing else to give, but I offer you myself,' and Socrates answered, 'Nay, do you not see that you are offering me the greatest gift of all?'"

102. Cf. Jaeger, *Paideia*, vol. 2, 29. Diogenes Laertius describes Socrates as "independent and

explains in a variety of ways, was not a pure sense of duty, but the pursuit of what he considered to be the greatest good possible, not only for himself but for the entire city.[103] It is so, of course, because it is absolutely, and not merely relatively, good. There is a paradox here, which cannot be overlooked, and it belongs to the essence of love and goodness: supreme goodness is something greater than the one who desires it, so that desire for it includes the possibility of extreme consequences. The *Republic* alludes to these consequences in Glaucon's challenge, which proposes that the test of whether justice were truly good in itself would be if someone adhered to it at the greatest cost conceivable, the most extreme situation the imagination could contrive. Socrates has already claimed at the beginning of the *Republic,* the moment Thrasymachus jumps in to call into question his true aims in the conversation, that the value of justice is such that one ought to be willing to do anything for its sake (336e). Socrates shows himself willing. At the opening of the *Republic,* he never calls the supremacy of justice into question; it is something to which he has always already devoted himself.[104] After Glaucon and Adeimantus issue their challenges in book II, he confesses it would be impossible to defend justice against such an attack, but that, "[o]n the other hand, I can't not help out. For I'm afraid it might be impious to be here when justice is being spoken badly of and give up and not bring help while I am still breathing and able to make a sound. So the best thing is to succour her as I am able" (368b–c).

The implications of Socrates' remark are greater than it would appear at first. A person might be inclined to say that *possibility,* understood in terms of practical feasibility, should present the ultimate horizon of action and thus determine the meaningful limits of a thing. This inclination is in a certain respect perfectly reasonable. But to accept this horizon without further qualification would be to reduce goodness to its realizable form, which ultimately means reducing it to its practical consequences, insofar as "realizable form"

---

dignified" (αὐτάρκης ... καὶ σεμνός). Notice again the inner completion (the word "independence," here, is literally "self-sufficiency") we have been associating essentially with goodness.

103. *Ap.,* 38a, 31a–b.

104. We could say that the "always already having devoted oneself" is the adequate subjective correlate to the absoluteness of goodness, though the relativity it implies requires at the same time the "realization" of this devotion in a particular, once and for all, decision. This is what distinguishes Socrates (and philosophers like him) (519c) from the universal desire for goodness that must be presupposed in everyone. See 505d–e, and 518c.

signals the actual impact or effectiveness a thing may have. As reasonable as the assertion appears to be, it nevertheless ultimately surrenders the absolute character of goodness, and so reduces it to relativity.[105] As we shall see at greater length in the following chapter, this proposal simply undermines reason precisely to the extent that the absoluteness of the good is the essential foundation of reason. We recall that the scholastic dictum *quidquid recipitur recipitur in modo recipientis* ("whatever is received is received in the mode of the recipient") cannot be unqualifiedly affirmed without compromising the reality of truth. Socrates' approach is radically different from the simple acceptance of what is actually possible: it is impossible to defend justice, he says, but he has no justification for attempting anything else so long as he has breath. If he accepted anything less than this impossibility, he could not be said to be a lover of the good. And it is just this love that assures the truth of things.

He must save justice, one wants to say, or else die trying. The irony here is of course essential: Socrates does die in his attempt to succor justice, if we can interpret his apologia as an insistence on adhering to justice regardless of practical consequences. The irony, then, is that it is ultimately this death that ends up "justifying" justice (i.e., sharing its absolute and unconditional goodness), and so what he had claimed was impossible turns out in a paradoxical way to be possible—without contradicting Socrates' claim. At issue is the absoluteness of goodness. There is no better way to show that the good is absolute than by showing that what one prefers to it is . . . absolutely nothing. Further, there is no way to show this than a willingness to give up everything one has and is for it. And, finally, there is no way to show that one is willing to give up everything other than to be willing to die.[106] Death is, af-

---

105. At 472c–473a, Plato states that the realization of a thing in practice will always fall short of the ideal, i.e., the truth of it, but aiming at anything less than the ideal is irrational.

106. Figal claims that Socrates' death is *not* a philosophical martyrdom or a "staatsburgerkündliche Lektion" that Socrates wishes to share with the Athenians, but simply the sole possibility Socrates has of remaining one with himself, and therefore good. *Sokrates,* 119. Figal is correct that Socrates is not trying to "show" something to the Athenians, but it *is* nevertheless the case that he is concerned not first with fidelity to himself, but rather is faithful to himself *in order* to be faithful to goodness. In this case, we can and ought to speak of a martyrdom in the etymological sense, i.e., a "witness." The whole of Socrates' life was to be a witness to goodness, and his death gives expression to the truth of his life. It is interesting to note, however, Figal's association of goodness with remaining one with oneself, which we have proposed is an essential dimension of the good's causality.

ter all, absolute, insofar as it represents the elimination of everything all at once.[107] By revealing that his own life means less to him than the good, Socrates wholly relativizes himself *to* it; he makes himself absolutely relative, as it were, which is another way of saying he becomes a relative manifestation of the absolute, in a manner that compromises neither the relativity of the relative nor the absoluteness of the absolute.[108] We might say that what was always implicit in Socrates becomes explicit, in Greek fashion, in the "contest" of the trial.[109]

There is an infinite difference between Socrates' willingness to die for goodness' sake and acts of self-immolation and the like, which are mistakenly referred to on occasion as acts of martyrdom. Though this is not the appropriate context to enter into a long discussion of the difference, it is worth pointing out that Socrates *does not seek death*. Indeed, he claims that it is impious to do so,[110] because this would put one's life principally in one's own hands, when it in fact principally belongs to the gods. In our terms, such an act would be the diametrical opposite of Socrates', for it would place the absolute wholly under the judgment of the relative.[111] Thus, instead of seek-

107. We might think in this context of Socrates' description of philosophy in the *Phaedo*: practicing death. According to Friedländer, the "path of knowledge, the path of love, and the path of death" are ultimately the same. *Plato: An Introduction*, vol. 1, 64. They are the same because they all represent the staking of oneself on the ab-solute.

108. In his "Eloge de la philosophie," Maurice Merleau-Ponty claims that what the philosopher essentially teaches is, if not absolute knowledge itself, then an *absolute relation* between this knowledge and the student. See Merleau-Ponty, *Eloge de la philosophie et autres essais* (Paris: Gallimard, 1960), 10–11.

109. We recall that Plato suggests such a dramatic sense of truth in the *Timaeus*, where he points to struggle, conflict, or contest as what allows the display of inner qualities for others to see (*Ti.*, 19b–c), in a way impossible with a mere "static" image. Here, again, we see a reason for the dialogue form.

110. *Phd.*, 61c–62c. Here he says that a philosopher should be willing to die but should not bring his death on himself.

111. One might think of G. K. Chesterton's characterization of suicide in this context: "Not only is suicide a sin, it is the sin. It is the ultimate and absolute evil, the refusal to take an interest in existence; the refusal to take the oath of loyalty to life. The man who kills a man, kills a man. The man who kills himself, kills all men; as far as he is concerned he wipes out the world. His act is worse (symbolically considered) than any rape or dynamite outrage. For it destroys all buildings: it insults all women. The thief is satisfied with diamonds; but the suicide is not: that is his crime. He cannot be bribed, even by the blazing stones of the Celestial City. The thief compliments the things he steals, if not the owner of them. But the suicide insults everything on earth by not stealing it. . . . Obviously a suicide is the opposite of a martyr. A martyr is a man who cares

ing death, Socrates simply seeks the good, wherever it may be and wherever it may lead. The truth of one's pursuit of the good would show itself, not in the abrupt cutting short of discussion with others, but in the desire to argue things out in patience with others as far as possible and be proven wrong when necessary,[112] while the fanaticism expressed in self-immolation invariably dispenses with discussion.[113] In order to show the absoluteness of the good, we might say, one must occupy one's entire life with it (*Rep.* 367d–e), and not only make it the putative theme of one's death. Suicide for the sake of the good would represent the false sort of absolutism that excludes the relative and thus does violence to it, as distinct from the genuine devotion to the absolute, which necessarily implies—precisely to the extent that it is genuine—a patient and free openness to the relative however it may present itself, insofar as goodness is manifest even there.[114]

The content of a life occupied with the good will be characterized especially by *obedience*, the other feature of Socrates' mode of being that makes the absolute manifest. Alcibiades, once again stung by the goodness in Socrates, blurts out: "I don't know if any of you have seen him when he's really serious. But I once caught him when he was open like Silenus's statues, and I had a glimpse of the figures he keeps hidden within: they were so godlike—so bright and beautiful, so utterly amazing—that I no longer had a choice—I just had to do whatever he told me."[115] The ex-propriative perception of genuine goodness entails an immediate inclination to obedience.

---

so much for something outside him, that he forgets his own personal life. A suicide is a man who cares so little for anything outside him, that he wants to see the last of everything. One wants something to begin: the other wants everything to end. In other words, the martyr is noble, exactly because (however he renounces the world or execrates all humanity) he confesses this ultimate link with life; he sets his heart outside himself," *Orthodoxy* (New York: Image Books, 1990), 72–73.

112. Socrates "stayed at home and engaged all the more keenly in argument with anyone who would converse with him, his aim being not to alter his [dialogue partner's] opinion but to get at truth," D. L., II.22. Socrates claims that the greatest good that exists for human beings is to spend every day discussing virtue (*Protag.,* 38a). On this, see Francisco Gonzalez, "Giving Thought to the Good Together. Virtue in Plato's *Protagoras,*" in *Retracing the Platonic Text,* edited by John Russon and John Sallis (Evanston, Ill.: Northwestern University Press, 2000), 113–54. We might compare Socrates' disposition, once again, with that of Thrasymachus, who desired to leave the moment he made his point, as we discussed in chapter 1.

113. Cf. Charles Griswold, "Style and Philosophy," 535.

114. Cf., again, *Rep.,* 402c.

115. *Symp.,* 216e–217a.

As we interpret it here, obedience in the philosophical sense means "heter-onomy" rather than "autonomy"; or, more adequately, it means (if an awk-ward coinage might be excused) "agathonomy," which includes both heter-onomy and autonomy in an asymmetrical unity that never eliminates their difference. In other words, obedience means taking as one's *own* measure a measure that comes in a certain respect from *outside* of oneself, and in the most fundamental respect fashioning one's activities first in accordance with this outside measure rather than forcing everything outside of one to adapt to one's own activity. To put it another way: it means adapting to the whole by finding one's place in it rather than forcing the whole to adapt to one's own closed prior determination. Significantly, Socrates introduces the good into the discussion with Glaucon and Adeimantus precisely under the guise of the "most precise measure" (504b–c). Ferber, we recall, gathers evidence from the dialogues suggesting that measurement is in fact the determinant feature of the good.[116] We have proposed, in chapter 2, an understanding of the relationship between goodness and intelligibility that would flesh out this suggestion: if knowledge is a relation, absolute goodness is what makes the reality to which the soul is ordered the measure of that relation. Good-ness is in this respect the foundation of genuine "objectivity." But this im-plies that a subordination of the soul to its proper other is constitutive of knowledge and truth. This subordination, furthermore, requires at its heart the discontinuity of the reversal that makes genuine transcendence possible. Thus, the intentionality of one's soul (i.e., one's desire or love), is reversed: it is no longer that whatever I love is good; rather, I now love what is good. But this reversal is the structural expression of obedience. Rather than first de-termining myself what it is that I want, I instead give a certain preference to what is presented to me, by another, as good. We saw such an endlessly pa-tient deference to the other in Socrates' interaction with Thrasymachus in book I. If this reversal lies at the heart of truth, then there is no knowledge outside of obedience.

It is no wonder, then, that the *Republic,* which is fundamentally about the transcendence that makes knowledge, and only therefore justice, possible should be constantly occupied with the themes of law, obedience, authority, power, and even persuasion and compulsion. These are intrinsically related to the epistemological and metaphysical inquiries of the book, so much so

116. Ferber, "Did Plato Ever Reply to Those Critics?" 53–58.

that, if we fail to see the connection, we have failed to understand the *Republic*. If, by contrast, we are alive to this connection, we become aware of the wonderful irony in the quotation from Homer that Socrates cites in relation to the philosophers who get free from the cave: they would much prefer "'to work the earth as serf to another, one without possessions,' and go through any suffering, rather than share their opinions and live" as those in the cave (516d). Socrates has already described the guardians as essentially having nothing simply of their own (419a). The alternatives presented here are either to live the life of opinion or to live, possessionless, as the servant of another. The contrast sets into relief a theme we have addressed from various angles already, insofar as it associates the lack of wealth and obedience to a measure outside of oneself with liberation from the cave of opinion. Opinion, we recall, represents the cognitive appropriation of reality according to one's own measure, and is thus simultaneously comfortable and essentially limited. The movement beyond the relativity of one's own point of view requires the decentering ex-propriation of being laid claim to by another. A further paradox thus arises here. The people Plato depicts in the cave allegory as willing to be serfs are precisely those who are genuinely free. To be sure, what Plato means by freedom in this context is not the conventional modern liberal definition of the absence of constraints on choice, a form Plato himself describes as the highest value in the democratic regime (562b–c), but instead the self-transcending involvement with what is really real, the open-eyed pursuit of the good, which in fact gives the identification of freedom with "doing what one wants" a full and precise meaning.

It is not merely the subtle irony of the passage from Homer, however, that connects the genuine philosophical life with obedience. In fact, Plato underscores this association quite explicitly in the dialogue. On the one hand, he explains that it is precisely the *law* that looks after the happiness of the whole rather than the exceptional well-being of a single class (519e).[117] The law is, at least in principle, nonrelative;[118] it has a suprapersonal scope. The philosophers who leave the cave do not simply decide for themselves to return, but do so as obliged by an order that transcends them. This does not mean that they do not *want* to return, but their desire, as we have suggested,

117. The impartiality of law thus represents a perfect contrast to the pleonexia that Thrasymachus champions in book I.

118. The law by nature is not a regarder of persons, though of course Thrasymachus is right to say that the law can be manipulated and made to serve the specific ends of the ruling party.

has the structure of obedience, and only as such does it comprehend more than is individually possible. Note the coincidence of obedience and desire in Plato's wording:

"Do you suppose our pupils will disobey us when they hear this and be unwilling (οὐκ ἐθελήσουσι) to join in the labors of the city, each in his turn, while living the greater part of the time with one another in the pure region?" "Impossible," he said. "For surely we shall be laying just injunctions on just men. However, each of them will certainly approach ruling as a necessary thing (οὐκ ἀναγκαῖον, i.e., as something they are compelled to do)—which is the opposite of what is done by those who now rule in every city." (520d–e)

They are willing, *and* they obey what is compulsory, and this because they are devoted to the good. For this reason Socrates repeatedly uses forms of the word ἀνάγκη and the impersonal verb δεῖ in speaking of the philosophers' supreme role in this section: they must be *compelled* to take office, because it is *necessary* for the good of the city and thereby for their own. The language of obedience becomes most insistent at this particular moment of the *Republic,* since we are speaking directly of the discontinuous reversal by which the good becomes manifest in its absoluteness, but we note that the same language attaches to the project of education all along the way. It thus brings to light the essential meaning of education: an introduction to reality.

Obedience is the decisive characteristic of Socrates' self-understanding.[119] Moreover, it is what essentially distinguishes Socrates' form of "not knowing" from that of those he unmasks. We will pursue this particular aspect further in the following chapter, but it is worth noting, in this context, that Socratic ignorance is not the dismissal of truth one might interpret it to be. Instead, it is a constantly renewed acknowledgment that the measure of

119. Cf. Kahn, *Plato and the Socratic Dialogues,* 96–97, where Kahn describes Socrates' pervasive sense of obeying a divine mission. It is crucial to note, however, that Socrates' total obedience is by no means blind. See Curtis Johnson's discussion in *Socrates and the Immoralists* (Lanham, Md.: Lexington Books, 2005), 37–53. There is an identity between obeying reason and obeying what is best. (See *Cri.,* 46b.) In this case, insofar as what is best includes the priority of an order that is larger than the particular person (but of course includes him), it can be perfectly reasonable to choose what one ordinarily would not choose, i.e., what one would not normally find reasonable in relation to oneself (as we will see in the next section, which raises the question of Socrates' consenting to his execution). In this respect, there is a sense in which obeying one's *own* reason is nevertheless obeying an *external* authority. (See Johnson, *Socrates and the Immoralists,* 44.) In the *Sophist,* Plato presents reason as a royal authority that issues commands (*Soph.,* 235b–c).

truth lies beyond himself. There is thus, in this, a kind of obedience to reality that shines forth in frequently disconcerting ways in his interaction with others. He would at every point rather see the way things are than the way he takes them to be, even if it means being dispossessed of his own intellectual "wealth." This fundamental disposition of obedience lends a special weight to his self-description in the *Apology*. The whole drama of his life, he insists, has a single explanation: his obedience to the god.[120] He showed his obedience to the city in remaining at his posts at Potidea, Amphipolis, and Delium, in spite of the danger to his physical well-being; how much more, he says, does he owe obedience to the god who stations him in the philosophical life.[121] He admits the great cost of the obedience, pointing again to his poverty and the precariousness of his social position—and yet never indicates, in either his words or his manner, anything else but that he is better off than anyone in Athens. Having nothing, we might say, he has nothing but the good. Only thus can we understand the freedom he displays before his accusers.

In short, freedom from what is lower comes at each stage only through a love for, and thus dependence on, what is higher. Love always means some kind of dependence. It is impossible to avoid loving *something* most, and thus making oneself dependent in an absolute way on *something* (even if it happens to be, for example, one's own immediate gratification). To be free in the most total sense does not mean to be utterly independent—for this would necessarily mean to be without love for anything, which is impossible in any event—but to be dependent only on what is *in reality* highest, with all this dependence entails. Perfect freedom is thus identical to absolute obedience to what is absolute.[122]

Justice and Obedience

The totality of his obedience offers a way to explain Socrates' extraordinary behavior in the *Crito:* while he seems to have both the ability and good

---

120. *Ap.,* 23b.

121. *Ap.,* 28e–29a.

122. As Heidegger puts it in his discussion of the cave allegory: "Comportment to what *gives* freedom (the light) is itself a *becoming* free. Genuine becoming free is a projective *binding of oneself*—not a simple release from shackles, but a binding oneself for oneself, such that one remains always bound in advance, such that every subsequent activity can first of all become free and be

reason to escape prison before his execution, he abides in the place the city has put him.[123] He has an obligation, he says, to obey the laws of Athens.[124] But here we encounter a troubling question, and reflecting on its implications will bring out a further dimension of the philosopher's descent. Glaucon has affirmed the philosopher's willingness to obey the command to go down because "they are just things commanded to just people." However, Socrates acknowledges that his condemnation and execution are unjust.[125] Why, then, does he accept obedience even to this order, at such a cost to him, his family, and his friends—indeed, as he claims, to the whole city of Athens?[126] One might argue that, even if he disputes the justice of the trial's outcome, he does not explicitly question the trial system by which the decision was made. One could say he is submitting to a just system, which happened to reach an unwanted decision in this particular case. He cannot reject the decision without rejecting the whole system that produced it.[127] But, though this argument is not without some grounds, the reality is more complex than the argument assumes.[128] We have to consider that Socrates regarded the popular vote upon which such a court system rests as intrinsically incapable of rendering just judgments[129] and also seems to have had doubts about the present regime in general. Is it not the case, in any event, that the absoluteness of the good stands higher than the fate of a particular city (precisely because it stands higher than absolutely everything else)? We

---

free," *Essence of Truth*, 43–44. Heidegger, however, stresses the binding of *oneself* more than Plato, i.e., views freedom more "egologically" than Plato does. For the latter, it is first of all the good that binds.

123. For a concise presentation of the problem this dialogue raises (especially in relation to the *Apology*), and references to the pertinent literature on the problem, see Curtis Johnson, "Socrates on Obedience and Justice," *Western Political Quarterly* (1990): 719–40, here 719–20.

124. *Cri.*, 54b–e.

125. *Ap.*, 38c–39b.

126. *Ap.*, 31a–b; cf. *Cri.*, 45c–46a.

127. Indeed, the Athenian laws tell Socrates that he will destroy them, and by extension the whole city of Athens, if he rejects the court's judgment. See *Cri.*, 50a–b.

128. Consider Woozely's observation: "The simple claim that a single act of lawbreaking by a single individual (e.g., Socrates), will have as its immediate effect the collapse, like the walls of Jericho, either of the particular law broken or of the system of law to which it belongs, is too silly to take seriously," *Law and Obedience: The Arguments of Plato's* Crito (Chapel Hill: University of North Carolina Press, 1979), 112. Woozely ends up judging that the arguments Socrates gives are not the strongest, and proposes another, more modern argument, that would justify Socrates' acquiescence, namely, the obligation to remain fair to others who are bound to law. See 135–40.

129. *Cri.*, 44d, 47c–d.

are thus led to wonder why he would submit to the city's judgment, particularly when he claims to obey the god rather than the people. On the face of it, complete obedience to the god would seem to require the overthrow of any corrupt order. Is his remaining in prison part of his fundamental obedience to the good, or is it in some sense a compromise of it?

Perhaps a clue to the response is to be found in a rarely noticed phrase in Plato's description of the philosopher's return to the cave: he is to "share the labors and honors" of the prisoners, "whether they be trivial or more serious" (519d). When Plato speaks of the philosopher-king, one typically envisions a person who, by virtue of his presumed absolute knowledge, would hold absolute sway over the many, one who would rule in a form indistinguishable from, say, the power of the tyrant, even if the content of the rule, the nature of the decisions, would be fundamentally different. In other words, we tend to assume that the philosopher would have the same power as anyone else who was given rule, but that he would *use* that power in a different way. We are familiar with Sir Karl Popper's claim that Plato's *Republic* expresses an essentially fascistic spirit.[130] From this perspective, if it is the case that the philosopher's return to the cave represents his assumption of the office of rule, the image of the philosopher-king just described would lead us to expect a triumphalistic descent, a true condescension, by which the philosopher would simply take charge, manipulating the prisoners as much as any tyrant or sophist, but always with the sincere assertion that it is for their own good. But this is decidedly *not* what Plato presents. The returning philosopher does not destroy the puppets or banish the puppeteers or become a puppeteer himself. (The latter being, of course, the office Thrasymachus's tyrant would seize if given the choice.) Instead, *he takes his place next to the prisoners.* He takes up and shares with them their labors and honors, no matter how banal or important they may be. We have to wait for the next chapter to unfold the surprising significance of this point; even here, though, we may offer an interpretation appropriate to the present context.

A *leitmotif* of this book has been the paradoxical twofold nature of the good: its absoluteness is not exclusive of, but necessarily *inclusive* of, relativity. An absolute obedience to this absolute good, then, rather than to a relative good such as personal gain or public opinion, by virtue of its absolute-

130. Karl Popper, *The Open Society and Its Enemies,* 5th ed. (London: Routledge, 1966).

ness must make room for a relative obedience to every relative good. This does not entail, of course, that one sanctions the existing order and everything within it. But it does seem to imply that one begins with things as they are, that one enters into them rather than descending violently upon them, and one sets them into order with what is highest through appeals to the inner logic and intrinsic goodness of things, as well as to others' own freedom and goodwill (i.e., desire for the good).[131] In other words, relation to the absolute, properly conceived, does not simply eliminate what is relative or partial. If it did, then the absolute and relative would exist as competing members of the same class, as it were, and the absolute would thereby cease to be what it is. Instead, what is relative and partial gets integrated into an order that both transcends and includes it and it thus acquires a necessity it would otherwise lack. This would mean not rejecting an existing order, but accepting it as far as possible (which means, to be sure, never definitively) within a spirit of obedience to the comprehensive order governed by what is in fact highest.

Viewed from this perspective, obedience proves to be the existential key to the concrete integration of the absolute and the relative. In obedience, one *transcends* the particularity of one's individual nature precisely without eliminating that particularity. Let us consider the soul's movement that Plato describes in the fourth segment of the divided line. Here we have (relative) hypotheses that are (analogically) opened up to the absolute beyond them and (katalogically) confirmed by that absolute without being eliminated. They are, in other words, both preserved and transformed through being considered in the light of what lies above them.[132] The structure of obedience displays a similar movement: instead of simply asserting the particularity of one's individual's will, making a claim for oneself and drawing the consequences from that claim without "testing" it in itself (and thus absolutizing the relative), one instead submits one's will to judgment in light of the absolute good. In this way, the particularity of one's will becomes simultaneously relative and absolute: it acquires, while remaining individual, all of

131. We will see in the next chapter that it is impossible to appeal to the intrinsic goodness of things unless one appeals likewise to the freedom of one's interlocutors.

132. Here we see how reason can be ultimate while at the same time subordinating itself to the ever-transcendent goodness. Again, this is the kind of obedience Socrates expresses in the *Crito* (46b), and also the " method" he follows in the *Phaedo:* a trust in reason that arises from an absolute commitment to what is absolute (see 89d–91c; 96e–102a).

the indisputable weight and authority of the whole that requires the particularity of one's will such as it is. Likewise, a part or partial order is not necessarily eliminated by being judged against the absolute good, the good of the whole; instead, it acquires its proper place and function in relation to everything else within the comprehensive order and thus, *in its particularity*, it becomes absolute in a manner appropriate to it. Again, this allows us to see the philosopher's return not as the revolutionary establishment of a new regime, but the in-breaking of a light, both profound and subtle that opens things up organically to their truth.

As soon as we begin to consider obedience along these lines, we see that it provides a fascinating way of interpreting Socrates' definition of justice.[133] There is something decidedly anticlimatic about the scene in book IV in which Socrates finally unveils what is ostensibly the goal of the entire dialogue: an adequate statement of what justice is. Though he tries to excite dramatic anticipation by drawing out a prelude that actually *acts out* a hunt (432b–e),[134] the definition he proposes—basically, justice means "minding one's own business" (433a)—invariably disappoints the reader. Not only does it turn out to be a variation on the first point made about the city-in-speech way back in book II (369dff.), but it seems positively uninspiring. It is interesting to note, too, that Socrates undermines this very proposal as a way of understanding virtue through his criticism in the *Charmides*,[135] which suggests there must be "more to it." To make matters worse, there is no indication of how such a definition meets the challenges made by Glaucon and Adeimantus. Moreover, there is the puzzling fact that what is offered as an answer to the dialogue's central question comes before the dialogue is half-finished. But our discussion of obedience reveals an unsuspected depth to this definition; the words prove to be like the statue of Silenus, opening up to marvelous depths when perceived in the proper context.[136] One of the

133. Curtis Johnson presents a strong argument that, for Socrates, justice ultimately *is* nothing but obedience. See *Socrates and the Immoralists*, 37–53. Cf. his article, "Socrates on Obedience and Justice," 719–40, esp. 721n5 and 724: "'To be just,' then, is very nearly identical in meaning for Socrates to 'to obey one's superior.'" Cf. Gerasimos Santas, *Socrates: Philosophy in Plato's Early Dialogues* (London: Routledge, 1979), 43–56.

134. On Plato's regular use of a "buildup" to heighten interest, see Greene, "Paradoxes of the *Republic*," 205–7.

135. *Chrm.*, 161b–162b.

136. Rosemary Desjardins's observation regarding the validity of definitions is pertinent here. She suggests that, for Plato, even correct words are not sufficient for knowledge, because

trickiest aspects of the problem of justice, for Plato, involves the difficulty of overcoming simple relativity, which is what links justice to the fundamental question of knowledge and the good. In relation to this problem, "minding one's own business" means doing what one does, *not* as a function of one's whimsical desires, but instead as a function of one's nature in relation to the needs of the whole.[137] In other words, it is the reception of one's particular and relative place in obedience. This makes it simultaneously relative and absolute: one overcomes one's partiality, not by rejecting that partiality or absolutizing it as a substitute for the whole (which is what it would mean to be a tyrant), but by embracing the partiality *as* partiality, i.e., by *perfectly* relativizing it. In this sense, justice becomes the in-breaking of the absolute good, which casts a transformative light on even the most trivial of activities.

But let us notice the brilliance of Plato's mode of presentation, which fulfills the very meaning it presents.[138] Socrates claims that this notion of justice was there from the beginning, only they couldn't see it because of the "stu-

---

these can be understood in different ways. (See her essay "Why Dialogues?" 110–25.) This is why Plato prefers concrete discussion to written words, and also points to a supra-propositional foundation for knowledge. She thus argues that the dramatic dimension of the dialogues is essential to " provide necessary parameters of interpretation that will allow us to cut through the ambiguity of the discursive level" (119). Desjardins's interpretation accords with Plato's resolution of the different views of language presented in the *Cratylus*. As he shows in this dialogue, there has to be some access to things beyond language in order for knowledge to be possible (*Cra.,* 438d–439c).

There is obviously a great contrast between Desjardins's reading of Plato and, say, Derrida's ("Plato's Pharmacy," in *Dissemination,* translated by Barbara Johnson [Chicago: University of Chicago Press, 1981], 63–171): Derrida recognizes the relativity of words, but denies access to any solid ground of meaning. Thus, for him meaning is endlessly deferred, which makes the oral discourse that Plato prefers simply a derivative form of writing, rather than vice versa. It is significant that Derrida's well-known essay on the *Phaedrus* does not mention the word eros: eros implies a constant movement, but toward a particular goal. But this is just what is lacking in Derrida. While thought for Plato is always "on the way," for Derrida it is always merely "on the move." If eros means the constant relativizing of the relative, and thus requires an absolute in relation to which things can be relativized, the lack of eros in the Platonic sense will necessarily mean a tendency to absolutize the relative itself, which means that Derrida's "différance" is ultimately totalitarian in a way that Platonic transcendence necessarily avoids. On this, see Catherine Pickstock's critique of Derrida along analogous lines. *After Writing,* esp. 3–46. See also Perl, "The Living Image," 191–204.

137. Notice how Socrates founds the first city in speech. 369cff. He begins with the basic needs (food, housing, clothing), which are universal, and then bases the division of labor on the natural differences among people. The articulated whole thus receives its determination from common need and natural aptitude.

138. Again, such an approach is typical of Plato. See Brumbaugh, "Digression and Dialogue," 92–94.

pid state we were in" (432d). The statement of justice, then, is not the introduction of something altogether new, but rather a deeper grasp of the same
thing that was present before, a grasp enabled by the philosophical progress
that has been made through the discussion that Socrates, the philosopher,
leads. In other words, we increase our understanding of a thing by seeing it
recast in terms of an increasingly "bigger picture." What we have here, moreover, is a concrete example of the "degrees of reality" displayed in the images of the central books of the *Republic*. As we argued earlier, they depict levels of manifestation of a single reality, which are dependent, in some sense,
on the state of the soul of the perceiver. In this respect, we can read Socrates'
claim that they were initially in a "stupid state" as an image of the prisoners
in the cave.[139] "Minding one's own business" thus is essentially the same notion that started off the discussion, but it now has a fundamentally different
meaning because it is grasped at a "higher level" of reality. Does this make
the articulation of the definition in book IV a sign that the cave has already
been left behind? No: the movement to true knowledge requires the light of
the good, and the good has not yet explicitly entered the discussion. Socrates
therefore expresses an appropriate reticence about the definition when he articulates it at this point, which suits this level of reality precisely: "'Well, then,
my friend,' I said, 'this—the practice of minding one's own business—*when
it comes into being in a certain way* (τϱόπον τινὰ γιγνόμενον), is probably
justice'" (433b, emphasis mine). Though we are now at the *intelligible* level of
a definition, Socrates presents it in a decidedly hypothetical mode, as something conditional. The real significance of the definition, as we have discovered, awaits the radical reversal of the presence of the good, that which confirms the hypothetical and makes it real.

The paradigmatic fulfillment of this definition comes, then, with the philosopher's return, insofar as this return is the manifestation of obedience to
the greatest good, i.e., a function of the good of the whole *rather than* the exclusive good of the part, and only thus also a function of the good of the part.
And it is precisely this paradox of obedience that leads the philosopher to
submit himself to the relative *in a certain sense on the relative's own terms*. We
saw precisely this in Socrates' relation to his conversation partners in book I.
He does not simply—violently—impose himself from above, but rather en-

---

139. In fact, Socrates says that the reality was there but their eyes were turned in the wrong
direction (432e), which is an image that points directly to Socrates' description of the cave.

ters into the particularity of a situation from below. Socrates always insists on listening first.[140] With respect to the definition of justice, we see that Socrates begins with what is most immediately given, and follows each thing through on its own terms as far as they go, allowing either the inner logic of the matter at hand, or the interruptions, questions, and requests of his companions, to bring to light the inadequacy and prompt the movement upward. In this context, it is interesting to note that, in his description of the philosopher's training in the second half of book VII, he shows that the ascent to reason from the perceptible is not an artificially contrived movement, but follows an intrinsic necessity, an impulse from below that springs from the nature of things (522e–526c). Judgment from a higher perspective—for example, the judgment of the visible from the perspective of the intelligible—arises only when judgment from within the lower order itself proves inadequate (523a–b). The perceptible, thus, provokes thought of its own accord when it appears contradictory at the level of perception (though we have to add that thought is required to see the contradiction in the first place). The judgment, then, arrives as both a fulfillment and a transcendence of the lower level. To put it somewhat figuratively, thought allows perception to show itself to be inadequate *as* perception, and brings its judgment not as an artificial imposition but as a resolution that reconfigures things within a higher order. Socrates describes the philosopher as gazing on and judging the shadows on the wall with everyone else (520e), and this is in fact what he does. He does not, for example, simply tell Thrasymachus that he is wrong, but patiently shows how Thrasymachus's presuppositions about reality will prevent him from obtaining what he wants. More generally, we can see that the philosopher, though he is wholly centered on the absoluteness of the good to the extent that he is a philosopher, nevertheless takes up the life of those in the cave and *shares* it.

But this puts the philosopher in a very strange light. On the one hand, he is indistinguishable from others insofar as he is sharing their labors and honors. He does not claim any special authority, at least in the usual sense. At the same time, however, he is absolutely different from all the rest. He is present and absent, seeing what they see but judging by altogether different standards. He seems ridiculously incompetent in tasks of great urgency, and yet shows unsurpassable skill in things that are useless. Aristotle calls the philosopher a serious man; Plato says he is like a child at play. The best attitude to have toward

140. *Laches,* 181d.

things that matter, in fact, is a playful seriousness or serious playfulness;[141] and this ought to be the philosopher's normal attitude. The philosopher lends weight to the most trivial things,[142] and at the same time shows a disarming nonchalance about the most weighty, including his own life. He appears to enjoy the most extreme freedom imaginable, and yet at the same time lives an obedience that strikes the average person as harsh to an obscene degree. It is again the paradoxical nature of the good that brings this about: the most radical transcendence is seen not in the one who restlessly struggles to get out and stay out of the cave, but in the one who shows up, surprisingly,[143] in the least expected corners of the cave, radiating a noble generosity and conversing with an indomitable irony.[144] If he is serious, Callicles asks, "won't this human life of ours be turned upside down, and won't everything we do be the opposite of what we should do?"[145] In short, "standing" on the good, he stands at once inside and outside the cave.[146] He thus embodies the poet Hölderlin's favorite description of divinity: *non coerceri maximo, contineri tamen a minimo*.[147] Is it not precisely this that makes the philosopher "difficult to see"?

Showing the Philosopher's Invisibility

Plato apparently planned at one point to compose a dialogue called the *Philosopher,* which would have completed a trilogy with the pair of dialogues the *Sophist* and the *Statesman.* It was never written. Each of the two dialogues that did appear mentions the proposal to have three conversations, the aim of which would be to define in turn the sophist, the statesman, and the phi-

141. *Letter VI,* 323d. On Plato's philosophy as an integration of seriousness and play, see the interesting analysis by Mauro Tulli in *Dialettica e scrittura nella VII Lettera di Platone* (Pisa: Giardini editori, 1989), 36–40. Tulli suggests that Plato's condemnation of Dionysius may be due to the latter's inability to reconcile these two aspects.

142. In *Alcibiades,* Socrates says that the details of Alcibiades' life are of little concern to anyone—except for Socrates himself (*Alc. I,* 122b).

143. Cf. *Chrm.,* 153b.

144. "Irony is then the noble dissimulation of one's worth, one's superiority. We may say, it is the humanity peculiar to the superior man: he spares the feelings of his inferiors by not displaying his superiority," Strauss, *City and Man,* 51.

145. *Grg.,* 481c.

146. Ranasinghe observes that Socrates is able to go back and forth freely between the cave and reality, and that this freedom is due to eros (*Soul of Socrates,* 101). He adds, incorrectly, that such eros is lacking in the *Republic* and must be sought in the *Symposium.*

147. "To be unable to be bounded by the greatest of things, and yet to be contained by the

losopher.[148] It is impossible to determine why the third dialogue was never written, but we can presumably rule out a lack of time, since, even with the latest possible dating of the two extant dialogues (assuming that it is in any event possible to determine the chronological order of their composition, an assumption we will discuss in the coda), Plato had time to write the massive *Laws* and a few other dialogues. We also can likely rule out a loss of interest, since the nature of philosophy was a constant concern for Plato. A variety of explanations have been proposed for the nonexistence of this dialogue.[149] Though it is impossible to solve this question in any definitive way, there seems to be internal evidence suggesting he never intended to write it—"internal" both in the sense of presented inside the two extant dialogues and in the sense of following naturally from the view of the philosopher we have been developing in this chapter.[150]

As a reflection of the good, Socrates possesses qualities that are impossi-

---

tiniest of things." Cf. Hölderlin's "Fragment von Hyperion," in *Sämtliche Werke und Briefe*, vol. 1 (Darmstadt: Wissenschaftliche Buchgesellschaft, 1998), 489. This text is known as "Loyola's Epitaph," composed by an unknown Flemish Jesuit to sum up the spirituality of St. Ignatius.

148. *Soph.*, 216d–217a; *Plt.*, 257a.

149. See Francis M. Cornford, *Plato's Theory of Knowledge* (London: Routledge, 1935), 168–69. Diskin Clay suggests that the reason it was not written is that the "philosopher" is not a "type," but a unique individual: namely, Socrates. *Platonic Questions* (University Park: Pennsylvania State University Press, 2000), 54. Griswold proposes that writing a definitive statement about the philosopher would contradict the essentially dialectical—and therefore occasional—nature of Platonic philosophy. "Plato's Metaphilosophy," in *Platonic Writings, Platonic Readings*, 162. Egil Wyller, *Der späte Platon: Tübinger Vorlesungen 1965* (Hamburg: Felix Meiner Verlag, 1970), 7–8, claims that the missing dialogue is actually the *Parmenides*, apparently because this dialogue concerns the One, which is central for the philosopher. Jacob Klein proposes that "the trial of Socrates, the Philosopher, replaces the dialogue about 'the philosopher,'" *Plato's Trilogy*, (Chicago: University of Chicago Press, 1977), 5. Mitch Miller makes a very interesting argument in this regard in *The Philosopher in Plato's Statesman*. Like Klein, he proposes that the "trilogy" (*Tht., Soph., Plt.*) is a more philosophical replay of Socrates' trial. Miller draws attention, as we do here, to the fact that the "philosopher" cannot be considered on a par with the other two figures, and that a separate dialogue called the *Philosopher* could not therefore be written. Instead, the "young Socrates" in the *Statesman* is being put to the test to see if he can become philosophical, if he can embody the Socratic "essence," in which case a new dialogue would not be necessary. Notice the implication that *knowing* what the philosopher is requires *being* a philosopher, i.e., it requires a movement beyond the dialogue into the existential order.

150. Cf. Michael Frede, "The Literary Form of the *Sophist*," in Gill and McCabe, *Form and Argument in Late Plato*, 135–51, here 49–51, for indications of the existence of the philosopher already in the *Sophist*. Frede, however, suggests in contrast to us that there is no philosophical necessity for Plato's having "hidden" the philosopher in this dialogue.

ble to describe in a completely adequate manner. The last chapter argued that the absoluteness of the good causes it to reverse any analogy that intends to explicate it, breaking it open in a surprising way, and thus bringing forth an unanticipated reality. The beginning of the present chapter pointed to a similar effect of the person of Socrates himself. Alcibiades cannot speak about Socrates without betraying his love,[151] which is an irrepressible reaction to an unmistakable reality. More generally in the dialogues, philosophical problems tend to resolve dramatically in relation to him. Such is to be expected precisely to the extent that he manifests, in his person, the goodness of the good, and to the extent that goodness is intrinsic to intelligibility. We therefore need to take quite seriously Alcibiades' claim that there is no comparison to be found for him.[152] Just as Plato does not place the good on the divided line, since that would make it essentially relative to other things and no longer absolute, so too he suggests that the one who reflects the good in a real way will somehow stand beyond comparison. It is only this that makes him, in principle, relative to everyone, which is how Socrates presents himself. At the same time, this absolute relativity gives his words an incontrovertible weight and power. One can gainsay an argument with another argument, Evagrius Ponticus once said, but how does one gainsay a life?[153] Now, we begin to see that Plato does not mean to present Alcibiades' claim as the exaggeration of a drunken buffoon, because he repeats a similar observation, this time coming out of the sober mouth of Socrates, at the beginning of the *Statesman* and thus directly after having defined the sophist in the dialogue of that name:

"I'm really much indebted to you, Theodorus, for introducing me to Theaetetus, and also to our visitor." "And perhaps, Socrates, your debt will be three times as great, when they complete both the statesman and the philosopher for you." "Well, yes and no: shall we say, my dear Theodorus, that we've heard the best arithmetician and geometer putting it like that?" "How do you mean, Socrates?" "Because you assumed that each of the three were to be assigned equal worth, when in fact *they differ in value by more than can be expressed in terms of mathematical proportion.*"[154]

---

151. *Symp.,* 222c.

152. *Symp.,* 221d. It is worth noting that something analogous would have to be said about anyone who loves goodness in an absolute sense—which means that many people could be, in principle, similarly incomparable, so to speak.

153. Even those who are not to be convinced by arguments tend to be persuaded by deeds. *Ap.,* 32a.

154. *Plt.,* 257a–b. Italics added.

Anything that can be expressed in terms of proportion is essentially relative. To suggest that this third type is beyond proportionality means it is beyond relativity. A kind of incomparability is not simply an idiosyncratic mark of Socrates; it is, rather, an essential characteristic of what Socrates most perfectly represents for Plato, namely, the philosopher.

If philosophy were simply comparable to other things, there would be no difficulty in speaking about it just as one would speak about anything else. But if philosophy *does* in fact represent a different level of experience, it will necessarily come "as a surprise" to the normal course of things. It is significant that Plato is inclined to introduce a discussion of the nature of philosophy and the philosopher as a *digression* from the conversation at hand. He confesses, however, that side issues often turn out to be the central issue.[155] The central books of the *Republic* in which the philosopher makes his appearance, as we have noted, seem to emerge incidentally, as the discussants stray from their topic. Similarly, as Brumbaugh has shown, *Letter VII* enters onto its most philosophical theme as a digression.[156] Another example is the *Theaetetus,* in which Socrates pauses as he sees the figure of the philosopher beginning to emerge, saying, "But I see, Theodorus, that we are becoming involved in a greater discussion emerging from the lesser one."[157] However, Theodorus presses him into what turns out to be an account of the philosopher, and Socrates artificially breaks off the "digression" (πάρεργον) with the comment that there would be too much to say about him.[158] In his brief but excellent account of this recurrent feature of Plato's style, Brumbaugh points out that this digression lies at the symmetrical center of the dialogue.[159] Just as the digression does not seem to belong, but turns out in reality to be essential, so too does Socrates in person present an unanticipated response to the discussion that seems to find no solution:

In the *Theaetetus,* according to one widely accepted reading, the philosophic issue seems to be what happens if one tried to define *knowledge* without reference to Platonic Forms. Theaetetus tries out one model after another equating knowing with sensation, perception, and opinion. But each time, quietly standing by, there is someone present in the dialogue itself who has a kind of "knowledge" that his sophistically affiliated models cannot explain.[160]

155. Cf. *Plt.,* 302b.
157. *Tht.,* 172b–c.
159. Brumbaugh, "Digression and Dialogue," 85.
160. Ibid.

156. Brumbaugh, "Digression and Dialogue."
158. *Tht.,* 177c.

This feature of Plato's style accords with what we have described as a *dramatic* structure: there is a discontinuous rupture, which proves to be a necessary fulfillment. It also accords with what we have argued is the essential nature of the philosopher: an "invisible" presence that does not allow genuine truth to be presumed within a merely immanent order, but requires that order to break open and beyond into a more comprehensive, and concrete, reality to realize its aim. Such a presence can *only* be communicated indirectly. As commentators regularly suggest, to make sense of the words in a Platonic dialogue requires one to go beyond those words. There is a parallel here between Plato's hesitation to offer a conclusive definition for nobler things with an intrinsic relation to goodness such as virtue and his hesitation to provide a straightforward account of the philosopher: they both require the concrete act of tying together various threads into a whole that includes the reader's active participation and thus serious interest. In other words, they require a movement toward the good.

Turning back now to the question of the absence of the *Philosopher* from Plato's trilogy, we see that there may be good reason for it. In fact, if we consider the evidence in the dialogues more closely, we discover that the philosopher is already there.[161] Plato seems to have presented the nature of the philosopher in the only manner adequate to his conception.

In the first place, both of the dialogues of the "trilogy" remark on the elusive *hiddenness* of the philosopher: the *Sophist* compares the philosopher to the disguised gods in Homer. Though they are present, they are not recognized as who they are but are mistaken for something else because of people's ignorance.[162] Some people, he says, take them for sophists, and some take them for statesmen, while in fact the philosopher dwells at a higher level. The Visitor tells us he is always here, but we have to look for him.[163] In the *Statesman,* when Theodorus presents the three types of people as mathematical units, Socrates objects: one of the three does not admit of a mathematical

---

161. Heidegger claims that "it is precisely the dialogue on the sophist that accomplishes the task of clarifying what the philosopher is, and indeed it does so not in a primitive way, by our being told what the philosopher is, but precisely Socratically," *Plato's Sophist,* translated by Richard Rojcewicz and André Schuwer (Bloomington: Indiana University Press, 1997), 169. Eric Voegelin argues that "if the project of the third dialogue is no more than an obscuring device, there is no distinction to be drawn between the Statesman and the Philosopher," *Plato and Aristotle,* 150. Our claim is that both Heidegger and Voegelin are correct.

162. *Soph.,* 216c–d.

163. *Soph.,* 253e.

proportion to the other two.[164] In other words, the philosopher is a reality of a different order. It would thus make sense that there could not exist a dialogue called the *Philosopher* that could simply be juxtaposed to those called the *Sophist* and the *Statesman*. The philosopher cannot appear *as a philosopher* within the cave—that is, within the language of the dialogues—but takes on a different appearance depending on the state of soul of the onlooker.

What Plato says here suggests that we ought not look for the philosopher somewhere else, but instead ought to look more closely at what is already in front of us. When we do, it turns out that the philosopher *shows up in an unanticipated way in both of these dialogues*. While attempting to give yet another definition of the sophist, the Visitor inadvertently stumbles upon the philosopher instead.[165] It is here that he comments on the philosopher's invisibility in relation to that of the sophist. Similarly, in the *Statesman*, the constitution that is separated out from the others, the seventh, and thus is not even comparable to them,[166] is that in which the ruling statesman is the philosopher.[167] Thus, the prediction that begins the "unfinished" trilogy comes true: the philosopher was present in both cases but only made an appearance through increased understanding. We could say that sophists and statesmen are not so much different "types" to be compared to a third "type," the philosopher, as they are relative images of which the philosopher is the reality.

But this image-reality relation is displayed in a remarkable way in the very dramatic setting in which the two conversations take place. As if to bring the point home, Plato contrives a situation that is virtually unique to this pair of dialogues: Socrates is *present*, and yet he *remains silent* through the whole discussion, while an *unnamed visitor* takes over his customary role.[168] At the same time, an "image" of Socrates stands in for him in each of the two dialogues: in the *Sophist*, it is Theodorus who is said to *look* like Socrates, and in the *Statesman*, there is a young student *named* Socrates who responds to questions. At the beginning of the *Statesman*, Plato draws attention to the fact that these both resemble Socrates in different ways[169]—just as, one might say,

164. *Plt.,* 257b.

165. *Soph.,* 253c.

166. *Plt.,* 303b. It is as distinct as the god from men, he says.

167. *Plt.,* 293c, 294a. Cf. Klein, *Plato's Trilogy,* 177.

168. Socrates also stands relatively silently by in the *Timaeus*.

169. *Plt.,* 257d–258a. See Miller's observations in this regard in *The Philosopher in Plato's Statesman,* 6–7.

the sophist and the statesman resemble the philosopher. Plato has thus made Socrates present and absent in the conversation at the same time. His presence is felt throughout the conversation without ever being made explicit. In other words, he stands above the discussion, while various images of him carry it forward, just as the philosopher is said to occupy a realm above the sophist and the statesman.[170] And this is something we may observe about the Platonic dialogues as a whole, and about the *Republic* in particular; the unique flesh-and-blood personage of Socrates pervades every conversation, and his presence lends them their weight, casts a new light on them, and thus provides the interpretive key.[171] The *Philosopher* could not be written because it entails something not necessary to the conventional views of either the sophist or the statesman: the good-drenched reality of a wholly committed life.

The Invisible Author

There is someone who is even more silently present in the conversations than Socrates himself. Apart from the most incidental of allusions,[172] Plato makes no appearance on the stage of his dialogues—in contrast to, say, Xenophon, who always relates his Socratic dialogues in his own voice. Plato's failure to appear has opened up the widest range of interpretive possibilities, to the delight of some readers and to the chagrin of others.[173] The herme-

---

170. Indeed, we could say even more accurately that Socrates stands above *both* the philosopher (the Visitor from Elea, who is presented as an accomplished philosopher. *Soph.*, 216a), and the images—just as the good lies beyond both forms and their appearances, the intelligible and the sensible realms.

171. Compare our reading to that of Ruby Blondell, who argues that Plato reduces Socrates' role in these later dialogues in order to put Socrates in his place and free himself from his "father," to show that Socrates isn't enough. "The Man with No Name: Socrates and the Visitor From Elea," in *Plato as Author: The Rhetoric of Philosophy,* edited by Anne Michelini (Leiden: Brill, 2003), 247–66. Apart from the various (and dubious) psychological needs she implies, Blondell's argument rests on the suggestion that philosophy transcends individuals, and so Plato must ultimately leave Socrates behind. Her suggestion is, I believe, the distortion of an important truth; it fails to see that true transcendence always "recovers" particularity, as we will see in our coda to this book.

172. *Ap.,* 34a, 38b; *Phd.,* 59b. See Hyland, *Finitude and Transcendence,* 142: "Plato never speaks in his own voice; he is both always present and always absent." The author adds in a footnote: "Or in the singular case of the *Apology,* present but silent." Cf. Diskin Clay, *Platonic Questions,* x.

173. For a brief but well-documented sketch of the history of modern Plato interpretations, with particular attention to the questions raised by Plato's anonymity, see Gerald Press's introduction to *Who Speaks for Plato?* 1–11.

neutic space created by his "absence" is no doubt one of the reasons for the incomparable fruitfulness of his philosophy. Perhaps such a fruitfulness is it-self a sign of the goodness at its heart.[174] In any event, among the various interpretations of this absence that have been offered, a unique possibility emerges from the line we have been following here: a kind of invisibility is the very mode proper to philosophy. From the perspective we are present-ing, we could say that Plato's style is thus not an idiosyncrasy, and not even simply a function of his own approach to the philosophical life, but is a para-digmatic expression of philosophy as such, to the extent that intelligibility is rooted in goodness and philosophy is thus concerned, not with an aspect, but with the whole of reality.

Socrates never wrote a word.[175] In the *Theaetetus*, he describes himself as a midwife who helps bring truth to birth in others rather than generating it himself.[176] We will explore in more detail in the next chapter the philo-sophical significance of this description, but we may nevertheless draw out some implications in the light of this chapter's discussion. To reject the title of teacher, as Socrates does, is to confess a kind of intellectual poverty that we may interpret in the positive sense of poverty indicated earlier. Posses-sion, as we have suggested, can never escape a kind of limited relativity. In this respect, to grasp the ultimate as ultimate must necessarily mean to allow oneself to be grasped *by* the ultimate. A grasp of this sort will therefore have the structure of expropriation and obedience. In not making a claim on truth of his own, insofar as this gesture is not the skeptical rejection of the possi-bility of truth, Socrates makes manifest a truth that is greater than himself. But it is precisely this that is required to transcend the cave of relativity, it is precisely this that brings the absolute to bear *in* its absoluteness. Socrates' philosophical "non-authorship"—inasmuch as "author" means "authoritative progenitor"—is what opens up the ground, we suggest, of intelligibility.

174. Fruitfulness is, after all, the consequence of the vision of the beautiful/good in the *Sym-posium*. It is significant that, according to our analysis, the "highest stage" of the philosopher's as-cent is not a final appropriation of the good, but a fruitfulness in it: the "always greater" character of the good never disappears.

175. According to Figal, this is precisely because his philosophy is so inseparably bound up with his life. *Sokrates*, 13.

176. *Tht.*, 149a. Interestingly, Socrates discloses his practice of this art to Theaetetus as a guarded secret: "Only don't give me away to the rest of the world, will you? You see, my friend, it is a secret that I have this art" (149a). The majority of people believe he simply creates confusion; but Socrates sees this as a means to bring them to truth.

But, in spite of appearances, Plato is no more an author than Socrates; or perhaps he is, like Socrates, an author in the etymological sense of the word: one who "augments" or "makes grow." In *Letter VII*, Plato explains that there will never be a book on philosophy with his name on it, not least of all because knowledge cannot be communicated with words alone.[177] The true mode of disclosure, or the mode of disclosure adequate to truth, requires a pointing away from oneself and what is one's own. It is perhaps significant that the two thinkers in the Western tradition "notorious" for having hidden their authorship behind pseudonyms, (Pseudo-)Dionysius the Areopagite and Søren Kierkegaard, both had, just like Plato, an acute sense of truth's rootedness in the good and the subsequent necessity for a transformation of one's relation to reality in order to come to knowledge of it. Kierkegaard spoke of the necessity of "gesticulating with one's whole existence"—i.e., becoming wholly transparent—as the only adequate way to speak of truth.[178] Dionysius likewise insisted that "we should declare the Truth, not with enticing words of man's wisdom, but in *demonstration of the power* which the Spirit stirred up in the Sacred Writers, whereby, in a manner surpassing speech and knowledge, we embrace those truths which, in like manner, surpass them, in that Union which exceeds our faculty and exercise of discursive, and of intuitive reason."[179] While Plato did not write under a pseudonym, like these later authors, his thought was shot through with the conviction that one presents truth best by becoming, as it were, a window that opens onto it, and his display of the philosophical life through the complexity of a dramatic inquiry rather than the two-dimensional elaboration of a treatise serves this purpose in an exemplary manner. The first reason a sixth-century interpreter gives for Plato's style is that "the dialogue is a kind of cosmos"—unless we ought to say instead that "the cosmos is a kind of dialogue."[180]

As we briefly discussed in the introduction to this book, there are some who see Plato's disappearance behind other characters as intending to show

177. *Letter VII*, 341C, 344C.

178. Source unknown. Kierkegaard also famously presents Socrates as the greatest teacher for having mediated a relation to truth and then disappearing: "Nor is the teacher anything more, and if he gives of himself and his erudition in any other way, he does not give but takes away," *Philosophical Fragments*, translated by H. Hong and E. Hong (Princeton, N.J.: Princeton University Press, 1985), 11.

179. Dionysius the Areopagite, *Divine Names*, translated by C. E. Rolt (England, Kessinger, n.y.), 51. Emphasis mine.

180. *Anonymous Prolegomena to Platonic Philosophy*, 28.

that philosophy is an open-ended process, and thus Plato *has* no particular philosophy.[181] Others claim he does have a philosophy, but one that for reasons of prudence needed to be kept hidden from the many.[182] Our interpretation, however, suggests that hiddenness is not a political strategy but the very essence of the life of the philosopher. The dialogues, from this perspective, are not a screen held up to the ignorant many, behind which Plato whispered his true ideas to his intimates; they are rather the very means by which the hidden can be manifest without eclipsing the invisibility *(sic!)* that makes it what it is. The dialogue presents a *definite idea,* rather than simply showing people having conversations in order to inspire us to have our own equally aimless conversations. The definite idea, or as Press calls it, the vision, *theoria,*[183] to which the dialogues introduce us requires an intellectual space greater than the mind of a single individual—because the heart of this vision is a truth in relation to which one must forget oneself. Socrates communicates this truth through his maieutic art; Plato does this by not laying bare his own thoughts as his own, but by creating, as it were, the stage on which Socrates has the freedom to point beyond himself to a truth that comprehends both himself and his interlocutors. Neither Socrates nor Plato alone could show the truth for what it is, because a truth that is one man's possession is simply no truth at all. *Comprehensiveness* is the very mode of truth, if the *Republic* has it right. What these philosophers cannot communicate as individuals they communicate in a dramatic interaction that seems to be unique in history. We have here—to use Kierkegaard's terms—at once both the hero and his poet.[184] By each of them pointing away from themselves, they communicate jointly something infinitely greater than the two of them, like the mirrors that endlessly reflect against one another the energy of light until it acquires the piercing force to pass beyond them, the force of a laser beam.[185]

181. See, for example, Randall, *Plato,* 1–5; Robert Wardy, *The Birth of Rhetoric: Gorgias, Plato and Their Successors* (London: Routledge, 1996), 53–54.

182. See, for example, Strauss, *City and Man,* 50–62.

183. Press, "Plato's Dialogues as Enactments," 146–47.

184. See the first paragraph of the "Speech in Praise of Abraham," in *Fear and Trembling,* translated by Alastair Hannay (London: Penguin, 1985), 49–50.

185. The image of mirrors reflecting off of one another and gaining in intensity is one Plato uses for friendship. *Phdr.,* 255a–e. Legend connects Plato and Socrates even more deeply than the teacher-student (or hero-poet) relationship: the days reported for the births of Socrates and Plato are the sixth and the seventh of Thargelion, respectively. The former was celebrated as the birthday of Artemis, the latter, of Apollo—the divine twins. See Riginos, *Platonica,* 15–17.

CHAPTER FIVE

THE TRUTH IS DEFENSELESS

*Or: How the Truth Viewed as Indemonstrably and
Thus Indefensibly Good Provides a Response to
the Sophistic Logic of Violence*

Guarding Reason

The *Republic* introduces the philosopher in the guise of a guardian. The beneficiary of this guardianship is, of course, the ideal city. But the philosopher's task raises an immediate question: against whom does the philosopher guard the city? A "real" city must protect itself against its warring neighbors, but a "city-in-speech," occupying "no place" (utopia), has no such neighbors. If we consider that a city in speech is in fact the rational ordering of a common life—the city is made, as Plato puts it, "from the beginning by reason" (τῷ λόγῳ ἐξ ἀρχῆς ποιῶμον πόλιν, 369c)—then the most direct enemies of this city would be the enemies of reason. The philosopher's task would be to defend the life of reason against whatever forces threaten it.[1] Clearly, for Plato, the principal threat to reason comes from the institution of sophistry and its hyperrationalism. Had Thrasymachus not assailed Socrates in book I, the *Republic* would have come to an end shortly after its beginning, and the group would have been able to catch the torch-lit horse race after all. At the moment of the attack, Socrates had just led Polemarchus to understand the significance of the difference between being and appearance and the nonrelativity of goodness (334c–335e), and had persuaded him to join Socrates' side in battle (335e). The impetus of the dialogue as a whole thus arises first of all from Thrasymachus's aggression. From this perspective,

---

1. On the philosophers' need to "put time in as warriors," and the significance of *thumos* even for the specifically intellectual ends of the city, see Patrick Coby, "Why Are There Warriors in Plato's *Republic?*" *History of Political Thought* 22.3 (2001): 377–99.

the *Republic* begins to look like a defense of philosophy against the sophists. There is no doubt warrant for the view sometimes proposed that Plato wrote this dialogue in part to give Socrates a more substantial apologia than he was permitted to give in the courtroom.

If we agree to view the *Republic* as a defense of the life of reason against its enemies, we run up against a series of difficult questions, which the present chapter intends to engage. First, is it in fact possible to defend the life of reason, if this means to give a rational defense of rationality? To enter into this question, we will discuss the account of knowledge that Plato presents in *Letter VII,* which agrees in the most decisive points with the interpretation we have offered of the *Republic,* and then consider the significance of the inference Plato draws in light of this account, namely, that true knowledge cannot be defended, at least not directly. The second question is: If reason cannot be defended directly, can it be defended indirectly, and what would this mean? In other words, what sorts of things must be defended in order to defend the life of reason, and how are they to be defended? To respond to this question, we will consider the modes of reasoning and engaging others and the attitudes toward reason expressed in both philosophy and sophistry. Because of the nature of the problem, the confrontation between philosophy and sophistry will turn out to be a confrontation between two fundamentally different modes of life and conceptions of the nature of reality. Our discussion of this issue will draw from the numerous dialogues that depict the contest between these two views of reason, especially the *Gorgias.* The third question is: If fruitful engagement presupposes joint assent to certain principles, can there in fact be any discussion between reason and its enemies, between philosophy and sophistry? If the answer is negative, as it seems to be *prima facie,* does this imply the impotence of reason and thus the victory of sophistry?

We ought to point out, however, that the purpose of this chapter is not simply to attempt to give discrete answers to these questions. Instead, our engagement with these questions serves the more basic purpose of fleshing out the nature of reason that follows from its ultimate ordering to the good. As will become apparent, the attitude toward reason that is expressed in the manner a person engages with ideas and in discussion with others and more generally orders his life has an intrinsic connection with his conception of the structure of reason. Typically, when one studies Plato's notion of reason, one attends to his explicit accounts of the "mechanics" of thinking in, say, his presentation of dialectic, and one gives little weight to the subtle revelations of the meaning of reason in the more dramatic and literary elements of the dialogue. But if drama depicts the interaction of various pursuits of ends, and if Plato is right that what one pursues is invariably the good in one guise or another, then we may consider dramatic action to be a "moving image" of the good, just as time is a "moving image" of eternity.[2] And if it is necessary to know the good in order to know anything else, then the concrete expressions of one's view of goodness will have a direct bearing on one's understanding of knowledge and reason more generally. Our contrast of philosophy and sophistry is thus meant to bring into relief a few of these more concrete aspects of the life of reason as Plato understands it. Along these same lines, the chapter will conclude with a reflection on the philosophical significance of Socrates' profession of ignorance, and how the view of reason it implies represents a more comprehensive response to the problem of sophistry than is generally recognized.

Real Knowledge and Ecstatic Reason

In the philosophical digression of *Letter VII* (341b–344d),[3] Plato offers a sketch of the incremental stages of reason's approach to its proper object. His description of the rational ascent, though it differs in several basic respects

---

2. Cf. *Ti.,* 37d.

3. There has, of course, been controversy since the nineteenth century over the authenticity of this letter (see R. S. Bluck, *Plato's Seventh and Eighth Letters* [Cambridge: Cambridge University Press, 1947], 174–81), a controversy we will not enter into here, except to note a few things. While scholarly opinion has shifted back and forth since the issue was first raised, at present a strong majority of modern interpreters defend its authenticity—and this after apparently all of the conceivable means of evaluating and adjudicating the question have been pursued at length. (See Sayre, *Plato's Literary Garden,* xix.) The most comprehensive stylometric analysis done on the letter comes out in favor of Plato's authorship. (See Gerard Ledger, *Re-counting Plato: A Computer Analysis of Plato's Style* [Oxford: Clarendon Press, 1989], 148–50, 199.) Moreover, as we noted in an earlier chapter, Brumbaugh has shown that the philosophical "digression," which some have taken to be a later insertion even if the rest of the letter is genuine, is representative of one of the most unique aspects of Plato's writing, his "stylistic fingerprint" (see Brumbaugh, "Dialogue and Digression"). It is impossible to come to a definitive conclusion on the matter, but it seems to be the case, as Gonzalez has observed, that the final issue is whether the letter is philosophically consistent with Plato's thought expressed more generally in the dialogues (*Dialectic and Dialogue,* 246–47). We will show that it seems to be quite consistent, and indeed on a fairly subtle point. For all intents and purposes, we will in the present context assume Plato to be the author, and agree with Drew Hyland that it must have been written, if not by Plato himself, at least by someone with a profound understanding of Plato, which suffices for our purposes. Hyland,

from the description given in the divided line, is nevertheless distinctly analogous to the view portrayed in the *Republic* and brings to expression something left implicit in that account.[4]

The description of reason's approach to its object comes in the context
of Plato's explanation of why he, in contrast to Dionysius II, is suspicious of
the possibility of writing when it comes to philosophy. The reason he offers
concerns the nature of true knowledge and the way to obtain it. In his words,
"For every real being, there are three things that are necessary if knowledge
of it is to be acquired: first, the name; second, the definition; third, the image; knowledge comes fourth, and in the fifth place we must put the object
itself, the knowable and truly real being."[5] Plato presents the first three things
on the list as prerequisites for knowledge; they represent necessary *but not
sufficient* conditions for knowledge. The fact that Plato distinguishes between
possessing a definition (second level) and possessing knowledge (fourth level) indicates quite clearly that one can have a definition of what something
is without having knowledge of it. Nevertheless, to accept this distinction is
not to deny that a person who *does* have knowledge ought therefore to be
capable of giving a definition, or at least of distinguishing it in reason from
other things.[6] It simply implies that something beyond the statement of the

---

"Why Plato Wrote Dialogues,"49n5. Cf. Margherita Isnardi-Parente, "Per l'interpretazione della
VII Epistola Platonica," *La parola del passato: rivista di studi classici* 97 (1964): 241–90, here 242.

4. The most obvious difference is that *Letter VII* presents five levels where the *Republic* has
only four. But this is easily accounted for by context: the letter concerns the relationship between
words and thought while the *Republic* concerns the relationship between the sensible and intelligible in relation to the good. In spite of this difference, they both express a similar view of reason as "ascending" to the really real in itself and so beyond any merely relative manifestations, be
they in language or in sense experience. Glenn Morrow points out the following differences: the
Letter makes no use of the terms "idea" or "dialectic," and instead employs a technical distinction
indicated here between ποῖόν τί and τί, which doesn't occur anywhere else in Plato. (Mauro
Tulli, however, draws our attention to a passage in the *Republic*, 438c–439b, which elaborates the
difference between the condition of being ποῖόν τί and ἁπλῶς or δι' αὐτό. *Dialettica e scrittura*, 30; cf. Isnardi-Parente, "Per l'interpretazione," 282.) Moreover, there is no explicit distinction between knowledge and opinion. Morrow himself does not believe these differences present
any obstacle to taking the *Letter* as genuine, primarily because the view of coming to know reality expressed here accords so well in its substance with what Plato expresses in other dialogues.
(And wouldn't a forger be sure to use terms like "idea" and "dialectic," and to employ the distinction between knowledge and opinion?) See *Plato's Epistles*, translated and with critical essays and
notes by Glenn R. Morrow (New York: Bobbs-Merrill Company, 1962), 60–81.

5. *Letter VII*, 342a–b.

6. It is thus that the inadequacy of definitions can be harmonized with Plato's regular insistence that a person who can't give a definition can't be said to know something. See Wieland,

essential properties of a thing is required to reach knowledge of it. Plato does not specify here what constitutes the difference, but it is not difficult to imagine what he has in mind. A definition is in the end simply *words*, which a person can memorize without understanding their meaning. Understanding, by contrast, would seem to imply some acquaintance with the thing being defined.[7] From this perspective, a definition, like a name or an image, would provide not an end point but a stepping stone toward the final goal, namely, knowledge itself.

But here we encounter a surprise: it turns out that *knowledge is not reason's destination*. Instead of presenting knowledge as the end, Plato adds a further step. After knowledge comes *the real being itself*, which is knowable (ὅ ... γνωστόν τε καὶ ἀληθῶς ἐστιν ὄν).[8] The fourth level, knowledge, is included with the three preliminary levels as "what she [the soul] is not seeking," while the fifth is the *essence* (τὸ τί), which is the soul's true end.[9] Before we consider in detail what this assertion might mean, it is helpful to look at the general picture of reason it implies, because it represents a radical departure from familiar views of reason and its objects. We tend to picture the act of reason as Aristotle does: it terminates *within* the soul (ἐν ... τῇ ψυχῇ) because it is there that intelligible objects have their proper existence.[10] When Aristotle goes on to say, then, that the soul becomes *identical* to its objects when it knows them, the locus of this identity must lie formally within the soul itself.[11] It is perhaps not coincidental that such a view of reason corresponds to Aristotle's view of love. As he explains in the *Nichomachean Ethics*, self-love is the paradigm of love because it represents an absolute unity that other forms of love can only defectively imitate.[12] The soul's

---

"La Critica de Platón a la Escritura y los Limites de la Communicabilidad," 26–27; Gonzalez, "Non-propositional Knowledge in Plato," 239 and 280.

7. For a concise account of this in the *Theaetetus*, see R. S. Bluck, "'Knowledge by Acquaintance' in Plato's *Theaetetus*," *Mind* 72 (1963): 259–63.

8. *Letter VII*, 342b.

9. *Letter VII*, 343c.

10. Aristotle, *De Anima*, II, 5, 417b18–24.

11. Cf. 430a19–21, III.7.431a1–2. What thinks and what is thought, he says, are identical in the absence of matter (*De Anima*, III, 5, 430a1–10); though knowledge *begins* with the really existing, sensible thing outside the soul, abstraction allows the soul to bring the (matterless) form into itself in a perfect sense. This is what it means for the soul to be, in a certain sense, all things (III, 8, 431b20–432a14).

12. Aristotle, *Nich. Eth.*, IX, 4, 1166a10–1166b2.

perfect unity with itself is thus, for Aristotle, the beginning and end of both reason and love.[13] In contrast to this, as we have argued above, Plato espouses an essentially *ecstatic* notion of love, expressed in the soul's transcendence toward its object, a transcendence that necessarily includes a moment of expropriation. For a soul to join with its object, it does not take the object into itself (as it seems to in Aristotle), but goes out in some sense to enter into the object.[14] In the *Republic,* Plato insists that a philosophical soul is specifically characterized by its "always stretching itself out to the whole and the all" (τοῦ ὅλου καὶ παντὸς ἀεὶ ἐπορέξεσθαι, 486a). Something similar is suggested in *Letter VII* with respect to reason: the act terminates not in the soul but in the real thing itself. In this sense, we could say that, for Plato, like love itself, *reason is essentially ecstatic.* Reason, in other words, comes to an end outside of itself. What does this mean exactly?

We can spell out more precisely what Plato is saying here if we attend to a couple of ambiguities in his account. First of all, when he goes on to elaborate the various "stages" of reason's approach to its object, Plato groups together on the fourth level, which he had identified as the level of knowledge, a strange assortment of items: "In the fourth place are knowledge, reason, and right opinion (ἐπιστήμη καὶ ὁῦς ἀληθής τε δόξα) (which are in our souls [ἐν ψυχαῖς], not in words or bodily shapes, and therefore must be taken together as something distinct both from the circle itself and from the three things previously mentioned)."[15] Normally, Plato insists, of course, on a sharp distinction between knowledge and right opinion,[16] but he includes them at the same level in this case. Is this a sign of inauthenticity, or just confusion? Or is it perhaps the sloppiness that one might expect in a letter as

---

13. This affirmation should not be taken to exclude the genuine insistence in Aristotle that a friend be loved essentially for his own sake, and the analogy this love could have with reason. The details of this analogy await a future study.

14. Oddly, Ludwig Edelstein, one of the strongest recent defenders of the *Letter's* being by someone other than Plato, bases his rejection of authenticity on the fact that Plato makes knowledge immanent in the soul here in this letter, which is a clear departure from his exceptionless insistence in the other dialogues on the *transcendence* of the forms, the objects of the soul, in relation to the soul. See Edelstein, *Plato's Seventh Letter* (Leiden: Brill, 1966), 98–105. Edelstein disregards the letter's clear statement that the soul must move beyond itself to attain true knowledge of the being or essence (343c), which the author distinguishes from what he calls knowledge at the fourth level.

15. *Letter VII,* 342c. The word "soul" replaces the word "mind" in the English translation.

16. E.g., *Meno,* 98b.

opposed to a published work? In fact, Plato's including these things together at the same level makes good sense once we consider the specific point he intends to make. Plato wants to show that genuine philosophical knowledge cannot be put into words like other things, or perhaps better, that words, as essential as Plato makes them out to be, can never simply substitute for the reality itself.[17] What is it that *can* be put into words? He says it is the qualities of an object (τὸ ποῖόν τι), as distinct from its being (τὸ ὄν) (343b–c). As Gonzalez interprets it, the qualities of an object are all the things that can be said about it, while the being is the unity of the thing that transcends the plurality of attributes, the essence that can be known but not expressed as it is known.[18]

Now, Plato affirms that the four levels all present the qualities of a thing (τὸ ποῖόν τι), and only the fifth level corresponds to that which the soul in fact seeks, namely, the being itself.[19] It is in relation to this concern that we ought to understand Plato's ordering of the levels. If he groups knowledge and right opinion (along with νοῦς) together on a single level, it is because there is some feature they share in common, which distinguishes them from everything else. The feature Plato identifies is that they *lie in the soul*.[20] No-

17. Gadamer puts this point beautifully; for him it is the key point in the philosophical digression in this *Letter*, and represents the heart of Plato's philosophy: "That which seeks to present something cannot be the thing itself it is presenting. There lies in the essence of these means of knowledge the fact that, in order to be able to be such a means, they must possess an inessentiality [*Unwesen*] proper to them. It is at the same time their essence to be the non-being [*Unwesen*] of what they present," *Dialektik und Sophistik im siebenten platonischen Brief* (Heidelberg: Carl Winter Universitätsverlag, 1964), 25. Cf. Tulli, *Dialettica e scrittura*, 35–36, who suggests that there is something of the ἄπειρον and thus of τὸ ψεῦδος in every grasp of a thing prior to the absolute.

18. See Gonzalez, "Non-propositional Knowledge," 244–47. Bluck interprets ποῖόν, not as the accidental qualities of a thing, but as its *suchness*, i.e., "likeness," 126–27, which is to be contrasted with the *real nature* of a thing. Bluck's claim that τὸ ὄν does not mean "real *thing*," but rather "'the real *nature*' of a thing" (127) does not seem to take into account that the essential nature *is* the real thing for Plato. The heart of the matter, here, is a distinction between the thing taken in a particular respect and the thing taken simply in itself. Isnardi-Parente reduces the distinction to that between essential and accidental properties ("Per l'interpretazione," 281–86), but the difference is more fundamental, namely, between the reality itself and *any* of its qualities, any particular *aspect* under which it is grasped.

19. *Letter VII*, 343c.

20. Or, as Gadamer puts it, the distinguishing mark is that these are all things possessed *as one's own*: "das Eigensein (das So-und-so-sein, die Meinigkeit) einer Ansicht oder Erkenntnis," *Dialektik und Sophistik*, 24. Notice, it was *precisely* this character that Aristotle had ascribed to the proper objects of knowledge; and it is precisely what *distinguishes* inadequate knowledge from the complete form.

tice, Plato is here talking specifically about the *form* of the relationship implied between the soul and reality. He is not, in other words, talking about truth or falsity, stability or instability, which is typically at issue when he distinguishes between knowledge and opinion.[21] Instead, the significant issue in this context is *place,* i.e., the locus or terminus of the soul's movement toward reality. This is why he does not need to distinguish knowledge from right opinion in this particular context, because they both reside "in the soul." What is important to Plato in *Letter VII,* and the one thing he insists on here, is that they are distinct, both from words (names or definitions) and shapes (images) on the one hand, and from the reality itself on the other. Right opinion and knowledge may be "true" or correct in themselves—in fact they necessarily *are* by definition—but they nevertheless remain penultimate in relation to the soul's aspiration to the real. It is also precisely this that gives them the same "rank," as it were. Unless reason is essentially ecstatic, it would make no sense to line up knowledge and opinion next to each other.[22]

The second ambiguity in this brief passage concerns Plato's apparently inconsistent use of the word "knowledge," ἐπιστήμη. While he labels the fourth level "knowledge" at 342b, he speaks of "perfectly attaining" knowledge of the reality itself, level five, at 342e. The only way to make sense of this ambiguity is to assume that Plato does not mean ἐπιστήμη in a technical, i.e., univocal, sense, but is using the term here more broadly to designate two different "types" of knowledge.[23] If we accept the difference Plato just indicated between levels four and five, we could say that "level-four knowledge" is the understanding of something that the soul possesses in itself, can presumably carry with itself in the absence of the thing known, and can even, say, formulate in written or spoken words. "Level-five knowledge," by contrast, would represent what might be called immediate knowledge, that is,

---

21. See, for example, *Meno,* 97dff.

22. Of course, our interpretation faces the opposite problem of distinguishing between knowledge and true opinion in this case. Without entering into the details, which are not immediately relevant to our present discussion, we could suggest that a person might have a true opinion simply by virtue of having been told something, without seeing it for himself, and one might also see something for himself (knowledge) and nevertheless come to rest in his own grasp of the reality, rather than remaining open to the reality that remains more than just this grasp—in the manner of Socrates' faithful ignorance, which we will describe at the end of this chapter.

23. Plato often insists that philosophy should avoid an overly technical use of terms. see, e.g., *Plt.,* 261e. He was well known for varying his own terms: D. L., III.63–64.

the knowledge a soul has when it actually "connects" with a thing beyond itself.[24] This latter type of knowledge does not, of course, exclude the former, but it is also not reducible to it.

This explanation not only gives a natural meaning to an otherwise complicated passage, but it also accords in essential ways with the theory of knowledge presented in the *Republic,* as we have interpreted it. In chapter 2, we proposed that the twofold nature of the good implies two different—connected but distinct—ways of knowing: on the one hand, there is the relative knowledge of how something is good (an account of the benefit it affords or the purpose it serves), and on the other hand, there is the "absolute" knowledge that consists in the soul's "grasp" of a thing's intrinsic goodness, which is the soul's intimate intercourse with the reality itself. There is not enough evidence here to suggest that Plato had precisely the same thing in mind in the two cases, but there is an undeniable similarity. The two accounts completely agree in ascribing to reason some kind of self-transcending character, which plays a crucial role in both views of the structure of reason.

We have argued that the key to the good's function as foundation of both truth and being is its status as transcendent measure. There would be no way to escape the cave of relativism unless it were possible to find a criterion for knowledge that was not simply immanent to the mind. Somehow, mind has to get beyond mind in order for it to *be* mind: at the heart of Plato's most complete view of knowledge—if this is what we can take the *Republic* to represent—is the moment of discontinuity within reason's own trajectory. But such a trajectory is precisely what Plato describes in *Letter VII,* insofar as this passage presents the soul coming to its proper end and finding what it most seeks (343c) *beyond* the soul (level four) and in reality itself, viewed in relation to itself as distinct from its relation to the soul. And yet, somewhat paradoxically, he refers in both accounts to this final destination as a kind of knowledge. This indicates that the expropriative moment

24. This way of contrasting the two "types" of knowledge follows more immediately from the text than Gonzalez's distinction between propositional and non-propositional knowledge (*Dialectic and Dialogue,* 256), which he offers to clarify the disagreement between Nicholas White and Gadamer in their essays in Griswold, *Platonic Readings, Platonic Writings* (see Gonzalez, 383n38), but they are ultimately pointing to the same thing. One might also compare this distinction with Aristotle's distinction between first and second actualities in relation to knowledge. *De Anima,* II, 1.412a23–27. Here is the difference between the "possession" of knowledge, and its "employment." Wieland seems to interpret *Letter VII* along these lines ("La Critica de Platón," 26–27), but he stresses the practical aspect of this actualization.

does not destroy or eliminate reason, but rather completes it.[25] It is not a "mystical" vision that dispenses with knowledge, but is the true or complete form of knowing.[26] In this respect, we might consider that the ambiguity of the word ἐπιστήμη in this passage from the letter could correspond as well to the difference between the third and fourth segments of the divided line; while these two segments both represent the intelligible order (as opposed to opinion or imagination), the fourth alone includes the discontinuous moment of reference to an unhypothetical first principle, and so it alone is knowledge in the complete sense.[27] If it is true, according to the *Republic*, that we can have knowledge of a thing in an objective or real sense only if we see it as good in itself and not merely in relation to us, then it is also true, according to *Letter VII*, that we reach the real being of a thing only if the soul arrives beyond itself to something that does not lie simply "in the soul."[28] In short, there is a profound unity between the *Republic* and *Letter VII* on what it means, finally, to know.[29]

So, we could say that the fifth stage that Plato describes in *Letter VII* differs from the previous stages insofar as it marks the moment the soul makes genuine contact with reality *on reality's terms*. This difference implies two others. On the one hand, Plato says, everything at the first four levels is disputable: names are arbitrary, no particular definition, as a combination of

25. As Ferber observes, the "light" of insight that the letter refers to is neither suprarational nor irrational. *Die Unwissenheit des Philosophen oder Warum hat Plato die "ungeschriebene Lehre" nicht geschrieben?* (St. Augustin: Academia Verlag), 1991, 38. We might qualify this slightly: it is perfectly rational *because* it is in a certain sense suprarational.

26. Edelstein speaks of mysticism in *Letter VII*, which he claims to be another feature that separates this letter irrevocably from the rest of Plato's work. What he means by mystical, here, is that it is in the end a passion of the soul rather than knowledge that can be articulated. (See *Plato's Seventh Letter*, 106–8.) But Wieland points out that when Plato critiques writing, for example, it is not in relation to special experiences, but to the most ordinary realities. "La Critica de Platón," 22.

27. Cf. *Letter VII*, 342e.

28. Ferber points out that the *full* participation in the idea (level five) does *not* mean perfectly "possessing" it. *Unwissenheit*, 42. However, Ferber goes on to include the fifth level among the "defective" forms of access to reality (50); in other words, for Ferber, level five represents an "imperfect" grasp. Our interpretation, by contrast, is that "grasping"—whether perfect or imperfect—is a notion that does not apply in this case, because it is, as it were, beyond its own grasp.

29. Contra Edelstein, who points out that *Letter VII* refers to knowledge of *things* at the end of the philosophical trajectory, rather than the *good*, as the *Republic* has it (*Plato's Seventh Letter*, 94–95). In our interpretation, *Letter VII* simply expresses the *content* of what it means to know the good.

words, can be considered established once and for all, images must by necessity contain contradictory features, and one can always argue about claims to knowledge.[30] By implication, the fifth level would be the only one beyond disputation.[31]

On the other hand, Plato goes on to say that, while the contents of the first four levels can be defended and argued for, the fifth level *cannot be defended:*

> Now in those matters in which, because of our defective training, we are not accustomed to look for truth but are satisfied with the first image suggested to us, we can ask and answer without making ourselves ridiculous to one another, being proficient in manipulating and testing these four instruments. But when it is "the fifth" about which we are compelled to answer or to make explanations, then *anyone who wishes to refute has the advantage,* and can make the propounder of a doctrine, whether in writing or speaking or in answering questions, seem to most of his listeners completely ignorant of the matter on which he is trying to speak or write. Those who are listening sometimes do not realize that it is not the soul of the speaker or writer which is being refuted, but these four instruments mentioned, each of which is by nature defective.[32]

If we were to ask why the speaker's soul is not being refuted here, we would have to say it is because the soul is in this case no longer merely in itself (level four) but rather with the real being that is known. The very same thing that makes knowledge indisputable makes it indefensible as well, namely, its absolute quality. Whatever one "possesses" in one's soul will always exist there within certain determinate conditions, from a particular perspective.[33] When the soul takes something into possession, it is received according to the mode of the recipient, which entails some difference between the soul's

---

30. Although Plato includes the fourth level among the things that can be disputed (343a–b), he does not offer a specific reason for its disputability as he does for the other three levels. Instead, it falls under the general comment that the contents of the four levels can be easily contradicted by sense-perception (*Letter VII,* 343c).

31. The kind of knowledge Plato intends here, because it cannot be an opinion or definition capable of being sufficiently formulated in a proposition, cannot be true or false the way an opinion or definition can be. On this point, see Wieland, "La Critica de Platón," 28, and Gonzalez, "Non-propositional Knowledge," 240.

32. *Letter VII,* 343c–d. Emphasis added. The word "soul" has again been substituted for "mind" in the English translation, which corresponds to the Greek.

33. Cf. Gadamer, *Dialektik und Sophistik,* 24; Gadamer, *Dialogue and Dialectic,* Eight Hermeneutical Studies on Plato, translated by Christopher Smith (New Haven, Conn.: Yale University Press, 1983), 112.

grasp and the object to be grasped, to the extent that the soul is not the object itself. This difference is what makes the grasp able to be contradicted in some fashion—as Plato puts it, it is "easy to refute by sense perception"—because it takes only another perspective to show up the constitutive limitation of the first. And yet, precisely because it is something in one's possession, one is capable of defending it, arguing on its behalf.[34] To get beyond the relative conditions of one's grasp and thus to attain to an "absolute" perspective means surrendering one's possession of the object and therefore one's ability to argue in a fully adequate manner on its behalf. The problem with debates between skeptics and dogmatists, or, in modern language, between "coherentists" and "foundationalists" or perhaps between "relativists" and "absolutists," is that both sides typically assume that knowledge has no other form than that of a possession that is able to be formulated propositionally. One side claims that some of these formulations have absolute and universal validity, the other claims that none do. But neither sees the mode of knowledge that Plato indicates here is genuinely absolute: it is not the soul's possession of a thing, and so it is not a conceptual content that can be verbally formulated, but is rather the soul's dwelling with the *being* of the thing itself, a relation that, precisely because it transcends verbal formulation, provides in fact the only genuine basis for one's words.

There is an incredible tension here: the heart of a matter is what is most vulnerable; precisely what is most important cannot be said. And if it cannot be said, one can never give a fully adequate description of it or argument for it—at least not in words alone. We are reminded of Socrates' reticence in speaking about the idea of the good with precision at the very moment when he says precision is most necessary. It is the very nature of what is ultimate to be ultimately defenseless.[35] Whenever we make an argument for

34. Here we see the problem with White's interpretation of the "immediate" contact at level five, which he refers to as an intuition. He is right to say that it cannot be called "infallible," since that would be a category mistake ("Observations and Questions about Hans-Georg Gadamer's Interpretation of Plato," in Griswold, *Platonic Readings, Platonic Writings,* 255; cf. a similar observation by Gonzalez, *Dialectic and Dialogue,* 253–54), but he is wrong to say we cannot distinguish it from a hallucination: to make such an observation implies a too "immanentist" view of this contact, which is precisely the opposite of what Plato is describing, and resembles much more a modern epistemological horizon. Gadamer's response to this implication is illuminating. "Reply to Nicholas P. White," in Griswold, *Platonic Writings, Platonic Readings* 258–66.

35. According to Veggetti, Plato rejects the traditional views of the good by insisting it cannot be *appropriated,* either theoretically *or* practically. "L'Idea del Bene," 224.

something, we offer *reasons* for it. These reasons justify it, by explaining why it is good or necessary. But by justifying it in this way, we are implying that its own goodness or necessity is relative to these reasons. A verbal defense will be adequate to the extent that a thing's goodness is in fact reducible to these (relative) reasons that can be given for it. If such a defense succeeds, then it implies that the interlocutors accept the relativity of the thing's goodness. It follows that to assume that all things can be given justification by argument is to assume that there is nothing good in an intrinsic way, nothing good in a more than merely relative sense. Something that was good in an intrinsic sense would ultimately not be able to be justified in terms of anything but itself—and this includes any of its qualities, be they essential or accidental, which can be articulated in a proposition, for even an essential attribute is not the *being* of a thing, but the verbal sign of an aspect of it. Socrates can defend justice only by *being* just to the end.[36]

One can thus give powerful arguments on behalf of, say, justice, and defend them in a manner that keeps one from seeming "ridiculous," as Plato says, but all the while one remains at the penultimate level in relation to the being of justice. We can understand, then, why Socrates refuses to give an "adequate" verbal account of the good and insists that he can speak of it only in the mode of belief. In other words, he cannot speak as if what he is saying represents knowledge of it (506c), and so whatever he says remains an image rather than the reality itself (cf. 533a).[37] He thus shows himself in the *Republic* to be taking seriously what the author of *Letter VII* asserts; a modest silence about the heart of things is no false modesty, but a modesty that acknowledges what it means for something to be true in a more than relative sense. In this respect, *Letter VII* provides a decisive confirmation of our interpretation of goodness as the cause of truth: a thing is true because it exists in itself in a manner irreducible to its relations, and this is just what it means to participate in absolute goodness.

It is illuminating to see that a similar view of the soul's relationship to re-

36. We recall Adeimantus's demand that Socrates not simply defend justice *in words* with an argument about its benefits, but *show* what it means to be just. *Rep.,* 367d–e.

37. It is crucial to see that Socrates is *not* saying that the good cannot be known in some sense, but only that he cannot speak as if his statements *were* the knowledge itself. On Plato's emphasis on the "direct" vision, see Utermöhlen, *Die Bedeutung der Ideenlehre,* 99. We will see how Socrates' profession of ignorance is itself a revelation of the objective truth of things *qua* objective.

ality comes to expression in the connection between love and madness in the *Phaedrus* (and also, but less explicitly, in the *Symposium*). In this dialogue, Plato characterizes love as the wings that carry the soul into the realm of the really real reality, which is the home of truth, knowledge, and virtue. And yet, he describes the soul that makes this journey as essentially "out of its mind."[38] How does being out of one's mind bring one to truth, knowledge, and virtue? We can reconcile what appear to be opposites if we consider that, according to Socrates' account, the very reason for the intensity of love is that it is a response to absolute beauty.[39] We argued in chapter 2 that this is what explains the ecstasis of love; here, we wish to point out that the very same thing makes it, in a sense, "unjustifiable." Relative goods can be calculated and measured against one another. This is just how Socrates presents the work of "mundane" reason in his first speech in the *Phaedrus*: one can explain these relative goods in terms of self-interest, and thus in terms that makes sense, at a certain level, to everyone (even if doing so provokes the opposition of their own self-love). Genuine love, by contrast, cannot be "explained" exhaustively, which means that it cannot be "situated" in any manifest way relative to self-interest, precisely because it has an absolute character, or, rather, because it represents the relation to an absolute object. While the appearance of a relative good can always be accounted for in relation to the things that bring it about and the things that can be expected from it, something that is absolutely good is by its very nature in some sense a "sur-

38. Gregory Vlastos pointed out this "puzzle" and remarks: "This convergence of *mania* and *nous* in love does not seem to intrigue commentators. Few of them notice the paradox at all or, if they do, they seem bent on explaining it away," *Platonic Studies*, 27n80. Gerasimos Santas attempts to solve the puzzle in "Passionate Platonic Love in the *Phaedrus*," *Ancient Philosophy* 2 (1982): 105–14, by elucidating the difference between love of bodily beauty and that of divine beauty itself. The key, however, is the question why the passionate love of divine beauty is essentially "mad": Santas mentions this fact but does not offer a reason for it.

39. In a notebook written in 1880, Nietzsche offers an excellent—and altogether Platonic (!)—description of the essentially "infinite" character of that which inspires love: "Love arises when we are unable, in spite of all our efforts, to manage a complete overview of the goodness we owe to a possession. It is an overflowing toward something unlimited; it lacks the knowledge of the entire value of a thing or person, because no scale exists that would be big enough to measure [it]. One brings all of the highest things one knows into comparison with it; if we love, we constantly meditate on every sort of perfection, and because it always coincides [for us] immediately with the beloved object, we willingly confuse it with him," in Nietzsche, *Nachlaß 1880–1882*, in *Kritische Studienausgabe*, edited by Giorgo Colli and Mazzino Montinari (Berlin: Walter de Gruyter GmbH and Company, 1999), 63.

prise."[40] It is without ultimate explanation, and for that reason, it is without justification. However, it is crucial to add immediately that this does not make it irrational. Irrationality is the opposite of rationality, and if rationality is intrinsically connected with goodness, then irrationality is connected with its opposite. Thus, an irrational choice would be the choice of evil—or as Plato tends to put it, vice is ignorance.[41] A rationally justifiable choice is the choice of a relative good. But the love of which Plato speaks is the "choice" of an absolute good: far from being irrational, it is so fully and absolutely rational that one cannot ultimately explain why one chose it. This is why, in the experience of something in its absolute beauty, one never runs out of things to say. Again, we see the connection between this and the point Plato makes in *Letter VII* that the proper foundation for all speech cannot itself be adequately translated into words. While the *Phaedrus* seems to intend an almost "mystical" experience in contrast to the more ordinary acts of speech and reason that are presumably meant by *Letter VII*, it is important to see that the most extreme form of ecstasis in love remains analogous to any intellectual act that connects with a reality beyond the self.

Good Communication

From what has just been said, one might be tempted to take a tragic view of the life of reason.[42] If one cannot put the essential into words, then what is the point of talking? Genuine insight would seem to lie beyond anyone's

40. As Tulli puts it, the being of a thing is necessarily "unforeseen". *Dialettica e scrittura*, 36. Needless to say, we have a philosophical reason here why wonder should be the indispensable origin of philosophy, as Socrates says in the *Theaetetus*, 155e. Wonder represents an openness to what is greater than oneself, and this is the key, as we have seen, to the possibility of knowing the essence of things. Wonder is an intrinsic dimension of any properly philosophical knowing.

41. Of course, it is an extremely complicated question whether it is possible, in Plato's eyes, knowingly to choose what is bad. We cannot engage this question here, but consider: the objections typically presuppose that knowledge and goodness are extrinsic to one another, and one can have knowledge of something irrespective of the character of one's relationship to that thing. But this is a presupposition the present account of the connection between goodness and intelligibility squarely challenges. A vicious relationship always necessarily implies defective knowledge. See, in this regard, *Rep.*, 602a.

42. See David Roochnik, *The Tragedy of Reason: Toward a Platonic Conception of Logos* (New York: Routledge, 1990). Roochnik claims that reason can neither surrender its desire for knowledge, nor satisfy it, but must come to terms with its "conditional" goodness. We will address his position below.

control, and, once gained, would seem to have a purely private significance. One would be inclined to think of Wittgenstein as "Platonic," on this point at least. On such a view, moreover, fundamental knowledge would cut one off from others. This view of knowledge would ultimately be indistinguishable from the Protagorean relativism we discussed in chapter 1. If the essential were incommunicable and thus in some basic sense wholly private, we would lose any solid basis for discussion, insofar as discussion requires some common point of reference, as Socrates himself admits: "Well, Callicles, if human beings didn't share common experiences, some sharing one, others sharing another, but one of us had some unique experience not shared by others, it wouldn't be easy for him to communicate what he experienced to the other."[43] But entering the arena of general discourse would seem to require the embrace of relative expressions and forms of knowledge (levels one through four in *Letter VII*), the very things Plato claims are susceptible to manipulation and therefore hardly the foundation for genuine communication. Thus, the dilemma: what we *can* communicate is not worth communicating, and what we cannot, is. We ought not to be surprised, then, by the pessimistic tone that overcomes Plato when he addresses the question of genuine teaching, both in the *Republic* and in *Letter VII*.

But if communication in general contains an intrinsic tension, it seems to break down altogether in the face of fundamental challenges to reason. David Roochnik and Charles Griswold have discussed this collapse in Plato.[44] Griswold claims that Plato was obsessed with the problem of justifying philosophy (and thus reason), so much so that he never depicted mature

---

43. *Grg.*, 488c–d.

44. Roochnik, *Tragedy of Reason*; Griswold, "Plato's Metaphilosophy. Why Plato Wrote Dialogues," in *Platonic Writings, Platonic Readings*, 143–67. It is important to take issue with the term "metaphilosophy" that Griswold uses in this essay, a term he says was coined by a student of Wittgenstein. The term betrays a kind of *Philosophievergessenheit*. Philosophy itself is concerned essentially with the justification of philosophy (though this does not necessarily have to take the post-Kantian critical form that Griswold presents as the culmination of this philosophical impulse)—this has been one of its major themes from the very beginning—precisely because it is ordered to the foundations of reality. The notion that one steps outside of philosophy ("meta") to reflect on the question, What is philosophy? and also What is knowledge? assumes a reduced version of philosophy that would be foreign to classical thinkers like Plato, though of course somewhat common in Enlightenment and post-Enlightenment thought. *If* philosophy is one τέχνη among others, it would require a "metaphilosophy" for its justification. But Plato is evidently aware of philosophy's unique status in this regard. As we will see, it is just this status that makes it "useless" in comparison to sophistry.

philosophers in discussion with each other, but rather always philosophers in discussion with various forms of antiphilosophers.[45] The problem with such discussions, to use Rorty's term, is that they lack the "commensurating" principles necessary for dialogue to take place. Although Griswold shows how antiphilosophy cannot avoid being parasitical in some sense on the intelligible order philosophy represents, he suggests that it is ultimately impossible to mediate between philosophy and its stubborn critics.[46] The best one can do is draw on the sorts of "political," and thus prephilosophical commitments that bind one with one's interlocutor. In this respect, the task of justifying philosophy is never complete, and a justification for reason can never be stated in a definitive way. This explains the "occasional" character of Plato's dialogues, and why they tend to be provisional and open-ended.[47] By the same token, a "hardened" critic of philosophy is simply irrefutable, and his existence shows the limits of reason.

Along similar lines, Roochnik claims that Plato intends to portray reason as a kind of Sophoclean tragic hero. Reason aspires to greatness, as its nature compels it, but it is ultimately chastened by its failures and must in the end accept a humbled existence. *Logos,* Roochnik claims, *cannot* dialogue with the misologist, precisely because of the radical nature of the challenge he presents to reason: "The point is that if the issue is what counts as legitimately significant discourse, the argument must be circular: That mode of discourse must itself be used in order to establish itself as significant. There can be no philosophical dialogue concerning the nature of significant discourse itself."[48] Thus, through its failed attempts, *logos* finally comes to an insight: "It cannot refute its opponents, its accusers, those who hate it. It cannot even enter into dialogue with them. This it now sees. And such seeing brings with it a recognition of a previous blindness."[49] Rather than assuming the kingly role, logos must therefore accept the fact that it plays a kind of self-enclosed "game" with rules that cannot be justified to those outside, even though it can and ought to insist on those rules for any who wish to enter it. The game need not be considered trivial, Roochnik adds, just because it can make no claim on reality as such.[50] But it is a game nonetheless. Again, the confrontation with non-reason reveals reason's limits. We have to recognize the implications of this concession of the limits of reason: it implies the victory of sophistry.

45. Ibid., 152–54.   46. Ibid., 165.
47. Ibid., 156–57.   48. Roochnik, *Tragedy of Reason,* 151.
49. Ibid., 164.   50. Ibid., 164–76.

Before responding to the serious questions provoked by these two authors, let us first note that to say that the essential cannot be put into words *in its essential form* does not mean that it is simply incommunicable. It is possible, as we saw in the last chapter, for words and images to mediate an immediate relationship with the essential, that is, to communicate more than they contain. As the *Phaedrus* puts it, words function most properly when they "remind" the soul what it always, in some sense, already knows.[51] Thus, while a word simply taken in itself, in isolation from other things, does not "contain" knowledge (how could it?), nevertheless, *if truth is rooted in the good*, the word can become the bearer of what transcends it to the extent that it is, so to speak, a "good" word. In this context, being a good word means, on the one hand, arising in the context of a life fundamentally ordered to the good. On the other hand, it means analogously being properly rooted in a well-ordered whole, insofar as a part that accepts the place suited to it in a whole becomes a "partial" reflection of that wholeness, i.e., the intrinsic meaning or goodness of a thing. We see here why an artistically formed dramatic dialogue would give individual words more weight than a straightforward treatise, and why a living dialogue with a true philosopher would be best of all.[52] The status of true knowledge that Plato describes in *Letter VII* would result in a tragic sense of the life of reason only if rationality were exhaustively translatable into concepts and concepts exhaustively translatable into words, because this would dissociate intelligibility from goodness. Paradoxically, the fact that they cannot be translated is precisely *why* genuine communication is possible. The rationalism that would take such exhaustive translation as an ideal thereby shows its ignorance of what makes rationality rational. The importance of this point cannot be overstated: as we have seen, if everything could be verbally justified, then there would be no *intrinsic* meaning to things, once again because intrinsic meaning is identical to the goodness that is absolute and therefore not ultimately justifiable. In other words, if everything can be justified, nothing can be justified. Typical talk of the "limits of reason" invariably ignores the connection between goodness

51. *Phdr.,* 275c–d. This statement ought not to be taken in a purely mechanical sense, in which an item simply triggers a reminder but is essentially unnecessary to that which is recalled. Such a view would follow if knowledge were ultimately a kind of information, a view that Plato quite clearly and emphatically rejects. If knowledge, by contrast, is rooted in a transcendent good that is both absolute and relative, the relative means of communication can be seen as participating in an intrinsic manner in the "absolute" or transcendent meaning it expresses.

52. *Phdr.,* 276a.

and intelligibility, and so fails to do justice to Plato's "nonrationalistic" view of reason.

But we are just beginning to respond to the difficulties Roochnik and Griswold raise. To say that communication is possible in principle still leaves open the question (among others) of the precise nature of the conditions of its possibility.[53] It is worth quoting the next paragraph of *Letter VII* at length:

By the repeated use of all these instruments, ascending and descending to each in turn, it is barely possible for knowledge to be engendered of an object naturally good, in a man naturally good (εὐ πεφυκότος εὐ πεφυκότι); but if his nature is defective, as is that of most men, for the acquisition of knowledge and the so-called virtues, and if the qualities he has have been corrupted, then not even Lynceus could make such a man see. In short, neither quickness of learning nor a good memory can make a man see when his nature is not akin to the object, for this principle (τὴν ἀρχήν) never takes root in an alien nature; so that no man who is not naturally inclined and akin to justice and all other forms of excellence, even though he may be quick at learning and remembering this and that and other things, nor any man who, though akin to justice, is slow at learning and forgetful, will ever attain the truth that is attainable about virtue. Nor about vice, either, for these must be learned together, just as the truth and error about any part of being must be learned together, through long and earnest labor, as I said at the beginning. Only when all of these things—names, definitions, and visual and other perceptions—have been rubbed against one another (τριβόμενα πρὸς ἄλληλα) and tested, pupil and teacher asking and answering questions in good will and without envy—only then, when reason and knowledge are at the very extremity of human effort, can they illuminate the nature of any object (ἐξέλαμψε ... περὶ ἕκαστον).[54]

Once again, we see that everything turns on the notion of goodness. On the one hand, knowledge occurs, if at all, essentially between a soul and an object that are good. Plato insists that the soul must be akin to its object to be joined with it in knowledge, which he specifies by saying it must possess justice and the other excellences. To things we normally take to be simply moral virtues, Plato ascribes an epistemological and metaphysical significance. It is natural to do so, of course, if the good is the ultimate principle of things.[55] On the

53. Griswold suggests that the dialogues *seem* hopelessly naive, observing that the dialogues never explicitly address the question of the conditions of possibility of dialogue between the philosopher and antiphilosopher (Griswold, "Plato's Metaphilosophy," 148–49). He nevertheless explains that they *display* a regular awareness of the question.

54. *Letter VII*, 343e–344b.

55. To be sure, Plato refers to the knowledge of vice here, which raises a fundamental

other hand, Plato suggests that the communication of knowledge requires, so to speak, a community in goodness between teacher and student. This entails a willingness to be tested through questioning, a willingness to respond, and in general, good will and lack of envy.[56] It is interesting to note that all of these characteristics point to the affirmation of a good beyond oneself, by which one is measured and to which one is responsible. If it is the case, as we have been suggesting, that an indispensable aspect of knowledge is the mode of relating to reality by which the soul subordinates itself to goodness, then it follows that substantial thinking and genuine communication cannot take place outside of the spirit created by a basic disposition toward goodness. The good, then, is the single condition of possibility of communication, insofar as it gives being to what is talked *about* and imposes certain demands, intrinsic to that being, on those who wish to know and thus to speak properly. In this respect, to teach in the fullest sense means to impart not just ideas but a relation to the good, and one can do so, and foster such a relation, only if one is in love with the good, as it were.[57] To communicate truth requires a love of beauty and goodness. Be good, then, and teach naturally.

To affirm the good as the condition of possibility for communication,

---

question regarding other things Plato affirms, namely, that the good is the cause of all being, etc. There is no room to investigate this fully in the present context, but it is essential to point at least in the direction of a response because the difficulty is so fundamental: we would have to say that vices are not things in themselves as such, but only relatively things in themselves—always relative, that is, to something good. (Tulli compares the issue here with the paradoxes of the reality of non-being in the *Sophist* and the theme of the "unlimited" in the *Philebus: Dialettica e scrittura*, 355.) Thus, the defect would never be known as such, but only indirectly (perhaps according to the "bastard reasoning" Plato refers to in the *Timaeus* that is necessary for grasping the "receptacle," *Ti.*, 52b) in relation to a positive good. This would avoid the obvious absurdity of inferring from the principle affirming the soul's need to become akin to the object it seeks to know the conclusion that a soul must become vicious to know vice. Clearly, the opposite is true: Thrasymachus does not understand the nature of injustice the way Socrates does, but Socrates understands it only in relation to the justice of which it is a defect.

56. Lack of envy seems to be, for Plato, one of the essential properties of goodness (see *Ti.*, 29e). There is a clear connection between this property and the metaphysical point that the absolute is always *also* relative. We will discuss this connection at greater length in the coda.

57. We refer again to Socrates' self-description as a midwife. To be "in love with the good" means to subordinate oneself to a higher reality and thus precisely *not* to make oneself the source of one's knowledge, which is what Socrates claims the sophists do. From this perspective, therefore, there is a necessary connection between the view of goodness as ground of reason and a "maieutic" conception of teaching. On this, see Mitch Miller's observations in "Platonic Provocations," 193.

however, seems only to quicken the problems that Roochnik and Griswold in different ways identified. Perhaps the very first thing an antiphilosopher would be willing to deny is that he is somehow bound to an objective or transcendent good. We have already suggested that no finally adequate argument can possibly be given for the good, while anything less betrays what is essential, and we have just seen that proper communication requires not only the right use of words but a genuinely good disposition on both sides. It seems that communication, from this perspective, is even more fragile than is usually understood. What does one do with an intractable refusal to acknowledge transcendent goodness? What if a person cheerfully professes surprise that something could be found that would interest him less? What about the possibility of insurmountable obstacles to commensurability? An obvious reply would be: Isn't the good by *definition* something that all things without exception have in common? In this sense, isn't goodness always the foundation for communication? We suggested in the introduction and chapter 1 that radical questions, even if they surrender the significance of the difference between truth and falsity, are still unable to avoid clinging to the difference between better and worse. Although, in the passage above, Plato expresses a certain pessimism about finding good souls—claiming in fact that the ἀρχή of knowledge (desire for the good?) is not to be found in alien souls[58]—he observes in the *Republic* that the power of intelligence, which is in fact a participation in the good's causing of truth, is present even in the most corrupt of souls. They do not need to be taught to desire goodness, but only to order that desire in the proper direction. It is impossible not to desire the good, however much one may deny it, and the one who insists on denying it will necessarily contradict himself.[59] While all of this is true, and must be true, there remains the evident fact that nearly all of the conversations Socrates has with those who are not already more or less on his side end poorly. Griswold is right that Plato tends to depict conflicts between philosophers and antiphilosophers, and often creates scenes of exasperation and hostility. Why does he do so? Is this a confession of the ultimate impotence of philosophy? Does Plato intend to chasten reason and lead it to respect its own limits, as Roochnik suggests? But how could this view be reconciled with the

58. *Letter VII*, 344a.

59. At *Grg.*, 482b–c, Socrates claims that, if Callicles denies absolute goodness, then it is not Socrates or reality that will contradict him, but Callicles himself. This can be affirmed only on the assumption that the good is absolute and thus the desire for goodness is universal.

indomitable power Plato ascribes to knowledge[60] and the absolute claims he makes on behalf of the life of reason from the beginning to the end of his work?

Responding to these questions requires a better sense of what reason is. Discussions of the problem of reason's self-justification to its critics, we propose, tend to take for granted a rationalistic notion of reason, which cannot help but founder on this problem. Part of the aim of the present book, however, is to develop a more ample notion of reason, starting from the principle that it is grounded ultimately in the good. Griswold claims that, while Plato cannot argue for reason, he can nevertheless "show" the viability of philosophy through the dialogues between philosophers and antiphilosophers, and thus provide indirect justification for it. This suggestion is illuminating. But we must be careful not to assume that these indirect proofs are, so to speak, "extrarational," or even in some sense "political" rather than philosophical in the strict sense. Our own claim, by contrast, is that these "indirect" proofs are *essential expressions of rationality,* precisely because reason is rooted in the good. It is the nature of reason to transcend the limits of reason, which is just another way of saying that reason is ecstatic. What seems to lie beyond the borders of the conceptual thereby turns out to participate intrinsically in thought, to be a *part* of thinking. Such a view of reason, as we will see, puts the challenge of dialogue with the antiphilosophers on an entirely new stage. Before we address that problem directly, however, we will try to flesh out some of the more concrete and subtle aspects of the life of reason that come to light most directly in the challenge reason's critics raise against it. Doing so will put us in a better position to see the significance of this challenge.

War and Battle

The great "contest" carried out in the *Gorgias,*[61] the dialogue that begins with the ominous words, "war and battle," is of course the contest between the philosopher and the sophist. This essential contest concerning goodness is in fact "greater than it seems" (*Rep.,* 608b); it is in fact a contest between two fundamentally different conceptions of reason. At stake in this contest, moreover, is the basic order of the universe.[62] The question around which these two conceptions of reason wage their battle, as Plato makes explicit

60. *Prt.,* 353c–d.   61. *Grg.,* 526e.
62. Cf. *Tht.,* 176e–177a.

during a climactic moment in the *Gorgias*,[63] is whether goodness lies at the center of things or not. The reason Socrates claims in the dialogue that nothing is worse than injustice[64] is that, if justice did not exist, then there would be no good and thus no order of intelligibility to things. The elimination of justice entails the collapse of reason. This means, in turn, that the order of life implied in the concept of justice—and excellence (ἡ ἀρετή) and beauty (τὸ καλόν)—is intrinsic to the life of reason. To bring the significance of this affirmation home and make it more concrete, let us consider the contrast between philosophy and sophistry on just a few points that are seldom taken to hold immediate significance for theories of knowledge. We will see that the implications of these two views of reason make themselves felt everywhere in the style, mood, and content of the *Republic*.

Power

The difference between the two conceptions of reason, the philosophical and the sophistical, comes to expression perhaps most directly in the relationship each implies to power. According to both the *Republic* and *Letter VII*, as we have interpreted them, reason is ordered to the real being of things, which means it has its terminus in something absolute and irreducible. To put the same point negatively, if a thing were ultimately reducible to its relations, it would no longer possess its own intrinsic being ("the verb 'to be' must be totally abolished"),[65] and by the same token, it would not represent an object for reason. In this case, there would be no basis for distinguishing reason from opinion or perception. Thus, if there is no being, there is no reason, and vice versa. But for anything to exist in an absolute way, i.e., as irreducible to other things, implies for Plato that there "be" absoluteness itself—implies, that is, the good. Here, again, we see the function we have been claiming for the good in providing a foundation for being and intelligibility. Now, one of the implications of reason's reciprocal relation with the absoluteness of being is that *reason itself* must be in some respect absolute in order to be reason. As *ordered* to what is absolute, in other words, it cannot be subordinated to anything else within the order of meaning without surrendering its own integral structure.[66]

63. See *Grg.*, 507a–509e.   64. *Grg.*, 509a.
65. *Tht.*, 157b.
66. We recall, however, that such a conception of reason is not inimical to obedience, but in fact requires it: see the section on "justice and obedience" in the previous chapter.

We thus see the relevance the question of power has for epistemology. On the one hand, as we saw in *Letter VII*, we cannot say that reason has "power" over its object, since attaining to its object at all requires the discontinuous moment of expropriation and ecstasis, by means of which reason adopts the measure of the thing itself rather than forcing that thing to adopt to *its* measure. On the other hand, nothing else can have any "power" over reason without making reason a relative instrument, and thus no longer reason. Thus, reason must be at the same time more powerful than anything else and essentially "powerless" in itself, if it is to exist as reason at all. The question of the integrity of reason in relation to its own specific work cannot be divorced from the place reason has in the general order of life: if it is given a subordinate role in this order, it will cease to be an "absolute means" by which the truth of things becomes manifest. As we recall, the being of things can become manifest only to a *lover* of wisdom, which means to a person "guided by truth," who must "pursue it entirely and in every way or else be a boaster who in no way partakes of true philosophy" (490a). In other words, in a society in which power trumps reason, things will no longer have a horizon, as it were, against and within which to manifest their intrinsic meaning.

The ecstatic nature of reason that follows from the connection between goodness and intelligibility is therefore incompatible with an individual's seeking of power for his own sake. We see why Plato was so occupied with the question of power: it is no exaggeration to say that the nature of reality is at stake in this question. Plato depicts the philosopher as one specifically without a desire for the power implied by political office (cf. 347d, 521b), and in spite of the perhaps overly optimistic hope he pursued of bringing about a philosophically founded polis in Sicily, he was well known to have kept aloof from politics.[67] There is, in Plato's mind, an ultimate and exclusive choice to be made: either one pursues truth, i.e., the intrinsic meaning of things beyond one's control, or one pursues power in some form or another, i.e., the capacity to manipulate things for ends one determines oneself. Significantly, in the *Symposium*, Plato presents Alcibiades—whose choice in this matter is well known—as *electing himself* to be the one in charge at the banquet: "Friends, you look sober to me; we can't have that! Let's have a drink! Remember our agreement? We need a master of ceremonies; who should it be? . . . Well, at least till you are

---

67. See *Letter V*, 322a–b. Cf. Bluck, *Plato's Seventh and Eighth Letters*, 3. According to Gadamer, the whole of Plato's work can be seen as one long *apologia* for his not entering politics. See *L'anima alle soglie del pensiero nella filosofia greca*, 29, cited in Benvenuto, "Lo Specchio della Potenza," 27.

all too drunk to care, I elect . . . myself!"[68] Self-election could be said to be the *symbol* of the pursuit of power and expresses in a nutshell why it is the opposite of truth. In contrast to this perfect reduction of the order of things to one's own determination (pure relativity), truth is comprehensive and essentially irreducible to such relativity. It is not an accident that the dialogue that contains Plato's most elaborate presentation of knowledge and the forms begins with the sharp contrast between Socrates, who shows little interest in power, and Thrasymachus, who takes it to be the highest good.

Nevertheless, it is important to see that Plato refuses to give the last word to the renunciation of power.[69] Ultimately, he says, truth and power must coincide. But the only way for them to coincide without eliminating the exclusive alternatives just presented is for the ruling office to be imposed on one who has renounced it, that is, to be a thing *received* rather than *seized*. In this way, power becomes not the opponent but the servant of truth, insofar as it is embraced within the obedience that is intrinsic to reason's ecstatic nature. There is an analogy between this reconciliation of truth and power and the reconciliation of being and appearance, which we will elaborate in our final chapter. The heart of both is the philosopher's obedient return to the cave. Now, as our previous discussion of that return already suggests, the philosopher's entry into politics, his acceptance, as it were, of ruling office, does not have to be interpreted in the straightforward sense of becoming king, but can—and perhaps ought to—take a much more subtle form. The identification of power with explicit office may be seen as connected with sophistry. Let us consider another alternative. We have proposed viewing Socrates in the *Republic* as the philosopher who "goes down." This would make him, by the same token, the paradigm of philosophy's entry into the public and political sphere. The fact that Socrates expresses no interest in politics makes him, in Plato's eyes, the "perfect candidate" for ruler: *Plato thus "imposes" rule on Socrates by making him the founder of the ideal city.* It is significant, in this regard, that Plato has Socrates claim to be the only person genuinely interested in politics in all of Athens.[70] Perhaps the best way to interpret this is that the political dimension of the philosopher's rule takes the form of bringing the

68. *Symp.,* 213e.

69. In addition to the *Republic*'s insistence on the descent into the cave (of the public order), see *Letter VII,* 328c: the main reason Plato offers here for his going to Sicily is to avoid being a "pure theorist."

70. *Grg.,* 521d. It is interesting to note, in this regard, that Plato is said to have learned his political philosophy specifically from Socrates. D. L., III.8.

authority of the good to bear in the public sphere in a manner appropriate to it. Here, we recall the significance of the philosopher's "invisibility," discussed in the last chapter. This way of understanding the philosopher's rule would not exclude in principle the actual assumption of office in an explicit way— Socrates does his duty,[71] and Plato responds to the possibility of helping to bring about a "philosophical regime" in Sicily—but it would refuse to limit the political dimension of philosophy to such things. To make power a servant of reason rather than the reverse is to transform the meaning of power.

Reasoning with others, of course, is one of the political dimensions of philosophy, and it is here that we also find an expression of reason's relationship to power. We raised aspects of this issue in the first chapter but are now in a position to view the significance more comprehensively. It is the very nature of sophistry to aim at victory in conversation, in the precise sense of dominance over one's opponent. The sophists with whom Socrates speaks always assume—as they must, given the horizon their view of reason sets— that Socrates shares the same aim: "'You love to win, Socrates.' 'But it's not for love of winning that I'm asking you. It's rather because I really do want to hear.'"[72] In fact, though his questions are notoriously aggressive and penetrating, Socrates always refuses to defend his own position *as* his own.[73] "If you will take my advice," he says, "you will give but little thought to Socrates but much more to the truth."[74] Typically, rather than assert his own position, he *questions*. The reason he offers in the *Gorgias* for doing so is illuminating: "And why, when I have my suspicions, do I ask you and refrain from expressing them myself? It's not you I'm after, it's our discussion, to have it proceed in such a way as to make the thing we're talking about most clear to us (ὡς μάλις' ἂν ἡμῖν καταφανὲς)."[75] As he shows here, Socrates questions rather than asserts because of the end to which reason is ordered: not dominance over the other, but the manifestation of its object to all parties present. The contest of positions against each other implies that truth is, of its essence, something an individual can possess *qua* individual. Such a dispute thus concerns the question whether one position is "better" than another;

---

71. For example, serving as a member of the Council. *Ap.,* 32b.

72. *Grg.,* 515b. Compare to *Rep.,* 336c.

73. "'Then it's the truth, my beloved Agathon, that you are unable to challenge,' he said. 'It is not hard at all to challenge Socrates'" (*Symp.,* 201c).

74. *Phd.,* 91b–c.

75. *Grg.,* 453c.

in other words, it concerns the "value" of relative perspectives, or perhaps more to the point, their "strength."[76] Considered in relation to the account of reason Plato offers in *Letter VII*, such comparisons can occur only at penultimate levels.[77]

By contrast, to get to the thing in itself is to get beyond any particular position in relation to that thing. This does not mean that one will have an absolute grasp, or that one will no longer have a perspective, which would amount to the denial of the finitude of the human mind. Instead, reason's ecstatic accomplishment of its aim requires ceasing to identify one's relative perspective with the thing itself. Reason can reach its proper end only by pointing to a supraindividual reality, a publicly objective truth. A truth of this nature can become clear only through the joint inquiry of other-subordinated souls, i.e., the "pupil and teacher asking and answering questions in good will and without envy."[78] By contrast, to *win* an argument between intellectual positions *qua* individual possessions is to eclipse a truth of this sort. It is for this reason that Socrates shows no desire to overpower Thrasymachus and that he, as it were, renounces any victory at the end of book I. It is, furthermore, why he says that a philosopher would rather be *defeated* by sophistical arguments than to defeat others with them,[79] and why philosophy cannot engage in competitions at this level.[80] Because reason is ecstatic, it does not first assert itself but rather joins in seeking *with* others. This joint search requires on the one hand helping others "let go" of their own asser-

76. The charge against him that Socrates denies is that he, like the sophists generally, makes "the weaker argument the stronger" (*Ap.,* 18c).

77. Sebastián Trías Mercant fails to understand the nature of Plato's philosophy on this point, and thus presents the philosopher as seeking domination, indeed, in a far more subtle and therefore dangerous way than the rhetorician. see "Platon y una Gramatica del Poder," *Pensamiento: Revista trimestral de investigación e información filosófica* 37 (1981): 287–312, here 293 and 310–11. Mercant, just like Thrasymachus in book I, assumes an essentially private notion of reason, and thus can interpret discussion solely in terms of a struggle for power. The same could be said for Chris Rocco, who accuses Socrates of hiding his "will to power" behind a facade of truth. "Liberating Discourse: The Politics of Truth in Plato's *Gorgias*," *Interpretation* 23.3 (1996): 361–85, here 380. He ultimately shows that all truth claims eventually turn into a power struggle: 383.

78. *Letter VII*, 344b.

79. *Euthd.,* 303d. In this passage, Socrates is criticizing the sophistical arguments of Euthydemus and Dionysodorus, stating with obvious irony that, because most people don't understand their arguments, "I feel sure they would be more ashamed to refute others with arguments of this sort than to be refuted by them."

80. See *Alc. I,* 119c.

tive claims, which we see for example in Socrates' exchange with Meno: "So now I do not know what virtue is; perhaps you knew before you contacted me, but now you are certainly like one who does not know. Nevertheless, I want to examine and seek together with you what it may be."[81] On the other hand, it implies a *desire* to be corrected by them, to be as subordinate to them as the good will allow:

So, I'm afraid to pursue my examination of you, for fear that you should take me to be speaking with eagerness to win against you, rather than to have our subject become clear. For my part, I'd be pleased to continue questioning you if you're the same kind of man I am, otherwise I would drop it. And what kind of man am I? One of those who would be pleased to be refuted if I say anything untrue, and who would be pleased to refute anyone who says anything untrue; one who, however, wouldn't be any less pleased to be refuted than to refute.[82]

We will return to the great significance of being defeated in argument toward the end of this chapter.

Freedom

A further reason that truth can have a connection with power only by radically transforming it is its dependence on *freedom*. One cannot force another person to acknowledge the truth of something. Notice: it is not that one "ought not" but that one "cannot." It is impossible because of the very nature of truth, Platonically understood. If a person is forced to see something, then what he sees will be something other than the truth. Why? The truth of a thing, according to the *Republic*, is most fundamentally its "in-itself" being, which comes to light only when the thing is viewed not in relation to a relative good, but in light of the absolute good, and thus as a thing absolute in itself. To view it thus, however, requires the "turning around" of the soul, away from the relative to the absolute (which of course also implies a return to the relative). But this act, though it must be provoked by something outside of oneself, must necessarily be a free act insofar as we define freedom as doing what one wants. To want something is to take that thing as one's good. It thus follows that, if one is forced to "turn around" without at the same time *wanting* to do so, one is taking one's good as lying elsewhere than in the absolute good. This means in turn that, whatever appearances may suggest, one hasn't in fact "turned around." Thus, one can see the

---

81. *Meno,* 80c–d.   82. *Grg.,* 457e–458a; cf. 506a.

truth *as* truth only in freedom. The being of things can manifest itself only to the free desire for absolute goodness. This is in part why Plato says children ought not to be forced to learn, but should learn through play (536e–537a).

Conversely, given this same view of freedom, one can be free *only* in relation to the truth.[83] Plato *shows* that this is so in the cave allegory, in which the liberated are those who see things as they really are, but the point warrants explanation. If it is true, as Plato supposes, that we want what is genuinely good and therefore ultimately absolute goodness itself, then one is not in fact doing what one wants to the extent that one fails to do what is good. This is a basic theme in many of the dialogues (e.g., *Gorgias, Protagoras, Theaetetus, Crito, Apology,* etc.) and of the critique of the tyrant in book IX of the *Republic* (cf. 577e).[84] Furthermore, if one cannot be said to do something freely when one does it without knowing what it is, then knowledge of the truth of things is a prerequisite for a free choice. In this case, if we distinguish between force and persuasion, and understand persuasion as necessarily including the person's freedom, then truth alone can persuade in the strict sense.[85] The attempt to bring a person to assent to anything other than what is good, no matter how "knowingly" the person makes the assent, is a form of manipulation or force.[86] There is a mutual dependence, as it were, between freedom and truth: one cannot affirm truth except in freedom, and one cannot be free except by affirming truth.

The fact that truth thus depends on freedom explains from another angle the inexpungible vulnerability that lies at the heart of philosophy. In his at-

83. Cf. R. F. Stalley, "Plato's Doctrine of Freedom," *Proceedings of the Aristotelian Society* 98 (1998): 145–58, here 145, 151.

84. Cf. Curtis Johnson, "What Is Liberty For? Plato and Aristotle on Political Freedom," *Skepsis* 12 (2001): 78–94, here 82–83.

85. Wardy concedes that freedom would be able to be found in reason alone *if* it were possible to pursue shared truth through dialectic. *Birth of Rhetoric,* 65.

86. It is useful to reflect on Socrates' first speech in the *Phaedrus* in comparison to Lysias's speech, both of which were supposed to persuade the boy to give himself to the nonlover. Lysias's speech claims that, outside of eros, there will be more freedom for the boy, and he will thus be able to get what he himself wants with little risk. Socrates, however, begins his speech with a prelude that exposes the presumed "nonlover." The nonlover appears to offer the boy a means to pursue freely his own self-interest, but in reality he is manipulating the boy, and making him the (willing) unwilling servant of the nonlover's own self-interest. In the end, however, even the manipulator turns out to be a slave in Socrates' eyes. One might also consider the parallel dynamic played out brilliantly in Shakespeare's *Coriolanus* between the tribunes and the people: it is *precisely* those endeavoring to give the people "their own voice" in the public order who are the ones most clearly manipulating them.

tempt to make the *Republic* more accessible, in his translation Cornford not only paraphrased some of the passages, which he thought could be expressed more felicitously than Plato expressed them, but also eliminated many of the simple responses by the interlocutors—the "Yes, of course, Socrates," "That is most true, Socrates!," and "How could it be otherwise, Socrates!," and so forth—that seem to add nothing of any substance to the ideas being articulated.[87] His decision reflects a common frustration regarding these "supposed" dialogues, particularly among young readers: the interlocutors come off quite often as mindless "yes-men," who offer no insights of their own or indeed any resistance at all to those of Socrates, even his most outrageous.[88] Now, those who chastise Cornford for his decision typically do so because they insist that the subtle differences in the responses in varying contexts can have enormous philosophical significance if we attend to the dialogue as a literary drama and not as a mere vehicle for argument. This complaint is no doubt true; however, there is a more basic complaint to make: even in cases where the responses fail to reveal anything additional even to the most subtle eye in terms of the substance of the matter discussed, the very *fact* of their existence bears significantly on the *form* of thought, and therefore on the nature of thought's object. As mentioned in passing in the first chapter, Socrates never makes a point without asking for assent from his partner and regularly confesses that he cannot proceed without his partner's willingness.[89] In this way, he places himself in dependence in some respect on the other's freedom. But he thus makes himself vulnerable insofar as the "success" of this relation depends in turn on the other's goodness. As he says in the *Sophist,* agreement and assent

87. "Much more space has been saved by leaving out many of the formal expressions of assent integrated by Glaucon and Adeimantus, and thus allowing Socrates to advance one step in his article in a single connected speech," *The Republic of Plato,* translated by Francis M. Cornford (New York: Oxford University Press, 1941), vii.

88. To such an extent that some commentators say the later dialogues could probably have dispensed with the conversational form altogether and been presented simply as treatises. See, e.g., Christopher Rowe, "The *Politicus:* Structure and Form," in Gill and McCabe, *Form and Argument in Late Plato,* 153–78. See, by contrast, Leonardo Tarán, "Platonism and Socratic Ignorance," 90.

89. When the partner steadfastly refuses, he still does not "lecture," but carries out both sides of the dialogue himself. See *Grg.,* 505cff. According to Benvenuto, while we think that Socrates' conversations are not real dialogues because they seem one-sided, in fact "if he didn't have an interlocutor, Socrates wouldn't be able to think," "Lo Specchio della Potenza," 9. Benvenuto goes on to point out how the teacher, for Socrates, *depends* on his pupil. The dialogue form is not an accidental use of reason, but represents its *essential* structure. Even the internal use of reason has a dialogical form. See *Tht.,* 189e.

have "authority" only for a good person.[90] He likewise cannot impose his own views, but has to accept whatever the other gives him and try to "make the best" out of it.[91] This attitude is, as we saw in the last chapter, an implication of the philosopher's return to the cave—a relative obedience to the relative in order to bring to expression the absoluteness of the absolute.

But it is also a function of the absoluteness of truth. It is not possible for truth to take a purely private form; to the contrary, it must be "structurally" public.[92] This implies that one obstructs one's own grasp of the truth *precisely to the extent that one excludes others from one's own pursuit of it.* We recall that in book I Socrates drew particular attention to Thrasymachus's lack of regard for others, and we suggested this was a necessary function of his epistemology. By contrast, Socrates shows that in his pursuit of truth, he is in effect as much responsible to it for others as he is for himself (*Rep.,* 450d–451a). In a certain respect, Socrates is dependent on the goodwill and freedom of others even for his own relationship to real being.[93] It is not, by its nature, something he can pursue merely on his own. As we saw in the passage cited from the *Gorgias,* the pursuit of truth is a joint venture, because the manifestation of truth is a public event. The locus of truth, according to *Letter VII,* is not in the soul, but in being itself, in reality. The one who desires this truth necessarily desires at the same time the freedom of others in relation to it.

To sum up, we could say that absolute truth is essentially vulnerable for several reasons: it cannot be put adequately into words and thus cannot be (merely) verbally defended or "secured" by argument; moreover, it is *public* rather than private, and so requires a joint possession and all of the dependence that such an interconnection implies; and, further, because absolute truth can be acknowledged only in freedom, as a thinker one is, so to speak, at the mercy of the goodwill of one's interlocutors.

If philosophy is thus dependent on freedom, sophistry is of course by its

90. *Soph.,* 246d.

91. *Grg.,* 499c. Literally "to make good what is present as given." Socrates, of course, means this "old proverb" in an ironic sense: not that he must pretend that what he is given is the best though he really would have wanted better, but that he must take what the other offers and bring it into relation as far as is possible with the good.

92. This does not deny the essentially intimate form of knowledge we argued for in chapter 2. Rather, it makes explicit that such a form of knowledge cannot be understood merely relative to a private individual.

93. We see here a more radical reason why Socrates rejects the possibility of exile in the *Apology* and the *Crito.* Being a part of a community is intrinsic to philosophical thinking.

very nature, and because of the nature of what it seeks to communicate, contemptuous of freedom. Socrates frequently mentions the sophistic tendency to present long speeches rather than to submit to questioning by one's interlocutors.[94] To speak at great length can be a form of laying hold of power for oneself; it subordinates the other and does not allow the other to be a mutual participant in the idea.[95] As we showed above, such a subordination is an elimination of freedom. Socrates makes an ironic allusion to the freedom of speech at Athens, which is the home of many well-known sophists. He explains that he will discuss with Polus only on one condition:

"That you curb your long style of speech, Polus, the style you tried using at first." "Really? Won't I be free to say as much as I like?" "You'd certainly be in a terrible way, my good friend, if upon coming to Athens, where there's more freedom of speech than anywhere else in Greece, you alone should miss out on it here. But look at it the other way. If you spoke at length and were unwilling to answer what you're asked, wouldn't I be in a terrible way if I'm not to have the freedom to stop listening to you and leave?"[96]

The irony here is that Gorgias had praised specifically the *power* of oratory as the greatest source of freedom.[97] It is so, Gorgias goes on to explain, because it can produce "persuasion" in others—a persuasion indifferent to goodness or truth. Oratory gives a person power over others, which is what Gorgias means by freedom. The problem, however, is that the exercise of power so conceived entails the eclipse of transcendence, insofar as it makes the person himself the ultimate arbiter, and this means that there is no true measure, i.e., no good. But if there is no good, what appears to be power turns out to be complete impotence.[98] By the same token, then, "freedom" of this sort turns out to be the most miserable slavery because it cannot by definition do what it wants, namely, attain to anything genuinely good. In short, manipulating others through sophistry makes one a slave. We return in this case to the image of the prisoners in the cave: Plato presents them as isolated from what they want *precisely because* their desires lack the constraint of a measure, which is something that the goodness they want necessarily entails.

One of the implications of this conception of freedom and truth is a re-

94. Cf. Blondell, *The Play of Character*, 41.
95. Cf. Mercant, "Una Gramatica del Poder," 296–98, who compares lecturing to law-giving.
96. *Grg.*, 461d–e.   97. *Grg.*, 452d.
98. *Grg.*, 466b.

versal of conventional views. It is generally assumed that the only way to protect the freedom of the other is to keep at bay any claim to objective or absolute truth, because such a claim seems to lead necessarily to oppression. In fact, the very opposite is the case. Violence and the imposition of points of view is *always and in every case* the result of a failure to affirm absolute truth in its absoluteness, for the reasons we have just shown. Tyranny is the identification of a partial view with the whole, and thus an injustice to other parts. But the opposite of this is not a "healthy" relativism, as conventionally understood, since genuine relativity requires the affirmation of an absolute to which everything is relative. Without such an affirmation, one's relativity becomes itself absolute and thus essentially unjust. Talk of relativism prompts a question that rarely receives explicit attention: relativism in relation to *what?* Relativity necessarily implies a reference point *to* which things are relative, and this point, in being taken as a reference, is by the same token taken to be absolute.[99] When no reference point is identified, the implicit one tends to be the particularity of an individual's experience, perception, or opinion. But this means that the individual is absolutized *as* an individual, and this is the definition of tyranny. There is no ultimate difference between tyranny and the usual understanding of "relativism."[100] The only relativism that preserves and cultivates freedom is that which takes what *is* absolute *to be* absolute and thus is founded on truth. By failing to acknowledge an absolute, sophistry lacks any means of distinguishing genuine persuasion from forceful manipulation.[101] Moreover, it lacks any grounds for social interaction other than varying degrees of such manipulation. Relativism and skepticism, as conventionally understood, are as much an enemy of freedom as is tyranny.

Totality: Everything and Anything

There is also a fundamental difference between philosophy and sophistry regarding the relationship each bears to the whole. Plato has defined philosophy in the *Republic* as love for the *whole* of wisdom. This is, as we have suggested, intrinsically connected with reason's being ordered to the good

99. Kelley Ross shows why some implicit absolute knowledge is therefore required for relativism to be able to remain self-consistent. See "Non-intuitive Immediate Knowledge," 167–69.

100. On their connection see Miller, *The Philosopher in Plato's* Statesman, 49–53.

101. See *Soph.,* 222cff., where Plato draws an analogy between the sophist's art and "piracy, enslavement, tyranny, [and] everything that has to do with war," which he groups under the label "hunting by force."

as such, which takes it in principle beyond any a priori limits. But there is an important qualification that must immediately be registered: though reason is ordered to the whole, it always remains subordinate to it. Paradoxically, this subordination necessarily implies that it never makes itself absolute but accepts a certain relativity. Or, to put it more adequately, if also more paradoxically, reason must be relative *because* it is absolute; it can "grasp" the whole that is its most proper object only by taking its relative place within that whole, and conversely, by taking its relative place, it becomes absolute in a manner appropriate to it. Thus, Plato makes reason the natural ruler of the whole (441e), and at the same times makes the ruler the subordinate servant of what it rules (342e). This implies that reason's being ordered to the whole of wisdom makes it responsible for everything.[102] In relation to power, we have suggested that reason's absoluteness is coincident with a subordination to its proper object. But if reason's proper object is the whole of reality in all of its parts, then reason is in some respect the servant of everything. It is responsible, that is, for the good of whatever is "under" it even more than that particular thing is responsible for itself. (Again, we can think of Socrates in book I, who shows himself, as one who embraces reason, to be arguably more concerned with Thrasymachus's happiness and well-being than Thrasymachus himself is.)

We see that the structure of the *Republic* and the movement of the dialogue reflects this comprehensive responsibility. The argument unfolds slowly over the course of the dialogue, with due attention given to particulars as far as required—for this is justice[103]—but all the time with a view to the whole. Socrates *plods* through the discussion, asking at every turn whether the account is adequate, a question that has no real meaning except in terms of care for the whole. Reason is shown from the beginning, then, to have a responsibility both for details and for seeing how they fit together in terms of the larger picture. Being responsible for everything means giving everything its due place, so that it most perfectly expresses what it is and also so that it serves the whole. Reason, according to Plato, seeks the fulfillment of each part of the soul (442c, 441e).

102. And, conversely, that irrationalism means being concerned only with a relative part *rather* than with the whole. See Nicholas White, "Rational Prudence in Plato's *Gorgias*," in *Platonic Investigations,* edited by Dominic O'Meara (Washington, D.C.: the Catholic University of America Press, 1985) 139–62, here 162.

103. See *Rep.,* 506b–507a.

As Plato says in the *Phaedrus*,[104] a speech must have an organic form, analogous to a living thing: the coordination of parts is what makes a whole come alive, as it were. In light of the *Republic*'s view of reason, we could say that a speech (*logos*) needs to have such an organic form precisely because it is an expression of reason. The *Republic* itself is just such an expression of reason. There is, in this sense, an intrinsic connection between the extraordinary order of the *Republic*, its translucent quality, its being about justice (a place for everything and everything in its place), its focus on the transcendent good, and its presentation of the nature of reason and knowledge. The perfection of the dialectic the *Republic* presents as the philosophical ideal lies in its ability to integrate all aspects into a synoptic view of the whole, rooted in being (537b–c). The convergence of form and content, to say it again, is not accidental to the meaning the dialogue intends to communicate. It is interesting to consider, as a contrast, the disorder that Socrates observes in the sophist Lysias's speech, which is—not coincidentally—about false love. Its failure to present an organic and thus hierarchically structured whole, Socrates says, is *due to its author's lack of interest in the subject*.[105] In other words, it is due to his not catching sight of the transcendence of the beautiful that is the cause of all interest.

If philosophy is essentially occupied with everything, sophistry represents a false imitation of this universality: it is occupied with *anything*. Plato emphasizes the pseudouniversality in a similar way in both the *Republic* and the *Sophist*: the image-maker is able fabricate the sun, the things in heaven, himself, animals, plants and everything else (596d–e). Sophists are moreover those who make "spoken copies" of "absolutely everything"—everything, that is, "but the truth."[106] The reason for this pseudouniversality is the sophist's superficiality.[107] There is a connection between sophistry's sev-

---

104. *Phdr.*, 264c. Cf. *Grg.*, 505c–d, where Socrates insists on the completeness of a discussion, which requires that it have a head (i.e., a principle) and that it unfold through interchange with another person.

105. *Phdr.*, 234e–235a.   106. *Soph.*, 232c, 233c.

107. A comparison with Nietzsche's criticisms of the falsely educated is appropriate here. In his complaint against the rationalistic positivism that severs form from content, which he detected in the German scholars of his time, Nietzsche writes: "Suppose one of them is engaged with Democritus, I always feel like asking: why not Heraclitus? Or Philo? Or Bacon? Or Descartes?—or anyone else. And then: why does it have to be a philosopher? Why not a poet or an orator? And: Why a Greek at all, why not an Englishman or a Turk?" "On the Uses and Disadvantages of History for Life," *Untimely Meditations*, translated by Hollingdale (Cambridge: Cambridge University Press, 1983), 86. On the separation of form and content, see ibid., 77–82.

erance of appearance from reality and its being a univocal technique that can be applied indifferently to everything and anything. It can be filled with anything whatsoever because it is essentially empty. Once again, we see here the appearance of power, insofar as such a technique presents itself as a mastery of all things. There is in sophistry a similarity to precisely what some praise as the value of symbolic logic: in knowing logic a person in principle knows everything, because there is nothing that can't be argued in it. Plato has the Visitor in the *Sophist* make the same observation: "In fact, take expertise in disputation as a whole. Doesn't it seem like a capacity that's sufficient for carrying on controversies about absolutely everything?"[108]

The difference between philosophy and sophistry on this point could perhaps be summed up by saying that, while sophistry represents an abstract universality, philosophy's universality is essentially concrete. Sophistry is indifferent to content, and this indifference prevents it from integrating what it knows into a well-ordered and meaningful whole. If this is true, then an analytical approach to the dialogues that would aim at reducing them as far as possible to their formal arguments *in principle* falsifies their meaning, however accurately it construes their arguments. Sophistry can "know" this or that, but it cannot see how these things hang together or how they fit into the cosmos, because to do so would require genuine knowledge of the good.[109] But then, if he attained such knowledge, the sophist would at that moment betray his disguise and show himself to have been a philosopher all along.

Time

The difference between concrete and abstract universality, between depth and superficiality, bears on the soul's relation to time. Plato regularly emphasizes *speed* when he refers to sophistry. "But the greatest thing of all," Socrates tells a couple of sophists, "is that your skill is such, and is so skillfully contrived, that anyone can master it in a very short time. I myself found this out by watching Ctesippus and seeing how quickly he was able to imitate you on the spur of the moment. This ability of your technique to be picked up quickly is a fine thing."[110] By contrast, a serious farmer—who possesses *nous*—does not look for *immediate* results from his work, but expects to wait

---

108. *Soph.*, 232e.
109. See Lachterman, "What Is 'the Good'?" 149–52, 159.
110. *Euthd.*, 303e–304a.

for the appropriate time.[111] In other words, he subordinates his expectations to the greater order. But it is not just the time required to learn the skill of sophistry that is at issue; instead, different relations to time in general characterize the whole of lives ordered around the practice of philosophy or its opposite. Plato describes the philosopher as having, so to speak, all the time in the world, while the sophist is *by nature* "stressed":

> Because the one man [i.e., the philosopher] always has what you mentioned just now—plenty of time. When he talks, he talks in peace and quiet, and his time is his own. It is so with us now: here we are beginning on our third new discussion; and he can do the same, if he is like us, and prefers the newcomer to the question in hand. It does not matter to such men whether they talk for a day or a year, if only they may hit upon that which is. But the other—the man of the law courts—is always in a hurry when he is talking; he has to speak with one eye on the clock.[112]

The difference between the modes of their relationship to time does not result from the relative quality of time-management skills, but a *difference in the nature of reason's object*.[113] On the one hand, the *telos* of sophistical reason is the practical consequences of ideas. A discussion is "measured" by what it accomplishes. In the light of our interpretation of the *Republic*, we would say that such thinking reduces its objects to their relative qualities; it does not look at things themselves, but rather stations itself at best on the third segment of the divided line. It turns away from realities and toward that which they produce. There is a connection, for Plato, between the "merely" relative and the "merely" temporal, and what is merely temporal is constantly undergoing change.[114] As Nicholas White has argued, Socrates' argument against sophistry in the *Gorgias* turns on the essentially momentary and opportunistic focus of its desire for an object, irrespective of its goodness, while consideration of goodness by contrast necessarily transcends the immediate and involves looking to the past, present, and the future.[115] If the object of the soul's interest in things is their relative qualities alone, one's soul, Plato con-

---

111. *Phdr.*, 276b–277a.

112. *Tht.*, 172d–e.

113. On sophistry as essentially time-bound, see Bruce McComisky, *Gorgias and the New Sophistic Rhetoric* (Carbondale: Southern Illinois University Press, 2002), 21–31. McComisky takes this as its positive contribution to the essentially constructivist notion of truth needed to pursue the constantly changing ends of democratic postmodernity.

114. *Tht.*, 157a–c.

115. White, "Rational Prudence," 155. See *Tht.*, 186a–b, and *Rep.*, 437a–439a.

tinues, becomes "small and warped,"[116] because one makes oneself dependent on the immanent chain of consequences.

Notice what happens, by contrast, the moment one asks, not what does X do, how will X affect me, and so forth, but simply, "What is X?" Immediately, the chain of consequences is interrupted and transcended. One is no longer dependent on relativity, but sees through the relative to the thing in its intrinsic and absolute meaning. This is not meant to imply that one attains the insight simply by raising the question. Instead, the claim is that one thereby reorients one's soul by making this insight the *telos* of one's rational interest. This reorientation can occur, we have suggested, only within the deepening of desire. To be "freed" from the love of practical consequences, either in relation to me (i.e., love of gain), or to how they impress others (i.e., love of honor), one must love knowledge, the truth of things in themselves, which means ultimately a love of the good. Because the *being* of something is not subject to change to the extent that it is irreducible to the relation that change implies, even while its actual existence and its practical consequences are constantly undergoing change, then philosophical reason is likewise free from time in the precise sense that it does not receive its final measure from what is time-bound.[117] People tend to "temporalize" eternity as something that comes "after" death. For Plato, knowledge of ideas is already a share in eternity.[118]

At the same time, however, and precisely insofar as it is rooted in the good, this freedom *from* time implies in another respect a greater responsibility *to* time, which expresses itself existentially as a certain *patience*. Desire for the goodness, i.e., the real reality, of a thing is a desire for the whole of it. But though the whole is revealed in one respect "in a flash,"[119] in another respect it does not show itself all at once but *takes time*. Something great,

116. *Tht.,* 173a.

117. It is important not to separate the absolute and relative being of things into a dualism. The point here is that there remains a distinction between the two, however paradoxically they may be intertwined. See *Soph.,* 249d.

118. Plato describes the philosophers as, in some sense, dwelling on the "Isles of the Blessed," (the traditional name for the soul's postmortem place of rest) while still among the living. See 519c and 540b. In Ferber's words, "Platos Himmel ist auch auf Erden," *Platos Idee des Guten,* 55.

119. See the instantaneous moment that Plato describes in the *Parmenides* (156d–e) that marks the transition from absoluteness to relativity. On this, cf. William Lynch, S. J., *An Approach to the Metaphysics of Plato through the* Parmenides (Washington, D.C.: Georgetown University Press, 1959), 139–45.

Plato explains, cannot come to be in a short time (608c). The "sophistry" that Plato associates with image-making (596d) is in fact characterized by a certain indifference to time. Everything a sophist does, he does *quickly*. Plato uses a form of the word ταχύ five times in the space of four Stephanus lines in his description of the art of image-making (596d–e). The reason image-making is so *quick* is that it involves no real difficulty (οὐ χαλεπός),[120] and it involves no difficulty essentially because it is superficial—it does not seek to get to the *core* of things but is content to capture how they appear (cf. 598b).[121] One does not have to go very far beyond oneself, we could say with a view to the cave, to reach appearance. Thus, along these lines, Plato observes that the sophist is able to teach anyone anything in a short time.[122] Socrates criticizes Alcibiades for "rushing" into politics, and attributes this haste to his being "wedded to stupidity."[123] It may be, however, that there is no other way to enter politics, as Alcibiades understands it, than by rushing, and that politics by its nature simply moves too fast. From a philosophical perspective, going too quickly forward actually brings one more slowly to one's destination.[124] The free play of time in leisure is necessary to reveal the full significance of a decision (619c).

The reason for the ease and speed of sophistic image-making, such as Plato presents it, is due to an indifference to reality. But if image-making is easy, the good is by nature hard (*Rep.,* 435c and 497d).[125] In the *Sophist,* Plato explains that appearances in argument are *corrected* by actual relations to things suffered in experience over time.[126] Patience is, indeed, a kind of suffering. It is so in the deep etymological sense of "undergoing" or "bearing" what is other than oneself (*patior,* πάσχω). In this respect, patience becomes an intrinsic part of a "methodology" that arises from the connection between goodness and intelligibility. Like love, patience is essentially relational or intentional. If knowledge requires a transcendence of self, as we have argued, then real knowledge cannot come quickly. In *Letter VII,* Plato claims that to reach the fifth level that represents the soul's genuine contact with reality on

---

120. *Rep.,* 596d.; see also *Soph.,* 251b–c. At 234a, Plato also points out how quickly one can make images.

121. In the *Sophist* (234c–235a), Plato discusses the ease of fooling and being fooled by *superficies,* the remedy for which is *aging,* i.e., the suffering of time.

122. *Euthd.,* 272b, 273d, 303e, 304a.   123. *Alc. I,* 118b–c.

124. *Plt.,* 264b; cf. *Rep.,* 528d.

125. See also *Hp.mai.,* 304e, *Cra.,* 384b, *Soph.,* 259c, *Phdr.,* 274a–b.

126. *Soph.,* 234d–e.

reality's terms requires "long and earnest labor."[127] True to this assertion, the educational program Plato outlines in the *Republic* lasts fifty years. Indeed, the kind of tedium that such a view of education immediately suggests to the mind is built into the dialogue itself. There is something exasperating about its constant self-revision and lengthy digressions, and this is part of the very methodology Plato intends to express *in* the dialogue. The patience this method calls upon is a function of the soul's acknowledgment of a measure outside of itself, which is, as it were, the very definition of truth. When the question arises whether the company ought to take the time to pursue an apparent digression in arguments rather than assuming something is understood and simply proceeding to further implications, Glaucon asserts, "For intelligent men . . . the proper measure for listening to such arguments is a whole life" (450b). This is not hyperbole. It is *literally* true: to the extent that one assumes one has complete and adequate possession of a thing in knowledge, one's soul is no longer outside of itself with real being but has reverted to a derivative level and thus is no longer "intelligent" in the strictest sense. Even before Socrates raises questions about the sorts of things Alcibiades plans to do, he first criticizes him for assuming he already understands the nature of what he intends.[128] The same thing comes to an especially dramatic expression in Euthyphro, who proceeds to carry into action what he believes he understands about piety *before* taking any interest in what piety *is,* regardless of Socrates' questioning him. Euthyphro responds: "Some other time, Socrates, for I am in a hurry now, and it is time for me to go."[129]

In short, the impatience and stress that follow from the subordination of things to their practical and temporal consequences undermine intrinsic meaning and eliminate justice. They indicate the collapse of reason.

Use and Gratuity

Because sophistry wields power, because it is indifferent to freedom, takes no essential responsibility for the whole, and aims at the timely impact of ideas, sophistry is extremely "useful." And being useful, it has no difficulty justifying itself and for that reason "selling" itself to others.[130] Philoso-

---

127. *Letter VII*, 344b. See Tulli, *Dialettica e scrittura*, 47, on *work* as the essential characteristic of philosophy.

128. *Alc. I*, 113b–e.

129. *Euthphr.*, 15e. Significantly, this is the last line of the dialogue.

130. *Ap.*, 19e–20c.

phy, by contrast, is basically "worthless" (cf. 487d). Though such accusations tend to come from "wise" critics of philosophy,[131] there is an essential truth to this observation. Or rather: this state of affairs follows directly from the essence of truth. If truth were nothing more than "correctness," one could make an obvious argument for its usefulness. A clear grasp of what and how things are allows for efficient action. Plato will often speak this way in his criticism of those who act without knowing what they are doing. But, as we have seen, his understanding of reason aims at a truth that is fundamentally different from mere correctness. Appearances, for Plato, fail to qualify as truth *not* because they are incorrect—a mirror image, after all, which he offers as an example is perfectly correct in its details—but simply because they are not the reality itself. The difference between reality and appearance concerns mode of disclosure, and truth thus is the presentation of the "heart" of things (511d–e). Again, we see the significance of the difference between absolute and relative intelligibility that we underscored in chapter 2: a teleological account—i.e., what something is good for—is crucial to understanding something, but it is not ultimate. A thing's essential truth is its irreducible being, its goodness in itself.[132]

But as we have suggested above, absolute goodness cannot be ultimately accounted for. It can likewise serve no further purpose. The disclosure of the truth of something, "itself by itself" as Plato often puts it, *must* be a singular and irreducible event. To be sure, something that is good in itself will necessarily be good for other things, but to reduce its goodness to these benefits is to eliminate its fundamental truth. In the *Republic*, Plato speaks of the "useless" studies (ἄχρηστα μαθήματα) that "purify and rekindle" the organ of the soul, which has been "destroyed and blinded by other pursuits," and by which truth alone can be seen (527d–e).[133] He goes on to say that such a thing is impossible to justify to those who do not already see it, but to those that do, such talk "seems extraordinarily good" (ἀμηχάνως ὡς εὖ δόξεις)—literally, "impracticably" or "uselessly" good. There is an essential connection between the uselessness of truth and the ecstasis of reason. Such

131. Cf. *Euthd.*, 305a.
132. Plato often uses the term "truth" to mean "reality". consider, e.g., *Symp.*, 218e. The truth of one's opinions depends on the truth of *being* (*Rep.*, 413a).
133. Specifically, in this context he is about to introduce the study of solids for their own sake (αὐτὸ καθ᾽αὐτὸ, 528a–b), regardless of their practical uses. This is part of the general education in philosophy.

a view of truth, moreover, explains the connection between philosophy and beauty. The *Phaedrus* can be seen as distinguishing between the (useful) mundane, calculative reason of self-interest and the (useless) ecstatic reason of philosophy. Its prologue, which elaborates the contrast between leisure (σχολή) and business (ἀσχολία: literally, the "absence of leisure"), provocatively proclaims philosophical discussion to be a "weightier thing than business" (ἀσχολίας ὑπέτερον πρᾶγμα).[134]

The very same thing that makes philosophy absolutely good makes it something more than a technique.[135] Every τέχνη, Socrates says in the beginning of the *Republic* (342c), is ordered to an end that is different from itself. It is just this that makes the various τέχναι both partial and relative. But the "art" that aims at the whole is itself necessarily its own end, and so there is no justification for it. This is what makes it useless—just as justice itself is "useless in the use of each and useful in its uselessness" (333d)—and also the science of all other sciences.[136] The totalizing of its aim and the absoluteness of its goodness has consequences for the philosopher. While sophists can be experts or professionals, a philosopher must be by nature an "amateur,"[137] and it is no accident that the word means not only nonprofessional but also "lover." An expert is one who has mastery over a thing. But to have mastery implies that the kind of "possession" we have seen corresponds only to a "relative" aspect of reality rather than to reality itself. Being occupied with the relative, and thus manipulable, aspect of reality enables one to produce results, and the ones who produce results are the ones who get paid. In this respect, one cannot be an expert in philosophy precisely because the truth cannot, by definition, be mastered. Callicles' comparison of being a philosopher and remaining like a child is thus full of significance.[138] If truth is root-

---

134. *Phdr.*, 297b.

135. According to Kube, *TEXNH und APETH*, 227–30, the sophists assumed virtue to be nothing more than an "Über-τέχνη," which provided the perfectly manageable means to serving one's own ends. Plato rejects this because it makes man essentially the measure. Every τέχνη aims at a particular good; that which aims at goodness itself—namely, philosophy—by definition cannot be a τέχνη (see 189–96).

136. The *Charmides* speaks of σωφροσύνη as a science of all other sciences including itself (i.e., a knowing of knowing), 166c. Interestingly, it is likewise said to be knowledge of the self (164d), the doing of the good (163e), and the doing of one's own business (161b). Moreover, Socrates concludes that the knowledge of knowledge is essentially useless (175a).

137. *Euthd.*, 282d.

138. *Grg.*, 485b.

ed in goodness, then a note of a kind of naiveté and inexperience will run through a life devoted to philosophy and will likely make its "practitioners" look ridiculous in matters of pressing practical concern.[139]

Along the same lines, we see how tightly philosophy is bound to wonder.[140] Insofar as wonder is the response to something greater than one, then the connection between truth and goodness makes wonder an indispensable part of the structure of the philosophical act, and not merely the spur to questioning it is often taken to be. Wonder, in other words, is not an instrument that produces results, but is the abiding principle of philosophy itself. The moment one ceases to wonder, one has ceased to look to the whole of which one is a part. And in that same moment, reason ceases to be philosophical, which means it ceases to be reason at all, and becomes instead a mere calculating machine.

In contrast to the gratuity of philosophy, sophistry is shown to be essentially "productive."[141] It constantly *makes* things.[142] It is just this that allows sophistry to make a kind of progress, while philosophy always seems to get stuck[143] and even in a way to go backwards: as Socrates' interlocutors regularly discover, not only have they not gained anything by his exposing them to philosophy, but they have in fact lost what they thought they had.[144] As Socrates says in the *Greater Hippias,* progress occurs specifically in the arts. It is modern craftsmen who make the ancients seem worthless by comparison, and sophistry is precisely an art in this sense.[145] Sophists claim to be "wiser" than the thinkers of the past, and in a technical sense they are no doubt right. But, notice, this both makes wisdom a "skill" and makes it subservient to ends other than itself, i.e., practically useful. Sophists are never therefore wise because it is good to be such, but always simply as "wise as they need to be."[146] This statement, of course, undermines itself. If wisdom

139. *Grg.,* 484c–486c.

140. *Tht.,* 155d. Socrates refers to the genealogy that makes Iris the daughter of Thaumas. Iris is the rainbow that binds together heaven and earth; she is an intermediate, messenger goddess. It is interesting to note that Iris is sometimes also taken in Greek mythology to be the mother of Eros. See Robert Graves, *The Greek Myths,* vol. 1 (Middlesex, Eng.: Penguin Books, 1960), 15b, p. 58.

141. See Kube, *TEXNH und APETH,* 33–40, for the connection between *technē* and the "Machbarkeit des Menschen."

142. Cf. *Soph.,* 234aff.   143. *Meno,* 80a–b.

144. Cleitophon shows his extreme exasperation when Socrates offers no response to his demand for a definition of the *skill* of virtue and the *product* of justice. *Cl.,* 409a, d.

145. *Hp.mai.,* 281d.   146. *Grg.,* 487c; *Euthd.,* 305e; cf. *Hp.mai.,* 283b.

receives its measure from something else, from some other human concern, it surrenders its absolute character and therefore its integrity. Wisdom becomes in this case an instrument, but this is no longer wisdom because it no longer concerns the disclosure of the being of things. Plato seems to suggest that if the "gratuitous" good is not fundamental, then "useful" relative goods will have sovereignty. Likewise, if there is no "useless" human activity that concerns the whole and the heart of things as such, then we are left with a series of relative skills. But, as we have suggested, relativity always implies an absolute reference point. What, then, is the common "useful" good unifying the relative benefits of the various τέχναι? In the absence of philosophy, the useless devotion to the good, Plato suggests that the only alternative is the "wage-earner's art" (*Rep.*, 346a–d). Absent the good, mastery of this art becomes the supreme sign of wisdom: "The mark of being wise, I see, is when someone makes the most money."[147]

One wonders whether honor could be an alternative to money as a relative common good. It seems, however, to stand in a sort of twilight for Plato. As we suggested in chapter 1, this is the significance of crisis. The appearance of virtue, on which honor depends, is rooted either in a desire for gratification or for genuine goodness, and it is the crisis that lets the truth be manifest.

The Indefensible Defense of the Defenseless

So what need is there to get to the heart of things if it is, in fact, useless? There is, of course, no adequate response to be given to this question. Indeed, there cannot be because of the very nature of what is at stake. Perhaps the best one can do is insist, as Plato does, that only a soul that has caught a glimpse of the really real can be defined as human: "As I said, nature requires that the soul of every human being has seen reality; otherwise, no soul could have entered this sort of living thing."[148]

If philosophy is the love of wisdom as a whole, then its disappearance means the eclipse of reality, the elimination of the center that holds all things together. Without philosophy, the cosmos begins to unravel. The love of goodness philosophy implies is the precondition for unity. Without such a love, "a man could not be dear to another man or to a god, for he cannot be a

147. *Hp.mai.*, 283b.
148. *Phdr.*, 249e–250a; cf. 248b–e.

partner, and where there's no partnership there's no friendship. Yes, Callicles, wise men claim that partnership and friendship, orderliness, self-control, and justice hold together heaven and earth, the gods and men, and that is why they call this universe a *world order* (κόσμον), my friend, and not an undisciplined world-disorder."[149] Thus, though philosophy is useless, indeed, precisely *because* it is useless in the specific way that it is, philosophy is indispensable. And to the extent that goodness has a causal role in the constitution of the world, philosophy has, so to speak, cosmological significance.

The account of philosophy that has been emerging in this study of Plato shows a dramatically different dimension from the conventional view. The existence of the philosopher is, above all, a sign of the world's fundamental goodness. The work[150] that is most proper to philosophy is not first to provide a solid foundation for the sciences, to marshal arguments about serious ethical matters, or even to raise fundamental questions about the meaning of life, but rather to bear constant witness to goodness. Or perhaps more precisely: it *is* to reason about life and to inquire into meaning, but only within the context of an existence devoted to the good, because only such an existence opens the horizon in which such reasoning and questioning makes "real" sense. To say this is not the same as saying that intellectual activities must be accompanied by moral character and that one ought always to put into practice what one learns. The point being made here does not concern the integrity of the moral life, as important as that may be, but the integrity of the intellectual life as such. Without an order that is transparent to absolute goodness, things lose not only their value, they lose their *intrinsic meaning*; they cease to be objects of the intelligence in the proper sense and be-

149. *Grg.,* 507e–508a.

150. "Work," here, in the sense Jacques Barzun gives the term. In criticizing the kind of drudgery mistaken for intellectual work, he writes (in an unmistakably Platonic spirit): "But is this not work? No, it is at best industry, a virtue not to be despised, but lacking the essential element of work, which is passion. It is passion in work and for work that gives it its dramatic quality, that makes the outcome a possession of the worker, that becomes habit-forming and indeed obsessional. Of all the deprivations that modern life imposes on intellectual man, the abandonment of work is the cruelest, for all other occupations kill time and drain the spirit, whereas work fills both, and in the doing satisfies at once love and aggression. That is the sense in which work is 'fun,' with an irresistible appeal to man's love of difficulty conquered—a pleasure altogether different from that for which educators have turned school subjects into activities and play. Under the habit of play, drudgery, when it comes, remains drudgery, instead of an accepted purgatory close to the heaven of work," Jacques Barzun, *The House of Intellect* (New York: Harper and Row, 1959), 125.

come instead raw materials for some other construction project. Plato was unable to imagine an intellectual life outside of the sort of community that arises from a common and living devotion to goodness; this is the heart of his critique of the kind of education ordered around the transmission of poetry without a living soul, as it were, to give that poetry a meaningful center. He challenges Homer's (and Hesiod's) title as "educator of Greece," because Homer didn't generate a group of followers passionately devoted to him (600c–e) as, of course, Socrates did.[151] It is interesting to reflect on the fact that reason came into its own in the rise of not just smart individuals but teachers and founders of communities, and that the great universities arose in the Middle Ages among the religious orders. The modern university appears to be the first institution of learning to think of intellectual life outside of the context of vocation—and, as we suggested in the introduction, seems also to be the first institution of learning to *teach* the contempt of reason and to embed this contempt in its methods and aims.

Let us finally return to the questions Griswold and Roochnik raised: What of the contest between reason and unreason? If it is the case that one cannot justify useless studies to anyone not interested in truth for its own sake (527c), if reason has its roots in the absoluteness of the good and can neither set its ultimate sights lower without ceasing to be what it is nor justify itself a this sense, what we have elaborated seems only to have cemented the incommensurability, and so left no real hope for finding a starting point for dialogue. Reason's being rooted in the good seems to make it ultimately helpless. Although Griswold and Roochnik offer rich accounts of reason and its resources, they both confess that reason has nothing finally to say to those who persist in a radical rejection of truth.

Behind the wall is, however, not the last place Plato stations the philosopher, and this inevitable failure is not Plato's final word on reason. Griswold claimed that Plato was obsessed with justifying philosophy and for this reason constantly called up the most serious challenges to it.[152] But, though this is true, one has to wonder why Plato would draw so much attention to philosophy's failures. Not only do a great number of dialogues end with reason's inability to "get anywhere," but Plato also regularly chooses to pit the philosopher against the nonphilosopher without ever having the philosopher

---

151. A more thorough discussion of the relationship between poetry and philosophy that Plato presents in this part of the *Republic* will be had in the next chapter.

152. Griswold, "Plato's Metaphilosophy," 153–54.

successfully persuade his opponent. How many "converts" do we find in Plato's dialogues?[153] If Plato wanted to justify reason in the obvious sense, one would expect him to show its triumph in these battles. If this was his aim, would he not, for example, have had Thrasymachus return to the discussion at the end of the *Republic* having decided, like Plato himself, to renounce power and pursue philosophy? The dialogue is, after all, basically a fiction, and Plato could have ended it in any manner that suited his purposes. Instead, the confrontation goes without any explicit resolution, and Socrates works out his views with those who are clearly already on his side. The moment in the dialogue where Socrates does seem to win someone "undecided" to his side, namely, Polemarchus, Thrasymachus charges in and breaks up the alliance. As if gloating over reason's futility, the dialogue *Cleitophon* simply rakes Socrates over the coals for being able to provoke interest in the question of justice but unable to say anything substantial and conclusive about it, so that those who are inspired by Socrates are left helpless and hungry and are eventually compelled to seek wisdom among the sophists like Thrasymachus.[154] What could Plato possibly have meant by writing this?[155]

The relationship between intelligibility and goodness that we have been developing here offers a surprising way to respond to this problem. The question of whether it is possible to persuade someone who refuses to listen to reason—the very first problem Socrates encounters in the *Republic*—typically takes for granted that *reason's primary aim is to persuade,* to such an extent that, if it fails to achieve this aim, its own integrity becomes suspect. But

153. If we accept Plato's authorship of *Alcibiades I,* which is the minority view (see *Plato's Complete Works,* 557–58), Alcibiades may be the exception that proves the rule. He leaves his discussion with Socrates by resolving to reform his life ("Yes, that's right. I'll start to cultivate justice in myself right now" [*Alc. I,* 135e]), but the readers of this dialogue would have known that his failure to cultivate this justice ultimately led to the downfall of Athens. The one figure who "converts" in the dialogue turns out to be Socrates' most catastrophic failure. On this, see Benvenuto, "Lo Specchio della Potenza," 25–27. Benvenuto suggests that Plato presented this obvious failure (for both Socrates and Alcibiades) in order to show that it is hopeless to enter politics and that philosophy is concerned therefore with something *more* than this.

154. *Cl.,* 410d.

155. There is some controversy over the authenticity of *Cleitophon,* but the strongest argument against it concerns the apparent baldness of the attack on Socrates, which goes unanswered. See *Plato: Clitophon,* edited by S. R. Slings (Cambridge: Cambridge University Press, 1999), esp., 227–34. After careful study of all the evidence, Slings takes it as genuine. The deciding question is whether it can be shown to be consistent with Plato's other dialogues, and we will propose a reason for thinking it does.

Plato is unequivocally clear that such an aim does *not* define reason, but only its sophistical counterfeit.[156] Reason's aim, by contrast, is simply the good. It was said that Socrates' goal "was not to alter his [interlocutor's] opinion but to get at truth."[157] While sophistry assumes reason to terminate in the individual's soul, philosophy understands truth to have its locus beyond the individual soul and, so to speak, in the world itself. Let us weigh the difference carefully. A person's perceptions and convictions are essentially *private* (ἴδιος) and therefore essentially relative in form, however "correct" they may be. To make such a conviction the goal of reason is necessarily to reduce the structure of reason to relativity. But Socrates insists that there is a decisive difference between "having learned" and "being convinced."[158] If reason is rooted in the absoluteness of the good, then measuring it by its capacity to persuade would undermine its own rationality. Philosophy cannot be ordered to persuade any more than it can be ordered to some practical aim without ceasing to be philosophy. One of the implications of the good's causing intelligibility is that reason acquires an essentially public dimension, as we have been arguing. What this means, in relation to the question at hand, is that reason seeks not first to persuade private individuals but instead to bring to light the truth of things as a *public*, a *common* good.[159] As Socrates says in the *Charmides*, "This is what I claim to be doing now, examining the argument for my own sake primarily, but perhaps also for the sake of my friends. Or don't you believe it to be for the common good, or for that of most men, that the state of each existing thing should become clear?"[160] The revelation of the truth of things is for the good of all. In other words, the truth that reason aims at cannot possibly be simply an individual's possession, nor can it be the possession of many individuals; rather, it is by its nature a comprehensive whole. Thus, the philosopher, in his dialogue with others, is primarily an instrument to make clear a truth that embraces them all.

A paradox arises once again: one of the most direct ways to make such a truth visible, as we saw in the previous chapter, is through the apparent failure of dialogue. Here we encounter an important implication of Plato's dialogue form. If truth is absolute rather than relative, and to that extent greater

---

156. *Grg.*, 453a. 157. D. L., II.5.22.
158. *Grg.*, 454d. 159. See *Grg.*, 453c.
160. *Chrm.*, 166d. Notice that the primacy of seeing its goodness for one's own sake corresponds to its absoluteness, while the goodness for others is the relativity this absoluteness necessarily entails.

than any individual soul, it is most clearly manifest *dramatically.* The straight-forward narrative of a treatise, for example, can at best transmit the sort of knowledge that can be expressed in statements and thus "possessed" in the soul—i.e., a merely relative form of knowledge. Plato's dialogues do not aim to articulate knowledge primarily in this form. Instead, as dramas, they present a truth that has a four-dimensional structure. The *Republic,* specifically, read dramatically in light of Socrates' *real* descent into the cave, "breaks open" to a concrete reality that transcends the simple written word. And the breakdown of dialogue can be in fact the most illuminating way for a dialogue thus to break open.[161] As Plato says in the *Timaeus,* contests of an extreme sort can be the best means of manifesting what is true beyond mere appearance.[162] This kind of contest presents perhaps the most intense form of "rubbing together" that *Letter VII* says is part of the essential method of illuminating knowledge. If this is true, we have a clear and convincing explanation for the agonistic character of so many of Plato's dialogues and also for the failure at the heart of the *Apology.* To debate on sophistry's terms is ignoble, so that—to the extent that the good is the point—even if you win, *especially* if you win, you lose. It is better, Plato says, to be defeated by such arguments than to defeat others with them.[163] Plato is simply stating what Socrates makes undeniably evident in the *Apology.* As this dialogue shows, if you lose on those terms, you "win." Philosophy cannot accept the terms of sophistry[164] but can win on its own terms by losing on the terms sophistry sets.

When Socrates is judged by the Athenian people, he says that they are in fact condemning themselves, or that justice itself condemns them.[165] He is right insofar as the confrontation brought forward the absoluteness of the good in the light of which their judgment acquired its true meaning, its

161. James Arieti offers a reading of the *Phaedo* in a similar spirit. The questionable nature of the arguments Socrates presents for immortality is intrinsic to what Plato intends to show about Socrates' relation to the world to come: "We see then that the arguments *had* to fail, not only because we cannot in this life know about our souls' longevity after death, *but because the drama of the dialogue requires them to fail,*" *Interpreting Plato,* 4–5. One ought to argue perhaps with his conclusion, but the mode of his interpretation is excellent.

162. *Ti.,* 19b–c.

163. *Euthd.,* 303d.

164. In *Alcibiades,* Socrates criticizes Alcibiades' willingness to "stoop to compete" with the sophists, *Alc. I,* 119c.

165. *Ap.,* 39b.

truth. The conflict that, in one respect, seems to present the failure of reason (viewed as an instrument of persuasion), actually, at another level, shows its supremacy (as that which makes fundamental truth manifest). Failure to convince becomes an occasion that manifests the truth in a more objective way. Thus, at the very limit of incommensurability in reason's confrontation with nonreason, Griswold and Roochnik, in different ways, end with the separation of two mutually impenetrable spheres, so to speak.[166] But this, again, assumes reason has an individual or private structure, and so this final result proves the victory of sophistry. It is significant that Roochnik's final image of reason is a chastened "hero" who must learn to content himself with his own "game," meaningful only for those within, and to surrender any aspiration to truth or universality. If, by contrast, truth is rooted in goodness, then insofar as the collapse of reasonable dialogue becomes an occasion for the philosopher to reveal the absoluteness of the good—as Socrates does paradigmatically in the *Apology*—the *sophist becomes a servant of truth in spite of himself.* Indeed, the sophist's resistance to truth makes the truth, dramatically understood, all the more evident. The "impossible" dialogues from this perspective represent the *privileged place* for the manifestation of the truth of philosophy, and we thus have a solid reason for Plato's apparent obsession with the disastrous encounter between reason and nonreason. Though the truth is defenseless, we could say it is so precisely because it needs no defense.[167]

166. Griswold claims that the "cheerful nihilist" is ultimately irrefutable, and that Plato was aware of this ("Plato's Metaphilosophy," 166–67). But we have to ask why he would show this impossibility so regularly. Griswold says that the setting of the dialogues reveals the significance of prephilosophical commitments. But, again, we have to ask: Would Plato call them such? Indeed, in his essay "Liberating Discourse," Chris Rocco points to the "extraphilosophical" means Socrates seems to resort to in order to justify philosophy, and argues that this shows the ultimate supremacy of rhetoric over philosophy. 377. But this is clearly not a Platonic position. It would seem that Griswold's interpretation would have no response to Rocco's argument. To respond in an adequate way, we would therefore need to show that the "extraphilosophical" is in fact genuinely philosophical, and that it is all at the service, not of winning the argument and persuading one's opponent, but of making truth manifest.

Roochnik, in the *Tragedy of Reason*, as we have already seen, ends with reason accepting the limits of its own game, in which it is at least entitled to call the rules, as arbitrary as they might be for outsiders. That such a perspective depends on a kind of subjectivism that would be alien to Plato needs no argument.

167. As Ross helpfully points out, the kind of truth represented by the forms for Plato is not a set of beliefs (with the subjective intuitive form this implies), but has a freer, more objective ground: "We thus do not *need* to be aware of our knowledge of the *Forms*, and it does not *need* to intuitively verify itself to us," "Non-intuitive Immediate Knowledge," 173. We could say, likewise,

It is necessary to point out immediately, however, that the truth's not needing to justify itself to others does not entail a disregard for one's interlocutors. Ultimately, if its indefensibility is due to its goodness, the very opposite is the case. Such a disregard would imply that one possesses the truth by oneself. But such a view follows from the *rejection* of truth's rootedness in goodness; it is the view that individual perception and convictions are the highest reason can achieve, which is the heart of sophistry. Reason that is ordered to the good, by contrast, participates in truth only with others, as we have seen. Whereas sophistry needs to produce the results of persuasion in others insofar as it is justified by its results alone, the reversal entailed in philosophy presents an extraordinary coincidence of gratuity and necessity. Truth, as rooted in the transcendent good, does not depend on the philosopher and his capacity to convince, and so he enjoys a complete freedom in his engagement with others. At the same time, just as what is absolute *includes* what is relative, the philosopher desires to participate in truth with every last person. We would have to admit, in fact, that his desire for others' participation is as intense as his desire for truth itself, which is by definition all-consuming (485d, 490a). There is something fundamentally disarming about Socrates' constant readiness to pursue any question with whomever it might be, as well as his audacity to call to account even the most powerful.

Moreover, by allowing the good to be manifest in an objective way, the philosopher becomes in his person a judgment on the antiphilosopher. But being judged, as we have seen, and as Socrates emphasizes repeatedly in the *Gorgias,* is a decisive method of being brought into relation with the good. In this sense, the philosopher's encounter with the sophist is an immediate way of bringing him, too, in relation to the good, and so embracing even the one who rejects it within the comprehending order of truth. In other words, the Socratic elenchus may be read as enacting the punishment that Socrates claims the unjust man most profoundly desires.[168] Bringing the unwilling party into the κόσμος may also explain the various acts of substitution Plato performs in the dialogues, substitutions that permit judgment to be carried out on the argument that the person himself is not in a position to make: consider Glaucon and Adeimantus's substitution for Thrasymachus, Socrates' taking Protagoras's part in the *Theaetetus,* his answering for the un-

___

it does not need to be *demonstrated* to its attackers, even if they can be shown to be wholly self-enclosed individuals for rejecting it.

168. See *Grg.,* 472e–479e.

willing Callicles in the *Gorgias* so that the discussion could continue,[169] or the Visitor speaking for the materialists in the *Sophist* and making them "actually better than they are."[170] Giving the argument careful articulation and then judging it in the light of reality is a way of extending the sovereignty of truth. In this sense, the philosopher does not view truth as a weapon,[171] or as a wall behind which to take shelter from the storm of society's unreason. Instead, it is essentially universal, not only in scope of application, but above all in form: *das Wahre ist das Ganze* ("the true is the whole").

The "Noble Risk" of Ignorance

Such a view of the nature of truth offers a new perspective on Socrates' regular professions of ignorance, which is interesting to consider as a conclusion to this chapter. The ignorance Socrates claims for himself is not a typical sort; the scholastics with good reason referred to it as a *"docta ignorantia."* The paradoxical character of Socrates' wisdom can perhaps be seen in the fact that the Academy, which ultimately had its origin, through Plato, in Socrates, alternated between espousing a form of dogmatism and being the home of skepticism. There is an ancient debate,[172] which has continued into modern times, over which of these two attitudes to truth best characterizes Plato, and how much of Plato's style was superimposed onto his "version" of Socrates. Often, one today attributes the dogmatic tendencies to Plato's legacy and envisions Socrates as being much more radically skeptical.[173] Without entering into the historical details involved in addressing that question, and instead attending exclusively to Socrates such as he appears in Plato's dialogues, i.e., Socrates as Plato understands him,[174] we can say on philosophical grounds that

---

169. *Grg.,* 505c–506c.   170. *Soph.,* 246c–d.

171. See *Symp.,* 219e.

172. D. L., III.51; cf. Empiricus, *Outlines of Pyrrhonism,* chap. 33, in *Selections from the Major Writings on Scepticism, Man, and God,* , 91: "Now, some have said that Plato is dogmatic, others have said he is dubitative, and still others that he is in one respect dubitative, in another dogmatic."

173. Typically, the negative elenchus is attributed primarily to Socrates; the elenchus, so the argument goes, was more present in Plato's earlier dialogues, and it begins to fade in significance in the later dialogues, which are more "dogmatic," and thus considered to be more "Platonic." See a discussion of the problems with this oversimplification in Tarán, "Platonism and Socratic Ignorance," O'Meara, *Platonic Investigations,* 85–109. We will propose a different way of viewing the relation of the dialogues to one another in the coda.

174. See Figal's observation. "Je genauer man sich an Platon hält, desto mehr wird man über Sokrates erfahren," in *Sokrates,* 22.

neither dogmatism nor skepticism adequately characterizes Socrates' position even in as "early" a dialogue as the *Apology*.[175] That Socrates *takes* a solid position of a sort, *pace* the skeptical school, is indisputably clear: he claims, in fact, to have been stationed by the god himself in his post and will remain more faithful to it than any hero in battle. He displays the unflappable confidence that one expects of someone with unshakeable convictions.[176] And yet, at the same time, Socrates tirelessly—and perhaps even tiresomely—claims that he knows nothing. It is significant that students tend to find him, at turns, both supremely arrogant and startlingly self-effacing. How are we to make sense of the human wisdom Socrates calls his ignorance?

The connection between goodness and intelligibility seems to supply a reason for the paradox. As we have seen, this connection implies an ecstatic notion of reason, which we have interpreted, following the divided line, the cave, and the account in *Letter VII*, as placing reason's own measure outside of itself. But if its measure lies outside of itself, reason can make its judgment only by being judged. The most complete form of reason will thus turn out to involve the confession of one's nonpossession of truth. Such a confession is itself a positive statement that truth has its proper place not in one's (private) mind but in the whole of which one is a part. If a dogmatist affirms that his own grasp of a thing is identical to its truth, then Socrates is not a dogmatist. But if the skeptic claims that there *is* no access to the truth as such, then Socrates is also not a skeptic. Instead, Socrates is one who bears witness to the fact that one can attain to truth only in renouncing one's own individual claim on it.[177] Skeptical ignorance would imply the simple indifference to truth that entails one's remaining, as it were, within the confines of one's own mind. It is this ignorance that Socrates sharply criticizes in both the *Symposium* and the *Meno*.[178] In this respect, his intellectual poverty keeps him, like love, always in pursuit of his object, and for that very reason always in its presence. His empty hands are open in constant gratitude for what is greater than they can hold. This is the reason Socrates expresses such a sublime freedom in his philosophizing: truth does not rest on him, but rather he

175. Assuming the *Apology* was early. We will discuss the problem of dating the dialogues in the coda.

176. Cf. J. C. Evans, who observes that Socrates *displays* the very virtues he claims not to know about and not to be able to practice without knowledge. "Socratic Ignorance—Socratic Wisdom," *The Modern Schoolman* 67.2 (1990): 91–109, here 91.

177. Cf. Evans, "Socratic Ignorance," 105–7.

178. *Symp.*, 204a; *Meno*, 81d.

rests on truth, and the intelligible order of things is sufficiently solid and objective to allow him to *risk* such an intellectual poverty.

Socrates in fact gives very concrete expression to an ecstatic notion of reason in his relationship to judgment. It is quite typical for Socrates to reach a certain point in his reasoning about a particular idea and then to leave it open. Whereas such an attitude might be expected in, say, the *Phaedo*,[179] where Socrates is more ambiguous about the ultimate possibility of knowledge, it is more surprising perhaps in the *Republic*, where the issue *is* a direct "vision" of the forms. But even here he says, after giving an account of the cave allegory, "A god doubtless knows if it happens to be true. At all events, this is the way the phenomena look to me" (517b), and later that the best he can offer is the truth as he sees it: "Whether it is really so or not can no longer be properly insisted on. But that there is some such thing to see must be insisted on" (533a). There are two things to notice here; first, a final and definitive statement of the matter *cannot* be given. If it could, we would in fact still be on the fourth level of the account of reason in *Letter VII*. The final stage, we have said, does not lie in the (expressible) contents of the mind but in reality itself. But this therefore means that reality *itself*, so to speak, makes the judgment of how things stand, rather than the knower's soul. Thus, as Socrates puts it here, the fact that he cannot make the definitive judgment of the way things are does not undermine any insight into the matter. To the contrary, it is the consequence of the very objectivity that makes genuine insight possible in the first place. The transcendence implied by an ecstatic notion of reason means that ultimate judgment is not the soul's to make, but, as Socrates says here and elsewhere, must be left up to the gods.[180] In other words, whereas the skeptic would deny the possibility of judgment at all, and the dogmatist would reserve ultimate judgment for himself, Socrates insists that there is a judgment, but that he himself is the one judged. He does not attempt to determine the final outcome of things, but *receives* their determination and thus allows himself to be determined by them.

Two characteristics of the "method" in the *Republic*, which would oth-

179. "No sensible man would insist that these things are as I have described them, but I think it is fitting for a man to risk the belief—for the risk is a noble one—that this, or something like this, is true about our souls and their dwelling places" (*Phd.*, 114d). In this dialogue, in fact, Socrates presents a kind of simultaneous openness to revision and complete certainty, such as we have been describing it here. See, for example, 100d–e.

180. Cf. Benvenuto, "Lo Specchio della Potenza," 24: Socrates' inconclusiveness is philosophy's opening up beyond itself to the transcendent.

erwise stand in tension with one another, show forth a certain convergence when seen from this perspective. On the one hand, there are the rather forceful statements concerning truth and the absoluteness of knowledge in contrast to opinion, and on the other hand, there is a modesty of expression and a constant readiness to revisit and revise. A reason ordered to a truth "outside of itself" will necessarily be both *certain* and *open;* it will be unshakably confident in its affirmation of truth and, for that very reason, never defensively insistent on its own perspective. It is significant that the *Republic,* like many other dialogues, presents its final statement of things as a *myth,* and specifically, a myth of judgment.[181] First of all, by presenting not only a myth, but in fact a vastly different one in each case, Plato expresses the same unwillingness that Socrates does to offer a definitive *account* of what is ultimate and to insist on its details.[182] Second, what these myths reveal is that, ultimately, all things will be judged, or perhaps we could say that what is ultimate about things is their being judged. Thus, the myth of judgment represents a fitting expression, in form and content, of Plato's theory of knowledge, for it is both the affirmation of an absolute measure and an acknowledgment that the measure, as absolute, lies outside of one's particular grasp. Again, the statement Socrates tends to make—"whether it is true, let the gods decide"—is an acknowledgment of the objectivity of truth.

It is very interesting, in the end, to consider the three things that Socrates *does* claim to have expert knowledge of. First, no matter how difficult the problem may be, Socrates expresses a conviction that there is a difference between correct opinion and knowledge: "However, I certainly do not think I am guessing that right opinion is a different thing from knowledge. If I claim to know anything else—and I would make that claim about few things—I would put this down as one of the things I know."[183] Notice that, from inside the cave, as it were, such a distinction makes no sense. Practically speaking, there *is* no difference between the two insofar as they produce

---

181. In addition to the *Republic's* "myth of Er" (614a–621d), there is myth in the *Gorgias* (523aff.), the *Phaedo* (107cff.), the *Phaedrus* (248eff.), and the *Laws* (904cff.).

182. According to Edward Ballard, myth is a *positive* expression of Socratic ignorance. *Socratic Ignorance: An Essay on Platonic Self-knowledge* (The Hague: Martinus Nijhoff, 1965), 167. For Ballard, however, it represents a sort of necessary irrationality, whereas we are suggesting it is a kind of suprarationality that perfects reason. We will elaborate this suggestion in the next chapter.

183. *Meno,* 98b. Along these lines, Socrates explains that his art of midwifery includes the capacity to distinguish truth from falsehood, true births from "wind eggs" (*Tht.,* 150b–151d).

the same outcome. We might want to say that knowledge is more "trustworthy," but we would have failed to see the point: correct opinion is absolutely and unshakably trustworthy precisely insofar as it is correct. The difference becomes significant only in terms of the relation each implies between the soul and reality. More specifically, knowledge implies a contact with being, and thus reason's movement beyond itself. To *insist* on this difference, as Socrates does, is to show that one dwells in the "place beyond heaven,"[184] beyond the mind's own horizon. There would thus be a perfect coincidence between Socrates' confession of ignorance and his knowledge of the difference between knowledge and true opinion. In fact, as we have interpreted them, these are the same thing.

Second, Socrates admits to knowing what love is. When a vote is taken at Agathon's house whether to spend the evening discussing the topic, Socrates says: "How could *I* vote 'No,' when the only thing I say I understand is the art of love (τὰ ἐρωτικά)?"[185] But to claim to know love is not a compromise with his claims of ignorance insofar as love itself *means* the refusal to identify oneself with wisdom.[186] In other words, his expertise on love and his confession of ignorance are, once again, one and the same thing: the acknowledgment that one is embraced by a reality, a truth, a goodness, that one can never subordinate to one's own soul. There is no contradiction, then, between the insistence that he knows nothing but things related to love and that he knows there is a difference between knowledge and opinion. Indeed, it is the exclusiveness of this knowledge of love that sets the difference between knowledge and opinion in such clear relief.

Finally, the third conviction that Socrates expresses is the one that underlies everything else, namely, that the ultimate reality, the principle of all things, is the good. There are some who believe that Socrates' renunciation of any claim to knowledge implies a lack of conviction regarding the good.[187] But if we accept this, we have reduced Socrates to a skeptic. To the

---

184. *Phdr.,* 247c.

185. *Symp.,* 177d–e. Socrates makes a similar statement in *Theages,* 128b. He also claims to be able to discern whether a person is in love, and who he is in love with (*Lysis,* 204c). In the *Phaedrus* (257a), he refers to his "expertise on love" specifically as a gift from Love himself.

186. Cf. Kosman, "Platonic Love," 58.

187. In his interpretation of the *Laches,* Gonzalez argues that courage requires "uncertainty concerning the highest good" (*Dialectic and Dialogue,* 40). This is simply not true. While there may be some uncertainty about how best to live in accordance with the highest good in a particular set of circumstances, Socrates never shows a trace of doubt about that goodness itself.

contrary, Socrates is free to renounce all "possessive" claims to knowledge precisely because of an absolute conviction regarding the good. People are fond of admiring Socrates' apparent willingness to question everything and everyone. However, there is not the slightest evidence anywhere in any of the dialogues or stories about him that Socrates ever called into question the fundamental goodness lying at the center of the cosmos.[188] Conventional cynicism would claim that he, alas, was not in the end as radical as he could have been—as radical, that is, as our cynics are. But Socrates himself both knows and says—"I would contend at all costs both in word and deed as far as I am able"—that questioning will come to an end if there is no intelligibility and truth,[189] both of which, as we have seen, depend ultimately on the good. Far from putting a limit to inquiry, such a conviction alone opens up the horizon wide enough to allow real questioning.[190] As any consideration of the ancient texts will show, Socrates is more thoroughly aware of the relativity of his own thoughts than any skeptic—because he knows that to which they are all relative. When he receives his sentence at the end of the *Apology*, he confesses that he does not know in any precise detail what his fate will be after death and does not know what is to come. But there is one thing he has no doubt about: whatever it is, it will be *good*.

188. See Blößner (*Dialogform und Argument*, 55), who points out that Socrates never calls the absolute goodness of justice into question for a moment.

189. *Meno*, 86b–c.

190. Ross shows that Socratic ignorance *necessarily presupposes* absolute knowledge (of an immediate, nonintuitive sort), which does not mean it can be adequately—absolutely—articulated (which Ross suggests is Plato's temptation). Less satisfactory is Hyland's claim that we "intuit," but don't "know," the intelligible *archai: Finitude and Transcendence*, 177.

RESTORING APPEARANCES

Or, How an Ecstatic Conception of Reason Makes
Images at Once Inadequate and Indispensable

"All of a sudden, he recovered his sight and saw that it was morning."
—*Republic*, 621b

Is Plato a Platonist?

Raphael's famous painting *The School of Athens* imaginatively illustrates a conventional belief regarding the two greatest Greek thinkers: Plato, the "idealist," points upward to the heavens; Aristotle, the "realist," gestures down toward the earth. Plato himself uses the directional metaphor to characterize the different relations to reality implied in the various μαθήματα. According to this metaphor, philosophy is essentially an *upward* path. As the standard interpretation has it, to lead the soul upward, ἄνω, means to lead it away from the realm of becoming, which is in flux, to the realm of being, which remains eternally the same. The movement away from becoming is likewise a movement away from the senses, since the senses are tied to this lower realm. But the senses are also bound up with the life of the body and its natural desires. In the conventional interpretation of "Platonism," there seems to be not only a tension but an outright opposition between the aspirations of philosophy and the body's natural τέλος. When Socrates describes philosophy as practicing death,[1] he does not mean merely preparing oneself for whatever is to come after life in this world. Instead, if death is the separation of the soul from the body, then philosophy *is* death, pure and simple, and our practicing for death would in fact be a practicing for philoso-

1. *Phd.*, 64a.

phy itself, that is, an always imperfect attempt to achieve that state in which the soul enjoys the untainted vision of the invisible reality of the forms themselves, finally free from the body's limitations. From the perspective of this state, it appears that the body, far from being filled with life, is in fact a "tomb" (the σῶμα is a σῆμα).[2] Socrates insists that the reality of the human being is not the body-soul composite, but the soul alone,[3] and *this* reality receives its life by feasting on that which lies beyond the senses,[4] and which is therefore completely independent of and even inimical to the body.[5]

It is no doubt because of this line of thinking, which leaves traces throughout the Platonic corpus, that Plato is generally taken to be the father of the various dualisms that are said to define Western thought.[6] In intellectual and cultural histories, the tag "Platonism" has largely come to designate not only universalist epistemologies, but also currents of disdain for the temporal, changing, and bodily aspects of human existence. Such currents, of course, generated powerful reactions in the nineteenth and twentieth centuries. Nietzsche took Plato to be the seed of the nihilism he found in the roots and branches of every modern institution.[7] In a passage from his notebooks written in the spring of 1888, Nietzsche referred to Socrates as "a moment of the deepest perversity in history."[8] The reason for his judgment springs di-

---

2. *Grg.,* 493a. Compare this, however, with Plato's allusion to the *other* meaning of σῆμα, namely, "sign": "Thus some people say that the body (*sōma*) is the tomb (*sēma*) of the soul, on the grounds that it is entombed in its present life, while others say that it is correctly called 'a sign' (*sēma*) because the soul signifies whatever it wants to signify by means of the body," *Cra.,* 400b–c.

3. *Alc. I,* 130c.

4. *Phdr.,* 247c–e.

5. For an excellent treatment of the alleged "body-soul" dualism in Plato, see de Vogel, *Rethinking Plato and Platonism,* 171–90. After showing that Plato does not pit the soul against the body (beginning with reference in the *Rep.,* to Plato's insistence that one not neglect the body in one's education of the soul, 535c–d), de Vogel nevertheless admits that Plato seems to have undergone a change from a more negative view (cf. *Phd.*) to a more positive view (cf. *Ti.*) of the body in its relation to the soul (177–78). Our proposal, which we shall elaborate, is that the two "sides" of the understanding are *equally essential* in Plato's philosophy, depending on the place each holds in relation to the good at the center.

6. If Plato is the father, then Parmenides, whom Plato refers to in a sense as his own intellectual father (*Soph.,* 241d), would be its grandfather.

7. Cf. Heidegger, *The Will to Power as Art,* vol. 1 of *Nietzsche,* translated by David Farrell Krell (San Francisco: Harper, 1991), 151–61.

8. Nietzsche, *Nachlaß 1887–1888,* vol. 13 of the *Kritische Studienausgabe,* edited by Giorgio Colli and Mazzino Montinari (Berlin: de Gruyter, 1999), 289.

rectly from what we have argued is the core of Plato's philosophy, namely, the absoluteness of goodness:

In praxi, it [Socrates' position] means that the moral judgments are uprooted from the conditionality *[Bedingtheit]* out of which they grew and in which alone they possess their meaning, uprooted, that is, from their Greek and Greek-political ground and soil, and, under the appearance of *sublimation,* they are denaturalized *[entnatürlicht].* The great concepts "good" and "just" are detached from the presuppositions to which they belong: and as "free-floating" ideas, they form the objects of dialectic. One seeks a truth behind them, one affirms them as entities or as signs of entities: in other words, one *fabricates [erdichtet:* poeticizes] a world in which they are at home, from which they come. . . . In summa: this disorder reached a peak already in Plato . . . and thus it became necessary to invent, in addition, the *perfectly abstract* human being.[9]

According to Nietzsche, when Plato thus "invented" truth and therefore the difference between being and appearance, a difference not to be found in the heroic age of the Greeks,[10] he began the spiritual decline of the West.[11] The very concept of truth, insofar as it depends in some respect on the "unconditional" and therefore on being's essential difference from appearance, is in Nietzsche's view necessarily an expression of contempt for what is real.

The thesis Nietzsche risked in the late nineteenth century has been accepted as a premise needing no justifying argument in postmodern thought. Derrida, for instance, has criticized the Western tendency to rely on "binary oppositions," a term drawn most directly from Structuralism, but which is, in Derrida's view, ultimately Plato's legacy.[12] According to Derrida, the "structural oppositions of Platonism" that have become ensconced in Western thought inevitably entail the privileging of one term and therefore the devaluing of the other. The differences between, say, Good and Evil, Being and Appearance, Truth and Imitation, and so forth, are essentially unjust

---

9. Ibid., 288–89.

10. "Those Greeks," he said, "were superficial—*out of profundity,*" Nietzsche, *Gay Science,* translated by Walter Kaufman (New York: Random House, 1974), 38.

11. His account of "How the 'True World' Finally Became a Fable," i.e., how the distinction between being and appearance eventually leads to nihilism, begins with Plato. see *Twilight of the Idols,* in *The Portable Nietzsche,* edited by Walter Kaufman (New York: Penguin Books, 1976), 485.

12. See Jacques Derrida, *Dissemination,* translated by Barbara Johnson (Chicago: University of Chicago Press, 1981), 85, 111, 149. By contrast, Thesleff has observed that the ancient Greek tendency, which continues in Plato, was to see opposites more as relational and complementary than as sharply polarized. *Studies in Plato's Two-Level Model,* 7–9.

and destructive. Making something positive always makes its opposite negative. We see a similar view expressed more recently by Martha Craven Nussbaum, who associates Plato's theory of knowledge and metaphysics with a
psychological need for purity.[13] The first speech on eros Socrates gives in the
Phaedrus seems to represent his typical rationalistic critique of human passions and all they imply. The second speech, however, signals in Nussbaum's
view a change of heart, a recognition of his previous one-sidedness. Nevertheless, she goes on to say, this self-criticism is not ultimately convincing:

> But we must now concede that Plato's will toward appearance was never unquali-
> fiedly good. The mood of recantation in the *Phaedrus,* its acceptance of limits, and
> its restoration to goodness of much in our nature that we associate with our finitude
> are connected, nonetheless, with a deep nostalgia for purity whose expression was
> never more moving than here. The complexities of the person are given greater re-
> spect; but Plato's deep discontent with our bodily nature, his sense that the body is a
> trap, a shell, are strongly present even in the speech of recantation (esp., 250bc). Dis-
> embodiment is a good even for the complex person (whose appetitive soul is taken,
> oddly to be separable from its bodily vehicle). Images of lightness, loftiness, clarity,
> and purity are used to characterize the soul's excellence. The person looks to this
> lightness as to a possible good; and, beyond this, he or she looks, as an impossible
> dream, to the imagined life of the pure divinities, drinking from the springs of un-
> blemished understanding.[14]

In the end, she suggests, to avoid the contempt for the body expressed in
such a Platonic dream, we must surrender not only the *possibility* of "pure"
knowledge, but even the desire for it.[15]

Now, this brief sketch of reactions to "Platonism" brings a dilemma into
view, one that has implications not only for philosophy but for the cultural forms that are inevitably rooted in it. On the one hand, it cannot be denied that truth implies a distinction between being and appearance, and that

13. Nussbaum, "'This Story Isn't True': Poetry, Goodness, and Understanding in Plato's *Phaedrus,*" in *Plato: On Beauty, Wisdom, and the Arts,* edited by Julius Moravcsik and Philip Temko
(Totowa, N.J.: Rowman and Littlefield, 1982), 79–124, here 117–18. Nussbaum's views on Plato are
expressed at greater length in *The Fragility of Goodness: Luck and Ethics in Greek Tragedy and Philosophy,* rev. ed. (Cambridge: Cambridge University Press, 2001), esp. 85–233. As Roochnik has
shown, Nussbaum's account of Plato's view of philosophy misses the subtleties that reveal that
heart of the matter, because she (ironically) overlooks the significance of the dramatic form. See
"The Tragic Philosopher: A Critique of Martha Nussbaum," *Ancient Philosophy* 8 (1988): 285–95.

14. Nussbaum, "'This Story Isn't True,'" 117–18.

15. Ibid., 118.

this distinction in turn implies a certain hierarchy of value: being presents a measure for appearance in a way that is not reciprocated. The postmodern critique of Platonism would therefore seem to have justified concerns that cannot be dismissed. We see the cause for concern in the characterization of Plato above: It does not seem possible to distinguish being from appearance without by that very gesture denigrating appearance. And this situation is of course contagious. Whatever has some relation with appearance becomes guilty by association, and we move quite quickly from a doctrine of forms to a contempt for what are undeniably essential aspects of human life, not only the *physical* needs of food, drink, and shelter, but also, for example, the familial relations that have their ground in sexuality. On the other hand, as we suggested in the introduction to this book, critiques such as those we just presented throw out Platonism only to let in misology. As we have shown at different points, misology turns out to breed its own kind of contempt, its own kind of violence, since its rejection of truth cannot avoid being a rejection of anything genuinely *common* and only therefore able to overcome a systematic fragmentation. Unnuanced critiques of Platonism have simply not faced up to the problematic implications of their own positions.

The dilemma appears to be fundamental: if we affirm the absolute difference between being and appearance that the notion of truth requires, there seems to be no way to avoid a condemnation of appearance and thus of all things bodily. But if we wish to "save appearances," we would seem to have to reject the Platonic notion of truth, and then suffer all of the consequences of this rejection. These are the alternatives that many prominent contemporary thinkers place before us. The question is: Are they adequate? Another way to put the question is: Is Plato in fact a Platonist?[16]

---

16. Gadamer, for one, responds to this question with a resounding 'No'. See the comment in his "Reply to Nicholas P. White," 260. So too does Stanley Rosen: *The Quarrel between Philosophy and Poetry* (New York: Routledge, 1988), 187. Drew Hyland elaborates a critique of just the sort of interpretation we saw in Nietzsche above in *Finitude and Transcendence*, esp. 165–95. It is important to see, however, that these defenses of Plato against Platonism tend at the same time to deny that he thought knowledge is, after all, possible, and thus they leave in place the alternatives that people like Nussbaum present to us as exclusive. They tend, in other words, to argue against any strong interpretation of forms or ideas in Plato's thought. But, as we will propose, it is not necessary to do so in order to preserve Plato against this charge: what is necessary is simply to recognize that absoluteness *always requires relativity*. The elimination of absoluteness in order to save relativity not only retains a problematic dualism but generates new problems of its own, not the least of which is the loss of relativity itself, as we have been arguing through the course of this

Our thesis, not surprisingly, is that "Platonism" is the name for a version of Plato that disregards the role of the good in his thought, and that it is precisely the good that allows us to avoid both horns of the dilemma just presented. The comprehensiveness of the good leads thought beyond both rationalism and irrationalism, beyond both "absolutism" and "relativism." Some of the broader issues associated with the relationship between being and appearance come into especially sharp focus in the question of the "ancient quarrel" between philosophy and poetry that Plato alludes to at the end of the *Republic* (607b), and so our discussion in this coda will center around this question. The issue of poetry arises as a sort of epilogue in the final book of the *Republic,* which is appropriate, as we will see, insofar as it serves to recapitulate many of the basic themes of the dialogue. It is likewise a fitting final question for the present book, since it gathers together in a summary way a number of the issues that have occupied us throughout. Plato's attitude toward poetry, and everything implied therein—namely, images, mythology, appearances, the senses, art, imitation, and the like—has been the object of countless studies. If we take it up yet again here, it is both with the hope that the connection between goodness and intelligibility can shed new light on this old theme and also with the desire to contribute one last argument for the importance of that connection for an understanding of the nature of reason.

In the following, we will first consider the apparent contradiction that studies of Plato regularly point to, namely, that Plato both condemns poetry and makes wide use of it. While some try to save Plato from this inconsistency by explaining it away, we will attempt to show that an ambivalence toward images is a necessary part of Plato's philosophy—intending the word "ambivalence" not in its usual sense of "subtle negative feelings toward," but in the original sense of a genuinely twofold attitude. We will argue that this ambivalence is a function of the twofold nature of the good and is reflected in the overall structure of the *Republic*. Images fall short of reality in one respect, but they also turn out to "add" something that mere abstract objects of thought do not possess. In chapter 3 we argued that the complex plot of the *Republic,* viewed in its integrity, serves to disclose the nature of the good; here, we will argue that it brings to light the essentially dual nature of images.

book. Holger Thesleff similarly affirms both the significance of forms or ideas in Plato *and* rejects a dualistic reading of Plato's cosmos: "The two-level model also implies a universal κοινωνία: there is no real χωρισμός between the two levels" (*Studies in Plato's Two-Level Model*, 123).

We will then elaborate the significance of the positive contribution that images make to thought and why the ecstatic conception of reason we presented in the previous chapter is impossible without them. This will put us in a position to make more general remarks on the importance of the "descent" in Plato's philosophy. We will conclude with a closer look at the *Republic's* concluding image, the "myth of Er," and what it reveals both about our general interpretation of the dialogue and about Plato's own relationship to it.

Contradiction in Appearance

Although the issue of poetry and poetic imitation had arisen already in books II and III, Plato's most thorough treatment occurs at the beginning of book X. To orient ourselves, let us first consider why he returns to the theme at the end of the dialogue. The discussion in book X comes to some extent as a surprise.[17] Indeed, it has been suggested that Plato had initially composed this consideration of the ancient quarrel between poetry and philosophy, as well as the other sections of book X, separately, and later joined it—some would say artificially tacked it on—to the *Republic* at the end.[18] There is some reason for the suggestion: the conclusion of book IX seems to bring an end to the driving concern of the dialogue, the difference between the just man and the tyrant. And yet, finishing with this, Plato proceeds to return to the question of poetic imitation, a theme he had dealt with at length already. Such a "reprise" might occur in a haphazard conversation, but it does not seem to belong to a dialogue that underwent several revisions. Moreover, once Plato presents the discussion of poetry in book X, he comes back once more to the difference between the just and unjust man (612aff.), which he apparently conclusively addressed at the end of book IX. The discussion of poetry thus stands as another digression, with nothing obvious to do with what borders it on either side.

But, as we have suggested before, digressions in Plato tend to hold great

17. Richard Lewis Nettleship claims that book X is "disconnected" from the rest of the dialogue, "the transition . . . is sudden and unnatural," *Lectures on the Republic* (London: Macmillan, 1901), 340.

18. The most elaborate argument for this position can be found in Gerard Else, *The Structure and Date of Book 10 of Plato's Republic* (Heidelberg: Carl Winter Verlag, 1972). As he puts it there, "Book 10 is a miscellany of four pieces, of different dates and with different purposes, and the whole never received a final editing from Plato" (65). See also Thesleff, *Studies in Platonic Chronology*, 185–86.

significance, and the present case is no exception. The discussion of the nature of imitation brings into focus for a last time what has been the governing theme of the dialogue as a whole, namely, the relationship between being and appearance. The central books of the *Republic* revealed justice to mean, in its deepest philosophical sense, the proper ordering of this relationship, and the justice of the state and that of the soul have shown themselves to be relative expressions of this essential meaning.[19] Plato underscores the pivotal importance of the theme of being and appearance by placing treatments of it at what are, structurally considered, the three most significant moments of the dialogue, namely, the beginning, middle, and end. The issue was first raised by Glaucon at the outset of the main discussion, it was the foundation for the presentation of the philosopher in the central books, and now again it appears at the dialogue's conclusion in the treatment of art. In this respect, we might view the discussion of appearance and reality in art as a recapitulation of the general argument of the *Republic,* which is a common feature in Plato's dialogues.[20] Indeed, if it is the case that, after reaching its peak in the ascent toward the good, the discussion descends through the degrees of imperfection (i.e., of distance from the good) in the various forms of government,[21] it is fitting that the dialogue should end with what Plato had presented as constituting the lowest segment of the divided line: art objects. Nevertheless, even if we acknowledge the structural balance this treatment in book X provides, one wonders whether the final treatment in fact contributes anything of substance to what Plato has already said in previous discussions. In other words, is this treatment of poetry there simply for aesthetic reasons, i.e., to bring closure to the argument by recapitulating its central theme, or does it carry any genuinely philosophical weight? In order to begin to respond to this question, it is first necessary to understand the nature of his critique of poetry in book X.

Book X begins with Socrates' exclamation that they were right to exclude from the city all imitative poetry, the reason being that imitation, as such, harms the soul:

---

19. At 368e–369a, Socrates suggests the idea of comparing justice in the city to justice in the individual soul in order to bring to light the "idea" of justice. See also 434e–435a. This idea itself would of course have to be different from each of its instances.

20. See, e.g., *Prm.,* 166c, *Lysis,* 222e, *Plt.,* 311b–c.

21. Cf. Sallis, *Being and Logos,* 450–54.

"And, indeed," I said, "I also recognize in many other aspects of this city that we were entirely right in the way we founded it, but I say this particularly when reflecting on poetry." "What about it?" he said. "In not admitting at all any part of it that is imitative (ὅση μιμέτιχη). For that the imitative, more than anything, must not be admitted looks, in my opinion, even more manifest now that the soul's forms have each been separated out." (595a–b)

First, let us note the unconditionality of the exclusion here. Some have claimed that Plato intends to banish from his ideal city not all art but only poetry;[22] others claim he is actually targeting only *bad* poetry.[23] But the fact that Plato uses the example of painting to illustrate the problem he sees in poetry (596e), compares artistic activity to reflecting things in a mirror (596d), and even makes allusion to the practice of sophistry in this context (596d), shows that he has in mind something quite basic and ingredient in all art, of whatever sort or quality: namely, the production of images *simpliciter*. The word ποίησις, after all, means most fundamentally "making," or "production," and the phrase "ὅση μιμετιχή," which Plato uses to qualify this making, means "insofar as it is imitative."[24] What is at issue here is the justification for derivative "realities" in relation to what is truly real, and poetry represents a paradigm case for this issue, not only because its practitioners are literally called "makers,"[25] and not only because it is essentially a fiction, but also because it

22. See Gallop, "Image and Reality," 115. Nehemas, "Plato on Imitation and Poetry in *Republic* 10," in Moravcsik and Temko, *Plato: On Beauty* 47. Nehemas takes 595b5–7 as a key text; it refers only to *listeners* and not to *beholders*. But the fact that Plato happens to be discussing poetry in this particular context does not necessarily mean that it is the only art he intended. It is especially difficult to make this case given the analogy between poetry and painting that forms the center of Plato's critique in this section.

23. Kurt Hildebrandt claims Socrates criticizes only imitative art, which is specifically to be distinguished from genuinely creative art. *Platon: Logos und Mythos*, 2nd ed. (Berlin: de Gruyter, 1959), 247. J. Tate, in his essay, "'Imitation' in Plato's *Republic*," *Classical Quarterly* 22.1 (1928): 16–23, makes a distinction between true and false imitation and claims that Plato condemns only the latter, which is superficial and seeks only to stimulate desires, thus introducing chaos into the soul. Julia Annas criticizes the view that Plato condemned only bad imitation. See "Plato on the Triviality of Literature," in Moravcsik and Temko, *Plato: On Beauty*, 1–28, here 19. As G. R. F. Ferrari puts it, "Let us, finally, not disguise from ourselves that it is the very greatest poetry that Plato would banish," "Plato and Poetry," in *Classical Criticism*, vol. 1 of *The Cambridge History of Literary Criticism*, edited by George Kennedy (Cambridge: Cambridge University Press, 1989), 92–148, here 141.

24. Cf. Heidegger, *Nietzsche*, 177–79.

25. For Plato, "poetry" represents every kind of productive activity: "After all, everything that

is exceptionally compelling and wielded a significant cultural power in Plato's Athens.[26] To raise the question of imitative art, then, is not to divert attention to a secondary matter, but to address directly the nature of reality and the subsequent relationship the soul ought to have to it, which has been Plato's central philosophical concern in the *Republic.*

After his introductory remark, Socrates goes on to confess a special love for Homer, but says that he must not thereby be dissuaded from elaborating his critique of poetry because "a man must not be honored before the truth" (595c). If we understand "truth" here to mean the real reality of things, Socrates' comment presents an anticipatory enactment of his critique of poetry, and indeed an echo of the philosopher's transparency to the real that we presented in chapter 4. Socrates here gives precedence to truth over a relative presentation of it, and he is about to censure poetry for reversing this priority.

Let us look at the main features of Plato's critique of the production of images specifically with a view to the question of their ontological status. There are three parts to the critique Plato presents: first, concerning the nature of the thing itself (595c–598d); second, concerning the sort of knowledge the artist possesses (598d–602b); and third, the effect that artistic imitation has on the soul (602c–606d). His criticism of the nature of art itself is well-known: art stands at a third remove from truth. The background of this account is Plato's view of the relationship between realities and their likenesses. Any time there are many things called by the same name, they necessarily share in something that is itself identically one and at the same time present in each. His example, here, is a couch, of which there cannot be more than a single idea (because if there were two, they would each share something that identifies them as the form of couch, and *this* would be the single idea).[27] This idea is brought forth, he says, by the "nature-begetter"

---

is responsible for creating something out of nothing is a kind of poetry; and so all the creations of every craft and profession are themselves a kind of poetry, and everyone who practices a craft is a poet". *Symp.,* 205b–c.

26. Collingwood has the target of Plato's criticism exactly right. "Plato's Philosophy of Art," *Mind* 34.134 (1925): 154–72, here 154–59. On the power of poetry, see Nehemas, "Plato on Imitation," 66–69.

27. Plato makes the argument for the necessity of *unique* ideas at 597c. Heidegger's interpretation of this argument (*Nietzsche,* 183–84) is clearly off the mark. For Plato, the uniqueness of ideas is a logical, and indeed metaphysical, necessity, but Heidegger attributes the insistence on the singularity of ideas to Plato's notion of divine creativity. It appears that Heidegger has in mind here his general critique of the "ontotheology" of Western metaphysics.

(φυτουργόν) (597d), or as he puts it elsewhere in this section, the "god" (e.g., 597b). Physical couches, of which there are many, are imitations of these, produced by human craftsmen. The painter, then, falls below the craftsmen, insofar as he does not imitate the idea, but only its physical appearance, the way it *looks*. He thus makes an imitation of an imitation.[28] Plato affirms that, because imitations in sound are similar to imitations in look, the poet shares essentially the same rank as the painter (597e), and a remark from Glaucon places sophists in the same group (596d). What unites them all is a focus on seeming rather than being.[29]

Now, it is important to see the relationship between unity and multiplicity implied in this hierarchy. The further we move from the divine idea, the greater the multiplicity. There can be only a single idea for any kind of thing; for each particular idea, there can be in turn an endless series of imitations; and for any of these physical instantiations, there can be an additional infinity of "pictures," insofar as one can take any number of perspectives on a thing, each of which, as relative, is different from the others (598a). From our discussions in chapters 1 and 2, we know that the irreconcilability of particular aspects *in* their particularity was a fundamental problem both ontologically and epistemologically for Plato, a problem that could be solved only in relation to a unity that transcended the individual aspects. We will return to this point in a moment. Plato draws attention to the poet's distance from reality in this context precisely by pointing to the universal scope of the

---

28. It is important to note that "imitation" does not mean simple duplication here, as Collingwood shows ("Plato's Philosophy of Art," *Mind* 34.134 (1925): 157): images for Plato are never a second reality juxtaposed to the first, but merely *appearances* of the one reality, being itself, and thus they represent a wholly different order from the forms, as we saw in chapter 2.

29. On the shift Plato here effects in the meaning of the verb μιμεῖσθαι, "to imitate," which originally meant "to represent," "to express," or "to act like," see Nehemas's comment: "Plato, however, wants to argue in *Republic* 10 that the poets, even when their imitations are successful, can do no more than imitate the look, not the nature, of things. To make this controversial point, to argue that poetry really is not just imitation in the sense of *likeness* but imitation of *appearance*, Plato appeals to painting, which can easily be said to be an imitation of the look of its subjects, considers it as representative of all imitation, and applies its characteristics to poetry as well," "Plato on Imitation," in Moravcsik and Temko, *Plato: On Beauty*, 58. It is interesting that the isolation of appearance *as* appearance occurs through reference to an essentially static art, namely, painting; the movement of drama seems to ensure that appearance will always be in some sense more than itself, that is, an "expression," even if the appreciation of this expression can drift toward the merely phenomenal. This may explain why Plato does not elaborate the distinction between being and appearance specifically in relation to poetry, which Annas points to as a weakness in his argument. "Triviality of Literature," 8–9.

poet's art.[30] While craftsmen each master only a single art, the poet is able to represent *all* of them indiscriminately (596c). But a strange problem emerges from this way of presenting the matter, which Plato simply ignores. Insofar as he produces *all* of the original realities, the god would seem to possess as multifaceted a creativity as the artist. If the forms are each one, and if reality is essentially connected with unity, we would expect the producer of the forms to be even more unified than the forms themselves; and yet the implication of Plato's argument is that the god represents as much multiplicity as he does unity. Whether or not Plato was explicitly aware of this implication, we will see that it bears significantly on the role the good plays in the being-appearance relation.

The second part of the critique concerns the various degrees of knowledge represented by the different levels of reality Plato has presented. Here, again, there is a hierarchy of three; however, this time the terms have altered slightly but significantly. Instead of the god, Plato places at the top the person who *uses* the things that are made, a person he quietly introduces for the first time at this point of the discussion: "For each thing there are these three arts—one that will use, one that will make, one that will imitate" (601d). The one who uses a thing, Plato contends, has the best knowledge of it, and is in a position to dictate to the craftsman how it ought to be made. The most superficial knowledge, of course, belongs to the imitator, who lacks even a correct opinion about the things he represents (602a).[31] If a person had genuine knowledge of things, Plato claims in the light of this hierarchy, he would always prefer to be the doer rather than the imitator.[32] In this context, Plato criticizes Homer for being himself a leader neither in war nor in education (600a–b), while he is admired by warriors and praised as the educator of

30. We are reminded here of course of the sophists' universal τέχνη, which we discussed in the previous chapter.

31. Cf. Paul Woodruff, "What Could Go Wrong With Inspiration? Why Plato's Poet's Fail," in Moravcsik and Temko, *Plato: On Beauty*, 137–50, here 142–44.

32. In this respect, Tate is right to point out a harmony between texts that seem contradictory: in book III, Plato approves the imitation of a good deed (396c), but in book X he rules imitation out altogether. In fact, a good person who "imitates" a hero or good deed unites himself with a *reality*, and one that is in fact not essentially different from him. Thus, there is here none of the "distance" between reality and appearance that presents the general problem with art for Plato. See Tate, "Imitation," 17–18. Cf. also Ferrari, "Plato on Poetry," 124–25, who makes a similar point, but is clearer than Tate that this imitation is *not*, in fact, *imitative*, which is why it receives Plato's approbation. One ought, in other words, to say that what *seems* like imitation in this case turns out not to be imitation, rather than drawing a distinction between true and false imitation.

Greece (599e–600a, 606e). For Plato, a book that does not arise out of a life devoted to what it speaks about cannot be an adequate source of wisdom.[33] In this criticism, we see that Socrates again stands as a contrast, because his words and deeds are a reflection of one another.[34] In this respect, he is not different from what he "imitates" in speech.

Finally, the third part of Socrates' critique concerns the effect imitation has one the soul. It is here that we see the significance of the multiplicity we just mentioned. Plato's critique of poetry is not in the first place a *moral* one, as it may have seemed to be in book III, where Socrates worried about the impression made on children by the depiction of gods doing bad things. Rather, the concern here is primarily ontological. The digression on the nature of philosophy at the center of the *Republic* has allowed us to return to the same theme at a much deeper level.[35] We have seen that wholeness has been a fundamental theme in the *Republic* from the very beginning (cf. 351cff.), and that this is the case because of the essential link between goodness and integrity. Such a view of goodness compels a question regarding the nature of multiplicity. To the extent that multiplicity presents itself in abstraction from a unifying order, the differentiation it implies cannot help but reduce to the mutual exclusion of parts. Multiplicity entails relative opposition, and if there is nothing but the relative, there is nothing but opposition. We recall that this fragmentation was the key to the problem of both Protagorean relativism and Thrasymachus's pleonexia. As Plato shows in book VII, sense-experience taken merely in itself is inherently contradictory (523e–524b),[36] which is why the unity of thinking is required to make sense of it. If this is indeed the case, it follows that imitation would create "factions" in

33. See *La.* 817b, where Plato contrasts the *real* drama of a well-ordered city to the fictitious drama of the poets.

34. See *Laches*, 188c–189b. Cf. Jaeger, *Paideia*, vol. 2, 36: Socrates was *in person* the new Attic drama. Contrast this with Moravcsik's observation that there cannot be a philosophical drama according to Plato. "Noetic Aspiration and Artistic Inspiration," in Moravcsik and Temko, *Plato: On Beauty*, 29–46, here 40. Jaeger's judgment clearly presupposes a certain transformation of the notion of drama, but he seems to be closer to Plato's position: philosophy represents the *perfection* of drama rather than its elimination.

35. Nehemas suggests that the treatment in book X is thus not a return to a theme already resolved, but a raising of "the question in a systematic form for the first time," "Plato on Imitation," 51. Cf. William Chase Greene, "Plato's View of Poetry," *Harvard Studies in Classical Philology* 29 (1918): 1–75, here 53.

36. See also *Phd.*, 59a and 60b–c, where Socrates observes that the opposites pleasure and pain always seem to be mixed up with one another in concrete experiences.

the soul of anyone who participates in it, exactly to the extent that imitation is occupied with nothing but appearances.[37] A person who involves himself with imitation will therefore necessarily surrender his interior unity:

> Then, in all this, is a human being of one mind? Or, just as with respect to the sight there was faction and he had contrary opinions in himself at the same time about the same things, is there also faction in him when it comes to deeds and does he do battle with himself? But I am reminded that there's no need for us to come to an agreement about this now. For in the previous arguments we came to sufficient agreement about all this, asserting that our soul teems with ten thousand such oppositions arising at the same time. (603c–d)

If Plato goes on to criticize the fact that poetry allows people to indulge the parts of the soul they would normally keep in check—and he claims in fact that this is the worst aspect of imitation (605c)—he does so against the backdrop of the nature of reality. The lack of unity in the soul makes it impossible to relate to reality as a unified whole, and vice versa; the two are essentially connected and reciprocally reinforcing. It is not an accident that dramatic imitation tends in particular to depict these "partial" and oppositional emotions and desires, since poetry is by nature a partial representation, which "lays hold of a small part of each thing" (598b). By the same token, a truly good man tends not to be portrayed, because there is something inaccessible about unity, at least by these means (604e). One would never expect to see the contemplative life featured on a reality TV show. There is, as we saw in chapters 2 and 4, something "non-manifest" about true unity and therefore goodness.[38] Again, form and content converge. If philosophy

---

37. The qualifier is crucially important. None but a purely commercial artist would accept the idea that he was presenting only the physical appearance of things. Serious artists of every age have been interested in communicating a truth or an ideal of some sort, however they understand it, even the crassest of naturalists. Nevertheless, it remains the case that the tendency toward reduction to sense-experience is a greater danger in art and that one must be, as we will suggest further on, genuinely philosophical oneself to appreciate art as art (rather than as reality itself), which means that one must be moved by more than the immediate impression on the senses. Iris Murdoch, like Plato a great lover of art, shows an awareness of this danger. *The Fire and the Sun,* 387 et passim. James Urmson rightly insists that this danger is present even in the most sublime examples of art and artists. "Plato and the Poets," in Moravcsik and Temko, *Plato: On Beauty,* 125–36, esp., 132–35.

38. Which does not mean, of course, that goodness is *merely* non-manifest, as we have repeatedly argued. The paradox does not go away even here; it will account for the essential (and therefore *good*) ambiguity of images.

is the whole soul "coupling" with reality as a whole (490b), artistic representation is the imitation of this: "imitation, a petty thing (φαύλη) having intercourse with what is petty, produces petty offspring" (603b).

Such a description of imitation reminds us, of course, of the shadow-play
on the walls of the cave. If there is an intrinsic connection between form and
content, then we can understand, in light of the *Republic*'s aim to bring the
reality of things to light, why Plato's condemnation of imitation would be
unconditional. We recall that he insisted at the start of book X on "not admitting at all any part of it that is imitative." Book III criticized poetry primarily for telling lies about the gods; Socrates agreed there to allow the "unmixed imitator of the decent" into the city (397d). Plato's condemnation of
it in book X appears to be far more radical. It is important to note once again
that his strictures apply here, *not* to imitations of bad things, but to imitation
as such. Insofar as truth, and thus unity, is meant to be the city's foundation,
there apparently can be no room for those things that stand at such a distance from it and are, indeed, precisely *defined* by that distance.[39]

But, although the unconditional rejection of poetry seems required by
the *Republic*'s general argument about being and unity, this rejection creates
unease on several counts. In the first place, as scholars are fond of pointing
out, Plato makes a good deal of use of just what he criticizes.[40] Indeed, he is
no doubt one of the most "poetic" philosophers in history, not just because
of a certain literary quality to his style, but also specifically because of his
genre, which is after all the dramatic enactment of conversations. And within these dialogues, Plato constantly introduces metaphors, images, and even
myths, which are the poet's proper media. The imaginative element is undeniably a fundamental aspect of Plato's philosophizing.[41] The irony reaches a peak, perhaps, in the divided line at the center of the *Republic*, for here

39. As Collingwood says, art is not concerned with truth either essentially or accidentally
("Plato's Philosophy of Art," 162), because truth is the "invisible" reality of a thing.

40. "The most obvious paradox in the problem under consideration is that Plato is a great
artist," Murdoch, *Fire and the Sun*, 462; cf. Gallop, "Image and Reality," 113. Collingwood points
out that Plato was not only a great artist; he also clearly took *a lot* of care with the specifically artistic details of his work. "Plato's Philosophy of Art," 168.

41. Mitchell and Lucas claim that this is precisely *why* he spoke so vehemently against it: he
was uncommonly susceptible to beauty and thus had to fight with himself for rationality more
than most philosophers. *Engagement with Plato's Republic*, 154. Cf. Collingwood, "Plato's Philosophy of Art," 169–70; John Fisher, "Plato on Writing and Doing Philosophy," *Journal of the History
of Ideas* 27.2 (1966): 163–72, here 170.

we have an elaborate visual image communicating to our thinking the notion that one ought not to use images in one's thinking. Attuned to this irony, Alasdair McIntyre suggested that the fact that Plato so deliberately uses images at the end of the *Republic* after everything he said within it clearly indicates his intention to show that the dialogue does not transcend the third level of the divided line.[42] While there may be some point to this observation, it does not remove the problem, for we have to recognize that Plato ends up outlawing any imitative poetry at all in his city, while the divided line makes images a natural and necessary stepping stone to understanding. Robinson expresses the common reaction to this problem with all desired clarity: "On the face of it, then, there is an inconsistency between Plato's principles and his practice about images. According to what he says about them, he ought never to use them, yet his works are full of them."[43] Moreover, the *Republic*, "which emphatically condemns imitation (595C–597E), and demands a form of cognition that uses no images at all (510–511, cf. εἰχόνες 510E), is itself copiously splashed with elaborate images explicitly called 'images' by the speakers. . . . There is no passage in Plato's works which fairly explains or even describes this incoherence. Probably it never struck him nearly so sharply and forcibly as it is here stated."[44]

Let us enumerate more specifically the ways in which Plato seems to be contradicting himself, or at least introducing a tension:

1) On the one hand, Plato speaks of philosophy as the soul's intercourse, in complete independence from the senses, with "invisible" being. If this is true, the *Republic* does not qualify as a work of philosophy.[45] In fact, if poetry is an imitation of reality in words, the *Republic*, as well as Plato's other dialogues, are examples of poetry. Socrates compares himself to a painter at several points over the course of the dialogue (414a, 488a, 501c, 548d), and uses just this comparison to characterize the poet's distance from reality.[46]

---

42. MacIntyre, *After Virtue*, 82. Our argument has been that the dialogue both *does* and *does not* transcend the segment, i.e., once we see that it does not transcend the segment, we in fact transcend it, which is part of the argument the dialogue itself is making and simultaneously enacting. See chapter 3.

43. Robinson, *Plato's Earlier Dialectic*, 220–21.

44. Ibid., 221. See also Murdoch, who similarly observes that the "problem" did not appear such to Plato and has in fact been invented by scholars. *Fire and the Sun*, 462.

45. As Arieti puts it, "The dialogue, [Plato] tells us, is mimetic philosophy, not real philosophy," *Interpreting Plato*, 242.

46. Gonzalez, *Dialectic and Dialogue*, 324n10.

As Robinson shows, Plato introduces images regularly over the course of the dialogue. We have seen that Plato turns to an image just when he says images are most problematic, namely, in discussing the good. In short, the *Republic*, as a whole and in its parts, is a work of imitation, just what the same dialogue rejects.

2) In book V, just before introducing the philosopher-king, Socrates uses the analogy of a painter to argue that an idealized *image* is better than an imperfectly realized *reality* (472d) and, further, that speech (λόγος) about something gets closer to truth than any *action* (ἔργον) (473a). But in book X, he says just the opposite. As we saw above, he claims that the mere *speaker* remains at a remove from truth, because of the imitative character of words, while the *doer* attains to the reality that the words simply imitate. Socrates, in fact, criticizes Homer for not doing in reality what he describes, while the city Socrates founds in the *Republic* is nothing but a "city in speech."[47]

3) At the same time, though Plato criticizes the *form* of poetic imitation, and not merely the content, at the very end of his seemingly unconditional criticism, he appears to change his mind: after exiling the poets from the city, he leaves the back door ajar, as it were, for the poets who praise the gods and good men (607a).[48]

4) Furthermore, Plato describes the philosopher as one who loves reality and truth, and clearly presents Socrates as a paradigm, and yet has Socrates confess his "greediness for images" (488a) and his love for poetry (607e–608a), especially for Homer (595b). But if one desires reality, as the philosopher does by Plato's definition, doesn't one for that very reason despise any mere approximation to it (cf. 505d)?

5) Finally, if we wanted to radicalize our questioning of Plato's critique of imitation, we could point to a fundamental difficulty it introduces: if imitation *as such* is problematic, then on Plato's own terms, the call for exile would necessarily have to extend to the craftsmen.[49] They, after all, do not produce reality itself in Plato's sense of the word, but only an imitation, and, if a con-

47. On this point, see ibid., 135.

48. Tate points out that the unconditional condemnation in book X not only contradicts book III's concession to a certain kind of imitation, as many scholars claim (and it is a reason some take book X to be a later addition), it also contradicts book X itself; Plato says no imitation is permitted at all, but then allows the imitation of the gods and good men. See Tate, "'Imitation,'" 16.

49. Plato explicitly includes craftsmen under the term *poet* taken in its broadest sense. see his explanation of this point in *Symp.*, 205b–c.

test were held to determine who practiced the most convincing deception concerning reality, the craftsmen would wear the laurels every time. Indeed, assuming reality to be the invisible form, which exists "itself by itself," there is likely no human activity that does not, in *some* degree, imitate reality and thus stand at a distance from truth such as Plato conceives it—apart, perhaps, from the most sublime heights of philosophical contemplation. If Socrates were to enforce the ban of imitators in his city, it would be an easy way to get the philosopher to be king, because the city would ultimately turn out to be, in fact, a community of one.

But appearances by nature come into conflict with one another, and those that produce outright contradiction, Plato has said, make the best instigators to thinking (524d). We are thus led to reflect whether Plato is presenting us here with something other than confusion.[50] To get a proper perspective on this question, we need to return to principles we have addressed in earlier chapters.

Good Distance

The essence of our proposal is that, if there were no principle of reality higher than the forms themselves, the tensions, inconsistencies, and contradictions we just laid out would be insurmountable. As we argued in chapter 3, if the knowledge represented by the soul's direct contact with the invisible being of things were in fact identical with the good, then there would be no ultimate justification for anything other than a sheer ascent to the forms and an abiding with them alone. In this case, imitation could never be but an obstacle; the desire for truth, which defines the philosopher, would be identical with a desire to eliminate images. It is illuminating to consider everything that would have to be eliminated if we eliminated images. It is, of course, clear that *writing*—whether poetic or otherwise—would go, because it cannot be anything other than imitation. But even speech would have no real justification. As we have seen, speech is not knowledge itself, and the most fundamental knowledge cannot be put into words. Thus, all discourse, even that of the philosophical variety, would have to go. But without writing or speech of any sort, there is no justification for communication. In fact,

---

50. Which is what even sympathetic commentators take it to be: "Plato's criticism is a serious, though confused, one," Mitchell and Lucas, *Engagement with Plato's Republic,* 164.

the value of most forms of human relationship would be called into question. Perhaps association with another person could spur one on to the pure intercourse with the forms, but any contact after that would be a distraction. Friendship would be at best an instrument and at worst an obstacle. There are some who read the *Symposium*'s ladder of love precisely in this sense, and unless one qualifies the Platonism that makes the forms alone the object of the intelligence, there is a solid basis for such an interpretation.[51] As we suggested earlier, even things as ordinary as human crafts would be emptied of value, and of course, the body, with the desires nature gave it, would carry out its life under the perpetual shadow of suspicion. One thinks here of the Johnny Cash song: "You're so heavenly minded, you're no earthly good." Platonism would thus be quite obviously guilty of the life-denying nihilism of which Nietzsche accused it.

Such a stark picture, though, contradicts not only our common sense, but also the palpable spirit of the dialogues; however much one may find expressions of such things in Plato's writing, they are always counterbalanced by pulls in the opposite direction. Is it not ironic that the philosopher infamous for his constant drive toward otherworldly ideals is also generally considered the most concrete philosophical stylist in history? There is good reason for the concrete spirit of the dialogues: this stark picture sets into dramatic relief the importance of the idea of the good in Plato's philosophy. Those who read Plato in the direction of a conventional Platonism typically disregard the implications this principle has for every aspect of his thought. We have argued at several junctures that the good is comprehensive; it is concerned with the whole rather than mere partial aspects. It is precisely this all-inclusiveness that makes the elevation of the good above the other forms so significant.[52] If the good were identified with the forms, at their level, then anything that lay "outside" of the forms or of the being that they represent—

51. This is essentially how Gregory Vlastos interprets Plato's theory of love. "Love in Plato," in *Platonic Studies,* 31–32. Individuals, in Vlastos's interpretation, are to be "used as steps." For a more substantial critique of this interpretation, see D. C. Schindler, "Plato and the Problem of Love: On the Nature of *Eros* in the *Symposium.*" *Apeiron* (forthcoming).

52. It should be noted that, while Plato does single out the good from the forms, he also on occasion includes it among the others in the intelligible realm (even if it remains the "last thing seen" in this realm). The good seems to be ambiguous in this respect: it can be known even while it transcends knowledge, as we have regularly affirmed. Similarly, it is a form or idea even while it is what founds all the other forms or ideas. Consider the variety of affirmations concerning its relation to the intelligible realm. 508b; 508e; 532a–b; 534b–c, and so forth.

as images or appearances do by definition—would by the same token lie beyond the scope of goodness, as it were. In this case, if the good concerns the whole of reality, appearances would have to be excluded from the whole of reality; they would have to be nothing. But Plato explicitly places them *between* being and nothingness.[53] By contrast, if the good were a "supra-formal" principle of reality, i.e., "beyond being . . . in dignity and power" (509b), there would be a clear justification for things "outside" of forms. The basic issue here is the fundamental question whether it is *good* that physical things, and by extension, images of any sort, exist or not. We receive an answer in principle by referring to the highest sense of the good as being good both in itself and in its consequences, which implies, we have argued, that the good is the ground for *both* being *and* appearance, in their unity and in their difference. Though the difference between the two, as the *Sophist* shows,[54] is what allows the possibility of deception, it does not change the fact that appearance as such is good.

We gather this response implicitly from what Plato writes and shows in the *Republic,* but there is a direct response in the *Timaeus.* It is the one time that Plato explicitly raises the question about the origin of the universe. Speaking of the divine craftsman, the Demiurge, Plato writes: "Now why did he who framed this whole universe of becoming frame it? Let us state the reason why: He was good, and one who is good can never become jealous of anything. And so, being free of jealousy, he wanted everything to become as much like himself as possible."[55] There are two things to note here. First, goodness itself is offered as the reason for the existence of the realm of becoming, as distinct from the eternal model, namely, the forms themselves. Second, Plato explains the causality of goodness in terms of its *not being jealous.* Jealousy means a refusal to share goodness, that is, to acknowledge the goodness of something or someone other than oneself. We recall that the highest (i.e, "good-est") good is good *also* in what comes from it; self-sharing is therefore an essential part of the meaning of goodness. To say that the physical world exists because its principle is good is to say that the

---

53. He sets opinion on that which lies between what is and what is not (478d), and opinion, of course, corresponds for Plato to sensible things. For a sophisticated account of how images can have no reality simply "of their own," and yet be distinct from nothingness, see Eric Perl, "Sense-Perception," 29–32, esp. 30n12; and Perl, "The Presence of the Paradigm," 346–55.

54. Cf. *Soph.,* 235c–236e.

55. *Ti.,* 29d–e.

otherness that makes the realm of becoming, which is *not* the realm of be-ing, possible has a positive foundation. Parmenides made Being the highest principle, and thus saw otherness, differentiation, and multiplicity, as sim-ply negative, i.e., nothing at all.[56] By making goodness the highest princi-ple, by contrast, Plato offers a positive ground for difference.[57] He thus af-firms that the visible universe is beautiful and good, as the effect of a good cause.[58] Moreover, if the intelligible forms are good, and likewise not "jeal-ous" of their goodness, then appearances, even as different from and lower than the forms, are themselves good in a relative sense, due to the positive ground of difference. The otherness of their goodness is not, so to speak, be-grudged them by the goodness of being.[59] From this perspective, while ap-pearances are indeed secondary, they do not represent a *fall* from what is pri-marily good, but rather in some sense a fruitful increase of it.[60]

The implication of this principle for the present problem should be clear. Often, those who have sought to reconcile Plato's apparent self-contradiction regarding the simultaneous use and censure of images have done so by show-ing that philosophical imitation is different from the poetic variety[61] and that

56. See Parmenides, DK 8, esp. lines 12–16.

57. In fact, in the *Sophist*, Plato posits a *form* for difference that is on a par with sameness (255c–d) and makes movement itself something divine (248e–249a). There remains, however, an ambiguity regarding the positive ground of difference. One may ask, for example, whether the form of difference is sufficient to account for the concrete *fact* of difference (or whether it simply defines *what* difference essentially is). On this, see D. C. Schindler, "What's the Difference? The Metaphysics of Participation in Plato, Plotinus, and Aquinas," *Nova et Vetera*, forthcoming.

58. *Ti.*, 28a, 29a.

59. As Miller puts it in his interpretation of the "vision of the heart of the *Republic*": "From its very nature, therefore, the Good gives of itself. This essential 'generosity' suffices for it to be cause of the forms (including itself) and of sensibles; it gives to the forms the perfection that each, to be itself, must have in its properly determinate way; and since each form thereby instan-tiates the Good, they too will be 'generous,' giving to sensibles the characters that these, to be themselves, must have in their properly determinate ways" ("Platonic Provocations," 190). It is not clear, however, in what sense the Good could properly be said to be the cause of itself.

60. The "fruitfulness" of τὸ καλόν is an underlying theme of the *Symposium*: Beauty, Plato says, is the true goddess presiding at childbirth (206d); the eternity that love wants is conceived by analogy with reproduction (206e–207b); and giving birth to "ideas and theories" is a response to the vision of the pure form of beauty (210d).

61. See Tate, "Imitation," 21–23. Gallop claims that the philosopher imitates the *forms* while artists imitate appearances: "The answer is simple. Socrates is no ordinary painter, but a phi-losopher artist. As such, he depicts the Intelligible rather than the visible world, Reality rather than appearances, Forms rather than particulars. Hence his strictures upon the painter do not apply to himself" ("Image and Reality," 115). Hermann Wiegmann claims that the philosopher

a philosopher can make a beneficial use of images, in contrast to, say, the sophists.[62] As helpful and as true as the distinctions may turn out to be, they fail to get to the root of the problem: Plato's difficulty with imitation arises principally because of the *distance* it implies from the truth, a problem that affects both its own ontological status and its effect on the soul. An apology for Plato's use of images that sought merely to show how one (namely, the philosopher) can eliminate the distance, through a special kind of enlightenment or inspiration, for example, abandons just what constitutes images *as* images. It is in this case not images (and thus art) that are justified, but only the philosopher who can, as it were, overlook them. With justifications of this sort, we remain stuck in "Platonic dualism." But if the good is the cause of being, truth, and knowledge, then the difference between being and appearance is not necessarily bad, and we can affirm it without in the least compromising the absoluteness of being and thus the absoluteness of its dif-

---

imitates the good while the poets imitate merely the beautiful. "Plato's Critique of the Poets and the Misunderstanding of His Epistemological Argumentation," *Philosophy and Rhetoric* 23 (1990): 109–24. We might compare this argument with Woodruff's observation: if poets loved the *form* of the *kalon* (which he translates, following Moravcsik, as the "fine") rather than the *beautiful*, i.e., the sensibly manifest *kalon*, "they would be Platonic philosophers . . . and their love would find expression not in poetry but in life itself". "What Could Go Wrong?" 142.

62. This is Gonzalez's explanation. See chapter 5 of *Dialectic and Dialogue*, 129–49. Gonzalez's presentation of the complex aspects of this theme and his critique of certain attempts to interpret them is, as usual, excellent and illuminating. Nonetheless, there are two judgments that seem to us somewhat lacking. First, he argues that the philosopher's use of images is essentially nonpoetic, which is why Plato's dialogues would never make good theater: "The philosopher is a bad poet, but for precisely this reason he makes better use of poetry than does any poet" (145). Gonzalez's judgment here is true only in a popular sense of poetry. The ancients ranked Plato next to Homer in terms of the power of his style. See, e.g., Longinus's judgment: "Even before [Herodotus] . . . Plato especially channeled off to himself thousands of such sluices from the Homeric stream. . . . And, in my opinion, Plato would not have reached such an acme in the doctrinal opinions of his philosophy, and he would not have kept pace with such poetic material and phrasing as we find in him, if he had not competed against Homer for the first prize with (by heaven) all his soul," *On the Sublime,* translated by James Arieti and John Crossett [New York: Edwin Mellen, 1985], 82–84. Second, once Gonzalez affirms the philosopher's use of poetry, he explains that the philosopher can transcend images in a way that the poet cannot by virtue of a particular philosophical "inspiration" (146–49). Unless we can explain "inspiration" further, the response would amount to a *vis dormativa* à la Voltaire; the explanation raises more questions than it answers. What is lacking in Gonzalez's solution, I suggest, is any reference to the significance of the good for this question. Thus, he attempts to resolve the problems by pointing to a particular kind of *ascent* from images rather than seeing that the philosopher is most radically different from the poet by being able to *descend* into them. As we will see, it is just such a descent that allows images to be (positive) *expressions* rather than mere *imitators* of reality.

ference from appearance. But, in fact, we can go further: if it is true, as we have argued repeatedly in this book, that goodness cannot be absolute without *also* being relative, then it follows that not only is the difference between being and appearance not bad, but it is *intrinsically good and desirable.*

Let us consider how this affirmation serves to differentiate the philosopher and the poet. While the poet dwells, so to speak, in the medium of appearances, *as* a poet he does not transcend this medium. The philosopher, by contrast, does transcend mere appearance and so catches sight of its difference from being. So far so good. However, this is only one side of the difference between the two. Most attempts to explain the difference consider only this side, and thus aim basically to show how the philosopher succeeds in transcending images in his use of them. But the problem with this way of accounting for the difference is that it leaves a contradiction firmly in place: Why use images if one can transcend them? If one can give a reason why the philosopher is able to get beyond appearances, isn't that also a reason to leave them behind? In this case, why does Plato not only use images, but *end* his dialogue with a myth? To avoid this contradiction, we have to see the other side of the difference between the philosopher and the poet, which is typically neglected by commentators: because the philosopher has transcended appearances, he is in a position to descend back into them, *to relate to them, that is, in the mode of a descent,* which means to affirm them from the perspective of being and the goodness of being, a possibility that is not given to the poet because of the absence of transcendence in mere appearance.

There are two consequences that follow, which will no doubt seem paradoxical to the point of disbelief in relation to conventional versions of Platonism. We will state them here, and then attempt to give a fuller account in what follows. In the first place, the recognition of the absoluteness of the good puts the philosopher in a better position to affirm the goodness of image and appearance than even the poet himself. The poet can produce images, but does not have the distance, as it were, to see how the distance of images is good. In this respect, from a merely poetic perspective, images are not, as such, mediators of reality. But the philosopher, knowing the difference, can see images, not as opaque "things," but as radiant manifestations.[63]

63. We can think in this context of the well-known quotation from F. H. Bradley: "That the glory of this world in the end is appearance leaves the world more glorious, if we feel it is a show of some fuller splendour." *The Principles of Logic* (London: Kegan, Paul, Trench, and Company, 1883), 533.

Philosophy thus lends poetry in principle a dignity that it would not otherwise have. We might reflect on sophistry in this respect: sophists care, as
it were, *only* for appearances. But for this very reason, they have contempt
for appearances, to such an extent that they are willing to manipulate them
without hesitation to achieve whatever result they happen to seek. By contrast, it is precisely the philosopher, who allegedly gives little attention to
sensibles *qua* sensibles, who nevertheless proves to be in the position necessary *to take images seriously.*[64]

Second, once we come to a proper view of the connection between
goodness and intelligibility, it is no longer necessary to *excuse* the philosopher's use of imagery, which is the primary aim of most attempts to reconcile the tensions in the *Republic.*[65] Instead, we can say that images turn out
to perform a properly philosophical function that abstract reason alone cannot.[66] In other words, just as in Glaucon's list the *best* good is good both in itself and in its consequences, so too the best philosopher not only transcends
images, he also returns to them. *Poetry makes philosophy better as philosophy.*
As we will explain to say this does not compromise in any way Plato's customary insistence on the mind's absolute purity in its intercourse with being. It simply integrates this purity into a more comprehensive whole, an integration that purity itself requires. In other words, a grasp of the good as the
principle of knowledge implies *both* that things like writing and poetry are
inadequate and thus dangerous, *and also* that they make philosophy better.
Goodness gives sense *both* to Plato's unequivocal condemnation of poetry
and his use of it.

64. Dionysius of Halicarnassus reports that Plato paid extreme attention to stylistic detail,
continuously re-writing passage after passage. *De comp. verb.,* 25.209. Annas claims that there is a
tension in Plato's discussion of poetry: he seems both to consider it trivial and extremely important. See "Triviality of Literature," 1–28. Our argument is that this is no problematic tension, but
again a natural expression of the twofold nature of the good.

65. For example, Crombie shows how art can be in certain contexts harmless. *Plato on Man
and Society,* vol. 1 of *An Examination of Plato's Doctrines* (New York: The Humanities Press),
148–49.

66. Fisher observes that Socrates uses imagery "to hint at truths inaccessible to descriptive
analysis," "Plato on Writing," 172. We will elaborate this point in the section entitled "Conversio
ad phantasmata."

The Way Up and the Way Down

Context, then, is (just about) everything.[67] But to affirm this, we must recall, is just to say that truth is the whole; to be concerned with the whole is to pay attention to the arrangement of parts. We argued in chapters 2 and 3 that the twofold nature of goodness requires a dramatic presentation, that only a complex plot involving the ascending continuous pursuit and the discontinuous reversal, the surprise that is both unanticipated and fulfilling, can bring to light the "whole" of the good in a nonreductive manner. If this is true, it offers an immediate reason for the frustrations one sometimes finds in treatments of Plato's views on art: a particular position or statement is a part of a whole, and receives and reveals its significance only in relation to that whole. Thus, a consideration and comparison of the various statements on poetry and art made in the *Republic* as so many free-floating fragments will often give the appearance of contradiction. This is in fact a basic part of what Plato says in the *Phaedrus* constitutes the very danger of writing.[68] Apparent contradictions, however, will show a different face once considered in context.[69] Can this general claim be affirmed of Plato's seemingly disparate views on art?[70] Does Plato's *Republic* as a whole exhibit such a plot?

Though there is no room in the present context to examine the structure of the dialogue in great detail, a look at some of the judgments scholars have made regarding the overall shape of the dialogue suggests a confident "yes" to this question. Many scholars have remarked on the ascent-descent structure of the *Republic* as a whole and have interpreted the significance of this structure in a variety of ways.[71] Brumbaugh provides a solid guiding principle for interpretation, proposing that the *Republic*, like many of the later dia-

67. Drew Hyland shows an exquisitely subtle sense of the significance of situation, what he calls "place," in Plato's dialogues in view of Plato's understanding of the nature of reality and the human soul. See chapter 1 of *Finitude and Transcendence*, called "The Place of Philosophy," 13–33.

68. See *Phdr.*, 275d–e.

69. We refer again to Desjardins's observation that "the point of the literary dimension of the dialogues is not only (nor even primarily) to charm but rather to provide necessary parameters of interpretation that will allow us to cut through the ambiguity of the discursive level," "Why Dialogues?" 121.

70. In Greene's lengthy study of Plato's views, we find an alternative proposal: Plato was so torn between the attractions of poetry and philosophy that he could never come to any settled opinion on the status of artistic production. "Plato's View," 74.

71. See Voegelin, *Plato and Aristotle*, 46–52; Sallis offers a diagram of just this structure. *Being and Logos*, 455. In a curious book, John Bremer divides the *Republic* into 240 equal units, and

logues, reflects structurally the method the dialogue describes.[72] He notes, as others have, that there is a clear symmetry of structure: all the major themes discussed in the first half of the *Republic* receive another treatment in a slightly different form in the second half. All, that is, but the good: it is the only major subject treated just once, and its treatment lies in the center of the dialogue as a whole.[73] Brumbaugh proceeds to show how the dialogue in general dramatically embodies the schema presented in the divided line. Building on this insight, and making use of the ascent-descent movement Plato describes in relation to the line itself, we can propose a way in which this method fits into the basic principle guiding the dialogue: the "double treatment" of themes Brumbaugh has observed reflects the twofold nature of the good, which represents, then, the hinge of the entire dialogue. The first half, we could say, presents issues prior to the "in-breaking" of the good and the introduction of the philosopher. The treatments here will tend to possess a certain "provisional" character, unfolding the way things are from the perspective of *eikasia* and belief. The second half, by contrast, will unfold a view of the whole, from top to bottom, starting from the absoluteness of

---

shows how they present a symmetry in an ascending and then descending array. *Plato and the Founding of the Academy: Based on a Letter From Plato, Newly Discovered* (Lanham, Md.: University Press of America, 2002), 181–221. Charles Kahn shows the proleptic "buildup" of the early books of the *Republic* and their culmination in the center with the idea of the good (but doesn't discuss significance of having the culmination take place in the center rather than at the *end*, as it does typically in Aeschylus, to whom he compares Plato on this point). "Proleptic Composition in the *Republic*, 131–42, esp. 142. Helmut Kuhn, in "The True Tragedy: On the Relationship Between Greek Tragedy and Plato," *Harvard Studies in Classical Philology* 52 (1941): 1–40; 53 (1942): 37–88, provides the following outline of the dialogue's structure: (1) Prelude in World of Appearances (357a–368e); (2) Mediating part I: Best City Coming into Being (368e–397e); (3) Center: Transcendental Realm; (4) Mediating part II: Best City Disintegrates (543a–608c); (5) Postlude in the World of Appearance (608c–621d). He removes book I from the schema as a "prelude." If our interpretation of book I is right, however, it forms an even clearer part of the realm of appearances than the segment Kuhn refers to. Hildebrandt offers a schema quite similar to Kuhn's, but with more details. See his *Platon*, 393.

72. Robert S. Brumbaugh, *Platonic Studies of Greek Philosophy: Form, Arts, Gadgets, and Hemlock* (Albany: SUNY Press, 1989), 30–32. Kenneth Dorter has recently presented a very clear articulation of the same interpretation. See his essay "The Divided Line and the Structure of Plato's *Republic*," esp. 3.

73. Brumbaugh, *Platonic Studies of Greek Philosophy*, 32. Though Brumbaugh approaches the *Republic* from a different angle from the one proposed here, the conclusions he reaches confirm the interpretation offered in this book on many points; it would be fruitful to work out a longer comparison, which is unfortunately not possible in the present context.

philosophy. On the one side, then, there is a gradual ascent to the absolute, and, on the other side, a descent from the absolute to the furthest extremities of the relative—from philosophical rule, through governmental decay, to tyranny,[74] and then finally to the realm of pure appearance. Complete understanding, we recall, must also *descend* from the unhypothetical first principle; the philosopher must return to the cave.[75]

This broad-stroke sketch of the general structure of the *Republic* bears immediately on the relationship between image and reality.[76] This relationship takes on a different character depending upon its place in relation to the good. In a sense, we are watching here the unfolding of a *genuine* relativism. *Before* the "absolute" perspective has been introduced, images all possess a certain opacity. This means, on the one hand, that they will exert a kind of oppressive force that has its symbol, we might say, in the "noble lie"—the mythos that all the inhabitants of the city are brothers and sisters, which is meant to inspire unity among them—presented in book III (414c). It is "noble" in the sense that it aims at the good of the whole, and yet it remains a lie in that it has not yet reached the absolute perspective necessary (see 504b) to bring that aim to its proper fulfillment. There is thus a certain analogy between the kind of violence advocated in Socrates' presentation of the community of women and children and the violence represented by Thrasymachus in book I, even if the former intends a unity simply disregarded by the latter. Though the discussion in book V is better than that in book I, it is nevertheless still a relative approach to a totality. The presentation of the "ideal city" through book V remains provisional.[77] Until goodness itself appears,

74. See Sallis, *Being and Logos*, 450–54.

75. Cf. *Letter VII*, 344b.

76. Greene observes that the difference between Socrates' primarily *ethical* critique of poetry in books II and III and his more radical critique in book X depends on the appearance of the ideas and the good in the interim. "Plato's View," 41.

77. Unless we recognize this provisional character, we will have no way to understand how Socrates can propose a "noble lie" shortly after insisting that "all gods and human beings hate the true lie, if that expression can be used" (382a). To think that Plato advocates such a lie simply and without further qualification is a failure to grasp the significance of the structure of the dialogue. The "noble lie" seems to represent, for Plato, the educational function of poetry, which is second best, but which is necessary in a society without a properly philosophical foundation, and in any event is part of his own Greek society. That being said, Plato is clear about the provisional character of the first half of the *Republic*. Not only does he regularly "start over" when he finds a better point of departure—which indicates that the final view comes only when we reach the "best" point, the good, which does not appear until the end of book VI—but he refers to the

rather than its mythical and always imperfect images, social order cannot have a true foundation in truth. On the other hand, the trajectory of the dialogue on its way to the good will take us further and further beyond images. As we saw in book II, the "seeming" must be removed in order for being to show its absoluteness *as* absolute. The work of the dialogue is to penetrate through the various layers of relativity until that which *is* emerges in its distinct clarity. At this point, images are *not* reality itself. Once the good does make its appearance (which, we argued in chapter 3, is Socrates' "breaking into" the *Republic* as the realm image of the good), however, there is a radical shifting of direction. Now the relativity that was initially eliminated is returned. But it returns not as an opaque veil that eclipses reality; instead, having been judged in relation to reality, the possibility emerges for a relative image to be a transcendent manifestation of reality. The good that was *beyond* it turns out *therefore* to be present within it. The whole *Republic* in its general structure and in the details of its dramatic interaction and argument is needed to show forth the truth of goodness and thus the goodness of truth.

We see this shift of perspectives most obviously in the contest between the just and unjust man that frames the main body of the dialogue. In book II, Glaucon says that all appearances must be stripped away in order for us to reach the truth of the matter about justice: the only way to distinguish the second type of good from the third is to disregard all consequences. But when Socrates returns explicitly to this challenge in the concluding moments of the dialogue, he explains that *justice itself* demands that the consequences that were borrowed be returned:[78]

---

prior discussions as a "sketch" (504d) and says that an "adequate light" is needed to catch sight of virtue, implying that where they are even at this advanced stage of the discussion is "steeped in shadows" (432c).

Strauss's well-known interpretation, which takes the problematic form of the ideal city to be Plato's warning against idealistic philosophers taking rule, fundamentally misses the point. The warning is not against rooting the political order in the absolute, but trying to do so in an *inadequate form*. He is criticizing an *inadequate* idealism, not a true idealism. See Strauss, *City and Man*, 124–27.

78. The very first definition of justice offered in the *Republic* is to give back what was borrowed (331c). It turns out to be not simply false, but inadequate, and it is thus able to take its relative place once its inadequacy has been adequately demonstrated. Plato returns at the very end to recover a point made at the very beginning, a point that had seemed to be simply dismissed and left behind.

"[W]ill you give back to me what you borrowed in the argument?" "What in particular?" "I gave you the just man's seeming to be unjust and the unjust man just. You
both asked for it; even if it weren't possible for this to escape gods and human beings,
all the same, it had to be granted for the argument's sake so that justice itself could
be judged as compared with injustice itself. Or don't you remember?" "If I didn't,"
he said, "I should indeed be doing an injustice." "Well, then," I said, "since they have
been judged, on justice's behalf I ask back again the reputation it in fact has among
gods and among human beings; and I ask us to agree that it does enjoy such a reputation, so that justice may also carry off the prizes that it gains from *seeming* and bestows on its possessors, since it has made clear that it bestows the good things that
come from *being* and does not deceive those who really take possession of it." "What
you ask," he said, "is only just." (612c–e)

Notice, it was *for the sake of the logos* that the appearances/consequences were
removed, and now that it has found its completion, we can return to the *mythos*, the realm of appearances.[79] Notice, too, the restoration of appearances is
not a concession to degenerate desires or a compromise of the absoluteness
of the difference between being and appearance. In this respect, Friedländer's
disgust with this moment in the dialogue is entirely misplaced.[80] To the contrary, the restoration is *demanded by* the absoluteness of justice itself. Seen
as such, these consequences are no longer obstacles to the truth but expressions of it. The appearance is the manifestation of what is really true. In this
respect, the moment of restoration is an indispensable part of the whole argument. It follows from the logic of the argument just as the philosopher's
descent follows from the comprehensiveness of the good.

Thus, the central position of the good in the *Republic* provides a motive both for the critique of images through the ascent beyond them and
also for the affirmation of images and a descent back to them.[81] This two-

79. On this, see the insightful discussion in Claudia Baracchi, *Of Myth, Life, and War in Plato's Republic* (Indianapolis: Indiana University Press, 2002), 93–97. Baracchi attributes the return
to a radical inadequacy in *logos*; we read it more as an overflowing of its completion, which certainly is more consistent with Plato's view of reason.

80. See Friedländer, *Plato*, vol. 3, 131. Friedländer believes this to be an example of Platonic
irony. Cf. Annas, *Introduction*, 348–49: she asserts that there is no reason for this return to rewards, and sides with the interpreters who claim the section was not part of the original plan.
It expresses, she says, the artificiality and clumsiness of book X more generally. Such judgments
miss the overall structure of the *Republic*, which *requires* the return.

81. Ferber has made a very similar observation for a similar reason; he affirms both: *"Plato
can therefore condemn the metaphorical method . . . Plato can therefore also recommend and use the
metaphorical method,"* *Platos Idee des Guten*, 55.

fold relation to the good in fact opens up a new way of looking at the Platonic corpus as a whole. Though we have to leave aside a thorough exploration of this possibility for a future study, it is worth noting generally how the problem of apparent inconsistencies in the *Republic*'s attitude toward images corresponds to certain inconsistencies people have found in the variety of positions apparently articulated in the different dialogues. Plato, for example, seems to express a different "attitude" toward forms in what are called his "early," "middle," and "late" dialogues.[82] It is often suggested that Plato had a certain ambivalence about the theory of forms.[83] This view generally corresponds to a "developmental" interpretation of the Platonic corpus, according to which Plato begins as a Socratic, writing primarily aporetic dialogues, starts to articulate a more positive doctrine concerning the forms in his "middle" period, but then reveals misgivings about the forms in his "later" dialogues, affirming criticisms and qualifications of basic aspects of his theory of forms, and finally ends with more strictly mythical *(Timaeus)* or practical *(Laws)* writings. In a similar vein, it is said that the fact he never returns to the idea that the good is the cause of intelligibility after the *Republic* shows that he eventually decided against this hypothesis.[84] But there have been sharp criticisms of both the developmentalist approach to Plato

82. See the thorough account of attempts to date dialogues by Thesleff, *Studies in Platonic Chronology*, 1–17; E. N. Tigerstedt, *Interpreting Plato* (Uppsala, Sweden: Almquist and Wicksell, 1977); Thesleff, "Platonic Chronology," *Phronesis* 34 (1989): 1–26; Cf. Charles Kahn, *Plato and the Socratic Dialogue*, 42–48; Kahn, "On Platonic Chronology," in *New Perspectives on Plato, Modern and Ancient*, edited by Julia Annas and Christopher Rowe (Cambridge, Mass.: Harvard University Press, 2002), 93–127.

83. Indeed, Hyland, among others, suggests that there is no such "theory" in Plato, and that what Plato says about the "ideas" is far more sparse and unsystematic than the interpretive tradition would have us believe. *Finitude and Transcendence*, 165–95. Hyland is concerned to overcome the Platonic dualism that the ideas, as typically interpreted, would seem to entail. But we have been arguing that affirming their transcendence does not necessarily entail dualism at all, and that the ideas are necessary in fact to sustain the kind of "relativism" that Socrates clearly embodies. It may indeed be the case that Plato did not think of the ideas as "things" that can be logically demonstrated, but, in rejecting their demonstrability in *this* fashion does not require rejecting their *reality* or the significance of that reality for thinking. Ferber is right to contrast a *showing* of the ideas *(Ideendeixis)* to presenting a complete *teaching* of them *(Ideenlehre): Unwissenheit*, 50.

84. Greene observes that Plato does not mention "the idea of the good" after the *Republic*, and infers from this that Plato surrendered his already tentative thesis, in the *Republic*, that one could attain some knowledge of it. "Plato's Views," 49. Jim Robinson argues that the thesis of the *Republic* gave way to a more logical notion of intelligibility, expressed in the *Sophist*. See "Change in Plato's Conception," 231–41.

and also the attempt to detect the chronological order of the dialogues, the success of which is key for this approach. Holger Thesleff has pointed out a host of difficulties that would impede any attempt to come to definitive conclusions about chronology.[85] Jacob Howland and Charles Griswold Jr. have raised substantial questions regarding the presuppositions undergirding stylometric analysis.[86] But even if it were possible to "date" the dialogues,[87] it would be legitimate to read changes in the perspectives expressed therein as signs of a "self-canceling" development in Plato's thinking only if the differences have no other explanation.[88] Charles Kahn, however, has shown that the dialogues generally accepted as early can be read "proleptically," as preparing for the *Republic*, and, indeed, as awaiting this dialogue in order to find resolutions for the questions that they had opened.[89] While Kahn can point only to the salutary effects of aporia and Plato's need to prepare his audience for the radical difference of his "otherworldly" view of reality as reasons for his apparently "gradual" revelation of his ideas,[90] the interpretation of the *Republic* being proposed here offers a more substantial explanation for this approach. An adequate manifestation of the good can occur only *dramatically*, only in the ascent that is reversed in order to reveal absoluteness and relativity at once. It is not possible in the present context to flesh out the proposal in any detail, but it is striking that the structure of the *Republic* can be seen reflected in observations often made about the relationships among the dialogues. Given Plato's profound concern about order generally, given his express views about the proper order of writing in particular, and given the incredibly sophisticated—and not immediately apparent—unities of structure in the dialogues that one after another study has shown in the past few

85. Thesleff, *Studies in Platonic Chronology,* 18–96.

86. See Jacob Howland, "Re-Reading Plato: The Problem of Platonic Chronology," *Phoenix* 45.3 (1991): 189–214; Charles Griswold Jr., "Comments on Kahn," in Julia Annas and Christopher Rowe, *New Perspectives on Plato, Modern and Ancient* (Cambridge, Mass.: Harvard University Press), 129–44.

87. Diskin Clay points to the remarkable overlap in what he refers to as the two most ambitious attempts to show the order of the dialogues, those made by Charles Kahn and Paul Friedländer, in *Platonic Questions,* 283–86.

88. Often, what appear to be significant changes of perspective in different dialogues turn out to be different articulations of the same view. See Perl, "Presence of the Paradigm," for an example of a coherent way to reconcile what appear to be differences in Plato's understanding of the forms' relations to images.

89. Kahn, *Plato and the Socratic Dialogue,* 59–65.

90. Ibid., 65–70. Kahn also offers no explanation for the dialogues that follow the *Republic.*

decades, we should be inclined to see the corpus not as a random series of "essais," à la Montaigne, but as philosophically interrelated parts.[91] There is, in short, reason to suspect that Plato conceived his literary production as a whole.[92]

The perspective we suggest here would offer a philosophical principle for some of the peculiar features in the dialogues: the good appears as the unhypothetical ἀρχή only once, not because Plato changed his mind about something so fundamental to his thinking but precisely *because* it is central, the organizing principle around which the other dialogues can be arranged.[93] It is entirely fitting, indeed necessary, that what is central appear only once. The *Republic* seems to stand in the center of Plato's writings viewed as a whole. Accordingly, it is possible to view the other dialogues as corresponding to the ascent-descent schema of the *Republic*. Thus, the aporetic "early" dialogues, like the *Republic*'s book I, point to the need for forms, as Kahn demonstrated. The so-called "middle" dialogues give an account of the forms as *different* from images, i.e., in their transcendence. And, after the *Republic*,

91. Howland criticizes the stylometric approach in contrast to ancient interpretations, which had little "historical" interest in Plato. The approach Howland seems to favor in the essay "Re-Reading Plato" is much more unsystematic. But, as Carol Poster has shown in "The Idea(s) of Order of Platonic Dialogues and Their Hermeneutic Consequences," *Phoenix* 52 (1998): 282–98, the ancient approaches tended to read Plato's dialogues, not "unsystematically," but according to a pedagogical order, one that was quite deliberately rooted in a theoretical or metaphysical interpretation. Indeed, the arguments Howland gives would also support a more organic, metaphysical ordering of the dialogues, which would seem too to be more in line with the obviously *kosmic* sense of order pervasive in Plato, as opposed to the "occasionality" one finds in Montaigne, for example.

In her survey of possible ways of ordering the dialogues, Poster presents the chronological approach and the dramatic approach (by which she means ordering them according to the history of their explicit setting, i.e., *Parmenides* first and *Phaedo* last), in addition to the pedagogical and metaphysical orders. Poster notes the difficulties in the chronological and dramatic approaches—though points out that the former is virtually the only one taken seriously in Anglo-American philosophy. She also shows that there will always be a certain circularity in one's justification for the approach one takes. Oddly, she concludes that we ought therefore to be suspicious of any approach that relies "on any one specific order as evidence of its validity" (295), though that criterion, too, would obviously require justification. A more natural conclusion would be that the principle of ordering is best that can show it derives from Plato's own philosophical principles. To be sure, such a criterion would hardly end argument, but it would be the most interesting place to begin argument.

92. See Jaeger, *Paideia*, vol. 2, 96; Kahn, *Plato and the Socratic Dialogue*, 41.

93. Cf. Jaeger, *Paideia*, vol. 2, 198; Paul Shorey, *Unity of Plato's Thought*, 78; Ferber, *Platos Idee des Guten*, 49, where he points to the good as the "center of gravity" in Plato's philosophy.

the emphasis lies much more on the "synthetic" moment: we noted de Vogel's observation that, though Plato retains a unified view of man throughout the dialogues, he seems to shift from a somewhat negative view of the
body, in the *Phaedo*, to a more emphatically positive view in the later dialogue the *Timaeus*.[94] Similarly, some commentators have remarked on the
positive significance of physical beauty in the *Phaedrus*—a dialogue generally
regarded as having been written after the *Republic*—that strikes a different
note than Plato's customary comments.[95] We might also consider the "new"
meaning of dialectic in the *Phaedrus*, which includes not only the "upward"
movement of unification, but also the "downward" movement of division.
The *Theaetetus* and the *Sophist*, moreover, seek to reconcile the immanence
of sensibles with the transcendence of forms, to reconcile both temporal
change and eternal sameness, rather than simply opting for one or the other. The problem at the heart of the *Parmenides*, too, is how to connect the
forms with images. The *Philebus integrates* both knowledge and pleasure into
a comprehensive view of goodness, and so forth. In this respect, we can read
these dialogues not as signs of Plato's changing his mind, but as the fruits of
the project envisioned in the *Republic*. The *Timaeus* and *Critias*, which seem
to be among the very last dialogues, make reference to the *Republic* at the
outset and propose to set this "theoretical" dialogue into motion.[96] Though,
again, it would require more argument and analysis to spell out the details
than is possible in the present context, we nevertheless can detect a general
drift in the body of work that corresponds to the *Republic*'s own movement,
a correspondence that is perhaps not entirely accidental: there is an ascent
beyond appearances toward the good, followed by a more synthetic and integrating tendency.[97] The relationship between forms and images has a dif-

94. De Vogel, *Rethinking Plato*, 177–78.

95. See, e.g., Greene, "Plato's View," 56–61. Greene sees this as an example that Plato didn't
mean his disparagement of art in the *Republic* to be taken seriously. See also Nussbaum, "'This
Story Isn't True,'" in which she reads the *Phaedrus* as "recanting" the *Republic*. Our interpretation
suggests that the "shift" is in fact *intended* by the view of reality presented in the *Republic*. The
Phaedrus, in this respect, is not a recantation but a fulfillment.

96. Cf. *Ti.*, 19b–20c. Socrates presents his interlocutors as, "by nature as well as by training,
. . . [taking] part in both philosophy and politics at once." It is also significant that the two dialogues are presented entirely as a *myth*: they thus echo in relation to the Platonic corpus the *Republic*'s concluding with a myth.

97. It is interesting to note, in this regard, Manuela Tecusan's observation that "images have a
didactic function which increases in importance as we advance toward Plato's last works," "Speaking about the Unspeakable: Plato's Use of Imagery," *Apeiron* 25.4 (1992): 69–87, here 69.

ferent character depending on its place in this general trajectory. That there is such a drift is not controversial; it is only the interpretation of the drift that is new here, its novelty consisting in an attempt to explain the movement in terms of the comprehensive consistency of Plato's philosophy.

This general drift comes to an end in the sensible world, in images. When Socrates banishes the poets in book X but then allows the return of all poetry that reflects genuine goodness, he is not backtracking or contradicting himself but bringing to expression the essential movement of the *Republic*. The banishment and return is an image of the ascent and reversal. Likewise, the poetic image of the myth of Er, far from implicitly undermining the argument of the dialogue and the structure of the divided line in particular, provides the finale that this philosophical drama demanded. As we will see, Plato could not have presented a more perfect conclusion. The same turn also explains the other tensions we highlighted in the *Republic*. The "need" that the absolute has for the relative, for example, explains the "greediness" Socrates professes for images and the passionate love he has for poetry. Although Plato distinguishes a lover of wisdom, as we saw, from the lover of sights and sounds (475c–e), the lover of wisdom loves the *whole* of wisdom, which of course *includes* appearances in their truth. One who loved forms *but not* images would in fact have a partial love comparable in a certain sense to those who love only sights and sounds. *Because* he loves the good, the philosopher loves every expression of it.[98] It follows that Socrates' greediness for images is a sign of his devotion to philosophy, and not a contradiction of it that must somehow be explained away. Similarly, we grasp the significance of the "remedy" (φάρμακον) Socrates spoke of with regard to poetic images (595b), namely, "knowledge of how [things] really are": it is a remedy that *saves* the phenomena rather than eliminates them.[99] One who sees the truth about being will see the truth about appearances and thereby reveal both a freedom from them and a desire for them. Finally, if the good is absolute, there is no contradiction between affirming the superiority of words over deeds on the one hand and the superiority of deeds over words on the other.[100] Each has a relative priority over the other depending on the con-

---

98. Cf. Sallis, *Being and Logos*, 382.

99. As Derrida showed in "Plato's Pharmacy," "φάρμακον" can mean either that which saves, or that which destroys.

100. Here we find a place for the insightful justification for images that Gonzalez offers, *Dialectic and Dialogue*, 129–49. He shows that Plato offers *two* hierarchies in book X: he initially

text: there is a need both for the contemplative vision of the ideal and its active embodiment, and each of these finds its proper place in relation to the one superiority that is never merely relative, namely, the superiority of the good itself.

The restoration of appearances at the end of the *Republic* is therefore an effect of the transformation of the nature of appearance that occurs in the center of the dialogue, a transformation we described in chapter 3 as the "breakthrough" by which Socrates becomes the real image of the good. It is helpful to refer back to this transformation in light of the present issue, insofar as it provides the explanatory paradigm. A host of things converge in this transformation: first, by pointing beyond to the "real" Socrates as the image of the good, Plato sets into shocking relief the inadequacy of words, images, and even his own dialogues, insofar as it reveals that the horizon of this written work, the *Republic*, cannot contain what it intends to communicate.[101] In this respect, Plato is offering us an image, the very content of which is that the image is *not* the reality itself. Here, we see the ascending moment that affirms, as it were, the good's inaccessible absoluteness. At precisely the same time, however, this image is *internal* to the *Republic*, it is an intrinsic part of the argument that dialogue is making. The absoluteness, then, has inserted itself into the immanent horizon of this written work, and it thus finds expression in logical arguments, in words, in images, in actions, and of course in the imitation of all of these things within the fictional drama that Plato fabricates. If we were asked whether this book adequately expresses the truth it intends to communicate, we would have to say both, with equal emphasis: "no, it doesn't" and "yes, it does." There is perhaps no major philosophical work in history that gives so much weight to the imaginative dimension of poetry than this one, a work that also attacks that same dimension. It is no accident that the "breakthrough" the *Republic* enacts occurs precisely in relation to goodness, and also no accident that the whole project of reason

---

presents the nature-craftwork-artistic image, and *then* he rates the user's knowledge above the maker's or the artist's. To explain the discrepancy here, Gonzalez argues that the *use* of a thing does not mean the instrumentalization of it, but the appreciation of its goodness. This is exactly right: a grasp of the good of a thing is not a merely intellectual act but involves a more comprehensive relationship that can be called a "use" of it. *This* is what it means to understand something in the light of the good.

101. We refer, again, to Arieti's observation: "We are to see Plato as challenging us. In attacking mimetic art, he is calling into question the authority of his own work. The dialogue, he tells us, is mimetic philosophy, not real philosophy," *Interpreting Plato*, 242.

thus becomes integrally concrete. The descent of philosophy into poetry implies the judgment of imagery, of course, but the judgment of imagery thereby justifies it. One could even say that, far from creating a community hostile to poetry, philosophy, as Plato here conceives it, opens a space for it that lends it a new dignity, insofar as it shows how images can be bearers of a reality greater than themselves.[102]

Conversio ad phantasmata

Our thesis is that the sovereignty of the good makes the "return" to images not a fall from a better place but a movement of internal completion. This implies, however, that images serve the intelligibility of things[103] and thus play an intrinsic role within the proper exercise of reason (although this does not imply at all any false dependence of reason on images, which is ruled out, among other things, by the account of dialectic, 532a). We have shown in formal terms the general place images have within the logical structure of the *Republic,* but we need still to explain their role more concretely. To this end, it will be helpful to consider, on the one hand, what imagery, and especially myths, contribute to the form of understanding, and, on the other hand, how images are necessary to the "ecstatic" notion of reason that we have argued lies at the heart of the *Republic.* Once we see the significance of imagery—and therefore by implication, sense-experience and the life of the body—we will understand why it is not proper to think of Plato as an "idealist" in the conventional sense.

Plato does not discuss the relationship between μύθος and λόγος in much explicit detail anywhere in his dialogues. We have passages that present the need to transcend images to grasp the truth of something;[104] Plato has Socrates show a dissatisfaction with the "monological" narrative of

102. In this respect, philosophy makes poetry "meaning-full," which does not mean, as we shall see, making it simply a dispensable vehicle for an otherwise abstractly articulatable meaning. Poetry is not a starting point for Plato, but an end point. See Versenyi on the "symbolic," i.e., disclosive aspect of art. "Quarrel between Philosophy and Poetry," *Philosophical Forum* 2 (1970–1971): 200–12, here 201–3.

103. Our argument is not that images add to the *intelligible content* of things, an affirmation that would necessarily lead to a form/image dualism. On this, Eric Perl's insistence is crucial. See "Sense-Perception," 21–23. Instead, the existence of images contributes to the *form* or *structure* of knowing that is proper for genuine knowledge, as we shall see.

104. See *Rep.,* 532b–c.

myths in comparison to the dialogical interrogation of elenchus;[105] in general, myths tend to fill gaps, to occupy places where there is no knowledge;[106] nearly all of the myths Socrates tells owe their origins to some "inaccessible" source, a priestess, a prophet, an inherited tale without an identifiable author.[107] Implied in all of these is the idea that myths and images are less than ideal, even provisional, viewed philosophically. They present an inadequate medium for the truth that reason seeks.[108] Given these generally negative attitudes, one cannot help but be surprised, in one of the only passages where the issue of the "rationality" of myths appears explicitly in Plato,[109] to see Socrates' criticism of those he refers to as the modern-day intellectuals who seek to distill a conceptual insight from myths rather than simply "believing" them.[110] In what way could a "belief" in a story be, as belief, superior to the conceptual truth that could be derived from it? Is this not a contradiction of the epistemology Plato lays out in the divided line and in his account of dialectic?

Understood from a richer view of Plato's notion of reason, what seems to be a failure turns out to be a positive feature. Let us consider the passage from the *Phaedrus* more closely. The problem that Socrates identifies here with the "boorish sort of wisdom" (ἀγροίκῳ τινὶ σοφίᾳ χρώμενος),[111] i.e., crass rationalism, that seeks to interpret the myth is that it never comes to an end. As he puts it, there is something inherently "laborious" about such an endeavor, because the myths contain a boundless multiplicity of details that present a rigorously analytic mind seeking to articulate them all with an imposing chore. He contrasts this endeavor with the simple effort to know oneself, which is "endless," we might say, in a fundamentally different way.[112] If we consider Socrates' apparently offhand observation in the

---

105. See *Prt.,* 329a–b; 335b–c.

106. See *Meno,* 99d; compare *Ion* 532d–e, where Socrates contrasts the *truth* of ordinary speech with the "wise" songs of the poets and rhapsodes.

107. On this point, see Jean-François Mattéi, "The Theater of Myth in Plato," in Griswold, *Platonic Writings, Platonic Readings,* 69.

108. At *Grg.,* 523a, Plato distinguishes *mythos* and *logos* precisely in terms of truth: "You'll think that it's a mere tale, I believe, although I think it's an account, for what I'm about to say I will tell you as true."

109. Plato does contrast *logos* and *mythos* in *Phd.,* 61b, *Prt.,* 324e, and *Ti.,* 26c.

110. *Phdr.,* 229c–230a. Cf. Friedländer, *Plato,* vol. I, 171–72.

111. *Phdr.,* 229e.

112. Cf. G. R. F. Ferrari, *Listening to the Cicadas: A Study of Plato's* Phaedrus (Cambridge: Cambridge University Press, 1987), 12.

light of our last chapter, we see that it is heavy with significance. The ratio-
nalist assumption that meaning can be exhaustively reduced to discursive accounts of that meaning—so that the whole of the meaning of a thing would
be strictly equal to the sum of statements made about it[113]—will necessarily undermine itself because the need for explanation goes on to infinity. It
is impossible to justify every detail of everything one affirms, and if one sets
off to make the attempt, one never comes back. Here again we see the inherent stressfulness of sophistry. If Socrates contrasts a "belief" in myth to the
rationalistic analysis of its details, he apparently assumes that such a belief
connects a person with the infinity of details in the myth in an "all at once"
sort of way.[114] While analysis is discursive, and thus takes things in a linear
fashion (discursive: "running through"), one after the other, the proper attitude to myth is a nondiscursive intuitive assent to a whole.[115]

Nevertheless, it would be far too easy to say that Plato is simply privileging so-called "holistic" thinking over the rigors of analysis. There are countless examples of his insistence on giving a precise account of a thing in order
to understand.[116] Instead, it would be best to say that there is an open tension in Plato.[117] On the one hand, μῦθος contains a wholeness that is lacking to λόγος, understood as discursive reason. On the other hand, λόγος
implies a conceptual precision and clarity that μῦθος cannot possibly possess by virtue of its imaginative form. Λόγος, moreover, allows one to take

113. Using syllable as an example, Plato presents the notion of a complex whole that is not
simply reducible to the sum of its parts (i.e., the letters that constitute it). *Tht.*, 203e.

114. On the momentary suddenness (ἐξαίφνης) that corresponds to myth, see Mattéi,
"Theater of Myth," 72. Manuela Tecusan argues that there is not always, for Plato, a metaphysical
argument behind the images he uses ("Speaking about the Unspeakable," 79)—presumably to
which the image could be reduced. Instead, an image can present an aspect of reality that *logos* by
itself cannot: namely, the *how* of a thing rather than simply the *what* of it (81).

115. Friedländer cites (*Plato*, vol. I, 210) a helpful text from Dante in this regard: "For we see
many things by the intellect for which there are no vocal signs, of which Plato gives sufficient
hint in his books by having recourse to metaphors; for he saw many things by intellectual light
which he could not express in direct speech" (from Dante, *The Latin Works*, translated by Philip
H. Wicksteed and A. G. Ferrers Howell [London, 1904], 347). It is crucial to see that, for all its
"intuitive" character, it is still an intellectual act, indeed, preeminently so.

116. We do not even have to go outside the *Phaedrus* for one such example: although the *Phaedrus* begins with a mythical account of love steeped in imagery, the second part of the dialogue
contains an insistence on the importance of rigorous analysis and the diligent work (πραγμα-
τεία) it entails. See 273e.

117. Friedländer observes that the *Republic* "hovers between reason (logos) and myth," *Plato*,
vol. 3, 139.

possession of an insight, while μύθος keeps one at a modest distance from it. But Plato wants precision of detail no less than comprehensive vision. He wants intimate possession no less than respectful modesty. Because μύθος and λόγος each contribute to this twofold need in a way that the other cannot, they must both be affirmed together, in their tension.[118] Neither can simply take the place of the other. Both serve different functions, but both serve philosophy as a whole.[119]

Plato makes this twofold need explicit in his explanation of dialectic in book VII. Dialectic, he says, is the capacity to ascertain the being of *each* thing, which entails a freedom from the senses (532a) and the separation of that thing from everything else (534b–c). At the same time, however, dialectic *also* grasps things in their "community and relationship with one another" (531d). Indeed, what Plato singles out as the mark of a true dialectician is *synopsis,* the ability to see all things together in a comprehensive whole:

"And the various studies acquired without any particular order by the children in their education must be integrated into an overview which reveals the kinship of these studies with one another and with the nature of that which *is.*" "At least, only such study," he said, "remains fast in those who receive it." "And it is the greatest test," I said, "of the nature that is dialectical and the one that is not. *For the man who is capable of an overview is dialectical while the one who isn't, is not.*" (537b–c, emphasis mine)

There is an obvious kinship between the "altogetherness" of an image and the totality of dialectic, a kinship signaled by the (significantly *visual*) term "synopsis." Julius Stenzel observed that Plato "gives to mere mythology the dignity of a religious metaphysic and demonstrates that it is the foundation of that synopsis of the whole of knowledge for which it strives; or rather that it is the foundation of all knowledge whatsoever."[120] Moreover, it is crucial to

118. Cf. Albert Cook, *The Stance of Plato* (London: Littlefield Adams, 1996), 104–5.

119. Luc Brisson likewise insists on the necessity of myth that is in some sense irreducible to *logos* (insofar as myth regards specifically that which cannot be verified or logically argued for). Nevertheless, Brisson reads myth essentially as a *logos manqué,* as it were, which is useful as a means for persuasion of non-philosophers in the realms of ethics and politics. See *Platon: Les mots et les mythes: Comment et pourquoi Platon nomma le mythe?* rev. ed. (Paris: Éditions La Découverte, 1994), esp. 144–51. Our argument, by contrast, is that myth serves a *specifically philosophical* purpose insofar as it preserves the ecstatic structure of knowing.

120. Stenzel, *Plato's Method of Dialectic,* translated by D. J. Allan (New York: Russel and Russel, 1964), 13. Stenzel goes on to say that the opposition that we take for granted between reason and belief regarding ultimate things would be foreign to Plato, who saw them as more organically united.

see that, while Plato singles dialectic out from other studies in its exclusive use of reason, he does not simply set dialectic alongside the other studies as one among many, as one study in contrast or opposition to all the others.[121] Instead, dialectic, though in one sense exclusive, in another sense *includes* all the other studies within itself, and if the other studies make use of imagery, then these become part of the comprehensive meaning of dialectic, even while they do not compromise its pure use of reason. Dialectic is the integration of all the others, but it is capable of integrating them all precisely because it transcends them.

We can get a more profound sense of philosophy's need for imagery and myth if we consider the nature of *ecstatic reason,* which we have argued lies at the heart of the *Republic.* To say that reason is ecstatic means that its proper end lies in a fundamental way *outside* of itself, which is another way of saying that there is something intrinsically rational about what is "suprarational."[122] From this perspective, the significance that nondiscursive myth and imagery have for reason becomes evident. On the one hand, ecstatic reason does not exist without the pure intelligibility of the forms. As we showed in chapter 2, if there are nothing but relative images, as sensible manifestations or appearances, then the soul never gets outside of itself in its perception of them but remains simply relative to itself. This would be Plato's critique of, say, Protagoras or Thrasymachus. The "in-itselfness" that defines the forms, according to Plato, demands the soul's self-transcendence, demands, that is, a movement beyond its self-enclosed relativity. The ascent beyond the cave and the forms depicts just this movement of transcendence. On the other hand, however, if the soul were able to grasp the form completely in a "merely" intellectual way (i.e., to lay hold of it in a manner that could be adequately translated into a discursive statement), the transcendence would, so to speak, come to an end, which means it would collapse back into immanence to the knowing mind. The *transcendence* of goodness demands *both* the (contemplative) movement out of the cave *and* the (imaginative/active) return to it.

121. Lachterman, "What Is 'the Good'?" 159.

122. Friedländer claims that myth leads intellect beyond where it normally can go. *Plato,* vol. 1, 189. He goes on to say, however, that it does so by giving a direction to the will (190). We are making a somewhat stronger claim: namely, that the "beyond reason" aspect of insight here is not an act belonging to the order of the will (which, of course, is not part of Plato's psychology in any event), but belongs to the essential nature of reason itself.

There is a dramatic difference between the sort of "objectivity" of knowledge that Plato envisions here and, say, Kant's view of the categories of the understanding and the ideas of reason. For Kant, these *must* be, by definition, part of the mind's own structure,[123] while for Plato, the objectivity of the ideas lies always *before* the mind, so that this objectivity is destroyed the moment the mind assumes it has complete possession of the idea in a way that reduces the idea to its immanence to the soul.[124] In Plato's case, we have an objectivity in the very *form* of the act of knowing, which is not the same thing as the simple universal validity we tend to identify with the term "objectivity." As we saw, Plato was unequivocally clear about the difference between knowledge "in" the mind and the thing itself in *Letter VII*, and this difference finds indirect expression in the dialogues, especially the *Republic*. But if it is true that reason's object is the thing itself that lies in some sense beyond the soul, the *nonconceptuality of this ecstasis is intrinsic to reason's integrity*. In other words, the pure intelligibility that defines the forms as objects for νοῦς alone requires the kind of nonpossession that is built into the structure of myths.[125] As Mattéi pointed out, there is a kind of "distance" that belongs to myths;[126] we wish to suggest that this distance is a constitutive part of the objectivity of truth and therefore a dimension that cannot be eliminated from an ecstatic notion of reason without destroying it. In a sense, we are simply recapitulating in a new context the conclusion we reached in the last chapter regarding Socrates' learned ignorance. Just as Socrates concludes with a profession of ignorance which indicates a "greater than I" aspect of truth, Plato concludes with a myth. In both cases, we have not the elimination or qualification of knowledge, but the perfection of it in its integrity. It

123. For Kant, the concepts or categories "spring, pure and unmixed, out of the understanding" (*Critique of Pure Reason*, A67, B92). These can be combined with intuitions to yield theoretical knowledge: "But *ideas* are even further removed from objective reality than are categories, for no appearance can be found in which they can be represented *in concreto*," ibid., A567, B595.

124. Edelstein argues for the "independence" of Platonic ideas from the soul or intellect. *Plato's Seventh Letter*, 97–105.

125. Cf. Edward Ballard, *Socratic Ignorance*, who insists that Plato meant to *include* what Ballard refers to as the "irrationality" of myth *within* philosophy, which entails a modification of the aspiration toward perfect intelligibility we normally associate with philosophy. Agreeing basically with this insistence, we would prefer to say that myth is "ecstatically" rational, and that the modification it entails is not a darkening of intelligibility, but the brilliance (ἐκλάμπειν, *Letter VII*) of the sudden insight due to the objectivity of the forms rather than the (essentially unsurprising) inference of demonstrative logic.

126. Mattéi, "Theater of Myth," 70.

is interesting to note that Socrates ends his life composing poetry, and does so specifically out of obedience to the gods.[127] Once again we hear an echo of the *Republic*'s obedient descent.

Let us compare Plato with Hegel on this point. Hegel affirms something like an ecstatic view of reason in his dialectic, insofar as *Geist* has to be alienated from itself in order to return to itself in an objective way. However, for Hegel, the distance of this moment of alienation needs to be ultimately overcome. The final form of reason strictly excludes the distance implied in image or myth, or as Hegel puts it, *Vorstellung*. Ultimately, philosophy supercedes religion because, while both share the same content, which is the truth of absolutely everything without remainder, philosophy takes that content up into the most perfect form, namely, the complete self-possession of absolute knowledge.[128] But, for Plato, reason does not end with complete transparency in the same way. Whereas Hegel concludes his *Encyclopedia* with the paragraph from Aristotle about the pure actuality of thought thinking itself—the "ultimate" in Aristotle's metaphysics—Plato ends his philosophical exposition with a myth about final judgment.[129] It is crucial to insist, however, that Plato's difference from a Hegelian notion of absolute knowledge is *not* what many people take it to be. Typically, one says that Plato recognizes the limits of knowledge, that reason is finite and can go only so far, that after this point comes ignorance, and thus that myth comes to be at the moment knowledge passes away.[130] The interpretation we propose here is significantly different: we contend that, for Plato, this distance is *intrinsic* to reason and thus part of its own perfection. Reason reaches a kind of completion in this nonpossession, because only here does the fundamental truth of things become manifest. In this respect, mythology is never simply some-

127. *Phd.,* 61a. Even though he contends here that philosophy is "the highest art," he agrees to compose *mythoi* rather than *logoi* out of deference to the god's command.

128. G. W. F. Hegel, *Lectures on the Philosophy of Religion*, vol. 1, edited by Peter Hodgson (Berkeley: University of California Press, 1984), 333. Cf. Hegel, *Enzyklopädie der philosophischen Wissenschaften* (1830), edited by F. Nicolin and O. Pöggler (Hamburg: Felix Meiner, 1959), §572, p. 450.

129. Hegel, *Enzyklopädie*, 463. There is admittedly some tension surrounding this point in Plato, insofar as he refers to the gods as possessing complete wisdom (*Symp.,* 204a), but also insists that what is ultimate cannot be solitary mind, pure and simple (*Soph.,* 248e–249d). The best we can say, perhaps, is that he did not explicitly engage this particular question, but nevertheless clearly presents the kind of ignorance we see in Socrates as displaying a certain perfection rather than being merely a provisional state that needs to be overcome.

130. e.g., Ballard, *Socratic Ignorance,* 161.

thing that needs to be overcome, but is rather an "interrupter" to reason that allows reason to be what it is, insofar as it is the nature of reason to affirm the soul-transcending *reality* of things. It is significant that the principle of truth, for Hegel, is *Geist,* while for Plato it is the good.[131] Goodness, as Plato says in the *Timaeus,* is *not* jealous,[132] while *Geist* cannot bear the existence of a truth it does not itself possess. The good, in other words, is not good without otherness, and so the reason that is ordered to it is not "allergic," as it were, to the distance and supraconceptuality implied by μῦϑος.

Mattéi is right, then, to associate Plato's use of μῦϑος with a contemplative, "theoretical" grasp of the whole in an "all at once" manner.[133] Philosophers, Plato says, are not those who have mastered argument—for these are sophists—but those who love the *sight* of the truth: τοὺς τῆς ἀληϑείας φιλοϑεάμενας (475e). Though Plato regularly identifies the realm of being with the invisible, he nevertheless makes broad use of the visual metaphors built into the language. The dialectician, as we saw above, is essentially *synoptic,* which means he "sees" things "together." In the remark from the *Phaedrus,* Plato seems to suggest that images have a special capacity to hold things together in a whole. It follows that, though reason is different from myth, properly understood they both serve the same end in different ways, so that a devotion to reason ought to incline one positively toward the mythical presentation of truth (as opposed to the sophist's deconstructivist tendencies), even while one never allows this presentation to substitute for reason's grasp. Among images, that is, the philosopher ought to remain in a basic sense both inquisitive and *naive.* One who wishes an overview will necessarily be "greedy for images" because an image is especially suited to providing a whole all at once. Let us consider a concrete example. In the cave allegory, Socrates instructs Glaucon to make an image (ἀπείκασον) so that he can "see" (ἰδὲ) what education

131. Once again, we see that Hegel is ultimately more indebted to an Aristotelian than a Platonic epistemology, though this affirmation runs counter to popular views of the German Idealist thinker. The Neoplatonists were right to point to the importance of the difference between Aristotle's and Plato's notion of God: Aristotle's is perfect νοῦς, Plato's is the principle of νοῦς. See Proclus, *The Platonic Theology,* translated by R. Baine Harris (El Paso, Tex.: Selene Books, 1985–1986), book II, chapter 4.

132. *Ti.,* 29e.

133. Mattéi, "Theater of Myth," 68, 76–79. Cf. Randall, *Plato,* 199–200, on "ideas" as object of the theoria engendered by a dramatic method. We might also think here of Press's proposal regarding the drama of the dialogues presenting a *vision.* "Plato's Dialogues as Enactments," 146–48.

is (514a). The image Socrates then displays is so full of implications that one never runs out of things to say about it, as the generations upon generations of commentaries can attest. It communicates its meaning with an incomparable power. Of all the things students read over the course of a semester's introduction to philosophy, what they most often carry out with them is a memory of Plato's cave. Plato cannot have been unaware of the power of this image, and it is perhaps why he explicitly "flags" it as an image, presumably to keep the reader from confusion (515a). Now, this image does not substitute for discursive reasoning, which we see already in the fact that Socrates explains the significance of various aspects of this image to his interlocutors. Without his explanation, the image would of course lie there dumb. But it is equally the case that a simple account of its meaning will never do complete justice to everything in it or exhaust its significance. Explanation and image, λόγος and μύθος, just like words and deeds, work in tandem to make manifest a "whole" truth, and it is this whole that the soul essentially desires.

But there is an obvious and important objection to make to this interpretation. If we say that reason works with images to attain its own end, are we not speaking about the third level of the divided line, which Plato characterizes in precisely these terms, and are we not thus speaking of reason at a derivative rather than a complete level? Here, we see once again the importance of context. If reason, shorn of any relation to the senses, were the final end of the soul's movement toward reality, the format of the *Republic* would have been quite different. Insofar as Plato meant to follow his own rules, and insofar as Brumbaugh is right that the divided line provides in some sense the method of the dialogue, we would have expected the *Republic* to begin with a heavy use of images, which it certainly does, and, after a purifying discussion of ideas, end with a purely abstract insight making no reference at all to images and sense-experience, which it certainly does not. The *Republic concludes* with the just man receiving all appearances of justice, and then with the myth of Er, which is the dialogue's most elaborate myth.[134] Similarly, if reason's departure from the senses were its final form, one would have expected that the central trio of images designed to communicate that which most completely transcends all appearances, namely, the good, would begin

134. Annas, in fact, expresses an annoyance with this "lame and messy ending," clumsily tacked on to "a powerful and otherwise impressively unified book," *Introduction*, 353. She considers the myth of Er crude and vulgar (349), and insists it reveals nothing of significance that would justify Plato's inclusion of it.

with imaginative allegories and culminate in the more abstract account of the divided line. However, not only does the sensually vivid allegory of the cave follow the line, but it *concludes* with the descent back into the cave—which is, after all, the cave of appearances![135] It is clear that the return to images, or as the medievals called it, the *conversio ad phantasmata,* in Plato's mind, brings reason's journey to closure in a way that what we might refer to as the abstraction of the forms does not.

How, then, do we reconcile this evident fact with the clear statements about the purity of reason on the divided line and elsewhere? There is an equally clear response to this apparent contradiction: images *as such,* however necessary they might be, are inadequate. The ecstasis of reason demands the unequivocally clear insight into the being of things beyond all appearances. There is, for Plato, an absolute difference between reason and belief or perception, and any insistence on the restoration of appearances cannot compromise this difference to any degree at all. The forms are *not* images, and this difference must come to manifestation with complete clarity before the relationship can be further qualified. We can thus insist both on reason's transcendence of images and its return to them and be equally unconditional about both moments. In other words, to put it more imaginatively, there is an infinite difference between the philosopher who returns to take his place next to the cave's prisoners and those who have never left, and the difference is the vision of forms as they are in themselves, taken as absolute and thus as wholly independent of images. The real knower is different from the dreamer, not because he remains outside the cave, but because he "believes there is something fair itself and is able to catch sight *both* of it and of what participates in it, and doesn't believe that what participates is it itself, nor that it itself is what participates" (476d, emphasis mine). Again, the true is the whole. The most comprehensive philosopher therefore "has to be like a child begging for 'both,' and say *that which is*—everything—is both the unchanging and that which changes,"[136] both invisible forms and tangible images.

To support the suggestion that a return to appearances is a *positive* movement for Plato, it is helpful to reflect on the nature of the myths he recounts, and especially the myths concerning the "afterworld." One's conception of

135. Cf. Wieland, *Formen des Wissens,* 222. Wieland points out that the return to the cave is in fact the final answer to the question posed concerning the "highest learning." Baracchi, too, points to the *descent* in which even the divided line culminates. See *Of Myth,* 96, 128n9.

136. *Soph.,* 249d.

what is last (ἔσχατον) is, so to speak, an expression of what one takes to be
ultimate. Conclusions reveal the end, the τέλος, of things. If we wanted to
address the question of the relation between reason and the senses, between
the soul and the body, in Plato, we could do so most directly by asking after
the character of his "eschatology." How does Plato envision the soul's final
state? Of course, Plato does not present a treatise on life after death, but tells
stories whose details, he says, are not to be insisted on.[137] We already pointed to the significance of this in the last chapter: in a certain respect, the best
account, the most adequate, is a mythological one. But, leaving aside the
details of the different myths he offers of the realm beyond death, a certain
feature common to them all emerges into view. If the soul becomes most
perfect when the body is eliminated—as the *Phaedo* seems to say, at least according to the usual interpretation—then its ultimate state would presumably be a kind of absorption into pure contemplation, in which any difference between knower and known would simply disappear. We find such a
state described, for example, in Plotinus, who spoke of the soul's desired
end as its flight from the world, alone with the Alone (φυγὴ μόνου πρὸς
μόνον).[138] Plato, however, never describes the final state of the soul in these
terms.[139] Instead, he presents different versions of what is called "reincarnation." Now, prescinding from any discussion of the extent to which Plato takes reincarnation literally—his philosophical principles would seem, in
fact, to make it doubtful[140]—we can at least affirm what comes to expression
in the idea of reincarnation: namely, that what is ultimate is not a disembodied soul but a whole human life, whatever that might mean in actuality. In
other words, Plato portrays the conclusion of the soul's journey invariably as
the embrace of an entire order of life, rather than, say, simply the experience
of the consequences of this one or a liberation from all things human. In the
Republic, he depicts the souls after death as being made to choose a life according to the lots they have drawn (617d–618b).[141] The choices are not sim-

137. *Phd.*, 114d.

138. *Ennead* VI, 9, 11. In Porphyry's arrangement, these are the final words of the *Enneads*.

139. On the difference between Plato and Plotinus in relation to this point, see Friedländer,
Plato, vol. 1, 80–84.

140. In a word, reincarnation taken literally implies what we might call a merely "horizontal"
transcendence, which is profoundly different from Plato's understanding of the forms' transcendence of images, for example.

141. More precisely, Plato says both that each will be required to choose a *daimon*, rather

ple objects of desire, but entire lives whose basic character is determined by that according to which they were ordered. Regardless of one's lot and thus one's order in the choosing, Socrates says, the wisest soul will choose the best life, the life of the highest good. And the highest good, as we well know, is good not only in itself but also in all of its consequences. To choose this is to choose everything, but—in contrast to the tyrant who *also* chooses everything in some sense—to choose it *well,* in the proper order.

Socrates *Redivivus*

It is not an accident that the image that concludes the *Republic* is that of a man who has been brought back to life. The final movement of Plato's philosophy, as we have pointed out, is the restoration of appearances, and Er's coming back to life is perhaps the most robust conceivable form of such a restoration. Just before telling the myth of Er, Socrates says that the argument has secured the truth and goodness of justice to such an extent that the soul will affirm it "whether it has Gyges' ring or not, and, in addition to such a ring, Hades' cap" (612b). Like Gyges' ring, Hades' cap has the capacity to make its wearer invisible.[142] Socrates is referring here, of course, to Glaucon's challenge in book II, which required the elimination of appearances. Now that appearances have been shown not to be ultimate, they have been justified and so can return to their rightful place. The argument has also justified a return to the account of punishments and rewards, which is given in the myth of Er. We recall that Cephalus begins with a tale of this sort at the start of the *Republic,* and Socrates now gives his own version in the end.[143] In the interim, rewards and punishments have been shown not to be decisive insofar as goodness has been isolated and manifest by itself, and this is what allows a more ample reconsideration of them. Indeed, Socrates' recounting

than the daimon's choosing him, and that each will choose a life (βίον), to which he will be bound by necessity. Cf. Heraclitus, DK 119. There is an interesting coincidence here of freedom and fate, choice and obedience. On the connection between freedom and necessity in Plato generally, and in the myth of Er specifically, see the essay by Julius Stenzel, "Das Problem der Willensfreiheit in Platonismus," in *Studien zur Entwicklung der platonischen Dialektik von Sokrates zu Aristoteles,* 3rd printing (Stuttgart: B. G. Teubner, 1961), 181–202, esp. 198.

142. Apparently even to the gods: ". . . but Athene put on the cap of Hades so that mighty Ares should not see her," *Iliad,* 5.844–45 (Murray and Wyatt translation).

143. The connection between the myth of Er and Cephalus's tale at the outset has often been remarked on. See, e.g., Brann, "Music of the *Republic*," 12, and Annas, *Introduction,* 349.

of the myth of Er seems to allude quite deliberately to Cephalus, and makes clear once and for all what was lacking in his perspective on justice. Socrates tells of a man who "lived in an orderly regime in his former life, participating in virtue by habit, without philosophy" (619c–d), and so having no fundamental reason to avoid choosing tyranny when presented with the possibility. Cephalus, we recall, rejoiced at his lack of eros (329a–d) because it allowed him to present the appearance of virtue. Viewed from an ultimate perspective, however, apparent virtue turns out to be none at all. Eros, we have seen, is essential to philosophy, and it is the intervention of philosophy that makes the difference between Cephalus's initial myth and Socrates' concluding one.

The role of philosophy in establishing this difference becomes especially apparent in Socrates' seemingly gratuitous mention of "Hades' cap." There would appear to be no purpose to this addition, practically speaking, because the cap performs the same function as Gyges' ring. But it in fact makes a powerful allusion that the ring does not. On the one hand, the name "Hades," as Adam points out, has an etymological connection with the word "invisible."[144] Plato himself plays on this resonance elsewhere to designate the realm of *being*, which is by nature the unseen.[145] As we saw in chapter 4, it is the realm in which the philosopher dwells. On the other hand, Hades is of course the name of the *eschaton*, the place where souls go after death. Er is just such a soul: Socrates' tale recounts Er's descent into Hades and return to this world, and as commentators remark,[146] Plato's allusion to Odysseus's story (614b) about his own descent into Hades and back is meant to underscore this connection. Odysseus in fact appears in Socrates' tale as precisely the one, of all the souls Er sees, who ends up making the correct choice (620c–d).

Plato, the philosopher, can be seen here to be both affirming and purifying Homer, the poet. Purifying, because while Homer's Odysseus is a master of deception and aims primarily at glory, Plato's Odysseus has "recovered from love of honor" through "memory of his former labors," i.e., because he has suffered through the whole of human experience and is now in a posi-

---

144. Adam, vol. 2, 430n12.

145. See *Phd.*, 80d; cf. *Grg.*, 493b. In the *Cratylus*, Socrates suggests the name Hades ought to be connected with the verb "to know" (εἰδέναι) rather than with the "invisible" (ἀειδής). *Cra.*, 404b.

146. See Bloom, *Republic of Plato*, 471n13; cf. Adam, *Republic of Plato*, vol. 2, 434.

tion to view it from an eternal perspective. But Plato *affirms* Homer in seeing Odysseus therefore becoming the quintessential wise man. He has worked through love of honor to love of wisdom, and has done this because he, more than anyone else, has "seen it all." Odysseus is one who has been to Hades and returned. In other words, he has gone to the utmost extremity of human experience and returned to recount it—to king Alcinous, in fact, who has interrupted the bard's poetic song in order to hear Odysseus's tale.[147] We are here presented with the essence of Plato's philosopher in a nutshell: just as the good is both absolute and relative, the philosopher, whose life is ordered around the good, not only goes to hell but returns from it. It is the comprehensiveness of reason's aim that makes philosophy ultimately a journey "there and back again." When Dante seeks to offer a view of the *whole* of human existence, he tells of a journey that encompasses both heaven and hell. Doing so, he draws on a tradition that begins, certainly, with Homer, but that passes through Plato.[148] In short, the myth of Er is once again a dramatic presentation of the center of the *Republic*: the philosopher not only ascends beyond the visible world into the realm of being, but returns to that world. Er's resurrection is a repetition of the philosopher's return to the cave. It is in *this* sense that the μῦθος is "saved" (621b), the rewards are returned (612b–c), and appearances are restored.

Among the many "eschatological myths" that Socrates recounts in the Platonic dialogues, the myth of Er is unique, and its uniqueness reflects the uniqueness of the *Republic* in the whole Platonic corpus (and, arguably, whole history of philosophy). While the other Platonic myths of the afterworld are speculations, stories received from prophets, priests, or unknown sources, Socrates presents the myth in the *Republic* as coming from someone who *has actually been there*. It is an eschatology given, in other words, as an eyewitness account! The extraordinary nature of this tale expresses the extraordinary "method" outlined by the dialogue. As we have argued, the fundamental challenge in the *Republic*'s account of knowledge is the question of whether it is possible to get beyond the relativity of the individual's perspective and attain to reality itself, a possibility depicted imaginatively as liberation from the cave. Contrary to conventional interpretations of Plato, ac-

147. *Odyssey,* 8.586ff.
148. On the *Odyssey* as the "subtext" of the *Republic,* see Jacob Howland's *Odyssey of Philosophy,* esp. 47–54.

cording to which Plato presents the liberation from the cave as an impossible ideal toward which one must nevertheless strive, we argued that if it is not possible to reach the absolute, then the very notion of levels in a cave collapses. Even relative differences make no sense except in relation to what is not relative. Without the actuality of the absolute, the typical refrain "Who's to say whose opinion is better?" becomes the final word on the matter. While the other myths can indeed be interpreted to some extent as fanciful stories with a message, Socrates tells this as a different sort of myth, as if to say that this is how it *really* is.[149] Instead of opposing the mythical and the true, he brings the two together: his is not, he says, a "tale of Alcinous" (614b), a phrase, referring to Odysseus's account of his extraordinary adventures, that had become an expression for any long-winded tale. There is, in short, a connection between this dialogue's uniquely bold claims about knowledge and the particular image that forms its conclusion.

Er's death, moreover, is an indispensable feature of this image; it is precisely what puts him in a position to see the way things are. We have argued in this book that the possibility of knowledge lies in a significant sense beyond the limits of human experience.[150] To lay claim to knowledge, as we propose the *Republic* does in a certain manner, does not deny the transcendent character of real reality. Instead, the emphasis on death brings to light in a striking way the *ecstatic* nature of reason. Reason's object *truly* lies beyond the soul, as Plato writes in *Letter VII*. Death is, of course, the most direct possible image for the ecstasis beyond the limits of human experience. By dying and returning from the realm beyond, Er transcends these limits but then returns to them. In this sense, the story told about him becomes another dra-

---

149. Of course, it does not thereby lose its mythical character, which is essential. Though he presents it as an eyewitness account, Socrates began the tale with the conventional "πότε," "once upon a time." Plato intends to make the mythical and the true coincide here, just as he seems to do, for example, in the prologue of the *Symposium*, where a story has been handed down but has its source in a real event.

150. Once again, it might be helpful to compare the basic positions of Plato, Kant, and Hegel in this regard. Kant remains from first to last within the *a priori* conditions of possibility and thus establishes an insurmountable "wall" between the finite and the infinite. Hegel eliminates the boundary and ultimately renders the infinite purely determinate and thus wholly circumscribed within reason's grasp. In contrast to both, Plato affirms the permanence of the (limiting) conditions of possibility, but makes these the stage upon which a dramatic conception of reason plays itself out, both preserving and transcending and returning to these conditions. The whole is thus far more complex than is typically granted.

matic expression of the ultimate meaning of things coming to expression in a relative and mediated way. According to the basic argument of the *Republic,* what knowledge requires is an image that "contains" the absolute in a relative manner without compromising its absoluteness. By being allowed to return to life without drinking from the river Lethe (621b), Er carries the "eschaton" back with him into this world. His return is, so to speak, *the entry of the infinite into the finite,* the insertion of the "beyond" into the "here and now." This, in Plato's eyes, is the very movement of philosophy. And it is no accident that the tale recounts a final judgment, for the role of philosophy, as Plato says repeatedly, is to judge from the best possible perspective, to take account of the whole, and to bring the universal meaning of things to bear on the particulars.

Now, as we argued in chapter 3, the movement of philosophy cannot be contained in an image, and the myth of Er is, after all, a story and nothing more. We would have slipped from the course along which Plato is leading us if we ended by taking an image for reality itself. In order for an image to be genuinely philosophical, it has to suffer a reversal; it has to break open. And we find just such a reversal, once again, in the *Republic's* concluding myth. If we have any doubts about Socrates as a real image of the good, we cannot help but be "persuaded" at the end: Socrates tells us that, if we are not persuaded by the story, we ought to be "persuaded by *me*" (621b–c), insisting on the first person singular and recalling for us its significance at the dialogue's beginning.[151] When we consider the insight that Er receives through death and his voyage to the "invisible" (Hades), it becomes clear that Plato wishes us to see him as an image of Socrates. Once again, in relation to what is ultimate, the narrative spills over itself into the really real reality. The question of death, of course, has "philosophical" significance not only for Er, but in an even more direct manner for Socrates himself. As we argued earlier, the absoluteness of the good became most dramatically manifest in Socrates' willingness to die for its sake, that is, to relativize the whole of his individuality to its absoluteness. It was just this willingness, which took concrete expression in the manifest ordering of his life, that opened up the horizon for the objectivity of truth, for the being of things to disclose itself *as* being, and for

---

151. Plato thus makes a fairly transparent allusion to Socrates' death at three junctures in the *Republic,* in the beginning (361e–362a), in the middle (517a), and at the end (614bff.), the three most important moments of the dramatic form.

the risk of intellectual poverty. The myth of Er thus sheds light on the life of Socrates, revealing it to be the bringing to bear of the good, the manifestation of its judgment, and therefore the light of intelligibility. In other words, it establishes him as the new Odysseus, the philosopher *par excellence*. Er points to Odysseus, and they both point to Socrates.[152]

Indeed, readers, from its first audience in Plato's Academy to those in ours, encounter Socrates in the *Republic* as one who has been put to death; his fate hovers in the background from the beginning to the end. The ἀπόλογον of Er cannot help but bring to mind the ἀπολογία of Socrates, which depicts what is, for Plato at least, the defining moment of Socrates' philosophical life and thus the moment that sets the horizon for all the dialogues. Socrates' words thus resound as if spoken, as it were, from the other side of the grave, just like Er's, and this lends them an incomparable weight. They become genuinely philosophical. In his *Letter II*, Plato explains that there never has been, nor will there be, any "writing of Plato's," but that which exists is "of a Socrates made beautiful and new"[153]—we might say, a Socrates *redivivus*. In the *Republic*, Plato brings Socrates back to life in order that he might say what is true.

Plato Goes Down

Thus, Socrates' recounting of the myth of Er turns out to be an image of Plato recounting the story of Socrates. If Er points to Socrates, Socrates finally points to the author of the *Republic*, to Plato himself. The myth of Er is only a story, and we ought to see that the *Republic*, too, is just a piece of writing. As such, it is a mere "pleasant amusement,"[154] and ought not to be substituted for real philosophizing. In this sense, we must see that the gesture by which Socrates breaks into the allegory of the cave is the same gesture that breaks the *Republic*, and the writing of dialogues in general, open to the life of philosophy embodied by Plato himself. He, no less than Socrates, understood the connection between goodness and intelligibility to imply that philosophy does not exist outside the context of a philosophical life, and that a philosophical life does not exist without a single-hearted de-

152. Cf. Howland, *Odyssey of Philosophy*, 160.
153. *Letter II*, 314c.
154. *Phdr.*, 276b.

votion to the good in community with others as part of a greater "whole."[155] Such a life entails a desire to understand things, to have an intimate contact with what is really real, but it also requires a willingness to return to the cave. On the one hand, we see that Plato could not dismiss the possibility of embodying philosophy in an actual polis through the invitation of Dionysius at Syracuse, in spite of the danger accepting this invitation entailed. He did not want to "appear to myself as a pure theorist, unwilling to touch any practical task."[156] It is significant that, having failed there, Plato nevertheless succeeded in establishing a philosophical community in the Academy, the first "university" in the Western world. On the other hand, and precisely because of the "communal dimension" of truth and the comprehensiveness this implies, a willingness to return to the cave entails the *obligation* of writing.[157] To write is to take the risk of embodying something true in a relative and thus essentially defenseless form.[158] But in the context of a genuinely philosophical life, the very risk can become a manifestation of the good, which, as ultimacy itself, is defenselessness. It is, paradoxically, Plato's dismissal of any ultimate significance to writing that lends his works such weight. His "transcendence" of the dialogues, that is, his invisibility as an author, makes his presence palpable throughout, which is no doubt one reason why his writing has the incomparable power that every new generation recognizes in it. The imperfection of writing, to borrow from the poet Leonard Cohen, is the crack by which the light gets in.

Once we recognize philosophy's intrinsic need for writing, the *Republic* yields one last secret to us. This need prompts us to read the first word of the dialogue as spoken not just by Socrates, but also, through him, by Plato himself: to take up his pen and fabricate a poetic image intended to say more than it says, and thereby to make truth public, is to "go down" into the cave of appearances.[159] It is to carry and carry out the delightful burden of

155. According to Gonzalez, the communal pursuit, through inquiry, of goodness is the very *meaning* of Platonic virtue. see "Giving Thought to the Good Together," 113–54.

156. *Letter VII*, 328c.

157. With a reference to *Symp.*, 209c–e, Ferber says that the desire for eternity that characterizes Platonic eros, and therefore philosophy, *demands* writing. *Unwissenheit*, 63.

158. "And when [a written discourse] is faulted and attacked unfairly, it always needs its father's support; alone, it can neither defend itself nor come to its own support," *Phdr.*, 275e.

159. According to Mitch Miller, "the Platonic dialogue is Plato's own descent for the sake of enabling others to join in ascent," *The Philosopher in Plato's* Statesman, xiii. Miller also makes the beautiful suggestion that Plato's writing is itself a (real) imitation of Socrates' own "defense" of

philosophy, the task implied in the exhortation that brings the *Republic* to a close: εὖ πράττωμεν. This verb means not only to be happy, i.e., to possess the good, but also to *do* it, to live it out in a concrete way and thus make it real.[160] If the first word of the dialogue *seems* to point to Plato, then this final word takes away all seeming: it is the word Plato always used to begin his personal letters—at least those addressed to his friends, those to whom he was bound in goodness.[161]

---

goodness through the practice of midwifery: "The dialogues would be his own distinctive way of practicing Socratic guardianship," "Platonic Provocations," 192–93.

160. Cf. Jaeger, *Paideia,* vol. 2, 146; cf. *Grg.,* 507c.

161. See *Letter III,* 315a–b. Reason ultimately shows in the light of the good that there is no one, in the end, who stands outside of this friendship (*Rep.,* 335d–e).

BIBLIOGRAPHY

Plato: Texts and Translations

Plato, *Respublica.* Edited by S. R. Slings. Scriptorum Classicorum Bibliotheca Oxoniensis. Oxford: Oxford University Press, 2003.

Plato's Republic: The Greek Text. Edited by Benjamin Jowett and Lewis Campbell. 3 vols. Oxford: Clarendon Press, 1894.

The Republic of Plato. Edited by James Adam. 2nd ed. Cambridge, Mass.: Cambridge University Press, 1963.

The Republic of Plato. Translated by Allan Bloom. 2nd ed. New York: Basic Books, 1991.

The Republic of Plato. Translated by Francis M. Cornford. New ed. Oxford: Oxford University Press, 1951.

Plato's Republic. Translated by Joe Sachs. Newburyport, Mass.: Focus Publishing, 2007.

Works in Twelve Volumes. Loeb Classical Library. Cambridge, Mass.: Harvard University Press, 1914–1927.

Complete Works. Edited by John M. Cooper. Indianapolis, Ind.: Hackett Publishing Company, 1997.

Phaedo. Translated by David Gallop. Oxford: Clarendon Press, 1975.

Plato's Epistles. Translated by Glenn R. Morrow. New York: Bobbs-Merrill Company, 1962.

Plato: Clitophon. Edited by S. R. Slings. Cambridge: Cambridge University Press, 1999.

Texts Cited

Albinus, Lars. "The Katabasis of Er: Plato's Use of Myths, Exemplified by the Myth of Er." In *Essays on Plato's* Republic, edited by Erik Nis Ostenfeld. Aarhus, Denmark: Aarhus University Press, 1998.

Alexander, Christopher. *The Phenomenon of Life.* Book one of *The Nature of Order: An Essay on the Art of Building and the Nature of the Universe.* Berkeley, Calif.: The Center for Environmental Structure, 2002.

Alighieri, Dante. *The Latin Works.* Translated by Philip H. Wicksteed and A. G. Ferrers Howell. London: J. M. Dent, 1904.

Annas, Julia. *An Introduction to Plato's* Republic. Oxford: Clarendon Press, 1981.

———. "Plato on the Triviality of Literature." In *Plato: On Beauty, Wisdom, and the Arts,* edited by Julius Moravcsik and Philip Temko. Totowa, N.J.: Rowman and Littlefield, 1982.

Anon. *The Anonymous Prolegomena to Platonic Philosophy.* Translated by L. G. Wester-ink. Amsterdam: North-Holland Publishing Company, 1962.

Arieti, James. *Interpreting Plato: The Dialogues as Drama.* Lanham, Md.: Rowman and Littlefield, 1991.

Aristotle. *The Basic Works.* Edited by Richard McKeon. New York: Random House, 1941.

———. *Metaphysics.* Translated by Joe Sachs. Santa Fe, N.Mex.: Green Lion Press, 1999.

———. *The Nichomachean Ethics.* Translated by H. Rackham. Loeb Classical Library. Cambridge, Mass.: Harvard University Press, 1999.

Ausland, Hayden. "Socrates' Argumentative Burden in the *Republic.*" In *Plato as Author: The Rhetoric of Philosophy,* edited by Anne Michelini. Leiden: Brill, 2003.

Ballard, Edward. *Socratic Ignorance: An Essay on Platonic Self-knowledge.* The Hague: Martinus Nijhoff, 1965.

Baracchi, Claudia. *Of Myth, Life, and War in Plato's Republic.* Indianapolis: Indiana University Press, 2002.

Barker, Andrew, and Martin Warner, eds. *The Language of the Cave.* Edmonton, Alb.: Academic Printing and Publishing, 1992.

Barzun, Jacques. *The House of Intellect.* New York: Harper and Row, 1959.

Baynes, Kenneth, ed. *After Philosophy.* Cambridge, Mass.: MIT Press, 1987.

Benvenuto, Sergio. "'Lo Specchio della Potenza': Eros e Volontà di Potenza in Platone." *Il Cannochiale* 2 (2002): 3–27.

Blondell, Ruby. "Letting Plato Speak for Himself: Character and Method in the Republic." In *Who Speaks for Plato? Studies in Platonic Anonymity,* edited by Gerald Press. Lanham, Md.: Rowman and Littlefield, 2000.

———. *The Play of Character in Plato's Dialogues.* Cambridge: Cambridge University Press, 2002.

———. "The Man with No Name: Socrates and the Visitor from Elea." In *Plato as Author: The Rhetoric of Philosophy,* edited by Anne Michelini. Leiden: Brill, 2003.

Blößner, Norbert. *Dialogform und Argument: Studien zu Platons "Politeia."* Stuttgart: Franz Steiner Verlag, 1997.

Bluck, R. S. *Plato's Seventh and Eighth Letters.* Cambridge: Cambridge University Press, 1947.

———. "'Knowledge by Acquaintance' in Plato's *Theaetetus.*" *Mind* 72 (1963): 259–63.

Bostock, David. *Plato's Theaetetus.* Oxford: Clarendon Press, 1988.

Bradley, F. H. *The Principles of Logic.* London: Kegan, Paul, Trench, and Company, 1883.

Brann, Eva. "The Music of the *Republic.*" *St. John's Review* XXXIX:1–2 (1989–1990): 1–103.

Bremer, John. *Plato and the Founding of the Academy: Based on a Letter from Plato, Newly Discovered.* Lanham, Md.: University Press of America, 2002.

Brisson, Luc. *Platon: Les mots et les mythes: Comment et pourqoui Platon nomma le mythe?* Rev. ed. Paris: Éditions la Découverte, 1994.

Bröcker, Walter. "Platons ontologischer Komparativ." *Hermes* 87.4 (1959): 415–425.

———. *Platos Gespräche.* 2nd print. Franfurt am Main: Vittorio Klostermann, 1967.

Brumbaugh, Robert S. "Digression and Dialogue: The *Seventh Letter* and Plato's Literary Form." In *Platonic Writings, Platonic Readings,* edited by Charles Griswold Jr. New York: Routledge, 1988.

———. *Platonic Studies of Greek Philosophy: Form, Arts, Gadgets, and Hemlock.* Albany: SUNY Press, 1989.

Burtt, E. A. *The Metaphysical Foundations of Modern Science.* Rev. ed. Garden City, N.J.: Anchor Books, 1954.

Campbell, Lewis. "On the Structure of Plato's *Republic* and Its Relation to Other Dialogues." In *Plato's* Republic: *The Greek Text,* edited by Benjamin Jowett and Lewis Campbell. 3 vols. Oxford: Clarendon Press, 1894.

Cherniss, Harold F. "The Philosophical Economy of the Theory of Ideas." In *Plato: A Collection of Critical Essays,* edited by Gregory Vlastos. Garden City, N.Y.: Anchor Books, 1971.

Chesterton, G. K. *Orthodoxy.* New York: Image Books, 1990.

Clay, Diskin. "Reading the *Republic.*" In *Platonic Writings, Platonic Readings,* edited by Charles Griswold Jr. New York: Routledge, 1988.

———. *Platonic Questions.* University Park: Pennsylvania State University Press, 2000.

Coby, Patrick. "Why Are There Warriors in Plato's *Republic?*" *History of Political Thought* 22.3 (2001): 377–99.

Collingwood, Robin George. "Plato's Philosophy of Art." *Mind* 34.134 (1925): 154–72.

Cook, Albert. *The Stance of Plato.* London: Littlefield Adams, 1996.

Cornford, Francis M. "Mathematics and Dialectic in the *Republic* VI–VII (II)." *Mind* 41.162 (April 1932): 173–90.

———. *Plato's Theory of Knowledge.* London: Routledge, 1935.

Cossutta, Frédéric, and Michel Narcy, eds. *La forme dialogue chez Platon: Évolution et receptions.* Grenoble: Éditions Jérôme Millon, 2001.

Craig, Leon Harold. *The War Lover: A Study of Plato's* Republic. Toronto: University of Toronto Press, 1994.

Crombie, I. M. *Plato on Man and Society.* Vol I of *An Examination of Plato's Doctrines.* New York: The Humanities Press, 1963.

———. *Plato on Knowledge of Reality.* Vol II of *An Examination of Plato's Doctrines.* New York: The Humanities Press, 1963.

Cushman, Robert E. *Therapeia: Plato's Conception of Philosophy.* Chapel Hill: University of North Carolina Press, 1958.

Demos, Raphael. "Is Plato's *Republic* Utilitarian?" In *Ethics, Politics, and Philosophy of Art and Religion.* Vol. 2 of *Plato: A Collection of Critical Essays,* edited by Gregory Vlastos. Garden City, N.Y.: Anchor Books, 1971.

Derathé, Robert. *Le rationalisme de J.-J. Rousseau.* Paris: Presses Universitaires de France, 1948.

Derrida, Jacques. "Plato's Pharmacy." In *Dissemination,* translated by Barbara Johnson. Chicago: University of Chicago Press, 1981.

Desjardins, Rosemary. "Why Dialogues? Plato's Serious Play." In *Platonic Writings, Platonic Readings,* edited by Charles Griswold Jr. New York: Routledge, 1988.

———. *Plato and the Good: Illuminating the Darkling Vision.* Leiden: Brill, 2004.

De Vogel, C. J. *Rethinking Plato and Platonism.* Leiden: Brill, 1988.

Diels, Hermann and Walther Kranz. *Die Fragmente der Vorsokratiker* (Zurich: Weidmann, 1985).

Dionysius the Areopagite. *Divine Names.* Translated by C. E. Rolt. England: Kessinger, n.y.

Dionysius of Halicarnassus. *De compositione verborum.* New York: Classic Books, 1910.

Dixsaut, Monique. *Platon et la question de la pensée.* Vol. 1 of *Études Platoniciennes.* Paris: Vrin, 2000.

Dodds, E. R. *The Greeks and the Irrational.* Berkeley: University of California Press, 1951.

Dorter, Kenneth. "The Divided Line and the Structure of Plato's *Republic.*" *History of Philosophy Quarterly* 21.1 (2004): 1–20.

———. *The Transformation of Plato's* Republic. Lanham, Md.: Lexington Books, 2006.

Edelstein, Ludwig. *Plato's Seventh Letter.* Leiden: Brill, 1966.

Else, Gerard. *The Structure and Date of Book 10 of Plato's Republic.* Heidelberg: Carl Winter Verlag, 1972.

Empiricus, Sextus. *Selections from the Major Writings on Scepticism, Man, and God.* Edited by Philip Hallie and translated by Sanford G. Etheridge. Rev. ed. Indianapolis, Ind.: Hackett, 1985.

Evans, David. "'Beyond Reality': Plato's Good Revisited." *Philosophy: The Journal of the Royal Institute of Philosophy* 47 (2000, suppl.): 105–18.

Evans, J. C. "Socratic Ignorance—Socratic Wisdom." *Modern Schoolman* 67.2 (1990): 91–109.

Ferber, Rafael. *Platos Idee des Guten.* 2nd ed. Sankt Augustin: Academia Verlag Richarz, 1989.

———. *Die Unwissenheit des Philosophen oder Warum hat Plato die "ungeschriebene Lehre" nicht geschrieben?* St. Augustin: Academia Verlag, 1991.

———. "'Da sagte Glaukon in sehr lächerlichem Ton . . .' (R. 509c1–2): Ein obszöner Witz Platos?" *Archiv für Geschichte der Philosophie* 75.2 (1993): 211–12.

———. "Did Plato Ever Reply to Those Critics, Who Reproached Him for 'the Emptiness of the Platonic Idea or Form of the Good'?" In *Essays on Plato's* Republic, edited by Erik Nis Ostenfeld. Aarhus, Denmark: Aarhus University Press, 1998.

Ferguson, J. "Sun, Line, and Cave Again." *Philosophical Quarterly* (1963): 188–93.

Ferrari, G. R. F. *Listening to the Cicadas: A Study of Plato's Phaedrus.* Cambridge: Cambridge University Press, 1987.

———. "Plato on Poetry." In *Classical Criticism.* Vol. 1 of *The Cambridge History of Literary Criticism,* edited by George Kennedy. Cambridge: Cambridge University Press, 1989.

Festugière, A. J. *Contemplation et vie contemplative selon Platon.* Paris: Vrin, 1967.

Feyerabend, Paul. *Farewell to Reason.* New York: Verso, 1987.

Figal, Günter. *Sokrates.* Munich: C. G. Beck'sche Verlagsbuchhandlung, 1995.

Findlay, J. N. "Towards a Neo-Neo-Platonism." In *Ascent to the Absolute: Metaphysical Papers and Lectures.* New York: Allen and Unwin, 1970.

Fine, Gail, ed. *Plato 1: Metaphysics and Epistemology.* Oxford: Oxford University Press, 1999.

Fisher, John. "Plato on Writing and Doing Philosophy." *Journal of the History of Ideas* 27.2 (1966): 163–72.

Foucault, Michel. *The Order of Things: And Archaeology of the Human Sciences.* New York: Vintage Books, 1994.

Frede, Michael. "The Literary Form of the *Sophist.*" In *Form and Argument in Late Plato,* edited by Christopher Gill and Mary Margaret McCabe. Oxford: Clarendon Press, 1996.

Freydberg, Bernard. *The Play of the Platonic Dialogues.* New York: Peter Lang, 1997.

Friedländer, Paul. *Plato: An Introduction.* 2nd ed. 3 vols. Princeton, N.J.: Princeton University Press, 1969.

Gadamer, Hans-Georg. *Dialektik und Sophistik im siebenten platonischen Brief.* Heidelberg: Carl Winter Universitätsverlag, 1964.

———. *Dialogue and Dialectic: Eight Hermeneutical Studies on Plato.*

———. *The Relevance of the Beautiful and Other Essays.* Translated by Nicholas Walker. Cambridge: Cambridge University Press, 1986.

———. *The Idea of Good in Platonic-Aristotelian Philosophy.* New Haven, Conn.: Yale University Press, 1988.

———. "Reply to Nicholas P. White." In *Platonic Writings, Platonic Readings,* edited by Charles Griswold Jr. New York: Routledge, 1988.

———. *Truth and Method.* Translated by Joel Weinsheimer. 2nd rev. ed. New York: Continuum International Publishing Group, 2005.

Gallop, David. "Image and Reality in Plato's *Republic.*" *Archiv für Geschichte der Philosophie* 47 (1965): 119–24.

Gauß, H. *Die Dialoge der literarischen Meisterschaft.* Vol. 2, part 2, *Philosophischer Handkommentar zu den Dialogen Platos.* Bern: H. Lang, 1958.

Gill, Christopher, and Mary Margaret McCabe, eds. *Form and Argument in Late Plato.* Oxford: Clarendon Press, 1996.

Gilson, Etienne. *Being and Some Philosophers.* Toronto: Pontifical Institute of Mediaeval Studies, 1952.

Gonzalez, Francisco. "Plato's *Lysis:* An Enactment of Philosophical Kinship." *Ancient Philosophy* 15 (1995): 69–90.

———. *Dialectic and Dialogue: Plato's Practice of Philosophical Inquiry.* Evanston, Ill.: Northwestern University Press, 1998.

———. "Non-propositional Knowledge in Plato." *Apeiron* 31.3 (1998): 235–84.

———. "Giving Thought to the Good Together: Virtue in Plato's *Protagoras.*" In *Retracing the Platonic Text,* edited by John Russon and John Sallis. Evanston, Ill.: Northwestern University Press, 2000.

———. "Socrates on Loving One's Own: A Traditional Conception of ΦΙΛΙΑ Radically Transformed." *Classical Philology* 95 (2000): 379–98.

———. "How to Read a Platonic Prologue: Lysis 203a–207d." In *Plato as Author: The Rhetoric of Philosophy,* edited by Anne Michelini. Leiden: Brill, 2003.

———, ed. *The Third Way: New Directions in Platonic Studies.* Lanham, Md.: Rowman and Littlefield, 1995.

González-Castín, Óscar. "The Erotic Soul and Its Movement towards the Beautiful and the Good." *Δαίμων: Revista de Filosofía* 21 (2000): 75–86.

Gordon, Jill. *Turning toward Philosophy.* University Park: Pennsylvania State University Press, 1999.

Gosling, J. G. "Δόξα and Δύναμις in Plato's *Republic.*" *Phronesis* 12 (1968): 119–30.

Graves, Robert. *The Greek Myths.* Vol. 1. Middlesex, Eng.: Penguin Books, 1960.

Greene, William Chase. "Plato's View of Poetry." *Harvard Studies in Classical Philology* 29 (1918): 1–75.

———. "The Paradoxes of the *Republic.*" *Harvard Studies in Classical Philology* 63 (1958): 199–216.

Griswold, Charles, Jr., "Style and Philosophy: The Case of Plato's Dialogues." *The Monist* 63 (1980): 530–46.

———. "Comments on Kahn." In *New Perspectives on Plato, Modern and Ancient,* edited by Julia Annas and Christopher Rowe. Cambridge, Mass.: Harvard University Press, 2002.

———, ed. *Platonic Writings, Platonic Readings.* New York: Routledge, 1988.

Hackforth, Richard. "Plato's Divided Line and Dialectic." *Classical Quarterly* 36.1–2 (January–April 1942): 1–9.

Hall, Dale. "Interpreting Plato's Cave as an Allegory of the Human Condition." *Apeiron* 14 (1980): 74–84.

Hare, R. M. "Plato and the Mathematicians." In *New Essays in Plato and Aristotle,* edited by R. Bambrough. London: Routledge, 1965.

Havelock, Eric. *Preface to Plato.* New York: Grosset and Dunlap, 1967.

Hegel, G. W. F. *Enzyklopädie der philosophischen Wissenschaften* (1830). Edited by F. Nicolin and O. Pöggler. Hamburg: Felix Meiner, 1959.

———. *Wissenschaft der Logik, erster Teil.* Edited by George Lasson. Hamburg: Felix Meiner, 1967.

———. *Phenomenology of Spirit.* Translated by A. V. Miller. Oxford: Oxford University Press, 1977.

———. *Lectures on the Philosophy of Religion.* Vol. 1. Edited by Peter Hodgson. Berkeley: University of California Press, 1984.

———. "Who Thinks Abstractly?" In *Hegel: Texts and Commentary.* Translated by Walter Kaufmann. 3rd printing. Notre Dame, Ind.: University of Notre Dame Press, 1986.

Heidegger, Martin. *The Will to Power as Art.* Vol. 1. of *Nietzsche,* translated by David Farrell Krell. San Francisco: Harper, 1991.

———. Platons *Lehre von de Wahrheit.* 4th printing. Frankfurt: Vittorio Klostermann, 1997.

———. *The Essence of Truth.* Translated by Ted Sadler. New York: Continuum, 2002.

———. *Plato's Sophist.* Translated by Richard Rojcewicz and André Schuwer. Bloomington: Indiana University Press, 2003.

Hildebrandt, Kurt. *Platon: Logos und Mythos.* 2nd ed. Berlin: de Gruyter, 1959.

Hitchcock, David. "The Good in Plato's *Republic.*" *Apeiron* 19 (1985): 65–92.

Hölderlin, Friedrich. "Fragment von Hyperion." *Sämtliche Werke und Briefe.* Vol. 1. Darmstadt: Wissenschaftliche Buchgesellschaft, 1998.

Howland, Jacob. "Re-Reading Plato: The Problem of Platonic Chronology." *Phoenix* 45.3 (1991): 189–214.

———. *The Republic: The Odyssey of Philosophy.* New York: Twayne Publishers, 1993.

Hume, David. *A Treatise of Human Nature.* 2nd ed. Edited by L. A. Selby Bigge and revised by P. H. Nidditch. Oxford: Clarendon Press, 1975.

Husserl, Edmund. *Formal and Transcendental Logic.* 2nd printing. Translated by Dorion Cairns. The Hague: Martinus Nijhoff, 1978.

Hyde, Lewis. *The Gift: Imagination and the Erotic Life of Property.* New York: Vintage Books, 1983.

Hyland, Drew. "Why Plato Wrote Dialogues." *Philosophy and Rhetoric* 1 (1968): 38–50.

———. *Finitude and Transcendence in the Platonic Dialogues.* Albany: SUNY Press, 1995.

Isnardi-Parente, Margherita. "Per l'interpretazione della VIII Epistola Platonica." *La parola del passato: rivista di studi classici* 97 (1964): 241–90.

Jackson, Henry. "On Plato's *Republic* VI 509d sqq." *Journal of Philology* 10 (1882): 132–50.

Jaeger, Werner. *Paideia: The Ideals of Greek Culture.* 2nd ed. 3 vols. Oxford: Oxford University Press, 1986.

Johnson, Curtis. "Socrates on Obedience and Justice." *Western Political Quarterly* (1990): 719–20.

———. "What is Liberty For? Plato and Aristotle on Political Freedom." *Skepsis* 12 (2001): 78–94.

———. *Socrates and the Immoralists.* Lanham, Md.: Lexington Books, 2005.

Joseph, H. W. B. *Knowledge and the Good in Plato's* Republic. Oxford: Oxford University Press, 1948.

———. *Knowledge and the Good in Plato's* Republic. Westport, Conn.: Greenwood Press, 1981.

Kahn, Charles. "Proleptic Composition in the *Republic,* or Why Book 1 Was Never a Separate Dialogue." *Classic Quarterly* 43 (1993): 131–42.

———. *Plato and the Socratic Dialogue.* Cambridge: Cambridge University Press, 1996.

———. "On Platonic Chronology." In *New Perspectives on Plato, Modern and Ancient,* edited by Julia Annas and Christopher Rowe. Cambridge, Mass.: Harvard University Press, 2002.

Kant, Immanuel. *Prolegomena zu einer jeden künftigen Metaphysik, die als Wissenschaft wird auftreten können.* In *Werke in Sechs Bänden.* Vol. 3: *Schriften zur Metaphysik und Logik.* Darmstadt: Wissenschaftliche Buchgesellschaft, 1998.

———. *Critique of Pure Reason.* Translated by Howard Caygill and Norman Kemp Smith. New York: Palgrave Macmillan, 2003.

Kersting, Wolfgang. *Platons "Staat."* Darmstadt: Wissenschaftliche Buchgeselschaft, 1999.

Kierkegaard, Søren. *Fear and Trembling.* Translated by Alastair Hannay. London: Penguin, 1985.

———. *Philosophical Fragments.* Translated by Howard and Edna Hong. Princeton, N.J.: Princeton University Press, 1985.

———. *The Concept of Irony.* Translated by Howard and Edna Hong. Princeton, N.J.: Princeton University Press, 1992.

Klagge, James, and Nicholas Smith, eds. *Methods of Interpreting Plato and His Dialogues.* Oxford Studies in Ancient Philosophy. Suppl. vol. Oxford: Clarendon Press, 1992.

Klein, Jacob. *Plato's Trilogy.* Chicago: University of Chicago Press, 1977.

Kosman, L. A. "Platonic Love." In *Facets of Plato's Philosophy*. Amsterdam: Van Gorcum, 1976.

Krämer, Hans Joachim. "Über den Zusammenhang von Prinzipienlehre und Dialektik bei Platon: Zur Definition des Dialektikers *Politeia* 534b–c." *Philologus* 110 (1966): 35–70.

Kraut, Richard. *The Cambridge Companion to Plato*. Cambridge: Cambridge University Press, 1992.

Kube, Jörg. *TEXNH und APETH: Sophistisches und Platonisches Tugendwissen*. Berlin: Walter de Gruyter, 1969.

Kübler-Ross, Elizabeth. *On Death and Dying*. New York: Scribner, 1969.

Kuhn, Helmut. "The True Tragedy: On the Relationship between Greek Tragedy and Plato." *Harvard Studies in Classical Philology* 52-53 (1941-42): 1–40; 37–88.

Lachterman, David. "What Is 'the Good' of Plato's *Republic?*" *St. John's Review* 39.1–2 (1989–1990): 139–71.

Laertius, Diogenes. *Lives of Eminent Philosophers*. Reprint ed. Vol. 2. Loeb Classical Library. Translated by R. D. Hicks. Cambridge, Mass.: Harvard University Press, 2000.

Lafrance, Yvon. *La théorie de la doxa*. Montreal: Bellarmin, 1981.

———. *Pour interpréter Platon: la ligne en République VI, 509d–511e: Bilan analytique des etudes (1804–1984)*. Montreal: Editions Bellarmin, 1986.

———. *Pour interpréter Platon: la ligne en République VI, 509d–511e: Le texte et son historie*. Vol. 2. Montreal: Editions Bellarmin, 1994.

Ledger, Gerard. *Re-counting Plato: A Computer Analysis of Plato's Style*. Oxford: Clarendon Press, 1989.

Lessing, G. F. "An Moses Mendelssohn, 9 Januar 1771." In *Lessings Briefe in einem Band*. Berlin: Afbau-Verlag, 1967.

Levinas, Emmanuel. "La philosophie et l'dée de l'Infini." *Revue de métaphysique et de morale* 62 (1957): 241–53.

———. *Totality and Infinity*. Translated by Alphonsis Lingis. Pittsburgh, Pa.: Duquesne University Press, 1969.

Lidz, Joel Warren. "Reflections on and in Plato's Cave." *Interpretation* 21 (1993–1994): 115–34.

Longinus. *On the Sublime*. Translated by James Arieti and John Crossett. New York: Edwin Mellen, 1985.

Luther, Martin. "Die letzte Predigt zu Wittenberg, 17. Januar 1546." In *Predigten*. Vol. 7 of *Luthers Werke in Auswahl*. 3rd printing. Berlin: Walter de Gruyter, 1962.

Lycos, Kimon. *Plato on Justice and Power: Reading Book I of Plato's* Republic. Albany: SUNY Press, 1987.

Lynch, William, S. J. *An Approach to the Metaphysics of Plato through the* Parmenides. Washington, D.C.: Georgetown University Press, 1959.

Mabbot, J. D. "Is Plato's *Republic* Utilitarian?" In *Ethics, Politics, and Philosophy of Art and Religion*. Vol. 2 of *Plato: A Collection of Critical Essays*, edited by Gregory Vlastos. Garden City, N.Y.: Anchor Books, 1971.

MacIntyre, Alasdair. *After Virtue: A Study in Moral Theory*. 2nd ed. Notre Dame, Ind.: University of Notre Dame Press, 1984.

Mahoney, Tim. "Do Plato's Philosopher-rulers Sacrifice Self-interest to Justice?" *Phronesis* XXXVII.3 (1992): 265–82.

Malcolm, J. "The Line and the Cave." *Phronesis* 7 (1962): 38–45.

———. "The Cave Revisited." *Classical Quarterly* 31 (1981): 60–68.

Manent, Pierre. *An Intellectual History of Liberalism.* Translated by Rebecca Balinski. Princeton, N.J.: Princeton University Press, 1995.

———. *The City of Man.* Translated by Marc LePain. Princeton, N.J.: Princeton University Press. 1998.

Marx, Karl. "Theses on Feuerbach." In *Marx-Engels Reader,* 2nd ed. Edited by Robert Tucker New York: Norton, 1978.

Mattéi, Jean-François. "The Theater of Myth in Plato." In *Platonic Writings, Platonic Readings,* edited by Charles Griswold Jr. New York: Routledge, 1988.

McCabe, Mary Margaret. "Myth, Allegory, and Argument in Plato." *Apeiron* 25.4 (1992): 47–67.

———. *Plato and His Predecessors: The Dramatisation of Reason.* Cambridge: Cambridge University Press, 2000.

McComisky, Bruce. *Gorgias and the New Sophistic Rhetoric.* Carbondale: Southern Illinois University Press, 2002.

McGinley, John. "The Doctrine of the Good in the *Philebus.*" *Apeiron* 11 (1977): 27–57.

McKim, Richard. "Shame and Truth in Plato's *Gorgias.*" In *Platonic Writings, Platonic Readings,* edited by Charles Griswold Jr. New York: Routledge, 1988.

McNeill, David. "Human Discourse, Eros, and Madness in Plato's *Republic.*" *Review of Metaphysics* 55.2 (2001): 235–68.

Mercant, Sebastián Trías. "Plato y una Gramatica del Poder." *Pensameinto: Revista trimestral de investigación filosófica* 37 (1981): 287–312.

Merleau-Ponty, Maurice. "Eloge de la philosophie." *Eloge de la philosophie et autres essais.* Paris: Gallimard, 1960.

Michelini, Anne, ed. *Plato as Author: The Rhetoric of Philosophy.* Leiden: Brill, 2003.

Miller, Mitch, Jr. *The Philosopher in Plato's* Statesman. The Hague: Martinus Nijhoff, 1980.

———. "Platonic Provocations: Reflections on the Soul and the Good in the *Republic.*" In *Platonic Investigations,* edited by Dominic O'Meara. Washington, D.C.: The Catholic University of America Press, 1985.

Mitchell, Basil, and J. R. Lucas. *An Engagement with Plato's* Republic: *A Companion to the* Republic. Burlington, Vt.: Ashgate, 2003.

Montaigne, Michel. "Apology for Raymond Sebond." In *Essays and Selected Writings,* translated by Donald Frame. New York: St. Martin's Press, 1963.

Moravcsik, Julius. "Noetic Aspiration and Artistic Inspiration." In *Plato: On Beauty, Wisdom, and the Arts,* edited by Julius Moravcsik and Philip Temko. Totowa, N.J.: Rowan and Littlefield, 1982.

Murdoch, Iris. *The Fire and the Sun: Why Plato Banished the Artists.* Oxford: Clarendon Press, 1977.

Murphy, N. *The Interpretation of Plato's* Republic. Oxford: Clarendon Press, 1951.

Nails, Debra. *The People of Plato: A Prosopography of Plato and Other Socratics.* Indianapolis, Ind.: Hackett, 2002.

Narcy, Michel. "Qu'est-ce que la science? Réponses dans le Théétèe." In *Platon: L'amour du savior.* Paris: Presses Universitaires de France, 2001.

Natorp, Paul. *Platos Ideenlehre: Eine Einführung in den Idealismus.* 2nd ed. Leipzig: F. Meiner, 1922.

Nehemas, Alexander. "Plato on Imitation and Poetry in *Republic* 10." In *Plato: On Beauty, Wisdom, and the Arts,* edited by Julius Moravcsik and Philip Temko. Totowa, N.J.: Rowan and Littlefield, 1982.

Nettleship, Richard Lewis. *Lectures on the* Republic. London: Macmillan, 1901.

Nietzsche, Friedrich. *The Gay Science.* Translated by Walter Kaufmann. New York: Random House, 1974.

———. *Twilight of the Idols.* In *The Portable Nietzsche,* translated by Walter Kaufmann. New York: Penguin Books, 1976.

———. "On the Uses and Disadvantages of History for Life." In *Untimely Meditations.* Translated by Hollingdale. Cambridge: Cambridge University Press, 1983.

———. *Götzen-Dämmerung.* In *Kritische Studienausgabe,* edited by Giorgio Colli and Mazzino Montinari. 2nd ed. Vol. 6. Berlin: Verlag de Gruyter, 1999.

———. *Nachlaß, 1880–1882.* In *Kritische Studienausgabe,* edited by Giorgio Colli and Mazzino Montinari. Berlin: Walter de Gruyter, 1999.

———. *Nachlaß, 1887–1888.* In *Kritische Studienausgabe,* vol. 13, edited by Giorgio Colli and Mazzino Montinari. Berlin: Walter de Gruyter, 1999.

Nussbaum, Martha. "'This Story Isn't True': Poetry, Goodness, and Understanding in Plato's *Phaedrus.*" In *Plato: On Beauty, Wisdom, and the Arts,* edited by Julius Moravcsik and Philip Temko. Totowa, N.J.: Rowan and Littlefield, 1982.

———. *The Fragility of Goodness: Luck and Ethics in Greek Tragedy and Philosophy.* Rev. ed. Cambridge: Cambridge University Press, 2001.

Nygren, Anders. *Agape and Eros.* Translated by Philip Watson. Philadelphia: Westminster Press, 1953.

O'Meara, Dominic, ed. *Platonic Investigations.* Washington, D.C.: The Catholic University of America Press, 1985.

O'Neill, John. *Plato's Cave: Desire, Power, and the Specular Functions of the Media.* Norwood, N.J.: Ablex Publishing Corp., 1991.

Osborne, Catherine. "Space, Time, Shape, and Direction: Creative Discourse in the *Timaeus.*" In *Form and Argument in Late Plato,* edited by Christopher Gill and Mary Margaret McCabe. Oxford: Clarendon Press, 1996.

Penner, Terry. "The Forms, The Form of the Good, and the Desire for the Good." *Modern Schoolman* 80 (2002–2003): 101–233.

Perl, Eric. "The Living Image: Forms and the Erotic Intellect in Plato." *American Catholic Philosophical Quarterly* 69 (1995): 191–204.

———. "Sense-perception and Intellect in Plato." *Revue de Philosophie Ancienne* 15.1 (1997): 15–34.

———. "The Presence of the Paradigm: Immanence and Transcendence in Plato's Theory of Forms." *Review of Metaphysics* 53 (December 1999): 339–62.

Pickstock, Catherine. *After Writing: On the Liturgical Consummation of Philosophy.* Oxford: Blackwell, 1998.

Polansky, Ronald. *Philosophy and Knowledge: A Commentary on Plato's* Theaetetus. Lewisburg, Pa.: Bucknell University Press, 1992.

Popper, Karl. *The Open Society and Its Enemies*. 5th ed. London: Routledge, 1966.

Poster, Carol. "The Idea(s) of Order of Platonic Dialogues and Their Hermeneutic Consequences." *Phoenix* 52 (1998): 282–98.

Press, Gerald. "Principles of Dramatic and Non-dogmatic Plato Interpretation." In *Plato's Dialogues: New Studies and Interpretations*. Lanham, Md.: Rowman and Littlefield, 1993.

———. "Plato's Dialogues as Enactments." In *The Third Way: New Directions in Platonic Studies*, edited by Francisco Gonzalez. Lanham, Md.: Rowman and Littlefield, 1995.

———, ed. *Plato's Dialogues: New Studies and Interpretations*. Lanham, Md.: Rowman and Littlefield, 1993.

———, ed. *Who Speaks for Plato? Studies in Platonic Anonymity*. Lanham, Md.: Rowman and Littlefield, 2000.

Proclus. *The Platonic Theology*. Translated by R. Baine Harris. El Paso, Tex.: Selene Books, 1985–1986.

Ranasinghe, Nalin. *The Soul of Socrates*. Ithaca, N.Y.: Cornell University Press, 2000.

Randall, John Herman, Jr. *Plato: The Dramatist of the Life of Reason*. New York: Columbia University Press, 1970.

Raven, J. E. "Sun, Divided Line, and Cave." *Classical Quarterly* 3 (1953): 22–32.

———. *Plato's Thought in the Making*. Cambridge: Cambridge University Press, 1965.

Rawson, Glenn. "Knowledge and Desire of the Good in Plato's *Republic*." *Southwest Philosophy Review* 12.1 (1996): 103–15.

Reale, Giovanni. *Toward a New Interpretation of Plato*. Washington, D.C.: The Catholic University Press of America, 1997.

Riginos, Alice Swift. *Platonica: The Anecdotes Concerning the Life and Writings of Plato*. Leiden: Brill, 1976.

Robin, Léon. *La théorie Platonicienne de l'amour*. 2nd ed. Paris: Librairie Felix Alcan, 1964.

Robinson, Jim. "A Change in Plato's Conception of the Good." *Journal of Philosophical Research* 18 (1993): 231–41.

Robinson, Richard. *Plato's Earlier Dialectic*. 2nd corrected ed. Oxford: Clarendon Press, 1966.

Rocco, Chris. "Liberating Discourse: The Politics of Truth in Plato's *Gorgias*." *Interpretation* 23.3 (1996): 362–85.

Roochnik, David. "The Tragic Philosopher: A Critique of Martha Nussbaum." *Ancient Philosophy* 8 (1988): 285–95.

———. *The Tragedy of Reason: Toward a Platonic Conception of Logos*. New York: Routledge, 1990.

———. *Beautiful City: The Dialectical Character of Plato's* "Republic." Ithaca, N.Y.: Cornell University Press, 2003.

Rosen, Stanley. "The Role of Eros in Plato's *Republic*." *Review of Metaphysics* (March 1965): 451–71.

———. *The Quarrel between Philosophy and Poetry*. New York: Routledge, 1988.

———. *Plato's* Symposium. Carthage Reprint. South Bend, Ind.: St. Augustine's Press, 1999.

———. *Nihilism: A Philosophical Essay*. 2nd ed. South Bend, Ind.: St. Augustine's Press, 2000.

———. *Plato's Republic: A Study.* New Haven, Conn.: Yale University Press, 2005.

Ross, Kelley. "Non-intuitive Immediate Knowledge." *Ratio* 29 (December 1987): 163–79.

Rousseau, Jean-Jacques. "De l'inégalité parmi les hommes." In *Du contrat social.* Paris: Editions Garnier Frères, 1962.

Rousselot, Pierre. *The Problem of Love in the Middle Ages.* Translated by Alan Vince-lette. Milwaukee, Wis.: Marquette University Press, 2001.

Rowe, Christopher. "The *Politicus:* Structure and Form." In *Form and Argument in Late Plato,* edited by Christopher Gill and Mary Margaret McCabe. Oxford: Claren-don Press, 1996.

Rudebusch, George. "Dramatic Prefiguration in Plato's *Republic.*" *Philosophy and Lit-erature* 26.1 (2002): 75–83.

Ruskin, John. *Unto This Last and Other Writings.* London: Penguin Books, 1997.

Sachs, David. "A Fallacy in Plato's *Republic.*" In *Ethics, Politics, and Philosophy of Art and Religion.* Vol. 2 of *Plato: A Collection of Critical Essays,* edited by Gregory Vlas-tos. Garden City, N.Y.: Anchor Books, 1971.

Sallis, John. *Being and Logos: Reading the Platonic Dialogues.* 3rd ed. Bloomington: In-diana University Press, 1996.

Santas, Gerasimos. *Socrates: Philosophy in Plato's Early Dialogues.* London: Routledge, 1979.

———. "Passionate Platonic Love in the *Phaedrus.*" *Ancient Philosophy* 2 (1982): 105–14.

———. "The Form of the Good in Plato's *Republic.*" In *Plato 1: Metaphysics and Episte-mology,* edited by Gail Fine. Oxford: Oxford University Press, 1999.

Sayre, Kenneth. "Plato's Dialogues in Light of the *Seventh Letter.*" In *Platonic Writings, Platonic Readings,* edited by Charles Griswold Jr. New York: Routledge, 1988.

———. "A Maieutic View of Five Late Dialogues." In *Methods of Interpreting Plato and His Dialogues,* edited by James Klagge and Nicholas Smith. *Oxford Studies in An-cient Philosophy,* suppl. vol. Oxford: Clarendon Press, 1992.

———. *Plato's Literary Garden.* Notre Dame, Ind.: University of Notre Dame Press, 1995.

Scheler, Max. "Ressentiment and Modern Humanitarian Love." In *Ressentiment,* trans-lated by W. Holdheim. New York: The Free Press of Glencoe, 1961.

Schenke, Stefan. "Der Logik des Rückstiegs." *Philosophisches Jahrbuch* 92 (1985): 316–34.

Schindler, D. C. "The Community of the One and the Many: Heraclitus on Reason." *Inquiry: An Interdisciplinary Journal of Philosophy* 46 (2003): 413–48.

———. "Homer's Truth: The Rise of Radiant Form." *Existentia: An International Jour-nal of Philosophy* 16: 3–4 (2006): 161–82.

———. "Plato and the Problem of Love: On the Nature of *Eros* in the *Symposium.*" *Apeiron* (forthcoming).

———. "What's the Difference? The Metaphysics of Participation in Plato, Plotinus, and Aquinas." *Nota et Vetera* (forthcoming).

Schleiermacher, Friedrich. *Introductions to the Dialogues of Plato.* Translated by Wil-liam Dobson. New York: Arno Press, 1973.

Sedley, David. *The Midwife of Platonism: Text and Subtext in Plato's* Theaetetus. Oxford: Clarendon Press, 2004.

Shorey, Paul. *The Unity of Plato's Thought.* Chicago: University of Chicago Press, 1903.

Sim, Stuart. *Contemporary Continental Philosophy: The New Scepticism.* Burlington, Vt.: Ashgate, 2000.

Sinaiko, Herman L. *Love, Knowledge, and Discourse in Plato: Dialogue and Dialectic in* Phaedrus, Republic, Parmenides. Chicago: University of Chicago Press, 1965.

Smith, Nicholas, and James Klagge, eds. *Methods of Interpreting Plato and His Dialogues. Oxford Studies in Ancient Philosophy,* suppl. vol. Oxford: Clarendon Press, 1992.

Splett, Jörg. *Denken vor Gott: Philosophie als Wahrheits-Liebe.* Frankfurt am Main: Verlag Josef Knecht, 1996.

Stalley, R. F. "Plato's Doctrine of Freedom." *Proceedings of the Aristotelian Society* 98 (1998): 145–58.

Stenzel, Julius. *Kleine Schriften: Zur griechischen Philosophie.* 2nd ed. Darmstadt: Hermann Gentner Verlag, 1957.

———. "Das Problem der Willensfreiheit in Platonismus." In *Studien zur Entwicklung der platonischen Dialektik von Sokrates zu Aristoteles.* 3rd printing. Stuttgart: B. G. Teubner, 1961.

———. *Plato's Method of Dialectic.* Translated by D. J. Allan. New York: Russel and Russel, 1964.

Stouffer, Devin. *Plato's Introduction to the Question of Justice.* Albany: SUNY Press, 2001.

Strauss, Leo. *The City and Man.* Chicago: Rand McNally and Company, 1964.

———. *Natural Right and History.* Chicago: University of Chicago Press, 1965.

Szlezák, Thomas Alexander. *Die Idee des Guten in Platons Politeia: Beobachtungen zu den mittleren Büchern.* Sankt Augustin: Academia Verlag, 2003.

Tanner, R. G. "Dianoia and Plato's Cave." *Classical Quarterly* 20 (1970): 81–91.

Tarán, Leonardo. "Platonism and Socratic Ignorance." In *Platonic Investigations,* edited by Dominic O'Meara. Washington, D.C.: The Catholic University of America Press, 1985.

Tate, J. "'Imitation' in Plato's *Republic.*" *Classical Quarterly* 22.1 (1928): 16–23.

Taylor, A. E. *Plato: The Man and His Work.* New York: Meridian Books, 1959.

Tecusan, Manuela. "Speaking about the Unspeakable: Plato's Use of Imagery." *Apeiron* 25.4 (1992): 69–87.

Thesleff, Holger. *Studies in Platonic Chronology.* Helsinki: Societas Scientiarum Fennica, 1982.

———. "Platonic Chronology." *Phronesis* 34 (1989): 1–26.

———. *Studies in Plato's Two-Level Model.* Helsinki: Societas Scientiarum Fennica, 1999.

Tigerstedt, E. N. *Interpreting Plato.* Uppsala, Sweden: Almquist and Wicksell, 1977.

Tindale, G. "Plato's *Lysis:* A Reconsideration." *Apeiron* 18 (1984): 102–9.

Tocqueville, Alexis de. *De la démocratie en Amérique.* Vol. 2. Paris: Garnier-Flammarion, 1981.

Tulli, Mauro. *Dialettica e scrittura nella VII Lettera di Platone.* Pisa: Giardini editori, 1989.

Urmson, James. "Plato and the Poets." In *Plato: On Beauty, Wisdom, and the Arts,* edited by Julius Moravcsik and Philip Temko. Totowa, N.J.: Rowan and Littlefield, 1982.

Utermöhlen, Oswald. *Die Bedeutung der Ideenlehre für die platonische Politeia.* Heidelberg: Carl Winter-Universitätsverlag, 1967.

Valiulis, David. "Style and Significance: A Note on Heraclitus, Fr. 62." In *Studies.* Vol. 1 of *Atti del Symposiums Heracliteum 1981,* edited by Livio Rossetti. Chieti: Università di Chieti, n.d.

Veggetti, Mario. "L'Idea del Bene nella *Repubblica* di Platone." *Discipline filosofische* 1 (1995): 207–30.

Velkley, Richard. *Being after Rousseau: Philosophy and Culture in Question.* Chicago: University of Chicago Press, 2002.

Versenyi, Laslo. "Quarrel between Philosophy and Poetry." *Philosophical Forum* 2 (1970–1971): 200–12.

Vlastos, Gregory. *New Essays in Plato and Aristotle.* Edited by R. Bambrough. London: Routledge, 1965.

———. "The Individual as Object of Love in Plato." *Platonic Studies.* 2nd ed. Princeton, N.J.: Princeton University Press, 1981.

———, ed. *Plato: A Collection of Critical Essays.* 2 vols. Garden City, N.Y.: Anchor Books, 1971.

Voegelin, Eric. *Plato and Aristotle.* Vol. 3 of *Order and History.* Baton Rouge: Louisiana State University Press, 1985.

Wardy, Robert. *The Birth of Rhetoric: Gorgias, Plato, and Their Successors.* London: Routledge, 1996.

Watson, Gerard. "Plato and the Story." In *Platonic Investigations,* edited by Dominic O'Meara. Washington, D.C.: The Catholic University of America Press, 1985.

Wheeler, Samuel. "Plato's Enlightenment: The Good as the Sun." *History of Philosophy Quarterly* 14 (1997): 171–88.

White, Nicholas. *A Companion to Plato's* Republic. 2nd ed. Indianapolis: Hackett Publishing Company, 1978.

———. "Rational Prudence in Plato's *Gorgias.*" In *Platonic Investigations,* edited by Dominic O'Meara. Washington, D.C.: The Catholic University of America Press, 1985.

———. "Observations and Questions about Hans-Georg Gadamer's Interpretation of Plato." In *Platonic Writings, Platonic Readings,* edited by Charles Griswold Jr. New York: Routledge, 1988.

Wiegmann, Hermann. "Plato's Critique of the Poets and Misunderstanding of His Epistemological Argumentation." *Philosophy and Rhetoric* 23 (1990): 109–24.

Wieland, Wolfgang. *Platon und die Formen des Wissens.* Göttingen: Vandenhoeck und Ruprecht, 1982.

———. "La Crítica de Platón a la Escritura y los Límites de la Communicabilidad." *Méthexis* 4 (1991): 19–37.

Williamson, Robert B. "Eidos and Agathon in Plato's *Republic.*" *St. John's Review* 39.1–2 (1989–1990): 105–37.

Wilson, J. R. S. "The Contents of the Cave." In *New Essays on Plato and the Pre-So-*

cratics, edited by R. Shiner and J. King-Farlow. Guelph: Canadian Association for Publishing in Philosophy, 1976.

Wittgenstein, Ludwig. "Lecture on Ethics (1929)." www.galilean-library.org/witt_ethics.html.

Woodbridge, Frederick J. E. *The Son of Apollo.* Boston: Houghton Mifflin, 1929.

Woodruff, Paul. "What Could Go Wrong with Inspiration? Why Plato's Poet's Fail." In *Plato: On Beauty, Wisdom, and the Arts,* edited by Julius Moravcsik and Philip Temko. Totowa, N.J.: Rowan and Littlefield, 1982.

Woozley, A. D. *Law and Obedience: The Arguments of Plato's Crito.* Chapel Hill: University of North Carolina Press, 1979.

Woozley, A. D., and R. C. Cross. *Plato's* Republic: *A Philosophical Commentary.* New York: Palgrave Macmillan, 1979.

Wyller, Egil. *Der späte Platon: Tübinger Vorlesungen 1965.* Hamburg: Felix Meiner Verlag, 1970.

INDEX

Plato's Critique of Impure Reason: On Goodness and Truth in the "Republic"
was designed and typeset in Arno by Kachergis Book Design of Pittsboro,
North Carolina. It was printed on 60-pound Natures Book Natural
and bound by Thomson-Shore of Dexter, Michigan.

CPSIA information can be obtained
at www.ICGtesting.com
Printed in the USA
BVHW072231240720
584638BV00001B/76